The Nez Perces in the Indian Territory

The Nez Perces in the Indian Territory

Nimiipuu Survival

J. Diane Pearson

Foreword by Patricia Penn Hilden

University of Oklahoma Press : Norman

Library of Congress Cataloging-in-Publication Data

Pearson, J. Diane
The Nez Perces in the Indian territory : Nimiipuu survival / J. Diane Pearson ; foreword by Patricia Penn Hilden.
p. cm.
Includes bibliographical references and index.
ISBN 978-0-8061-3901-2 (hardcover : alk. paper) 1. Nez Percé Indians--Wars, 1877. 2. Nez Percé Indians--Relocation. 3. Nez Percé Indians--Government relations. I. Title.

E83.877.P43 2008
973.8'3--dc22

2007037205

The paper in this book meets the guidelines for permanence and durability of the Committee on Production Guidelines for Book Longevity of the Council on Library Resources. ∞

1 2 3 4 5 6 7 8 9 10

Contents

ILLUSTRATIONS

FIGURES

MAP

Foreword

I begin with an origin story. A few years ago just days before the May graduation, Dr. Diane Pearson and I were standing in the corridor outside the offices of the Native American Studies Program at the University of California, Berkeley. Two Cherokee students approached Dr. Pearson, wanting to introduce their parents. Since I had had a less than salubrious relationship with one of the students—he earned a D in my class—and since it was graduation and a time for celebration, I stepped away, not wanting to mar the occasion. Dr. Pearson, though, was characteristically determined to include me and, after greeting the parents and saying what good students their children had been in her class, she reached out to me and said, "Do you know Professor Penn Hilden?" The father, who obviously had heard my name and who was not happy with his child's experience in my class, glared at me and said, "What tribe are you?" I replied, "Nez Perce." He then said, with some aggression, "Well, you must know X." I said, "No, I don't." He grimaced and said, "Well, he's the tribe's attorney. He's winning a lot of cases." I then explained that my people were not from the reservation in Idaho, that they were among those captured and sent to live in the Indian Territory. "We're Oklahoma Nez Perces," I told him. "There are no Nez Perce Indians in Oklahoma," he announced angrily and, grabbing his wife's hand, marched away.

"What was that all about?" Dr. Pearson asked me. And I explained, both about the near-failure in my class of one of the man's children and about his obvious ignorance of the history of the Nez Perce Nation, divided during the 1855 and 1863 treaty negotiations, and then divided again when whites moved in to take the entire northeastern Oregon valleys where many anti-treaty Nez Perces were living on their own land, in peace. Chased from their homes, the bands decided to travel to join Sitting Bull's Hunkpapas, who they knew were living just over the U.S. border in Canada. Men, women, children, and horse herds set off, hounded by U.S. Army troops with whom they were forced to battle over and over. In the end, after many had died, including chiefs, young warriors, children, and much of their treasured Appaloosa herd, the remaining Nez Perce people surrendered. Captives of the United States, they were sent to the Indian Territory, to live the story Dr. Pearson narrates within. In the Indian Territory, my family married other Indians and stayed. Always hostile to what they called the "treaty Indians," they took pride in worshiping in the old ways, speaking their language, and surviving in the white world in many of the ways Dr. Pearson describes here.

I did not know much more than my own family's stories: I knew that we were Wallowa Valley people, and I knew about the war and the terrible years of death in Kansas and Oklahoma. Although I learned which reservation people to disdain (the hostility continues between those who signed away the land and those who never did) and how to practice what we knew as "Indian religion," I knew little else. I had a few pictures, and my brother and I found more in the collections of the old Museum of the American Indian in New York City. Even our family memories were scattered and fluid: talking to my sister when I was writing a book about growing up "Indian" in the 1940s and '50s, I discovered that she had vivid memories of face-painting patterns, war bonnets, songs, and Nez Perce words I had forgotten. Neither of us knew much about the historical details. We knew that Dad had decided one summer to visit the Idaho reservation, and we thought he had perhaps reconciled with the despised "treaty" people. But when I followed him a few years later, I discovered that he had not met anyone, that no one had even seen him. I later asked him about this. "Oh, I didn't get out of the car," he said. "I just wanted to see, so I drove around and then went back to Lewiston to the motel."

But now Diane Pearson has forever silenced the hostile nay-sayers—Indian and non-Indian—narrating with painstaking detail the history of these people whose defiance of white conquest sent them into the death-dealing world of the Indian Territory. They survived, as she shows. They created new ways of living in the white world while maintaining their Indianness. They transformed their tightly held religious practices to fit this new place. Women continued their essential roles of supporting their families and their traditions while, as this book attests, moving successfully into the new world of the late-nineteenth-century capitalist United States. Many eventually returned: some to the Colville reservation in Washington, others to the Idaho reservation. But many did not. The little Nez Perce graveyard near Ponca City, Oklahoma, marks the place where so many died (notwithstanding Horace Axtell's claim that this graveyard is a fake, erected after the original burial place, with all its headstones, was plowed over by the white farmer who bought the land). And my family's history, like that of dozens of others, marks the still-living history of other, now "Oklahoma," Nez Perce Indians.

So thank you, Diane Pearson! For your energy—which amazed me as I watched the process of tireless research undertaken in the midst of a heavy teaching load—and for your dedication to finding the truth, to giving names when they can be found, to offering this history to the descendants of those Nez Perce people who fought and died and who fought and survived. Qey.ci.yew.yew, ta'c lawtiwa, Diane.

Patricia Penn Hilden
University of California, Berkeley

Acknowledgments

My debts are many, and my gratitude is profound for the support and guidance I have received while I worked on this book. Two of the people who encouraged this project to fruition are Professor William Willard and Professor Patricia Penn Hilden, and I thank them for introducing me to this fascinating and less-than-sterling moment in U.S. history. My heartfelt thanks go to Professor Willard for his unflagging interest, ideas, and wise counsel. He was committed to the idea that one small community could be traced through time and historical circumstances. I owe Professor Penn Hilden a debt of gratitude for her support and inspiration as she and her Aunt La Rue seek their family who remained in the Indian Territory. John Berry, Native American Studies Librarian at the Ethnic Studies Library at the University of California, Berkeley (UCB), answered my repeated requests for help, archival purchases, and pleas to negotiate national and international databases. Consequently, more than twenty-five hundred primary documents, papers, newspapers, reports, letters, Internet documents, and publications that form my research base will have a permanent home at that library.

I also owe my sincere thanks to the UCB interlibrary loan librarians, government documents librarians, and Bancroft librarians who provided essential support and services. Eric Fong, Ethnic Studies Department computer expert and technology manager, scanned maps and documents, photographs, and lithographs for presentations and the press and answered hundreds of questions about computers, websites, and technologies. Haruo Aoki, author of the *Nez Perce Dictionary,* offered me some of the best advice: try not to confuse historical Nimiipuu names any more than they have already been misinterpreted. Following his advice, I began with Lucullus McWhorter's work and moved from there to the 1878, 1879, 1880, and 1885 Nez Perce Indian Territory Census, Chief Joseph's lists of warriors and women dictated to James Reuben, the *Nez Perce Dictionary,* and Nez Perce tribal publications that were given to me by W. Otis Halfmoon. The list of "Personal Names" was composed from many sources, but the final resource was the 1885 census generated at the Oakland Agency. Otis shared telephone calls, family stories, e-mails, advice, and encouragement after my introductory articles were published in the 2004 edition of *Journal of Northwest Anthropology.* Thank you, Otis; I hope that this book is written for the American Indian point of view. And thank you, Phil Cash Cash, for including me on the Nez Perce Listserv. Phil and I are University of Arizona alums; "Go, Wildcats!"

Jesse Paul, Diana Mallickan, Robert Applegate, Nakia Williamson, Albert Andrews, and Steve Grafe deserve my heartfelt thanks for their comments, suggestions, and help. Jesse very graciously shared stories of his great-grandfather Jesse Paul and his great-great grandparents with me, and I treasure his support and encouragement. Diana and Robert plumbed the National Parks Service archives for photographs and advice, and Nakia's artistic abilities and artist's eye identified old photographs. Albert Andrews kindly answered my questions about the prisoners going home with Chief Joseph and about Nimiipuu horses. Consequently, I have used the term "horses" rather than "ponies," because Mr. Andrews agrees that "ponies" was racist rhetoric applied to American Indian horses. Steve located the impossible, traced visual and material culture, and has given the Nimiipuu in the Indian Territory a home at the Cowboy and Western Heritage Museum. Steve is unfailingly kind, retains his humor even in the darker moments, and is a "go-to" kind of fellow.

Steve and Connie Evans shared Lynus Walker's stories about his grandfather John Walker. Thank you for trusting me with Mr. Walker's stories, and thank you, Steve, for introducing me to Mylie Lawyer. I treasure my moments with Mylie Lawyer and mark her recent passing with sadness as the end of an era that I was privileged to share. Arthur Taylor and his mother deserve special thanks for the photograph of Jim Horn (Tewiispelu, James Horn Grant). Arthur amazed me with his innovative use of technology to provide that image. I accepted Arthur's kind offer to share the photograph by e-mail, he spoke with his mother in Idaho, and then he took a train to his doctoral classes in Chicago. The next day a beautifully scanned portrait arrived in my e-mail, and there stood Jim Horn. Loran Olsen literally brought Nimiipuu voices into my office and home. Thank you for the recordings, your encouragement, and the photographs of Levi Jonas. Hearing Levi Jonas sing and Jim Horn speak gave me goose bumps as I recounted their stories. And many thanks go to another interested author, George Venn, for timely conversations and help.

Archivists from Special Collections, the University of Idaho, Moscow; the Montana State Historical Society; the Minnesota State Historical Society; the North Dakota State Historical Society; and the Kansas State Historical Society offered invaluable and timely help, as did Mary Jane Warde of the Oklahoma Historical Society. Trevor Bond, Cheryl Gunselman, and Patsy Tate facilitated essential research with the McWhorter Collection at Washington State University, Pullman. Thank you all for the photographs, your enthusiasm, and your help. The McWhorter Collection is one of the great archival collections of northwestern history. Terry Harrison at the Mason City Public Library in Iowa helped me locate essential newspaper articles, and Dr. William W. Bottorff and Mary Ann Wortman gave new meaning to Kansas borderland history. They maintain detailed databases containing accurate copies of Cowley County newspapers that they publish online and in a series of volumes published by the Arkansas City Historical Society, and they share their resources with generous and unfailing support. Research conducted at the Fort Worth, Seattle, and Washington, D.C., national archives offices was facilitated by the generous and timely help of Meg Hacker, Patty McNamee, Mary Frances Ronan, and Daisy Njuko. The National Archives and Records Administration (NARA) archives and files and the National Anthropological Archives at the Smithsonian Institution are essential locations for primary source documents in American Indian history, and the archivists make the difference between meaningful research and frustration. Special Collections librarians at Michigan State University in Lansing heard my pleas for speedy research into collections of original Indian Bureau documents. Barbara Landis, Indian School biographer of the Cumberland County Historical Society, provided essential information about the Nimiipuu children at the Carlisle Indian Industrial School, and Bill Farr of the O'Connor Center for the Rocky Mountain West at the University of Montana, Missoula, located Joe Sherburne's photographs and records. Thank you, Bill; the photographs are terrific. Joe Sherburne was one of the good guys.

Last, but certainly not least, thank you to Jane Lyle for her enthusiastic and vital edit of my manuscript. Jane is every author's dream; she is intelligent, well informed, and eager to help bring the author's vision to fruition. And thank you to my former student Maria Cruz, who delved into special collections for missionary publications held by the University of Texas, Austin.

Funding for *The Nez Perces in the Indian Territory* was provided by a University of California American Federation of Teachers Professional Development Fund grant, and the numerous microfilms and other archival materials and copies purchased by John Berry, Native American Studies Librarian, Ethnic Studies Library, UCB.

J. Diane Pearson

Personal Names

Ale-we-tal-a-te-ket, Mary
Al-lul-ta-ka-nin or Al-lul-took-nim, Frank Buzzard; Lease Meeting 2/9/1884
Andrew, John
Andrews, Will
Andrews, Phillip
Armstrong, Ralph
At-ko-koo
At-tas-poo, or Ott-tas-poo, Went Forth, Abraham Wentforth
At-we-ya-we-non-mai, Mollie Hayes
Bear, Amos
Bear, Charles
Benjamin, Walter
Black Trail
Cayuse
Co-co-clum
Consuelo Blue (Yosyós, or blue); Consuelo Lip Trap
Coots Coots Ha-me-ai-cut, Kuts-kuts-tsa-a-me-yo-hat, Little Man Chief; Lease Meeting 2/9/1884
Davis, Elias
Eaw-se-cath Sa-cum
Ee-la-we-mah, Hi-aps-nin, Davie or David Williams; Lease Meeting 2/9/1884
E Lous See La Kat Tset, John Pinkham
Em-mo-tah, In mo tah, Mat Whitfield; Lease Meeting 2/9/1884

Es-pow-yes, Es-pa-we-yas, Is-pow-zah-as, Es pous, Light in the Mountain, George; Lease Meeting 2/9/1884
E-yal-ilp-pilp, Fleeting Red, Charlie Monckton
E-ya-lo-kaun
E-yal-lo-ka-win, Alexander Waters; Lease Meeting 2/9/1884
Eyes around the Neck
Fox-se-ap-poo
Gould, Dollie
Gould, Thomas or Tommy
Ha-hats-mox-mox-in, Ho hots mox mox, Yellow Bear; Lease Meeting 2/9/1884
Hayes, James; Lease Meeting, 2/9/1884
He Kah Koo Sowyeen, Luke Andrews
Hemean Mox Mox Khewn, Old Yellow Wolf, Yellow Wolf's maternal uncle
Heminish Húsus, Him-es-nim-huses, Him ish men houses, Wolf Head; Lease Meeting 2/9/1884
He-we-lee-ka-sat, Cornelius Baldwin
He Yoom Ya Tse Mock To Lu Ein, Um-tock-mul-in, Ye-yum-tak-mul-in, Grizzly Bear Hat, or John Fur Cap
He-yo-wa-pat-kekt, Eliza Moses
He-yum-el-pilp, He Yum Ilp Pilp, Um-ill-pilp, Umill pil pil, Red Grizzly Bear
Him-in-sl-pilp, Red Wolf; Lease Meeting 2/9/1884
Him-mits, Billy Williams
Hin-ma-to-we-yal-a-ket, Young Joseph, Chief Joseph; Lease Meeting 2/9/1884
Hohats Sumpkin or Ho-hats-somp-kin
Ho-ko, or Hoo-koo, Hair
Hoofs around the Neck
Hooper
Hoos tool, Tom Hill; Lease Meeting 2/9/1884
Ho-pope
Hum-lats
Húsus Kute, or Huses-ke-wit, Bald Head; Lease Meeting 2/9/1884

Húsus maqs maqs in, Huses-mox-mox-in, Houses mox mox, Yellow Head, John Walker; Lease Meeting 2/9/1884
In-wa-teumm She-cu, Eyes of Thunder, Thunder Eyes, Amos George
Ip-na-mat-we-kin, Ip-na-Not-Will-Ken, Ip-sa-nu-well wacket, Ip-na-wat to wicken, Dick Johnson; Lease Meeting 2/9/1884
Ip-na-som-wee-san-mai, Laura Minthorn
Ip-pits-ke-tit, Stephen Julius
It-sa-la-hi-ee-ta, Itsa la he yekt, John Red Wolf, elder son of Chief Red Wolf
Its-ca-tite (Ips-ket-tit, Susan)
Jackson, Frank
John Bull
Johns, Samuel
Johnson, Albert
Johnson, Eddie
Jonas, Julia; to Forest Grove Indian School, 1883
Jonas, Levi; to Forest Grove Indian School, 1883
Jonas, Lucy; to Forest Grove Indian School, 1883
Kah-pots, Kapoocha, or Kapack
Kal-la-tose, Peter Platter
Ka-moo, Rope
Kap Kap Pon Mi, Chief Joseph's daughter
Ke-ko-she-im, Isaac Lawrence
Ko-koh-tsis-kum, Coo-coo-chick-kim, Crow Blanket; Lease Meeting 2/9/1884
Kool-kool-mul-mul, Powder Horn, or Powder Horn Owl; Lease Meeting 2/9/1884
Kool-kool-Sneany
Kool-kool-Sni-niin
Kool-kool-sub-im, Kool-kool-sul-im, Jim Nat; dependent William Bull
Kool-kool-tick-lih-kin, Jay Gould; Lease Meeting 2/9/1884
Kool-luts-tah, Mary Wilson, Forest Grove Indian School 1883
Ko-san-yum, Luke Wilson
Ko-she-she-man, Harry Anderson; Lease Meeting 2/9/1884

Lah-pey-a-lute, La-pe-yah-lut, La-pe-yal-luts, Phillip Walker, Phillip Williams
Lawrence, Alice
Lawyer, Archie, Reverend
Lean Elk, Poker Joe
Littlewolf, Rebecca
Long Yellow Nose
Los-tso-kas-tin, Johnson; Lease Meeting 2/9/1884
Lydia Joanna
Mal-its, Edward Newman; Lease Meeting 2/9/1884
Man Who Had Eyes Like a Crane, The; or, The Man with Silver Eyes
Many Wounds (Sam Lott)
Mary, Anna
Met-tat-wap-tas, Three Eagles; Dependent "Susan" did not return to Lapwai with Three Eagles in 1883
Minthorn, Rob
Miyapkáwit, Baby, Captain George
Mo-Hos, Mo-has
Moses, Lilly
Newman, Lilly
Nick-yas-ko-hem, John Anderson; Lease Meeting 2/9/1884
Nots-no, Janet Rachel, Jeanette Rachel
Old Clark, Captain Clark, Daytime Smoker
"Old Man" Halfmoon
Op-has, Charley or Charlie Joseph; Lease Meeting 2/9/1884
Oto-kea, Pete
Ow-hi, Au-high, Benjamin Grant (Yakama); Lease Meeting 2/9/1884
Pahalawasheschit, Star Doctor
Pahit Palikt
Pa-ko-lee-ka-sat, Pack-al-lu-cutch-et, Five Times Over; Lease Meeting, 2/9/1884
Pa-ya-wa-hiekt, Pa-ya-wa-hickt, Hoof Necklace, Samuel Fleming; Lease Meeting, 2/9/1884
Penahwenonmi, Helping Another

Peo Peo Tholekt
Pe-wa-ya-ta-lee-ka-sat, Amelia Young
Phillips, Luke
Pie Wah, Jesse Paul
Pie-wa-we-e-ma
Porter, James; Lease Meeting 2/9/1884
Price, Ellen
Red Wolf, George W. (George W. Wolf)
Red Wolf, Harrison
Red Wolf, Josiah
Reuben or Reubens, James
Rivers, Henry; Lease Meeting 2/9/1884
Sa-caw-ta-she (Cayuse), Nimiipuu Warrior's Widow
Samuel, Silas
Seelo Wahyakt, Sa-lu-wa-kakt, Sur-li-I-hiakts, Eye Necklace, Eyes around the Neck
Shaw-we-haa, Albert Joe
She-wa-tas-hai-hai, She-wa-tis, White Cloud, Captain Jack; Lease Meeting 2/9/1884
Simon, Johnny
Skou-cum-Joe, Nez Perce Joe
Snow, Jacob
Snow, Jimmie
Stuart, Harriet Mary, Harriet Mary
Sul-in-mox-mox-in, Chutlum mox mox, Yellow Bull; Lease Meeting 2/9/1884
Sum-kain
Sup-poon-mas, Bugle, Blowing Instrument, Charley or Charlie Moses; Lease Meeting 2/9/1884
Sur-lee-i-haikt
Ta Mah Utah Likt, Josiah Red Wolf's mother
Ta-mai-yo-tsa-ka-win, Some Left on Top
Ta-ma-ya-to-wa-son-mai, Woman Riding, Carrie Schutt
Tam-mooks
Tel-ho-wich, Tulha-wits, Tell howich, Swift Runner
Te-ta-pin-ma, Leg Marrow

Tewiispelu, Ta-wes-pa-loo, Tow-as-plew, Tow as pa lew, Jim Horn, James Horn Grant; Lease Meeting 2/9/1884
The Man Who Had Eyes Like a Crane, or, The Man with Silver Eyes
Tim-sus-sle-wit, Ta-mus-ses-lee-wit, Rosebush
Tip-yal-la-nat-kekt, Tip-yal-la-na-kekt, John Andrews; Lease Meeting 2/9/1884
Tip-yal-la-na-tsis-kun, Eagle Blanket; Lease Meeting 2/9/1884
Tisca, Skunk, Polecat; Lease Meeting 2/9/1884
Tit-een, Having Teeth
Toko-ma-po, Jean
Toma Alwawinmi, Tom-ma-al-wa-win-mai, Magdellenia, Spring Time
Tom-chich-kim, Tom chi kin, Fog Blanket; Lease Meeting 2/9/1884
Took ka lickt se ma, Never Hunts
To-sa-im, Emma Ruth
Tsis-koop, Chick-coops, Ticklish, Adelia Emeline
Tuck-te-we-ta-la-sha, Rosie Martha, Mattie Rosie, Rosa Price
Tu-kai-sam-poo, Took-i-sam-poo, Belonging to a Hill, John Hill; Lease Meeting 2/9/1884
Tuk-ta-lats, Delia Mary
Tuktena Tuk Hayakt, Tuk-te-na-tuk-ke-ya-yekt, Daniel Jefferson; Lease Meeting 2/9/1884
Tuk-tu-lats, Delia Mary, Delia Parnell
Wah-La-Mut-Ki, Chief Joseph's grandfather
Wahlitis
Wahnistas Aswetesk
Wal-ly-tits or Shining Bear, John Minthorn, also known as Weyat-mas Wa-hakt or Swan Necklace; Lease Meeting 2/9/1884; 1880 census: 64 listed as Umtill-lipt, Shining Bear
Wal-we-yes
Waptastamana (Blacktail Eagle)
Wap-tas-wa-hiekt, Wap ta yhchitt, Feathers around the Neck, Frank Thompson; Lease Meeting 2/9/1884

Wa-tas-tsis-kum, Wa-tis-chi-kim, Frank Earth Blanket; Lease Meeting 2/9/1884
Wat-u-sa-kaun, Thomas Peters; Lease Meeting 2/9/1884
Wa-wook-ya-el-pilp, Wa-wak-zah-ill-pilp, Red Elk
We-ya-wes, Goose over Mountain, Lease Meeting 2/9/1884
White Owl
Williams, Mark
Wolf, Charlie, Charlie Williams
Wolf Head, Luke
Wolf Head, Mrs.
Yo-hoy-ta-mo-sat, Lame John, 2/9/1884

The Nez Perces in the Indian Territory

Introduction

With the Nez Perce Treaty of 1855, the Nimiipuu entered into a series of treaties and agreements that marked new protocols for dealing with the United States. Like other Native nations whose members were not yet U.S. citizens, the Nimiipuu experienced staggering losses of land, were segregated on reservations, and were subjected to restrictive laws and policies that did not apply to U.S. citizens. Regardless of the protections guaranteed by the Bill of Rights (the first ten amendments to the U.S. Constitution), the Nimiipuu struggled to protect their sovereign and civil rights after the Nez Perce nation was divided by another disastrous treaty in 1863 that abrogated the rights and properties of five nontreaty bands. Following more than a decade of turmoil involving broken treaties and discarded federal promises, separatist religious influences, settler and gold miner invasions, and an intrusive federal bureaucracy, the nontreaty bands were forced into conflict with the United States. Memorialized as the Nez Perce War of 1877, the resulting conflict left the nontreaty bands scattered across the West. And despite a surrender accord that guaranteed their return to Idaho in 1878, the prisoners who surrendered at the Bear Paw, Montana, on October 5, 1877, spent the next eight years in federal prison camps. War leaders, elder chiefs, and almost all of the experienced band leaders were either dead or in Canada. Younger men, such as Chief Joseph (Hin-ma-to-we-yal-a-ket), Yellow Bull (Sul-in-mox-mox-in), Yellow Bear (Ha-hats-mox-mox-in), and the Palus leader Húsus Kute

(Bald Head), matured in prison camps, where they faced almost unimaginable challenges.

The nontreaty Nimiipuu and their Palus and Cayuse allies joined the Modocs, Northern Cheyennes, and other Native nations in an era when the federal government used exile to the Indian Territory as a means of revenge against recalcitrant American Indians. The Nimiipuu, Palus, and Cayuse prisoners became the *tableaux vivants* of federal American Indian policies and were used to threaten other tribal nations with federal authority. The captives were to be permanently segregated in the Indian Territory, where they would become sedentary farmers and reconstructed English-speaking Christians who sent their children to federal American Indian schools.

Like other Native nations relocated to the western Indian Territory, the Nimiipuu prisoners suffered drastic population losses as a result of malaria, tuberculosis, and other viral and bacterial diseases. Dissension, destructive behaviors, and poverty were rampant in the prison camps, but such conditions were overcome by traditional governance and ceremonials, innovative intragroup action, personal sacrifice, and group cohesion, or they were simply endured. Intricate social relationships and experiences, complicated by conditions in the prison camps, laid the foundations for changing practices and expansion of spiritual beliefs. Spiritual practices included a dynamic new Presbyterian church, the old *wéset* (Seven Drums) faith, and Sun Dances.

Challenged with technologies that were intended to intimidate them, the captives instead used them to their advantage. They endorsed the telegraph and telephone, became the first American Indians to record their pro–civil rights platform on the Edison voice recorder, learned to manipulate the press and public opinion, and engaged in effective social and political interactions with non–Native Americans. Chief Joseph and Yellow Bull became respected public speakers and dedicated civil rights activists, while Tom Hill (Hous Tool), Yellow Bear, Húsus Kute, and many others demanded federal attention to their freedom. Yellow Bull and Tom Hill learned to speak English in order to avoid having to rely on federal interpreters; as Joseph and the community learned, those interpreters often promoted their own agendas or lied to the prisoners.

Young leaders, such as Chief Joseph, struggled to maintain predictable relationships in an era of constantly changing federal officials. Youngsters accepted responsibilities usually delegated to much older people because elderly, women, and children were dying in disproportionate numbers during this time. Although women were generally ignored by federal authorities, they established trade relationships; gardened, traded, and sold produce to provide a healthier diet; and transferred their arts, crafts, and other skills to new environments. Some captives made the most of available opportunities or engaged in the changing economic and social structures, while others avoided any outside contacts. Suffering from physical and psychological injuries, the exiles experienced depression that was offset only by their unremitting desire to return to their homelands.

Focused on civil rights, fulfillment of the Bear Paw surrender accord, and the theft of their Wallowa Valley homelands, Nimiipuu leaders joined with Ponca peace chiefs, American Indian rights activists, and Christian leaders to promote their freedom. They were subjected to the racism of post–Civil War Missouri at Quapaw, but relocation to the Ponca Agency in the western Indian Territory afforded the prisoners access to equitable judicial and economic systems. Guided by a few elderly survivors, some of the younger men served as American Indian police and as judges on the Court of Indian Offenses, while others accepted responsibilities that allowed leaders such as Chief Joseph to create new opportunities. Leaders of the prisoner population appealed to the president, to Congress, to the secretary of the interior, and to the commissioner of Indian affairs to circumvent dishonest American Indian agents, racism, and biased federal edicts, and forced the Bureau of Indian Affairs to act on their demands.

The captives took control of their lives whenever they could. They refused to allow General Samuel C. Armstrong and Lieutenant Richard Henry Pratt to remove their entire male population to Virginia or Florida from the prison camp at Fort Leavenworth, Kansas. Instead, they negotiated the admittance of their children to the Carlisle Indian Industrial School, the Chilocco Indian Industrial School, and other federal schools.

Although actively involved in the life of the western Indian Territory, the Nimiipuu, Paluses, and Cayuses never agreed to remain there. Subjected to intense federal pressures, leaders and their supporters argued for improved living conditions, decent homes, and their return to the northwest. They supported Indian rights activists who hoped to make them the Supreme Court test case of the *United States ex rel. Standing Bear v. Crook* decision. The exiles simply wanted to go home. Following years of consultations, federal promises and disappointments, appeals to politicians and religious leaders, federal funding delays, and western resistance, the Nimiipuu, Paluses, and Cayuses negotiated their release in May 1885. Supported by religious and political activists, eastern politicians, and a select group of army officers, Chief Joseph and 149 of his supporters continued their exile in the Washington Territory, and the other 118 survivors returned to the Nez Perce reservation in Idaho.

The Nimiipuu, Palus, and Cayuse captivity narrative is a microanalysis of American Indian survival, adaptation, civil and aboriginal rights, demographics, and decline. It is also a story of dedication to homeland and peoplehood, and of the lived experiences of federal Indian policies. The text is rich with stories, events, and places that are intended to guide further research. The stories hold a special place because they bring new dimensions to an eight-year period of U.S. history that has never been made clear to the Nimiipuu survivors.

Like the stories, language and Nimiipuu names are unique to American Indian history. "Nimiipuu" means "Nez Perce people" in the Nimiputimít language and is used throughout the text. "Nez Perce" is an assigned name that was utilized by non-Natives, treaty makers, and federal authorities and appears in the text in that context. English-language and Nimiipuu names provide another challenge. By 1877, many Nimiipuu had adopted English names, and after the war ended in October of that year, interpreters, army officers, federal officials, schoolteachers, and Christian religious leaders assigned English names to many of the Nimiipuu prisoners. It was also customary to assume English names when converting to Christianity, and schoolchildren often adopted their teacher's name. Spelling of the new names is problematical because translations were inconsistent. "Charley" often appears as "Charlie"; Shults becomes Schutt; Dolly may also be spelled as Dollie; and plural and singular designations are sometimes confused.

Phonetic English-language translations of Nimiipuu names are also perplexing. Interpreters, record keepers, and Indian Agency employees worked without Nimiputimít dictionaries, recording Nimiipuu names in accordance with their own constructs. It was also common for people to assume different personal names, leaving non-Native record keepers with a bewildering array of names. Consequently, we have settled on one version of each personal name in the text and have included a list in the front matter to provide the variations.

Another facet of the captivity narrative is distance. Faced with deportation and relocation across a significant portion of the United States, the Nimiipuu, Palus, and Cayuse captives were taken from Montana, Idaho, and other western locations to Fort Leavenworth, Kansas, then moved to the Quapaw Reservation in the Indian Territory, and finally transferred to the Ponca Agency, Indian Territory. Since there were many deaths and burials in the course of these travels, the map that accompanies this text indicates only the broad sweep of the journeys. Neither the text nor the map indicates precise locations of graves; the book is purposefully vague regarding exact travel routes and camps in order to avoid the exhumation of human remains or grave goods.

CHAPTER 1

Policy, Politics, and Administration

Prologue to Captivity

The Nimiipuu occupied an aboriginal land base of more than 13.5 million acres at the time of their first contacts with the United States in 1805 and 1806.[1] They had lived in the same plateau area for at least ten thousand years, and the Nimiputimít language stems from one of the oldest language stocks in North America. Sacred histories account for the origins of the people, their location in their homelands, and their connection to the land. Land provided subsistence, affluence, liberty, and power. In contrast to mechanistic concepts of land tenure, however, Nimiipuu individuals did not own land; rather, they shared intense communal and spiritual relationships with the land and its other inhabitants.

Bound together in a peoplehood of common language, a sacred history, shared ceremonials, and aboriginal territory, an estimated four to six thousand Nimiipuu engaged in seasonal hunting, fishing, and gathering activities throughout their homelands. In winter they came together in sedentary villages located along the Snake, Clearwater, and Salmon rivers. Related families and bands often wintered in the same villages; bands that were hunting in Montana either wintered there or snowshoed home. Ceremonials held in the winter villages formed the backbone of the Nimiipuu spiritual calendar.[2] Nimiipuu governance was loosely structured, and there was no organized central government or supreme chief. Each village typically followed its own leader. Village leaders participated in a band council for consensual decision making, although as legal scholar John K. Flanagan noted, the Nimiipuu remained autonomous at all levels.[3]

The Nimiipuu enjoyed healthy intertribal trading relationships, and they maximized the opportunities for transportation offered by swift-flowing rivers and streams. By the mid-eighteenth century, they had transitioned into a horse culture, adopting Spanish horses that filtered into their country from the south and east. The Nimiipuu practiced selective livestock breeding and were known for their superior horses. Women were heavily involved in the trade economy and provided the majority of the labor to sustain their families.[4]

For thirty years following the Meriwether Lewis and William Clark expedition in 1805–1806, the Nimiipuu participated in the global fur trade economy. Even though the fur trade initially offered few economic or sociopolitical advantages, the Nimiipuu made the most of their fiscal opportunities, and by the 1830s they enjoyed prestige, wealth, and independence as a result of their involvement with the trade.[5] Meanwhile, the United States and Christian missionaries were expanding their interests in the northwest. Jesuit priests and Protestant evangelists, such as Marcus Whitman, the Reverend Samuel Parker, and other missionaries, proselytized among the Nimiipuu, the Cayuses, and other Native nations.[6] Resident Presbyterian missionary Henry H. Spalding was sent to the Nimiipuu in response to their requests for teachers and textbooks, and settled near Lapwai Creek in 1836. Spalding, however, interfered with local governance and joined forces with medical missionary Elijah White to introduce new laws to the Nimiipuu. Designed by Spalding, the laws were not set down in federal or public statutes, but they were precursors to the Nez Perce treaty of 1855 and formal intervention in Nimiipuu governance. Delivered in 1842, the laws violated the Nimiipuu's civil rights and began to shift political power to the federal authority.

These laws also condoned capital punishment, supported the change to an agrarian economy, and granted Native leaders jurisdiction over American Indians. American Indian agents and non-Native authorities, however, adjudicated crimes committed by non-Native people in Indian Country. White also introduced the idea of a centralized head chief and the concept of majority rule to the Nimiipuu. He reinforced the idea that without treaties, the Nimiipuu were politically responsible to the United States. Meeting with twenty-two chiefs, headmen, and a group of Nimiipuu, White considered the men in attendance to be a majority empowered to change tribal governance.[7] The laws enacted by this council were intended to make the chiefs accountable to non-Native authorities for law and order.[8]

Unlike the traditional autonomous bands, the proposed government consisted of one governor or head chief, twelve subordinate chiefs of equal power drawn from the heads of different villages, and five officers to implement their orders. The federal authority sought to create new governing structures that marked a clear line of authority to facilitate later treaty-making processes. The council members were introduced to majority rule when they were told to select the new head chief. They were confused about the process, so after introductory speeches and remarks, the federal interpreter and other officials helped to select the first chief.[9] The officials and council members finally selected a young English-speaking stockman and farmer named Ellis who held no hunting or war honors. Untrained and facing community opposition, Ellis and his band eventually moved east to the buffalo-hunting country.[10]

Spalding was determined that once the Nimiipuu became farmers and had settled on small, permanent farms, their excess lands would be available for non-Native settlement.[11] The new laws also reflected the conflicts inherent to a community adapting to an agrarian economy and federal constructs. These laws were not overwhelmingly accepted by the Nimiipuu, although they were institutionalized by the treaties of 1855 and 1863. With those treaties, the federal government legitimized the head chief as a centralized figure of authority who received a federal salary and benefits.[12]

Federal treaty making was planned in advance, at pre-treaty councils, while surveys and expeditions provided federal officials with detailed reports about prospective treaty nations. In the case of the Nez Perce treaty of 1855, Isaac Stevens, governor and ex officio superintendent of Indian affairs for the Washington Territory, spent two years preparing for treaty councils with Native nations. As head of the Pacific Railroad Expedition and Survey, Stevens was charged with selecting and mapping the railroad route across the northern United States. He also controlled topographical and mineralogical surveys, interviewed prospective treaty nations, and filed voluminous reports. Convinced that Christian Indians would be easier to manipulate, Stevens believed that the Flatheads, the Spokanes, and the Christian Nimiipuu would honor nonviolent Christian ideals. He also intended to remove all of the northwestern Native nations onto consolidated reservations in eastern and western Washington Territory.[13] Commissioners of Indian Affairs Luke Lea, Charles E. Mix, and George Manypenny, who guided treaty making during this era, focused on acquiring land to facilitate Manifest Destiny and on placing American Indians on fewer, more compact reservations.[14] Stevens also planned to control American Indian resistance, to ensure compliance with federal authorities and edicts, and, most importantly, to control American Indians' interference with settlers or other non-Natives. As a result, he and Governor Joel Palmer of the Oregon Territory repeatedly threatened unrestricted settler invasions of the Nez Perce nation unless the Nimiipuu would accept their proposed treaties.[15]

The treaties of 1855 and 1863 reduced Nimiipuu landholdings by more than 13 million acres. The Nez Perce treaty of 1855 established the Nez Perce reservation; reserved fishing, hunting, and gathering to the Nimiipuu in their usual and accustomed places; protected water rights; and instituted "civilization" provisos that governed agriculture, education, flour mills or lumber mills, hospitals and physicians, and federal employees. Other stipulations called for federal payments and surveys, roadways, preservation of friendly relations with the United States, and the prohibition of alcohol. The treaty also attempted to restrict the Nimiipuu to certain areas of the reservation and to allot them individual farms, and it penalized those who abandoned their farms. The Nimiipuu were pledged to peaceful relationships and were required to defer differences with other Native nations to the federal government for adjudication.[16]

The treaty legitimized White's efforts to implement a centralized system of governance by stipulating that the person selected as head chief would become, in effect, a federal employee after ratification of the treaty. The head chief's duties were specified, and the government agreed to pay his annual salary of $500 for twenty years. The government also agreed to provide the head chief with a comfortable home and ten acres of plowed and fenced land. Education probably influenced the selection of Lawyer as the first head chief in 1855, and religion may have played a role as well. Lawyer was a bilingual English-speaking Christian, and Governor Stevens preferred dealing with Christians. Lawyer accepted the duties of head chief when he signed the Nez Perce treaty of 1855. He became responsible for tribal behaviors and was to notify the superintendent or the agent about crimes committed by the Nimiipuu against territorial citizens. Lawyer was also required to remand all accused non-Native people to the Bureau of Indian Affairs and to record and seek redress for injuries done to the Nimiipuu there. Assisted by advisory subchiefs and the military, the federal government agreed to support Lawyer's decisions. The superintendent of Indian affairs, however, reserved the right to terminate Lawyer's services if he did not perform to the superintendent's satisfaction.[17] Records do not show that a Nimiipuu council selected Lawyer as head chief, and there was some opposition to Stevens's choice. Despite selective resistance, Lawyer became head chief when the treaty was ratified in 1859.[18]

Governor Stevens reinforced the laws of 1842 in the treaties with a sliding scale of salaries and tangible benefits that bound head chiefs to the federal government. He also implemented the position of head chief in treaties with the Walla Wallas, Cayuses, et al., the Yakamas, the Kootenais, the Flatheads, and the Pend d'Oreilles in 1855.[19] Along with Lawyer, these men formed the nucleus of a system of head chiefs that became central to the colonization of American Indian governance. For example, Lawyer subsequently signed a series of treaties favorable to the United States, including the unratified peace and friendship treaty of 1858; the unratified treaty of 1861, which proposed opening vast areas of the Nimiipuu reservation to miners and prospectors; and the treaty of 1863, which cost the Joseph's band the Wallowa Valley. In 1867, however, Lawyer signed an amendment to the treaty of 1863 that protected reservation timber and eased restrictions on removal to the reservation for Nimiipuu farmers.[20]

The Nimiipuu tried to adjust to the terms of the treaty of 1855 because most of the headmen had signed the agreement. The southern Nimiipuu homelands remained intact, and by 1860, most Nimiipuu farmers remained on land off of the reservation in accordance with treaty provisions.[21] The events leading to the treaty of 1863 involved stolen Nimiipuu resources and a trail of land cessions and theft that led to war with the United States in 1877.

When gold was discovered on the Nimiipuu reservation in 1860, Idaho was still part of the Washington Territory, Abraham Lincoln was running for president, and development of western infrastructures held the attention of U.S. businessmen.[22] Sometime in 1854, a merchant from Portland, Oregon, purchased a few gold nuggets from a Spokane Indian. In response to rumors that there was gold on the Snake River, San Francisco entrepreneur Elias D. Pierce visited the reservation several times disguised as a trader, then returned in 1860 with a group of prospectors.[23] They found gold along the rivers, and Pierce made plans to inundate the area with prospectors. Federal troops failed to remove Pierce or his men from the reservation, and they moved farther into the Nez Perce nation. Claiming that he had a permit to cross the reservation, Pierce then hid for a few months before appearing elsewhere on the reservation. In May

1861, Pierce met with chiefs and leaders who did not want him on the reservation, but he remained there over the winter of 1860–61. The following March, one man in his party snowshoed out and shipped $800 worth of the Nimiipuu's gold to Portland.[24]

As Pierce had intended, West Coast newspapers soon provided directions to the Nez Perce gold fields, illustrated reservation borders, and voiced the public's determination to abrogate sovereign rights and treaties. It was understood that the gold was located on an American Indian reservation, but citizens presumed that the government would enact a favorable new treaty with the Nimiipuu.[25] Thousands of miners and prospectors flocked into the Nez Perce mining districts, and as news of the gold strikes spread throughout Oregon and California, towns sprang up on the reservation almost overnight. By the summer of 1861, sixteen hundred gold claims had been filed in the area that Pierce had explored. The mining towns of Oro Fino, Elk City, and Florence were founded in 1861, and despite Indian agents' protests, the town of Lewiston, Idaho, was also developed on the Nez Perce reservation. By October 1861, Lewiston contained about two hundred tenements and housed more than twelve hundred non-Natives. Shacks, cheap hotels, dilapidated rooming houses, and houses of ill repute were built along reservation roads leading to mines or anywhere there was water.[26] Indian Agency employees left their jobs for the gold fields, and miners rushing between gold discoveries disrupted reservation life. As the Nimiipuu warrior Yellow Wolf recalled, "Them white killers were never bothered from living on our lands. They were still there. Still robbing or shooting or hanging Indians."[27]

When the superintendent of Indian affairs proposed that the government negotiate free access to the gold fields and reduce reservation boundaries to exclude the gold districts, a new treaty was signed. Drawn between Superintendent Edward Geary, Indian Agent John Cain, Head Chief Lawyer, and forty-seven chief headmen and delegates, the treaty of April 10, 1861, was never ratified by Congress. Instead, a company of U.S. soldiers was sent to the reservation to preserve the peace. The army could not prevent miners from going into the country north of the Clearwater River, and by September 1861, an estimated seven thousand people had trespassed on the reservation. Matters deteriorated as the troops were withdrawn, and in February 1861, the Senate ordered negotiations for a new treaty to surrender the northern part of the reservation. The commissioner of Indian affairs agreed with the Senate, and in the summer of 1862, appropriations were authorized to negotiate another treaty.[28]

Idaho became a U.S. territory on March 4, 1863, and territorial officials developed legislative districts, law enforcement agencies, and infrastructures that seriously affected those Nimiipuu who were not living on the reservation. Off of the reservation, American Indians were subject to territorial and local laws that often ran counter to the federal protections afforded to them on the reservation. As ex officio superintendent of Indian affairs, the governor was a dual-purpose official who was expected to guard the interests of Native nations within his jurisdiction. Nevertheless, those nations often controlled the properties most desired by immigrants and non-Native voters. The first governor of the Idaho Territory, William H. Wallace, became the ex officio superintendent of Indian affairs after posting a $50,000 surety bond. The governor controlled all American Indian agencies and federal funds, treaty monies, and federal property on American Indian reservations within the Idaho Territory.[29] Whereas Wallace took no interest in Nimiipuu affairs, his successor, Caleb Lyon, was charged with "dereliction of official duty" after stealing $46,418.40 from the Nez Perce treaty funds. The theft was eventually deducted from Governor Lyon's $50,000 surety bond, and another governor spent his time in office tending to his business interests and mail contracts until President Ulysses S. Grant forced his resignation. When war broke out between the Nimiipuu and the United States in 1877, Governor Mason Brayman called for one hundred volunteers to fight against the Nimiipuu instead of protecting their treaty relationships.[30] Thus, territorial governors deprived the Nimiipuu of effective federal representation during a crucial period in their relationship with the United States.

Negotiations for a new treaty and cession of the gold-mining districts began when Congress refused to ratify the treaty of 1861. The resultant treaty of 1863, often called the "Thief Treaty," was a major cause of the war in 1877. It cost the Nez Perce nation $3 million in gold, which was not reimbursed until 1960. In addition to losses of more land, the treaty of 1863 upheld a centralized Nimiipuu authority and the majority-rule decision marked by the 1855 treaty. Federal authorities insisted that the signatories of the treaty represented a majority of the Nimiipuu people, so they considered the agreement legal and binding even though most of the five lower, or nontreaty, bands had not signed it. In retrospect, the non-Christian chiefs or lower band leaders may not have been notified about the treaty council and did not receive a copy of the treaty for their deliberation. Consequently, the nontreaty bands refused to accept payments or benefits from the treaty, invested no authority in majority decision making, and granted no one the authority to speak for them.[31] The five nontreaty bands that rejected the treaty were the Chief Joseph's or Wallowa band, Looking Glass's band, the White Bird or Lahmtahma band, the Palus from the Lower Snake River led by Húsus Kute and Hahtalekin, and Toohoolhoolzote's group from the high country between the Salmon and Snake rivers. The Paluses remained in their aboriginal homes along the Snake River despite federal demands that they relocate to the Yakama reservation.[32]

In addition to costing the Joseph's band their Wallowa Valley homelands, the "Thief Treaty" cost the band more than $15 million in gold, which was never repaid because it was extracted from their southern Wallowa Valley homelands after ratification of the treaty in 1867.[33] Contrary to rumors that the Nimiipuu did not value gold, they extracted the mineral to participate in the changing economy, and men such as Black Tail were said to have had more than $6,000 in gold coins by the end of the war in 1877.[34]

After the conflict of 1877, young Chief Joseph expressed his objections to the treaty of 1863:

> A chief called Lawyer, because he was a great talker, took the lead in this council, and sold nearly all the Nez Perces' country. My father was not there. He said to me, "When you go into council with the white man, always remember your country. Do not give it away. The white man will cheat you out of your home. I have taken no pay from the United States. I have never sold our lands." In this treaty Lawyer acted without authority from our band. He had no right to sell the Wallowa (Winding Water) country. That had always belonged to my father's own people, and other bands had never disputed our right to it. No other Indians ever claimed Wallowa.[35]

The treaty of 1863 contained additional stipulations that supported federal goals and programs. Individual allotments in fee title were not forced on the Nimiipuu until after passage of the Dawes Act in 1887. But as a prelude to allotment in fee title, Article 3 of the 1863 treaty provided for allocation of individual twenty-acre plots on the reservation. All men twenty-one years old or heads of families were to receive individual allotments. Allotted lands were exempt from taxes, levies, or sales and were alienable to the United States or to members of the Nimiipuu nation. The treaty also penalized Nimiipuu who avoided agriculture and preferred their freedom. Article 3 withdrew all federal payments or benefits to those who continued migratory ways of life until they took permanent homes on the reservation. Other provisions reinforced the shift to a sedentary agricultural lifestyle. The government agreed to pay the Nimiipuu $262,500 for an estimated 6.51 million acres of land, and at least $200,000 of that money was intended to support agriculture. Paid over four years, $150,000 was to be used to cover the costs of removal to the reservation and to plow and fence farms and fields, and $50,000 was supposedly designated for the purchase of agricultural implements, wagons, harnesses, cattle, sheep, and other livestock. Additional Nimiipuu capital was assigned to build flour mills and sawmills at Kamiah and to support education. The sawmill was to serve Nimiipuu home builders, and the flour mill was meant for Nimiipuu farmers.[36]

But not all of the Nimiipuu wanted to become farmers or sedentary residents of the reservation. Many participated in the conflict of 1877 because of the restrictions imposed by the 1863 treaty.[37] That treaty also presumed that the Nimiipuu desired to give up the seasonal lifestyle of hunting, fishing, and berry and root gathering that was reserved in Article 3 of the treaty of 1855. The new treaty did not abrogate the previous treaty, although it rewarded those who opted for a sedentary lifestyle. And $2,500 of the money generated by the sale of the ceded lands was to go toward building two Christian churches. Once again, majority decision making was not representative, because many of the Nimiipuu who were not at the treaty council were not Christians. Furthermore, none of the treaty funds were set aside for non-Christian practices or centers of worship. The nontreaty groups also resented being told to give up their portion of the 1855 reservation and that they must live on a reservation with the Christians. Yellow Wolf insisted that the Nimiipuu remained a people, even though different religious and spiritual beliefs would make it difficult to live too close together.

Treaty provisions reinforced federal power by giving the government the authority to build roads and highways on the reservation. The government also held the right to manage all ferries and bridges on the reservation and allowed hotels and stagecoach stands to be built along its public roads. Article 8 retained all reservation timber as the exclusive property of the Nez Perce nation, although the government reserved the right to use the timber free of charge to develop military installations. This article was amended in 1867, ending the military's free access to the Nez Perce's timber.[38]

Conditions continued to deteriorate after the treaty of 1863. The United States was involved in the Civil War and offered no effective military protection to the Nimiipuu. This was an era of federal misdeeds, broken treaties, dishonest politicians, and Indian agents who refused to meet their responsibilities. Non-Natives disregarded treaty provisions that allowed the Nimiipuu to live off of the reservation and let their livestock destroy Nimiipuu farms and fences. Soldiers stationed at Fort Lapwai imported whiskey into American Indian villages, and non-Natives sold alcohol on the reservation. Settlers resented the fact that the Nimiipuu were allowed to pasture their herds off of the reservation, whereas they were barred from grazing their animals on the reservation. Settlers also filed illegal claims for Nimiipuu farms or paid substandard prices for farms and improvements in the districts to be sold under the treaty. Nontreaty bands living off of the reservation experienced increasingly hostile encounters with incoming settlers, who often viewed them as illegitimate occupants of their aboriginal lands.[39]

Although circumstances in the Wallowa Valley were difficult, the treaty of 1863 had no immediate effect on Chief Joseph's band. When the band returned to the Wallowa Valley to hunt and fish in August 1872, however, they found that non-Native settlers and their livestock had moved into the area. Insisting that the sale of the Wallowa Valley was illegal, Joseph ordered them out of the valley. He was adamant that his father had not sold the valley when an Indian agent tried to arbitrate a temporary settlement. Trying to support the settlers and the treaties, the Indian agent instructed settlers to leave the Nimiipuu alone, because they were exercising their usual and accustomed hunting and fishing rights.[40]

Indian Agent John B. Monteith and Superintendent of Indian Affairs T. B. Odeneal met with Chief Joseph and his brother Chief Ollokot in an attempt to convince the men to move to the reservation. The Nimiipuu and the federal representatives finally reached a compromise. Because treaty making with American Indians had officially ended in 1871, federal agents recommended the creation of an executive order reservation for the itinerant Nimiipuu bands. President Grant agreed with the decision, but when the reservation was established on June 10, 1873, officials divided the Wallowa Valley along its north-south axis, even though the Nimiipuu required the grazing and livestock lands located along the east-west axis. The new reservation consisted of about half of the Wallowa Valley. However, yielding to pressure from western congressmen and politicians, the president revoked the executive order and returned the Wallowa reservation to the public domain two years later.[41] Governor Lafayette F. Grover of Oregon was a vocal anti-reservation advocate, declaring that majority rule was the recognized decision-making process, the 1863 treaty was legal, and title to the land had been established by treaty and force of law. He also insisted that the general land office had already surveyed the public lands in the Wallowa Valley and vicinity. In addition, he stipulated that there were already too many American Indian reservations in Oregon, and that citizens were against the idea of another reservation in the Wallowa Valley.[42]

Commissioners who consulted with the nontreaty bands on November 13, 1876, also warned that life in Oregon would be untenable for the Nimiipuu. They would be treated unfairly under state and local jurisdiction, and state laws would not protect them. Instead, they promised that land would be set aside for them on the Lapwai reservation, where the government would help build homes and fences, purchase farm implements, and provide other goods and services. The commission also assured the Nimiipuu that their hunting and fishing rights would be protected, inasmuch as they were compatible with a settled pastoral lifestyle. The Nimiipuu rejected the commissioners' suggestions, and Chief Joseph made it clear that he would accept no justification for non-Native settlement of the Wallowa Valley. Joseph based ownership of the valley not on the executive order but on aboriginal rights that the Nimiipuu had never relinquished.[43]

Legal scholar John K. Flanagan suggests that although the treaty of 1863 was upheld by the U.S. Court of Claims, it is invalid because of its insistence on imposed concepts of majority decision making. He states that the lower or nontreaty Nimiipuu did not sign the treaty and that the government should have established a compromise with each band without appointing a national principal chief. He also notes that General Oliver O. Howard and Major H. Clay Wood originally supported Chief Joseph's band's claim to the Wallowa Valley but then reversed their opinion and threatened military expulsion of the nontreaty bands to the Lapwai reservation. Flanagan concludes that the lower or nontreaty bands were left out of the 1863 treaty process altogether; thus they should not be held to that treaty, and their title to the Wallowa Valley was never legally extinguished. Flanagan also questions the amount of "just" compensation awarded the Nimiipuu in 1959 by the Court of Claims, because the court ignored the nontreaty bands' rights of occupancy, which had not been extinguished by the treaty of 1863.[44] There is also the possibility that the court's data supporting the value of the reservation gold and mining districts was prejudiced by conflicts of interest. The court employed an appraisal firm that was heavily dependent on government contracts, which may have cost the Joseph's band more than $15 million in gold claims and lost properties.[45]

Bigotry and pro-Christian biases also contributed to the war of 1877: peace commissioners paid lip service to religious freedom, then rejected Nimiipuu religious practices at the prewar conference held at the Lapwai Agency on November 13, 1876. Commissioners David H. Jerome, Oliver O. Howard, William Stickney, and A. C. Barstow blamed American Indian spiritual practitioners for dissension and problems with the council, asserting that they promoted spiritual quackery, and they erroneously blamed the Dreamer prophet Smohalla for the Nimiipuu's rejection of the 1863 treaty. Six months later, Howard ejected the Nimiipuu leader Toohoolhoolzote from a May 1877 prewar council for refusing to abdicate his non-Christian beliefs.[46] Many of the statutes that limited American Indian civil rights, terminated freedoms of speech, and granted the commissioner of Indian affairs or Indian agents extraordinary powers were not repealed until the 1930s. Consequently, late-nineteenth-century American Indian policies were guided by legislation and administrations that diminished American Indian land bases, abrogated tribal governance, restricted use of American Indian properties, and attempted to eradicate American Indian cultures and societies.[47]

Faced with American Indian resistance movements, the army, the Bureau of Indian Affairs, and the U.S. public were involved in a long-term debate over which federal agency should have control of the Bureau. Its forerunner, the Indian Department, had been established in 1824 as part of the War Department, but it was transferred to the Interior Department in 1849, at which time it was reorganized as the Bureau of Indian Affairs. By the late 1860s and 1870s, senior military officers and Secretary of War George W. McCrary were arguing that the Indian Bureau should be returned to the War Department. Civilian leaders, American Indian rights activists, and Indian Bureau employees wanted it to remain in the Interior Department. General Philip Sheridan supported the decision of President Grant's Peace Commission in 1867 to remove all American Indians to reservations. Sheridan also felt that as federal wards, American Indians should respect the law or face reprimands, such as wars of extermination and loss of their reservations. Once placed on reservations, he believed that they must remain segregated there or be considered hostile to the United States. Furthermore, Sheridan believed that Indian agents, superintendents, and the Indian Bureau should control American Indians but that they had failed in their duty to do so. He thought that he and the army should take immediate control of American Indians who left reservations.[48] Major General John W. Schofield supported continued civilian management of the Indian Bureau, but by 1875 he was so disgusted with the lack of control, poorly qualified Christian Indian agents, and Indian Bureau graft that he decided that the army should assume control of the Bureau. Other generals echoed the complaints, insisting that it was unfair to call on the army to settle problems caused by unjust agents and failed Indian Bureau policies. American Indian rights advocate the Reverend William H. Hare admitted that soldiers were rarely asked to intervene in American Indian affairs until situations were out of control.[49] McCrary and Sheridan also suggested that the War Department resume control of the Indian Bureau because the civilian institution was an enduring failure. According to Sheridan, American Indians should be fed and confined to reservations, where soldiers could force submission and control the "savages."[50] Transferring the Bureau to the War Department might also save the government $1.5 million a year. Other supporters of the move referred to Lieutenant Colonel George A. Custer's defeat at the Little Big Horn, Montana, in 1876 as the "Interior Department's War," brought about by failed Indian Bureau policies.[51]

The Board of Indian Commissioners and American Indian rights activists opposed the relocation of the Indian Bureau. At the core of the debate were President Grant's peace policy, the management of American Indian agencies and reservations by Christian missionaries, and control of a major government entity. Activists also resisted military supervision of civilian Indian Bureau employees. Speaking to the Board of Indian Commissioners in 1879, American Indian rights activist and former Indian Bureau superintendent Alfred B. Meacham warned that army officers serving as Indian agents would retard "civilization" programs. Addressing legislators, American Indian rights activists, the commissioner of Indian affairs, and the Board of Indian Commissioners, Meacham defended the Indian Bureau, which he said was modernizing and improving the administration of reservations. He promised that within the year, a new and improved organization would be functioning more efficiently.[52] Grant's peace policy was focused on "civilization" programs for American Indians, including removal to reservations, education, and conversion to Christianity. Meacham and most civilians supported the peace policy and the Interior Department, whereas military men, western businessmen, and frontier advocates promoted military control and management of American Indians.[53]

Both national political parties included campaign planks dealing with Indian affairs in the 1878 elections. Democrats condemned American Indian policies and held the federal government responsible for the recent problems with the Sioux, the Nimiipuu, and other Native nations. The Republican Party supported moving the Indian Bureau back to the War Department.[54] The struggle for power, money, and control was not settled during the Nimiipuu conflict of 1877; nor was it settled while the resistant Nimiipuu, Paluses, and Cayuses were imprisoned in the Indian Territory, even though they were at the heart of the debate.

Following a chain of command between Indian agents, the Indian Bureau, the secretary of the interior, and the War Department, federal officials legitimized military measures against the Nimiipuu. The nontreaty bands did not come onto the Nez Perce reservation in the turbulent decade following the treaty of 1863. Settlers moved into the Wallowa Valley in accordance with the treaty and into other treaty areas that they considered to be in the public domain. The nontreaty bands, however, refused to move onto the reservation, and Chief Joseph's band held to their premise that they had not sold the Wallowa Valley. In June 1876, General Howard proposed an interdepartmental commission to meet with the nontreaty bands. It was formed under the auspices of the Indian Bureau, the Interior Department, and the Board of Indian Commissioners, with Howard and Major Wood representing the army. Jerome, Stickney, and Barstow represented the Interior Department and the Indian Bureau. The commissioners met with Joseph's nontreaty band at Lapwai on November 13, 1876, where they presented a united front. Joseph reiterated that they had not sold the Wallowa Valley and insisted on their continued freedom. Even though intrusions into their holdings had increased and a settler had recently killed a Nimiipuu man, the band would not seek revenge. They would continue to live in peace, but they would live as free men. The band was warned that they would be placed on the reservation by military force if they did not move peacefully. Howard mentioned military involvement as the federal entities laid a legal foundation for military intervention. He reported to the general of the army that if the nontreaty bands overran settlers' lands or committed depredations on them or their properties, ample force would bring them "into subjugation." Gratified with the outcome of the meeting and the threats of military intervention, Howard suggested that the same treatment be applied to resistant bands of Yakamas and Umatillas.[55]

Warfare with American Indians was conducted under the rubric of national defense in accordance with federal and state statutes because Congress never declared war on a Native nation.[56] Consequently, Howard was careful to articulate the legalities of the police action against the Nimiipuu in accordance with these principles. "Under known interpretation of law our campaign against hostile Indians is not recognized as war," he said when he described the severity of the action against the Nimiipuu to the War Department in 1877.[57] In addition, the Nimiipuu, Paluses, and Cayuses who were captured or surrendered during the conflict were to be treated like prisoners of war, even though American Indians did not gain legal status or protection as prisoners of war until 1897.[58]

The Nimiipuu situation remained in limbo for the next six months, while civilian and military authorities remained within the parameters of legal authority. On February 9, 1877, Indian Agent John Monteith sent details of his activities to Commissioner of Indian Affairs John Q. Smith, telling Smith that he had sent four pro-treaty Nimiipuu men to confer with Chief Joseph and the Wallowa band. They carried instructions from the Indian Bureau to move onto the reservation permanently, but after careful consideration, Joseph repeated that they would not go onto the reservation until they were constrained to do so. Monteith worried that three of the other nontreaty bands might also refuse to go onto the reservation under the current circumstances. He then warned Joseph that the band must be on the reservation by April 1, 1877, or the military would force their removal. Having set the date, Monteith required Smith's confirmation of his decision and asked that Smith forward the request for military aid through the secretary of the interior and the War Department. Monteith was convinced that if Joseph and the nontreaty bands were not forced onto the reservation then, Joseph would never submit to the procedure.[59] Smith agreed with Monteith's plans to use force and submitted his agreement to the secretary of the interior. The secretary concurred with Smith, and on March 6, 1877, he asked the secretary of war to order federal troops to assist the Indian Bureau with the "peaceful" removal of the Nimiipuu to the Nez Perce reservation.[60] One week later, General Edward Townsend notified General Irwin McDowell that he was to assist the Indian Bureau with the relocation. General William T. Sherman's adjutant general, Townsend, and Assistant Adjutant General Samuel Breck agreed that the army would "protect and aid" the Indian Bureau. The army was not, however, to interfere with civilian authority and was not to initiate military action. The removal was a fragile operation that was to be conducted with prudence, and the Indian Bureau was in charge of the relocation. Townsend also relayed the message to various army officers that the Bureau was expected to resolve the question in accordance with the treaties.[61]

On May 21, 1877, General Howard telegraphed the War Department that everything was in order. The nontreaty Nimiipuu were aware of his thirty-day notice to move themselves and their livestock to the reservation and that troops were at Lapwai to enforce their compliance.[62]

CHAPTER 2

Lapwai to the Bear Paw

The Road to Surrender

The Nimiipuu's struggle to retain their sovereign and civil rights held center stage in the debate over national security and development of the western United States for four months in 1877. The press clamored for protection of the western frontiers as the War Department shifted into high gear to solve the "Indian problem." Following Custer's defeat at the Little Bighorn in June 1876, westerners were terrified of the Sioux, and federal authorities recommended that all recalcitrant American Indians be incarcerated at St. Augustine, Florida. Failing that, authorities advised that all American Indians located within the western states and territories should be relocated to the Indian Territory. The debates over control of the Indian Bureau accelerated, and General Philip Sheridan dominated a national media that vilified sentimentalism directed at the uncooperative Sioux.[1]

The situation only worsened in the West when the army attempted to force the Northern Cheyennes and Sioux onto reservations. Colonel Nelson A. Miles and the Fifth Infantry were in the field almost continuously after October 1876, and they engaged in a series of brutal winter marches and battles that culminated in the surrender of various bands of Sioux and

Northern Cheyennes. By July 1877, there were at least forty-eight lodges of American Indians living at Cantonment on the Tongue River (later renamed Fort Keogh) in Montana, including the Northern Cheyennes and Sioux who served as army scouts against the Nimiipuu. Miles was preparing to insert a military presence between the Sioux in Canada and the United States when he was ordered to keep his troops in the Yellowstone Valley. Within the month, Miles and the Fifth Infantry were chasing the Nimiipuu as they tried to escape into the Judith Basin in Montana.[2]

Federal officials involved in the prewar councils held at Walla Walla, Washington Territory, and at Fort Lapwai, Idaho, excluded Nimiipuu women from the meetings while granting army wives and non-Native dependents privileged access. Some of those women, including army surgeon John FitzGerald's wife, Emily, recorded details of the councils that differed from those of federal reporters. Even though her accounts were biased against the Indians present at the councils, she did acknowledge the presence of women at the meetings. Mrs. FitzGerald made it clear that she disliked the nontreaty Nimiipuu. She presumed that they were dirty and smelled strongly "Indian," and she even rejected their nonwestern clothing. She preferred the pro-treaty Nimiipuu, who wore western suits and clothing, cut their hair above their shoulders, and were not heavily painted.[3] Of the nontreaty men, Mrs. FitzGerald found Chief Joseph's brother Chief Ollokot especially repugnant, describing him to her mother as a "wretched looking Indian, hair, forehead, and eyes painted a bright red."[4] Paradoxically, she was rather fascinated by Joseph, whom she described as a "splendidly horrible looking Indian."[5] Mrs. FitzGerald also supported the assumption that federal policies would result in civilized American Indians. "The Nez Perce Indians are at war with the whites," she said. "What a blow to the theories of Indian civilization."[6]

Although non-Native women were allowed inside the church for the council, the Nimiipuu women were placed outside the building. Marking the event with their best clothing, they wore multicolored ensembles such as yellow skirts, blue scarves, and red dresses. Several were wrapped in handsome bleached robes made of buffalo hides that they had decorated with bands of beadwork. Interested in the artistic abilities that the women had demonstrated in producing the garments and regalia, Mrs. FitzGerald paid no attention to their intellects or thoughts. She questioned one woman about her beaded leggings but was ignored, and she commented on another ermine-trimmed outfit and an ornate horse headdress and decorated regalia. When the diplomatic efforts failed, Mrs. FitzGerald wanted Chief Joseph killed and the nontreaty bands consigned to the bottom of the Red Sea.[7]

Trying to avoid war, the nontreaty bands and federal officials arranged further meetings, which were recalled by Nimiipuu observers and Captain William C. Painter's young son Harry. In 1877, Chief Ollokot met with John B. Monteith three times between February 15 and 17, trying to convince the Indian agent that the nontreaty bands did not want to leave their homes and families and go to war. Concerned about previous councils and misunderstandings, the Nimiipuu arranged another meeting with General Howard at the Umatilla Indian Agency in March 1877. Howard encouraged the visit and then sent a young lieutenant to attend the meeting in his place. Years later, the warrior Yellow Wolf recalled that Ollokot was insulted by Howard's decision to substitute his subordinate. Harry Painter, whose father explained the historical nature of the gathering to his sons, remembered that Indian agent Narcisse A. Cornoyer and his father agreed with Ollokot that Howard's avoidance of the meeting was a mistake. They understood that the Nimiipuu deserved an informed response to their concerns. Howard was forced to hold another meeting on April 19 and 20 in Walla Walla, which he attended, but an ailing Chief Joseph missed that conference.[8]

Thanks to Dr. and Mrs. George M. Sternberg and Harry Painter, history has an alternate description of the assembly held at Fort Walla Walla on April 20. Chief Ollokot filled in for Chief Joseph at the council, and unlike Emily FitzGerald, Mrs. Sternberg appreciated Ollokot's strength, good looks, and forceful demeanor. A skilled diplomat, Ollokot was energetic and impressive when objecting to the injustices of the 1863 treaty. Seated on benches along one side of a long table, the Nimiipuu faced their non-Native counterparts, who were seated similarly across the table. Army officers, non-Native ladies, and the Sternbergs sat on the available chairs, while some of the Nimiipuu women were relegated to the floor.[9]

Harry Painter remembered the Walla Walla councils, thanks to his father's insistence that he understand their significance. Captain Painter explained to Harry that war was coming and that the Nimiipuu had been "willfully wronged." He then took Harry to Charles Phillips's studio so that the boy could see Chief Ollokot and the other leaders pose for their photographs. "I was young," Harry told historian Lucullus McWhorter, "but it all made an impression on my mind that has endured."[10] Accordingly, Harry never forgot the Nimiipuu gathered in front of the old Walla Walla courthouse or his father's recollections of the council. Ollokot held his ground with General Howard, who threatened to send federal troops to occupy their homelands in the Wallowa Valley. Howard argued that the Nimiipuu must agree to relocate to the Lapwai reservation, but Ollokot refused to make any promises and forced another meeting on May 3, 4, and 5 at Lapwai.[11] On March 24, 1877, about six weeks before the meeting, Howard had received orders to force the nontreaty bands onto the Lapwai reservation in accordance with Indian Bureau requests.[12]

Gathering for the meeting in May, General Howard's aide-de-camp Charles E. S. Wood, Emily FitzGerald, and several Nimiipuu participants remembered the bands and families as they entered Lapwai. Expectations of serious negotiations were fostered by the procession that circled the council grounds. Long lines of men clad in distinctive regalia rode horses decorated with elaborate beaded accessories and plumes made of eagle feathers. Women and children joined the chanting men and rode behind them in the protective order of the march. Once again, the women wore bright shawls or colored blankets, ankle-length skirts or colorful dresses, beaded leggings, and fiber hats. Many of the mounted women carried babies in decorated cradleboards, and older children rode small horses. Men displayed special ornaments made of eagle feathers or bear claws as the processional circled the camp three times. A large hospital tent was erected inside the compound, where delegates spoke with Howard and Wood or with the Indian agents and Lapwai Agency personnel. Resplendent in their finest clothing and regalia, the Nimiipuu were joined by army officers in dress uniforms and Indian agents wearing suits. Surrounded by their children, the women were arranged outside near the open tent flap and beneath the rolled-up tent sides. In later recollections, Howard voiced his concern that the chants sung during the procession ended on an affirmative, almost defiant note.[13]

Displeased with the results of the council on May 5, Emily FitzGerald favored forced removal of the nontreaty bands to the Nez Perce reservation. More fully attuned to the intricacies of the negotiations, the Sternbergs noted on June 14 that Joseph's band and their allies had agreed to remove to the reservation. In order to avoid war, the bands would try to make the best of conditions there. But the next day, Mrs. FitzGerald complained to her mother that the Nimiipuu had not gone to the reservation. Events spiraled out of control after several young Nimiipuu men killed a white man to avenge the murder of one of their relatives, and on June 17, 1877, troopers attacked a Nimiipuu group who were protected by a flag of truce. As a result, between June 17 and October 5, the nontreaty bands were involved in a defensive retreat and conflict with the United States. They fought eleven engagements and traveled almost two thousand miles trying to avoid federal troops before the final battle at the Bear's Paw, Montana.[14] Hundreds of families fled with the refugees, taking with them thousands of pounds of tepees and household goods, and about four thousand horses.[15]

American Indians throughout the West were drawn into the conflict, including Chief Crazy Horse of the Oglala Sioux, who was killed at Camp Robinson, Nebraska, allegedly because of his attitude toward the Nimiipuu. When asked if he and the Oglala would fight against the Nimiipuu for the United States, Crazy Horse was reported to have said that he would join and fight until all of the white men were killed. The interpreter, however, had misquoted Crazy Horse. The chief had promised to fight until all of the Nimiipuu were dead. He was killed while resisting arrest as a result of the false interpretation.[16]

The national press trumpeted the military news, including Colonel Custer's defeat and the post-Custer American Indian resistance movements. Correspondents and reporters wrung every detail out of the prewar councils and relocation meetings with the Nimiipuu. And with few exceptions, their accounts reordered the Nimiipuu resistance and its aftermath as predominantly male activities, ignoring women, Nimiipuu narratives, and non-governmental tales of the conflict.[17] Although male commissioners and authorities accorded Nimiipuu women no authority, women did attend the prewar councils and meetings. Even though federal officials seated them in unfavorable locations, Nimiipuu women normally attended community meetings and usually opted to remain silent. They did, however, influence subsequent decisions, and women who disagreed with a conclusion signaled their displeasure by leaving the meeting. Women also made their own political decisions. Toko-ma-po (Jean), for example, left her husband to support the Nimiipuu resistance. She felt that she must support a conflict that had been caused by non-Native encroachment on the nation's sovereign territory.[18]

During the Sioux and Nimiipuu campaigns, Colonel Miles's infantry marched more than four thousand miles, killing, capturing, or evicting nearly seven thousand Sioux, Northern Cheyennes, and Nimiipuu.[19] The army employed three divisions, and about two thousand men were assigned from six western military districts to pursue the Nimiipuu. Most senior officers were Civil War veterans, and many of them had recently served in the Cheyenne and Sioux campaigns after Colonel Custer's defeat. Surgeons and veterinarians cared for the soldiers and animals, while hundreds of technicians and engineers kept the equipment functioning. Transportation was provided by the quartermaster general and hundreds of teamsters, wheelwrights, and wagon masters. Steamboats delivered supplies up the western rivers, and the railroads brought men and materials to Bismarck, North Dakota, where the telegraph aided communication. Nevertheless, General Sheridan complained that the western and borderlands army was overextended, so Congress appropriated almost $1 million to expand the cavalry and recruited twenty-five hundred men for cavalry regiments. The War Department spent more than $495,000 for more than 6,100 cavalry and artillery horses and supplemental herds of mules and oxen. The animals were fueled by more than a million bushels of grain and many more tons of hay and forage.[20] The army was well prepared to hunt down the nontreaty bands.

On the Nimiipuu's side, women were the quartermasters and commissary generals. Men customarily supplied animal proteins for the Nimiipuu diet, while women provided the other two-thirds of the caloric requirements. Women processed and preserved the proteins and gathered and prepared roots, berries, and other vegetal materials for consumption or conservation. By mid-June, the women were heavily involved in seasonal harvests. They began gathering roots in the spring, and from early summer through August they picked berries. They processed the salmon harvests by mid-June and prepared beef and game animals for storage. The variety of seasonal fruits and vegetables, supported by the animal and fish proteins, ensured a rich and healthy diet. Spring and summer were busy times for the women, who also built the camps, cared for children and the frail elderly, tended to the wounded, and buried the dead.[21]

With few exceptions, reviews of the Nimiipuu conflict were conducted by men. According to Secretary of War George W. McCrary, American Indians constituted a force of some 260,000 "savages" by the middle of 1877, and it was understood that American Indian women made up a portion of this savage population. When General William T. Sherman mentioned the

Nimiipuu at war, he included them all under the general category of "Indians." His accounts were based on communications submitted by an all-male military, which made few distinctions between women, children, and fighting men.[22] Twenty days after the end of the Nimiipuu conflict, General Sheridan reported that Colonel Miles had captured about four or five hundred men, women, and children. Even so, the army did not count the prisoners until November 24, and the War Department was not required to record the names of the women and children. The army commonly included women and children in the "Indians killed" battle statistics, and American Indian women were always referred to in the racist vernacular as "squaws."[23]

General John Gibbon's report after the surprise attack on the Niimiipu camp at the Big Hole, Montana, on August 9, 1877, provides an illustrative example of the War Department reports. Gibbon regaled the War Department with troop movements and logistics, and praised his command. He then mentioned that Captain Richard Coomba had recorded eighty-three dead Nimiipuu on the field, and that they had found six more Nimiipuu bodies in a nearby ravine. Gibbon did not mention that most of the corpses were women and children who had been disinterred and mutilated by General Howard's Bannock Indian scouts. Howard had witnessed the mutilations and had finally ordered hastily reconstituted burials that left Nimiipuu graves open and partially disinterred bodies strewn around the Big Hole.[24] In contrast, Dr. FitzGerald's personal recollection was that there were at least thirty dead women and children on the battlefield, including several people he recognized from the April 1877 council. The woman who had refused to discuss her beaded leggings with his wife Emily and the man wearing the ermine-trimmed robe were both dead. Gibbon also reported that the troopers did not kill the "squaws" until several officers were wounded or killed, after which they shot every Indian in sight. Chief Joseph and the other leaders counted eighteen Nimiipuu men and fifty-one Nimiipuu women and children killed at the Big Hole.[25] Otis Halfmoon remembers that Kool-kool-Sni-niin's wife was one of the women killed there, and that his son was murdered by Assiniboin Indians while trying to reach Saskatchewan.[26]

General Gibbon employed the word "squaw" to describe American Indian women in attempting to justify his attack on the Big Hole. He spoke of "squaws" who tried to protect themselves and their children during the ambush. He then switched to the equally pejorative "poor wretches" to describe women who assumed submissive postures during the attack. According to Gibbon, suppliant women were not killed as long as they remained immobile, including a woman who had begged for her baby's life with a passive hand gesture. Gibbon spared her life because of her femininity; "her sex saved her," he said. Army scout commander George O. Shields justified the subsequent slaughter of the women whom Gibbon had spared. According to Shields, one of the dead women was holding a Henry rifle, and another woman's body was found near an empty revolver. Their deaths were acceptable, despite their appeals to Gibbon, because they allegedly had attempted to protect themselves. Women who were fighting for their lives exhibited the "desperation of fiends" and turned into "she-devils" who forced valiant troopers or scouts to defend themselves. Non-Native men, of course, were gallant leaders who "dealt death to many a redskin."[27]

Penahwenonmi (Helping Another), a ninety-eight-year-old survivor of the Big Hole, told a much different story about the women and warfare. According to her account, only one woman fought at the Big Hole, and that was Wahlitits's pregnant wife, who shot the trooper who had murdered her husband. Penahwenonmi insisted that the other Nimiipuu women did not fight but instead ran away, seeking cover in the brush and along the creek.[28]

Another function of post-battle essays and reports was to blame the victims. General Gibbon set the literary stage for his sneak attack at the Big Hole, telling of troopers crawling up the bluff above the Nimiipuu camp as barking dogs, crying babies, and distant horse herds broke the predawn silence. He was careful to point out that the deaths of women and children were unavoidable during surprise attacks. Gibbon also blamed the unnecessary fatalities on the early morning darkness and reiterated that submissive women and children hidden in the brush were not harmed. Failing to tell his readers about the deadly ambuscades fired through the tepees, Gibbon suggested that women and children trying to escape from the tepees were fired on because they were running away. In other words, if they had stayed in the flaming tepees, they would not have been shot. In a further attempt to justify the killing of so many women and children, Gibbon detailed specific instances in which women returned fire on the army. He praised one soldier who had shouted that the person in the distance was a woman and not to shoot. In reality, the soldier had cried, "Don't shoot the squaw, boys!" just before killing the old woman who had supposedly fired at him. Gibbon created the impression that killing noncombatants was an unavoidable consequence of the momentum of the attack. He also rationalized his role as a savior of submissive women, even though he ignored their subsequent murders. Gibbon was deaf to the screams of children burning alive in the tepees and said nothing about one lodge in which five sheltered children were murdered. He told readers of the *American Catholic Quarterly Review* and *Harper's Weekly* that the troopers torched the tepees, leaving out the part about the unarmed women and children trapped inside, and said nothing about soldiers who shot dogs and children who were hiding.[29]

General Gibbon left the impression that the situation on the battlefield was out of control, but he told his superiors that the troops had responded to his commands. Nimiipuu recollections also suggest that Gibbon could have stopped the unnecessary killing. Peo Peo Tholekt remembered two young boys who ran from a flaming tepee directly into the troops. Instead of killing the boys, one of the troopers gave them a gift, and the children were not harmed. A Nimiipuu child, Harriet Mary (Harriet Mary Stuart), recalled a trooper who took a baby from its dead mother and gave it to another woman. These gestures of humanity and Gibbon's comments suggest that the situation was not beyond his control.[30]

When studies of the war and the Big Hole are revisited, survivors' details enhance the narratives. Tom Hill recalled a love story, and others spoke of elders and of medicine men whose powers could not allay the carnage. Many years later, Hill spoke of his wife and of their wartime experiences to photographer Edward S. Curtis: "We got to our last camp. It was about nine o'clock when the soldiers charged on us. I had a wife whom I loved more than anything else. I took a horse and tied her to it, and told her to go fast. The soldiers were on all sides of us, and many of our people were soon killed or wounded."[31] Thanks to her husband, Mrs. Hill survived the attack. Owyen, Yellow Bull, and others remembered the elderly holy person Kah-pots. During the onslaught at the Big Hole, one woman asked the old man if he had any power to stop the carnage. Kah-pots cried that his powers were ineffective and that she must run away down the creek to save her life. Kah-pots, whose final medicine was working in him, could not go on, and Yellow Bull remembered that all they could do was leave him without the proper death prayers and songs. Historian McWhorter thought that Kah-pots might have asked to be left behind, so as not to slow the others' escape. Bannock army scouts killed Kah-pots as Yellow Bull and others looked back in alarm. Bannock, Cheyenne, and Sioux scouts who were allied with various army units murdered many of the frail elderly or wounded men and women left behind during the brutal march.[32]

Children recalled unimaginable memories of the war as well. Josiah Red Wolf spoke of his mother, Ta Mah Utah Likt, and his baby sister. In the heat of the assault on the Big Hole, Ta Mah Utah Likt sent her two older sons running for a willow grove. She then picked up her baby, took Josiah by the hand, and ran toward the willows. She and the baby were killed by a single shot. The anguished father could not tear the boy away from his dead mother, so he covered the terrified child with a buffalo robe, warning him to remain utterly silent. Pahit Palikt, the son of Lame John (Yo-hoy-ta-m-sat), watched from under piles of blankets and robes as a trooper killed his dog. After seeing their mother murdered, David Williams (Ee-la-we-mah) and his younger brother became moving targets as they scurried for shelter beneath a creek bank.

A number of women were injured at the Big Hole. Among them were El-liu-ta-lat-kit's wife; Mrs. Tom Hill; Many Wounds's aunt, Hin-math; Blacktail Eagle's daughter; Mrs. Mel-mel-lis-ta-li-kai-a; Ta-ko-ya-ya; Mrs. Es-pow-yes; Eiu-ya-tsits-kon, Freezing Weather Blanket's mother; and La-kau-tes-sin. Mrs. Hill, Hin-math, and Mrs. Mel-mel-lis-ta-li-kai-a survived the war and the prison camps in the Indian Territory. Chief Joseph's younger wife Spring Time and many other women, children, and elders were also wounded at the Big Hole. Chief Ollokot's older wife Aihits Palojami died of the wounds she received there, and her infant son was orphaned when Ollokot himself died at the Bear's Paw, where Josiah Red Wolf's father and his three sons witnessed the surrender.[33] The Nimiipuu, Chief Joseph said, "never make war on women and children; we could have killed a great many women and children while the war lasted, but we would feel ashamed to do so cowardly an act."[34]

Children harbored distinctive memories of the warfare. On a visit to Lapwai in 1923, retired general Hugh L. Scott met Jesse Paul (Pie Wah), who had been a small child at the Bear's Paw. Scott did not remember the little boy, but he recalled the children's wretched condition. Among those children was Harriet Mary, who witnessed the slaughter of the women and children at the Big Hole and who spoke of an encounter with tourists in Yellowstone Park. Josiah Red Wolf witnessed the deaths of his mother and sister at the Big Hole, then lost his brother George in an Indian Territory prison camp. George had not been old enough to fight in the war, although he carried messages to Colonel Miles during the surrender negotiations. Mr. Red Wolf wept when he remembered the terrible cold at the Bear's Paw and the soldier who gave his heavy coat to George. George wore that coat every winter thereafter until his death on February 14, 1883, when the temperature dropped to –20° F at the Oakland Agency in the Indian Territory.[35]

Recovering their weapons, the Nimiipuu took back the Big Hole by noon on August 9. Women stanched bleeding wounds with cold mud packs, while medicine men and women treated ghastly injuries. Women and men packed up the camp, and just after noon, the main cavalcade left the Big Hole. Several warriors and elderly men remained behind the main group, trying to locate injured people before the Indian scouts could kill them. Even the mortally wounded Gray Eagle stayed to help, and before his injured daughter In-who-lise left, Gray Eagle "tied her wounded arm to her breast, then her father and brother put her in a saddle and told her stepmother Mary to go with her and the other women and kids."[36] Injured women and children lay on horse-drawn travois or were tied into their saddles; other wounded women were held in their saddles by friends and relatives.[37] Gray Eagle died several days later. The Nimiipuu dead and wounded were hidden or carried away to confuse the military's efforts to estimate the numbers of warriors who had been killed or injured.[38]

As the battles with the army continued across Montana, many of the refugees tried to escape the violence. Their attempts to disengage often resulted in captivity or death, as with the group that sought sanctuary at the Gros Ventres and Assiniboin Agency at Fort Belknap, Montana. One morning after breakfast, a Gros Ventres man named Long Horse allegedly murdered a group of refugees at Fort Belknap, on a sandbar in the Milk River. A non-Native lady who told of the killings admitted that she did not know whether Long Horse feared Colonel Miles or if he was just mean-spirited. And according to In-who-lise, who was cared for over the winter by a Gros Ventres woman, Miles had promised the Assiniboin three blankets for every Nimiipuu male they captured. Trooper William F. Zimmer, however, maintained that a group of Gros Ventres and Assiniboin had camped together and killed the Nimiipuu for their horses. Trooper Thomas Woodruff confirmed the deaths on October 15, 1877, and General Howard also acknowledged the killings. The Indian agent at Fort Belknap, W. L. Lincoln, mentioned problems between the Nimiipuu and Gros Ventres but said nothing about the murders. Nevertheless, Nimiipuu historian Otis Halfmoon understands that the Assiniboin killed the refugees.[39] Indian Bureau and War Department records do not always assign correct names to American Indians, and the numbers of prisoners captured, transferred, or killed seldom agree with Nimiipuu recollections or other documents. Halfmoon's research thus fills the gaps in the federal record, and materials dictated by Chief Joseph and other prisoners in the Indian Territory in 1882 reaffirm the Assiniboin killings.

Other refugees were also dislocated. One woman and three youngsters were captured in the Gros Ventres country. Several fleeing Nimiipuu were also killed or wounded by Crow Indians near the Musselshell River and the Judith Basin. Joseph and other prisoners worried that a child who had been kidnapped by the Crows was being held at that agency.[40]

Nimiipuu, Palus, and Cayuse refugees were arrested regardless of their noncombatant status or their gender and were returned to Idaho or deported to prisons during 1877. Another deportation narrative tells of the Red Heart band, whose members were arrested at the beginning of the war. Opting to remain neutral, the group had gone home to the south fork of the Clearwater River, but General Howard incarcerated them as resisters regardless. Families were rounded up, horses and equipment were impounded, and the band was marched to prison at Fort Lapwai.[41] Sorrowing friends and families tried to visit the prisoners at the stockade, but orders were issued to move Red Heart's band farther away. Waves of grief swept the community as the prisoners left for Fort Vancouver in the Washington Territory on August 4, 1877. The stockade gates opened to a dismal sight when the weeping, shouting prisoners were marched out. Men tore ornaments from around their necks and decorations from their clothing, throwing them over the barricades to friends and family. In return, spectators tossed their beaded decorations toward the prisoners, hoping the unique items would land near a friend or relative. One banished mother tore the ornaments and beadwork from her clothing for her young daughter, and an older prisoner left his moccasin decorations for his wife. Crowds of non-Natives, including the Sternbergs and Emily FitzGerald, watched the convoy being driven from the post.[42]

Four months after the Red Heart prisoners reached Fort Vancouver, former government scout James Reuben visited them there. Citing his individual reputation and his service to the government during the Idaho campaign, Reuben, who himself was Nimiipuu, petitioned General Howard for their return to Idaho, asking for Howard's personal intervention. Reuben guaranteed the prisoners' good behavior and informed Howard that they had begged to be allowed to go back to Idaho.[43] Howard and Indian inspector Erwin C. Watkins both hoped to deport Red Heart's band to the Indian Territory, but the band of noncombatants, including the homosexual man Wal-we-yes and "Old Man" Halfmoon, remained at Fort Vancouver until the end of April 1878. One infant died in the prison there, and the rest of the band was returned to Lapwai by a federal order of April 22, 1878. Otis Halfmoon remembers family stories about how the prisoners were held in chains at Fort Vancouver and how miserable the prison experience was for the detainees.[44]

Other refugees were incarcerated and sent to prison after the war ended on October 5. Sup-poon-mas (Charley Moses) and John Fur Cap (He Yoom Ya Tse Mock To Lu Ein) were shipped from Fort Keogh, Montana, on October 28, 1877, and had joined the main body of prisoners at Fort Leavenworth, Kansas, by December 5. Sup-poon-mas had been at the Bear's Paw battlefield, but he escaped before the prisoners were removed to Fort Keogh. Information supplied by interpreter Arthur "Ad" Chapman, a U.S. Postmaster named John J. Manuel, and several nontreaty informants convinced Colonel Miles that these two men were extremely dangerous and should be arrested and deported to the Indian Territory. Sup-poon-mas and Fur Cap were sent to Fort Abraham Lincoln and then on to Fort Leavenworth, where they were guarded by Captain Andrew S. Bennett of the Fifth Infantry and Sergeant Miller of the Seventeenth Infantry. Speaking in Crow and using sign language and an army officer translator, Fur Cap was interviewed in Omaha, Nebraska. He spoke of settler intrusions, crimes, and robberies committed by non-Natives against the Nimiipuu, and about their desperate attempts to escape from the army. Miles planned to imprison the men as examples to the other Nimiipuu, but more understanding authorities allowed the men to join their families at Fort Leavenworth. Their status had earlier been based on information supplied by Chapman and other men openly hostile to the nontreaty Nimiipuu.[45]

Another group of Nimiipuu prisoners was held at Fort Missoula, Montana, from late August or September 1877 to early June 1878.[46] This group included John Hill (Tu-kai-sam-po), Amos George (Thunder Eyes, In-wa-teumm She-cu), and an old man referred to as Hopan or Honan.[47] John Hill was a neutral on his way home to join his family in the Bitterroot Valley, Montana, and George was a distinguished warrior and medicine man who had scouted for General Howard.[48] Hopan belonged to the band of neutrals led by Lean Elk (Poker Joe), who usually lived in the Bitterroot Valley.[49] Another man identified as Chief "Perische" was brought into the post on September 19, 1877, from Stevensville. George and Hill were released in early summer 1878. Hill had been in the army before and planned to remain neutral against soldiers he might have served with in the past.[50] General Sherman personally released Hill from the guardhouse, and General Sheridan ordered George released.[51] Two men nicknamed "Long" and "Short" were deported to the Indian Territory from Fort Missoula in June 1878.[52] These men were probably the elderly Hopan and Chief "Perische"; Hill apparently was rearrested and deported at a later date, because he was incarcerated in the Indian Territory prison camp by late October 1880.[53]

Later that year, a group of warrior-class Nimiipuu combatants were deported from Fort Lapwai to the Indian Territory. Among them were Yellow Wolf, Samuel Fleming (Hoof Necklace, Pa-ya-wa-hiekt), Henry Tabador, Dick Johnson (Ip-na-mat-we-kin), Little Man Chief (Coots Coots Ha-me-ai-cut), Weyoosecka-Tsa-Kown,

Seelo Wahyakt (Eye Necklace), and Ko-san-yum (Luke Wilson).[54] There were seventeen men in this group, including fourteen warrior-class males who were mentioned by Indian agent Monteith on November 4, 1878.[55] Sergeant Martin L. Brown escorted nineteen prisoners to the Indian Territory on a journey that resonates with experiences of the kind alluded to by contemporary Nimiipuu. After leaving Fort Lapwai, Brown's command sailed down the Snake River from Lewiston to the Columbia River, where they transferred to a steamboat that took them to Portland, Oregon. Transshipped down the coast to San Francisco, the party landed at Alcatraz Island, then ferried across the bay and boarded the Union Pacific train for Fort Leavenworth. They traveled by stagecoach from Fort Leavenworth to their final destination in the Indian Territory. Nimiipuu also remember a group of prisoners, including the young Palus warrior He Kah Koo Sowyeen (Luke Andrews), who were captured on their return from Canada and shipped to the Indian Territory from Pendleton, Oregon. Some of those prisoners died during transport on the train, and Nimiipuu memories make it clear that their bodies were not properly disposed of.[56] Other men deported to the Indian Territory from among the Canadian refugees were Wolf Head (Heminish Húsus), Yellow Head (John Walker), Long Yellow Nose, Phillip Walker (Lah-pey-a-lute, Phillip Williams), Daniel Jefferson (Tuktena Tuk Hayakt), Kowtoliks, To-was, and David Williams.[57]

Tom Hill's band was detained and turned over to the army on August 17 or 18, 1878, at the Blackfeet Agency, Montana. Hill's band consisted of four men, five women (including his wife), and two children. Hill served as the interpreter for the conference between Chief Joseph and Colonel Miles held on October 1, 1877. Despite a flag of truce, Joseph was bound and kept prisoner overnight at that meeting. After Hill saw how Joseph was treated, he left the main group of resisters and decided not to fight anymore. Miles then sent Hill out to locate hidden Nimiipuu and uninformed resisters to tell them that the conflict was over.[58] Hill and his band stayed in Montana about a year, until they were detained by Blackfoot Indian agent John Young. A trader and settler named Charles Aubrey reported Hill's location to Captain Charles C. Rawn at Fort Shaw, who sent Lieutenant Frederick M. H. Kendricks to arrest the group. Aubrey tricked the band into remaining in the area, then told Rawn to hang them or deport them to the Indian Territory, because he feared that Hill would whip him for his betrayal. Half-starved and out of ammunition for their Winchester carbines and their one 50-caliber Springfield musket, the members of the band were living on berries when they, along with fifteen broken-down horses, were picked up. Hill tried to explain to Rawn that they had been captured by accident, and he asked that they be sent home to Missoula.[59] Despite Hill's agreement with Miles, General Sheridan ordered the band deported to the Indian Territory and their guns and horses sold. The $250 generated by the sale was sent to General John Pope at Fort Leavenworth, although the records fail to show that the funds arrived with the prisoners. Standard army practice was for captured horses to be returned to the Indian Bureau, transferred to the quartermaster's department, paid to Indian scouts, used as cavalry and infantry remounts, or destroyed.[60]

Tom Hill's band arrived in St. Paul, Minnesota, on October 5, 1878, and the nine adults and two children were shipped to Fort Leavenworth two days later, arriving on October 9. From there they were sent by train to Baxter Springs, Kansas, then taken by wagon to the Quapaw Agency prison camp. General Gibbon recommended that Hill be returned to Missoula after the rest of the band was settled at Quapaw, but Hill and his wife remained with the other prisoners until 1885. The War Department did not regard the women and children as noncombatants or neutrals.[61]

Weyat-mas Wa-hakt (Swan Necklace) and a band of five men, two women, and two boys escaped to Saskatchewan. Captured in Montana near the Blackfeet Agency about a year later, they were sent to join the main body of prisoners in the Indian Territory. A prisoner who was referred to as "Bloody Joe" was captured with several other Nimiipuu at Crow Camp, Terry's Landing, Montana, on July 11, 1878. Insisting that Bloody Joe was dangerous, Colonel

Miles sent him to Fort Snelling, Minnesota, and from there he was transferred to Fort Leavenworth. The orders issued at Fort Snelling applied only to Bloody Joe and mentioned no other band members.[62] Bloody Joe seems to be the Nimiipuu man later identified as Skou-cum-Joe ("Nez Perce Joe").

A multitude of problems dogged the fleeing Nimiipuu and their Palus and Cayuse allies. Souvenir hunters had waited near the Bear Paw battlefield until the fight ended and then went into the deserted Nimiipuu camps. They did the same thing at the Clearwater and Big Hole battlefields. Nimiipuu goods and artifacts were deemed acceptable spoils of war. General Howard's chief of Bannock scouts, Captain Stanton G. Fisher, collected bows and arrows, a woven Navajo chief's blanket, and a pipe that he claimed had belonged to Chief Joseph.[63] Colonel Miles kept Joseph's damaged shawl and the rifle that he surrendered at the Bear's Paw. In the meantime, scavengers at Clearwater loaded boats bound for Lewiston with beaded ceremonial and horse regalia that they had taken from underground caches or stripped from Nimiipuu corpses and dead horses. The shipments included ornate feathered war bonnets, beaded and feathered hoop shirts, and even a tiny rag doll. Civilian volunteers waited at the Big Hole to gather buffalo robes from the carnage following General Gibbon's attack. One forager took thirty-two buffalo robes to Helena, Montana, where collectors paid the highest prices for the bloodiest garments.[64] Dr. Sternberg purchased four or five beaded garments from a battlefield relic hunter at Clearwater, including one with matching horse regalia and a woman's beaded dress. The doctor also took a few field trophies of his own, including an ornate saddlebag. Biographer John Gibson described Sternberg's activities and the scene after the battle:

> [It was] a souvenir hunter's heyday. Back of their lines the advancing troops found their camp intact, so hastily had they abandoned it. Indian blankets were there in profusion. So were buffalo robes, food of all kinds, and any number of articles of personal use. Buried deep in the ground but easily located by the souvenir-hungry visitors

> were artistically beaded ceremonial costumes, belts, robes, and trinkets of many kinds.
>
> [Sternberg] carried off two of those battlefield souvenirs, a beaded Indian robe and a bag which allowed the Indians to load additional equipment on the back of their ponies.[65]

The most bizarre souvenir story involved the owners of the Sawtooth Ranch in Montana. They filed a claim against the Niimiipu for a $700 piano that they insisted the resisters had stolen. Federal authorities testified that they had never seen a piano in any of the Nimiipuu camps, and additional research revealed that a grand piano had never existed at the Sawtooth Ranch.[66] The war was a convenient excuse to bill the government for such things as the mythical piano.

The Nimiipuu did, however, retaliate in kind; they viewed army supplies and animals as fair game during the conflict. There was a large freight storage area on the bank of the Missouri River near Cow Island, where the Nimiipuu attempted to buy some supplies. When purchase negotiations broke down, a fight broke out on September 23, 1877, and the refugees destroyed nearly fifty tons of freight. They carried away flour, sugar, and other foods, which were later reclaimed at the Bear's Paw by the Prairie Gros Ventres.[67] On another occasion, the resisters executed a nighttime raid on General Howard's horse herd. The herd was pastured around Camas Meadows, and in the early morning hours of August 20, 1877, Nimiipuu raiders sneaked in and cut loose the hobbled bell mares. Pandemonium ensued. Shooting, shouting, and waving blankets, the patriots drove approximately one hundred frightened animals ahead of them, thinking they had stolen a herd of cavalry horses. But the cavalry horses had been picketed for the night and had twisted their ropes and leads into a colossal tangle. The intrepid raiders had stolen Howard's pack mules. When daylight came, the truth was revealed to the raiders. "Eeh!" Peo Peo Tholekt recalled. "Nothing but mules . . . all mules!"[68] Peo Peo Tholekt had wanted Ad Chapman's powerful gray racing horse, but the horse escaped in the melee. Troopers managed to recover twenty of the mules, but the raiders made sure that Howard was not able to rescue any more of them. The mules were finally recaptured at the Bear's Paw, although by then, most of them were lame or injured.[69]

Horses and mules formed the backbone of the resistance, providing transportation and serving as tactical partners. Their corpses marked skirmish lines and military charges, and injured and dying horses littered the war trails. Abandoned and escaped horses and mules were scattered across Montana, and when troopers ran out of rations at the Big Hole, they ate the Nimiipuu's horses. The army offered a $30 reward for stray mules, and prospectors and travelers hoped to secure a free saddle mount when they found an abandoned horse. The Nimiipuu's horses carried equipment and families and were excellent swimmers, crossing water where army horses could not. They also towed rafts made of tanned hides and poles that were loaded with equipment and families. Pulled by two, three, or four horses guided by swimming men, the rafts were towed across rivers and streams. When the refugees used regular boats, saddle horses swam behind, attached by lengths of rope. General Howard complained that he could never train the army's horses to swim like the Nimiipuu's horses.[70] Howard relied on rafts, boats, or bridges and met with delays when those conveniences were not available.

Army pack mules fell to their deaths from cliffs and trails, and other animals became frenzied from the sounds and smells of battle. Yellow Wolf remembered that when Chief Joseph's younger wife Toma Alwawinmi (Magdellenia) tried to mount her horse to escape from the Clearwater River, the animal was nearly wild with excitement and would not let the mother mount while holding her baby. Yellow Wolf held the horse until she climbed on, and she and her child then raced away. Peo Peo Tholekt remembered another woman who drowned with her infant when her horse lost its footing while crossing the Clearwater River. Women with babies strapped to their backs in cradleboards or carrying children behind them in their saddles loaded and drove the packhorses. One Yellowstone tourist recalled the Nimiipuu women lashing herds of packhorses through forests littered with downed timber and granite chunks. The national park echoed with the shouts of the women and their whips as they dislodged horses that had become stuck between trees, smacking the animals in the head until they backed up and found another way. The grueling march was no place for tender feelings; crippled and dead horses, and trees and logs grimed with their blood, defined the line of the march.[71]

Horses went into battle and then carried the resisters away. Instructed by war chiefs and war leaders, teenage boys held horses for fighting adults. Red Feather of the Wing tended to spare horses and delivered fresh mounts to fighting men. He also returned limited fire with a six-shooter he had picked up from a dead trooper, although he was too young to manage a rifle. When war leader Toohoolhoolzote directed men to drop back and fire, he sent a group of boys to hold the warriors' edgy horses. When the fight turned against the men, the boys rode or ran for their lives. Women delivered fresh horses to the battlefield and then dismantled tepees and lodges, packed the horses and travois, and drove the herds and pack animals. Grandparents cared for children, and elderly men helped to tend the horses and to move the camps. Older men were camp criers who kept track of people killed during the day and repeated their names in the camps at night.[72]

Ad Chapman counted 1,531 horses that had been captured by the army at the Bear's Paw and agreed that Colonel Miles had awarded 300 of the animals to his Sioux and Northern Cheyenne scouts. Another 500 of the captured horses died or were lost or stolen during the march from the Bear's Paw to the Tongue River in Montana after the surrender. Thousands of the Nimiipuu's horses were never accounted for after the conflict, although individual narratives tell of personal losses. Lynus Walker recalled that his grandfather Yellow Head lost 100 horses during the war.[73] Toohoolhoolzote lost 20 horses during one engagement at Clearwater. In the end, Miles held about 1,200 horses at Fort Keogh, Montana, 700 of which had belonged to the Nimiipuu,

Paluses, and Cayuses. Many of the animals were crippled or footsore, and despite Miles's promises to Chief Joseph, the injured animals, all of the foals, and mean or spirited horses were shot. At least 229 of the best animals were transferred to the Fifth Infantry as remounts, and one carload of impounded horses was shipped east from Lapwai. More than 300 saddles and uncounted pieces of horse equipment, buffalo robes, and tons of camp equipment were confiscated and stored at Fort Keogh. At least 100 saddles were destroyed in a warehouse fire at Fort Keogh on November 29, 1877, and the items that were not destroyed became federal property.[74] The army was authorized to impound horses to support troops and military movements, and Indian agents were authorized by federal statute to impound and sell American Indians' horses at their discretion.[75]

The resistance of 1877 nearly bankrupted the Nimiipuu and their allies. Chief Joseph maintained that the nontreaty bands lost at least 4,000 horses during the conflict. He also argued that they would not need federal support after the combat ended if the government would repay the value of their lost or stolen horses.[76] The secretary of war, however, insisted that impounded horses, saddles, camp equipage, and household goods were considered spoils of war and were not subject to rebate. Although Colonel Miles had promised Joseph that all of their horses and impounded goods would be returned to them when they were sent back to Idaho in the spring of 1878, General Sheridan and Secretary of War McCrary denied Miles's authority to make such an agreement.[77] "Those promises," said McCrary, "were made without a shadow of authority."[78]

The trails to the final battle at the Bear Paw were lined with graves, dead animals, ruined equipment, and other distressing reminders of the march. A Montana pioneer named Jirah Isham Allen remembered a bundle of baby moccasins he found in an abandoned Nimiipuu camp and his melancholy assessment of the conflict. "It seemed sorrowful enough in thinking it all over," Allen wrote in his diary. "I could not repress a wish that the fleeing hunted creatures would get through all right."[79]

By the time the Nimiipuu reached the Bear Paw and the last battle of the war on October 1, 1877, those who would surrender with Chief Joseph faced years of exile and prison. Many others slipped away across the border into Saskatchewan, where Chief White Bird spent the rest of his life after predicting that the United States would never deal fairly with the resisters.[80]

CHAPTER 3

Fifty Days

The Bear Paw to Fort Leavenworth

Late in the afternoon of October 5, 1877, Chief Joseph surrendered an estimated 398 men, women, and children to Colonel Nelson A. Miles at the Bear Paw, Montana.[1] The surrender was completed with restrained handshakes and a sad smile. Joseph then walked to a small tent that the army had waiting for him; clad in buckskin leggings and moccasins, a blue woolen shirt, and a gray shawl riddled with bullet holes, he bore traces of bullet wounds on his forehead, wrists, and shoulders. The apprehensive young leader had brought the Nimiipuu refugees to the end of the conflict. The surrendered men wore no face paint or special war regalia, and Joseph's front braid was wrapped in otter fur.[2] No fires warmed the Nimiipuu camps that last night, and more refugees came out of the ravines and into camp when the trumpeter played the cease-fire.[3] As a steady stream of blind and injured men, women, and children straggled into the army encampment long after dark, a war correspondent wondered, "How could Joseph have traveled so rapidly with such maimed followers?"[4] The cold deepened as women heated army rations over willow twig fires, and silent captives warmed themselves near troopers' and scouts' fires. A squad of soldiers stood guard over the battle zone, where Nimiipuu women remained in the earthen bunkers to care for injured warriors. One warrior had been buried alive in the bunkers during the shelling, and another woman and child were smothered by a caved-in shelter pit. Early the next morning, Miles and General Oliver O. Howard inspected the defense sector and the carnage that had been exacted by the heavy shelling during the final battle at the Bear Paw. Miles ordered litter carriers into the trenches, and relief details moved the wounded warriors to the field hospital. Ministering to soldiers and wounded warriors, army surgeons extracted bullets and treated the injuries caused by exploding shells.[5]

War chiefs Looking Glass and Ollokot, war leader Toohoolhoolzote, and two other important headmen were all dead. Chief Ollokot and Toohoolhoolzote had died in the rifle pits, and Chief Looking Glass was killed near his tepee.[6] Chief White Bird had escaped to Canada, while the Palus leader Húsus Kute and some of his band remained at the Bear Paw. Responsible for the protection and care of the families during the conflict, Joseph assumed his place as peace chief. Of the more than seven hundred people who had started from Idaho in June, at least ninety-six were dead, including fifty-six women and children.[7] The non-treaty bands lost huge herds of livestock, caches of food and gold dust, and tons of equipment and tepees. Men surrendered Winchester rifles, several long-range Creekmoor guns, and their ammunition. The army seized their horses.[8]

When the Nimiipuu surrendered, they became federal prisoners. They were held for two days at the Bear Paw, where physicians treated the wounded and the dead were buried. The Nimiipuu had hidden their dead before the surrender, but burial details searched the battlefield for additional corpses. Hungry children were initially delighted when Colonel Miles fed them army rations, but the pork, bacon, and other unfamiliar foods soon upset their stomachs.[9] The cold, sleet, and blowing snow and the sights and smells of the battlefield assaulted the senses as Miles prepared to move the prisoners.[10] On the morning of October 7, Miles left the Bear Paw for Cantonment on the Tongue

COLVILLE
BLACKFEET
Bear's Paw Mountains
Snake River
LAPWAI
FORT HALL
Pocatello
0
100
200 miles

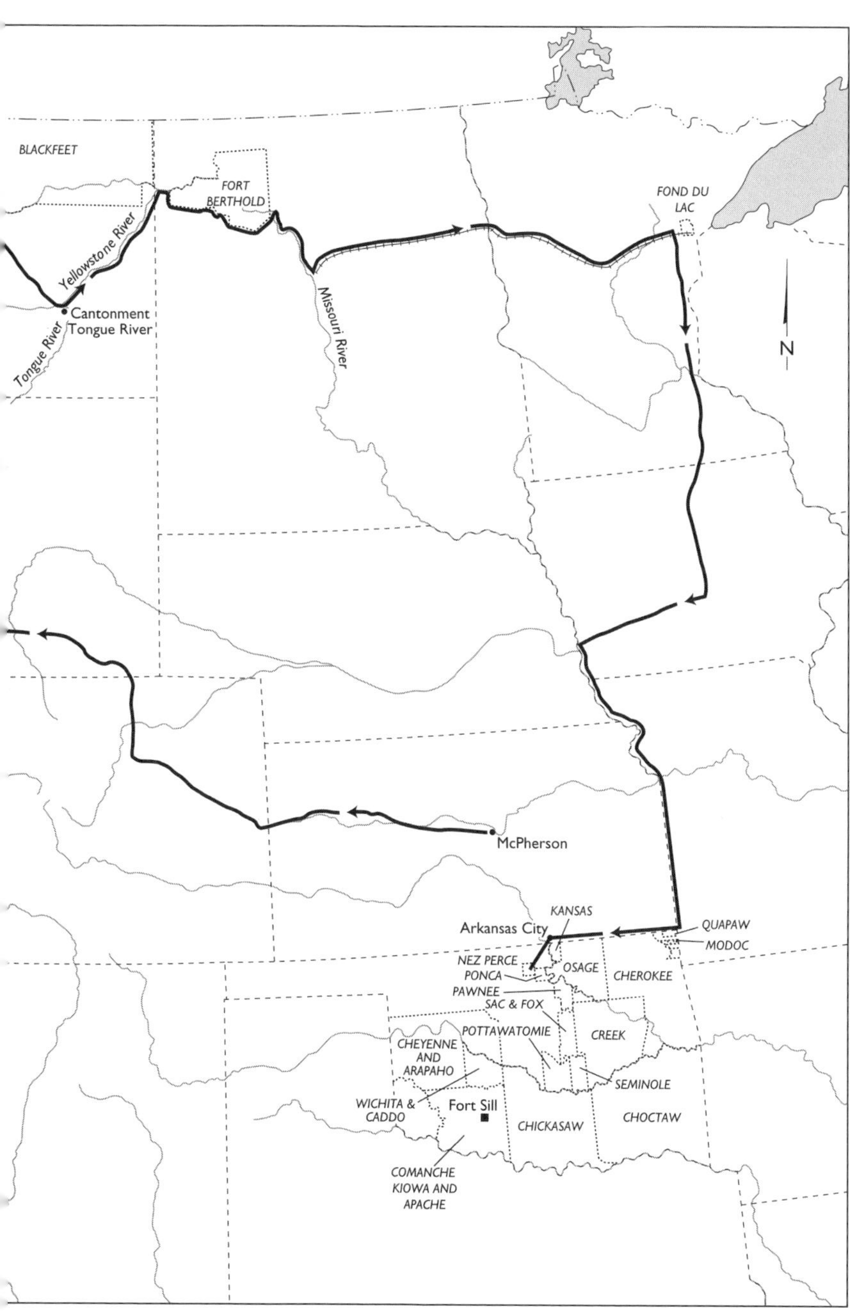

The Exiles' Trail. From the Bear Paw, Montana, on October 7, 1877, to the Indian Territory, and back north to Fort Colville, Washington, on May 27, 1885.

River in Montana with an estimated one hundred male captives and about three hundred women and children prisoners.[11]

More than forty wounded warriors were transported in brush-filled wagons, and two injured soldiers were placed in ambulances. One ambulance carried a trooper suffering from thigh wounds, and the other carried Lieutenant Henry Romeyn, who had been shot through the right lung. Soldiers cut sixteen-foot-long poles for two mule litters and for travois, but the poles were too short, and the litters were abandoned because the hind mules could not see to walk.[12] Five injured soldiers were placed on horse-drawn travois, and two extra army travois were assigned to the Nimiipuu wounded. Another fifty or sixty wounded warriors were taken away by the Nimiipuu on additional travois.[13]

A warrior who had been shot through the back was transported on a specially rigged saddle. Nimiipuu practitioners had affixed two four-foot-long sticks to it, the lower ends of which were tied to the O-rings of the cinch, then crossed over the saddle pommel, extending about eighteen inches above the horse's back. The medicine men padded the unique structure and then eased the injured man into the cradle. A buffalo robe was tucked around him, and a lariat was secured around the patient, the robe, and the frame and saddle. Surgeon Henry R. Tilton inspected the rig, even though the injured man had assured Tilton that he was all right. By the time the column reached Cantonment on the Tongue River, the patient had recovered enough to quit the support. Tilton felt that the poles of another travois were too short and that the patient being transported on it was cramped. That injured man also assured Tilton that he was not uncomfortable.[14] The prisoners did not trust the soldiers, so wounded prisoners hid their injuries whenever possible and tried not to complain to army doctors.[15]

Flanked by the captured horse herds, the prisoners rode or walked toward the Yellowstone River. Resembling a vast caravan, the command moved across the prairie behind the advance guard and the troops and herds. After them came the prisoners and ambulances, the pack trains and wagons, and the flankers and rear guard.[16] The command consisted of three companies of the

Seventh Cavalry and five companies of the Fifth Infantry, artillery, and the captives.[17]

Meanwhile, more than two hundred Nimiipuu refugees were trying to reach the Canadian border. The Red River Métis reported that thirty warriors and injured men with two hundred horses had already crossed into Saskatchewan, and Father Jean-Baptiste Genin and a party of Métis ministered to a group of injured Nimiipuu who had staggered into their hunting camp in far northern Montana. After learning that forty-five refugees were hiding at the Red River Métis camp on the Milk River, Colonel Miles dispatched a force to arrest them. Lieutenants Hugh L. Scott of the Seventh Cavalry and Marion P. Maus of the First Infantry and about one hundred infantrymen went to the Métis village, where the Nimiipuu families surrendered without a fight. Scott hired Red River Métis carters to transport the women and children and notified Miles that they would meet the main column at a camp near the Missouri River. The children wept through several cold, hungry nights because the soldiers carried only hardtack and no extra blankets. Scott then assigned a detail to kill several buffalo, and the children were wrapped in the raw hides and fed roasted buffalo meat.[18]

Traveling south from the Milk River, the prisoners entered the gruesome Bear Paw battlefield. The area was littered with animal carcasses, fresh graves, and a huge cavity where the Prairie Gros Ventres had unearthed a cache of Nimiipuu possessions. Heaps of flour, clothing, household items, and other provisions were strewn everywhere. The silence was shattered by the noisy parade of the Métis' carts and the mounted men, and a rifle shot rang out when Lieutenant Scott killed a deer on the battleground. The prisoners joined the main march at the Seventh Cavalry camp on the north side of the Missouri River, opposite the Musselshell River. Scott rejoined his unit, and the combined caravan of Nimiipuu prisoners and Colonel Miles's Cheyenne scouts continued on to Fort Keogh.[19]

Lieutenant Scott was interested in Native languages, and he used his time on the march to study the trade language known as Chinook Jargon, which functioned as a sort of lingua franca that made it easier for American Indians to communicate with Europeans and Americans. A young prisoner who referred to himself as Tipitt told Scott that he had attended a mission school, and he volunteered to teach the jargon to Scott. Scott was also interested in Tipitt's horse, which was branded with a large Mexican-style rooster, reminiscent of the Nimiipuu's trading days with John Sutter and the Sacramento, California, rancheros.[20] Once Scott's column joined the main cavalcade, the lieutenant spent several days riding with Chief Joseph and the interpreter in their wagon, asking the chief about the war.[21]

By the time the overland caravan neared the Missouri River, the prisoners were anxious to bathe and reaffirm their spiritual connection with water. Water is an intricate part of the *wéset* faith because it cleanses and heals, so as the caravan reached the river, many of the prisoners stripped off their clothing and plunged into the ice-covered water.[22] After Lieutenant Scott's group joined the main column, the convoy crossed the Missouri. They left camp on the south side of the river on the afternoon of October 16, 1877. The cross-country journey took seven days, and four wounded warriors died before reaching Cantonment on the Tongue River.[23]

One of the men was buried in the heavy underbrush near the junction of the Missouri and Yellowstone rivers. The thirty-year-old had succumbed to wounds received at the Bear Paw, coupled with the fatigue and exposure of the march. On the night of the burial, the old holy man George Washington conducted the *wéset* ceremonials. Called by a high-pitched cry, Washington responded in the same tone to mourners gathering at the grave. The warrior's body lay next to the fire-lit tomb, wrapped in buffalo robes and blankets. A small hand-bell was rung as the silent mourners stood near the grave, their blankets pulled over their heads. Representing the sound of the heart, the bell rang again, and then Washington sang the prayers for the dead. As each prayer ended, the bell was rung and the mourners chanted a response. Then the women intoned a dirge, and the grieving cries of the captives sounded again. The bell rang one last time, and the prayers were completed as the mourners disappeared into the darkness. Washington and two other men were standing near the grave when the army officers watching the service asked to see the dead man's face. After refusing their first request, Washington finally pulled back the shroud to reveal a handsome young man whose face was framed by long black hair and marked by clean, aquiline features. The officers agreed that the corpse was good-looking, and Washington reaffirmed that he had been a fine man. The other two men then laid the body to rest.[24] A fifth warrior died just before the column reached Fort Buford and was buried on the south side of the Missouri River before November 8.[25]

On October 23, the party reached the bluffs above the river across from the cantonment, and the caravan deployed into parade mode. Having spied the approaching column, jubilant men, women, and children rushed to the riverboat landing. Mounted on horses or riding in every available conveyance, the galloping horde was trailed by gangs of barking dogs. Joined by Colonel Miles's Sioux and Cheyenne scouts, those stationed at the cantonment hurried to greet the column as it ferried across the Yellowstone River. Riding prized Nimiipuu horses that they had taken to the cantonment in advance of the column, the scouts were "painted in gorgeous colors . . . [and were] shouting and crying the results of their prowess and victory"; the prisoners were taunted with their own horses.[26] Meanwhile the cannons boomed, and the Fifth Infantry band joined the uproar, belting out military and inspirational music. Soon after the column had crossed the river, the band played snippets of the popular song "Not for Joseph," the lyrics of which went "Not for Joe, not for Joe / If he knows it, not for Joseph / No, no, no, not for Joe / Not for Joseph, oh dear no." The prisoners did not understand the suggested sarcasm until interpreter Ad Chapman explained the insult to Chief Joseph. Joseph just pulled his blanket tighter and said nothing. Families living at the cantonment were not overly interested in the captives, beyond knowing that their loved ones who served in the army were no longer in danger. Alice Blackwood Baldwin, the wife of an officer who was stationed at the post, expressed the prevailing sentiment when she mentioned that Joseph was just another prisoner who had lost his fight for freedom and his aboriginal rights.[27]

Sometime between October 23 and 31, Chief Joseph, his companion Jackson, and two teenage boys were taken to John H. Fouch's photography studio at Fort Keogh.[28] Fouch took two photographs of Joseph, one of Jackson, and one of the boys. In these images, the toll of the preceding months' fighting and travel is clear. Joseph is pale and thin with bags under his eyes, and deep worry lines run from his nostrils to his mouth. Wrapped in a worn blanket, he is wearing a new shirt that appears to have been purchased from the post trader. The boys are brutally thin; one youngster's chest is skeletal, their toes are poking through their worn moccasins, and they too have deep circles under their eyes. Seated in front of a painted backdrop of leather tepees and happy woodland Indians, holding studio prop straw hats, the boys appear stunned and out of context. The photograph of Jackson was composed without romantic innovation in front of a blank canvas, with Jackson wrapped in a plain blanket. Identified as Joseph's aide, Jackson was recorded in the 1878 ration list as the head of a three-person family consisting of him, one woman, and a boy.[29] Joseph also posed for photographer Orlando Scott Goff in Bismarck, but by then he had gained weight, and the lines in his face were not as pronounced.[30] Although that image is in black and white, the sheen on Joseph's face suggests that he wore red face paint for this semiformal portrait.

On the evening of October 29, a courier rode into the cantonment bringing orders from General Alfred H. Terry to send the prisoners and Colonel Miles's Cheyenne scouts to Fort Abraham Lincoln, Dakota Territory.[31] Miles had promised Chief Joseph that the Nimiipuu would spend the winter on the Tongue River, but now he was being instructed to proceed regardless of the weather or other interference.[32] Joseph resisted the move, reminding Miles that he had guaranteed their return to the Lapwai reservation in the spring. Miles explained that supplies were low at nearby Fort Keogh and that it was more cost-effective to hold the prisoners over the winter at Bismarck, Dakota Territory. Joseph reluctantly agreed to move to Bismarck for the winter, assuming that the Nimiipuu and their allies would be returned to Lapwai from there.[33]

Following a day of hasty preparations, the captives were on their way to Fort Abraham Lincoln. Most of the men and some of the women were marched overland, while nearly two hundred women, children, elders, sick, and wounded were shipped upriver on fourteen flatboats. Fred Bond's boat, the *Leader,* transported twenty-two of the prisoners and their baggage, plus Bond's gear, the food, and other supplies. Bond normally traded in buffalo carcasses, but he had contracted with the army to deliver the prisoners more than eight hundred miles to Fort Buford and then on to Fort Abraham Lincoln. He recorded his saga of the river-bound captives in a self-aggrandizing, romanticized manuscript titled *Flatboating on the Yellowstone,* which has been published several times since 1877. When historian Lucullus McWhorter questioned Bond about the trip, he added nothing new to the tale and insisted that he had recorded the events honestly.[34] Despite the problems with the manuscript, which reinforce Bond's notion of himself as the captives' savior, it is an interesting source of information.[35] When the narrative is enhanced with data from army records and other materials, a representational view of the captives' experience emerges.

The flotilla of fourteen flatboats left Fort Keogh on October 31, 1877, on a late fall day marked by brilliant sunshine and cold temperatures. The Yellowstone River was running with slush ice as the boats hurried to reach Fort Abraham Lincoln before the rivers froze. On the trip upriver, the boats ran rapids and falls and covered about forty miles a day. One boat capsized in the Buffalo Rapids, and at least twenty captives were drowned, but no losses were recorded from the *Leader.*[36] Colonel Miles assigned two companies of infantrymen to guard the flotilla, and the rest of the army traveled overland with the captives and the horse herds. Miles sailed on the *Leader* for two days until the boat overtook the land party, and then he and Acting Assistant Surgeon R. G. Redd left the flatboats with orders to proceed as a group to Fort Buford. Dr. Redd, who had performed the postmortem identifications of Colonel Custer and the officers killed at the Little Big Horn, was reassigned to care for the Nimiipuu prisoners.[37]

The captive women faced special circumstances, and although Bond did not discuss their problems, he appeared to understand American Indian societal constructs. He selected the oldest prisoners to enhance his authority, including the woman who appeared to be the oldest female in the group. Bond described the elderly woman, whom he called Shades of Night, as tall and slender with white hair and a wrinkled complexion. When he placed her in charge of the women and children, it was a position that she probably already enjoyed. The elderly woman was also crucial to Bond's successful navigation, serving as the pilot who kept him from wrecking the *Leader.*

Bond ignored menstruation, pregnancy, and other issues affecting the war-weary women. Many of the women aboard the *Leader* may have stopped menstruating because of the stress, but others continued to cycle. The women hoarded every animal hide or bit of soft animal hair and found substitute plants to replace the milkweed and other components that were typically used for menstrual pads. Because menstrual remains were never incinerated, the women had to slip away from the *Leader* to bury them. Sacred and ultra-powerful when they were menstruating or giving birth, Nimiipuu women customarily retired to menstrual or maternity lodges during those times.[38] The captive women had no opportunities for this separation on the *Leader,* although they reestablished those practices as soon as possible.

Issued army rations at Fort Keogh, the flatboats carried dried pork and green coffee, sugar and hardtack, rice and navy beans, and flour. Aboard the *Leader,* the captive women boiled coffee on a pebble stove stoked with willow twigs. The women slept onshore and rose at dawn to build a fire, then prepared coffee and salt pork that was eaten with hardtack for breakfast. When the *Leader* stopped for lunch or for the evening, the women went ashore to gather bullberries.[39] Washington hunted deer when he had the chance, which the women processed and brought back to camp. According to Bond, Washington and the other prisoners hunted and fished whenever they could. At Fort Buford, Bond resupplied the *Leader* with potatoes and vinegar, and the army authorized additional rations and blankets for the second leg of the trip to Fort Abraham Lincoln.[40]

While at Fort Buford, the attractive younger women were at risk from soldiers who were waiting for a chance to fondle them as they were carried from the *Leader.* Fearing that the women would be molested, the post commander confined the *Leader*'s occupants to a log building protected by a twenty-four-hour armed guard. The prisoners were disarmed, except that Bond and Washington concealed their weapons, and Bond gave his dagger to one young woman for her protection.[41]

Bond controlled the food and the guns and was the only protection afforded the captives on the *Leader.* When Colonel Miles ordered the flatboats to proceed as a flotilla, he had expected them to stay together, so he had not provided individual protection for any of the boats. However, the flatboat pilots turned the journey into a race: the first pilot to deliver his captives to their destination was supposed to win an old silver watch. The boats ran neck and neck for a while, but Bond was eventually able to outdistance the others in the *Leader,* thus leaving his own passengers unprotected. Bond apparently enjoyed being in charge and in control. While sailing through the Badlands, he threatened the captives with tales of warlike Crows and Sioux in an effort to guarantee their obedience.[42]

When the *Leader* stopped at night, the women dug narrow sand trenches where they built low-smoking willow fires. Boys and injured men stood guard in the evening, and Bond and Washington stood the midnight watch. Bond claims that only he and Washington had access to a gun, while the other prisoners apparently stood guard armed with sticks or bows and arrows.

Leftovers were thrown into the river after meals, campfires were covered with sand, and the prisoners rubbed out their footprints. Bond feared roving bands of aggressive American Indians, and when the *Leader* approached the Mandan village near old Fort Berthold, he argued with two young men who tried to come on board. According to Bond, he swam out and pushed the men's bullboat into the river while the terrified prisoners huddled in the bottom of the *Leader.* Washington remained aboard the *Leader* with Bond's gun, prepared to defend the captives. Bond's quarrel with the strangers escalated until Indian traders and Mandan Indians stopped the fight. Concerned about the dispute, Colonel Miles asked Washington if he thought the Fort Berthold Indians were evil people. "Yes," replied Washington—the Mandans had stolen two blankets from them. But the Nimiipuu had settled the score by taking four large buffalo robes from the Mandans.[43]

The night the overland column reached the Indian agency at old Fort Berthold, Chief Joseph began his career as an intertribal diplomat. The Upper Missouri River and Plains nations knew about the Nimiipuu conflict and wanted to meet the patriots. Standing in the center of a fire-lit circle surrounded by more than fifteen hundred American Indians and a few non-Native men, Joseph faced the crowd. Speaking Nimiputimít and using eloquent sign language, he addressed the Nimiipuu, Sioux, Cheyennes, Crows, Arikaras, Mandans, Gros Ventres, and English-speakers present. He told of conditions leading to the war, of the war itself, and of their captivity. Speakers of eight languages understood the chief's dialogue, which was delivered without interpreters.[44]

The next day, the overland column set out again, and the flotilla continued down the Missouri River. The weather was stormy, with a brisk west wind, and the ice was closing the river when the *Leader* reached Fort Abraham Lincoln. The boat prisoners had grown increasingly apprehensive as they sailed farther east, and now, as they neared the fort, they were nearly immobilized by fear. When Bond pointed to the American flag, they did not even react. When a steam whistle blasted and the fort's cannons were fired, the prisoners fell to their knees in the bottom of the boat, crying and praying. After cooperating with Bond for almost eight hundred miles, they were too terrified to help him sail the *Leader* to the landing.[45] When an army officer demanded that the captives be hurried from the *Leader,* they could not move. A more experienced officer stepped in and tried to calm the situation, but by then the prisoners had to be carried from the boat up the bank and into the waiting ambulances.

The overland march from Fort Buford to Fort Abraham Lincoln took nine days and covered 250 miles. When the cavalcade was about 20 miles west of Bismarck, they were met by the mayor and a group of the town's leading citizens, who had arranged for Colonel Miles to parade the prisoners and troops through Bismarck. They guaranteed free food and alcohol for the soldiers and promised Miles that drunken soldiers would not be arrested. Most of the soldiers reported to Fort Abraham Lincoln before returning to Bismarck, and the overland captives were reunited with the flotilla delegations following the march through town. The prison camp was then set up along the Missouri River, and the officers camped near the railway depot.[46]

The Nimiipuu's blank faces and deepening depression puzzled Bond. Psychosomatic problems associated with warfare were not yet understood, and he could not comprehend why "his" captives expressed no joy or other emotion. On one occasion, he took a young female prisoner to a dance in Bismarck. He assumed that the girl was shy and silent because she spoke no English or was dazzled by the dusty splendor of Bismarck, when in fact she may well have been suffering from shock. Her reticence endeared her to the local ladies and to Bond, all of whom failed to consider that it might have been the circumstances that had caused her silence.[47]

Washington's lack of response to the triumphal parade of Nimiipuu prisoners marched through Bismarck also perplexed Bond. As the two men waited for their breakfast in a local café, the overland column of prisoners and troops led by Colonel

Miles and Chief Joseph came down the street. Everyone in town had gathered to watch the procession, and crowds stopped the pageant at Main and 4th streets to hand out food to the prisoners and express their sympathy. As they watched the stalled procession, Bond shook Washington's arm and exclaimed, "See!" White people were good after all. "They are white people and not soldiers," was the old man's response. When breakfast arrived, Washington could not eat it. He could only stare in silence as their waitress berated the soldiers for the prisoners' deplorable condition.[48]

The man commonly known as George Washington was about seventy years old. A large, white-haired man, he was active and dressed well, and he appeared to be uninjured, although his eyesight was limited by cataracts.[49] He was also a respected person whom the prisoners turned to for leadership, and a *wéset* practitioner who sang evening prayers and performed burials and other ceremonials. When the Nimiipuu expatriates recorded the names of the men who had participated in the war, they marked eight of them as "old." Several of those men could have been Washington, including Mo-Hos, Toke ka pats, Tstim meh hi, and Tuk le kas. Whoever Washington was, he accepted responsibility for the captives, spoke English, knew American Indian sign language, and was self-assured when dealing with the military. The old man was also a warrior who was prepared to fight when the hostile men threatened the *Leader.*[50] Unfortunately, he would not survive the prison camp at Fort Leavenworth.

Many priests of the old religion were with the captives, including the Palus celebrant who would come to be known as Star Doctor (Pahalawasheschit). Star Doctor surrendered with Joseph and endured the deportations to the Indian Territory until he ran away and rejoined the Paluses in the northwest. Another old *wéset* priest who spoke at the May 1877 prewar councils was also with the prisoners; General Howard had recognized him, although he did not record his name. This old man instructed the interpreter to work carefully to ensure that future generations would understand the meeting.

Bond was infatuated with a prisoner he called "Viola," who suited his romantic fantasies about American Indian women. If her father or another male relative was with her, he does not appear in Bond's narrative, although the girl's mother and the older women are noted as having watched over her. When Bond came too close or did something they considered improper, one of them pointed at the girl, who then broke eye contact with Bond. She had been reminded about her safety and about Bond's potential to harm her. Bond did not consider his constant attentions to the girl to border on sexual harassment, and he appears to have avoided overt sexual misbehavior. When he parted from the captives in Bismarck, he gave "Viola" a Bible inscribed with his name and his mother's address. Several years later, he learned that the young woman had attended the Carlisle Indian School and was serving as an army nurse in the Spanish-American War.[51]

As the Nimiipuu waited in Bismarck, Colonel Miles and several of his men were honored by the locals. Community members and army wives sponsored a dinner and dance in their honor at the Sheridan House Hotel on November 20, 1877. A late-night supper with music provided by the Seventh Cavalry Band was followed by a series of speeches and toasts by local dignitaries, Colonel Miles, Captain Frank Baldwin, Lieutenant Hobart K. Bailey, and scout Luther S. "Yellowstone" Kelly. Still worried about Colonel Custer's defeat the previous summer, city leaders congratulated Miles for protecting the northern Missouri River frontier. In return, Miles praised the developing frontier and the opportunities it offered settlers and immigrants. Then he addressed the question of Chief Joseph and the Nimiipuu prisoners. Miles recognized their honorable conduct of the war and hoped that the captives would be allowed to remain within the precincts of the Department of Dakota. The admission fee to the after-dinner dance was $10 in gold, with ladies attending free of charge. Local merchants stayed open all night while Bismarck partied until dawn, and the soldiers were drunk for days on the free alcohol.[52]

The next day, City Commission members Dr. Henry R. Porter, Colonel George W. Sweet, and William A. Bentley hosted a luncheon at the Sheridan House Hotel to honor Chief Joseph, Húsus Kute, Old Yellow Wolf (Hemean Mox Mox Khewn), and Yellow Bull. The luncheon was a booster event for Bismarck, which was the western terminus of the Great Northern Railroad and the regional center for frontier development. Dr. Porter, who had served with Major Marcus Reno's command at the Little Big Horn, and Sweet, who was an executive with the Great Northern Railroad, thanked the Nimiipuu for conducting a war free of the kind of savagery so dreaded since Colonel Custer's defeat. They also made certain that the Bismarck events were reported in the national press. Informal receptions were held in the Sheridan House parlors before lunch as men, women, and eager children met Joseph, Húsus Kute, Yellow Bull, and Yellow Wolf. Overwrought with the romance of the Noble Savage, one young woman kissed Joseph on the lips and pressed her wedding ring into his hand. The luncheon consisted of salmon and speeches that encouraged a lasting peace and an end to the "Indian Wars." Joseph and Húsus Kute expressed their desire for peace and encouraged recognition of their civil rights. They also pointed out that all people lived under the same sky, and that this should guarantee one system of laws applicable to everyone, including American Indians.[53]

The luncheon for Chief Joseph was not popular with everyone in Bismarck, although people who opposed the event aired their complaints out of town. In Minnesota, one correspondent informed the readers of a St. Paul newspaper that decent people rejected honors shown a savage whose hands were red with the blood of soldiers and innocent civilians. The author also defended the proper ladies of Bismarck, discounting rumors that certain females had displayed unseemly behavior toward Joseph, and wrote that Bismarck should have welcomed Charles Darwin's specimens of primitive man or an orangutan rather than "wild Indians."[54] The *Brainerd Tribune* contended that the prisoners were being pampered and pandered to by Indian-loving East

Coast elites, and that the conservative U.S. frontier was no place for sentimentalism or fervent liberals concerned with American Indian rights. The *Tribune* author also argued that the frontier must be purged of the "greasy savage" to make room for frontiersmen and their families, the backbone of the nation. Western resource development was another mantra of conquest as purported by the *Tribune.* And then, to seal the newspaper's anti-Indian sentiment, the *Tribune* insisted that Joseph was an impostor. Replaced by an innocent-faced youngster, the real Joseph supposedly was still in Idaho, where he would wreak more havoc. Another rumor identified Joseph as a Sisseton Dakota man named Black Thigh who had deserted from the army scouts after the 1863 Minnesota uprising. Black Thigh supposedly went west and was adopted by the Nimiipuu, who elected him chief because of his superior leadership abilities. Thus the Sisseton connection was the real reason the Nimiipuu had tried to join Sitting Bull in Saskatchewan.[55]

In Bismarck, Chief Joseph spoke with Colonel Miles twice on November 20, reiterating the surrender agreement that guaranteed their return to Idaho and pointing out that the Nimiipuu were relying on Miles to keep his word. But on the evening of November 21, following the luncheon and after Miles and Lieutenant Bailey had gone to St. Paul, Ad Chapman and the editor of the *Bismarck Tribune* met with Joseph in his tepee. The interpreter had been instructed to tell the chief that another move was expected, this time to Fort Leavenworth, Kansas. Miles had known about the transfer before his second meeting with Joseph on the 20th, but he had left Chapman to deliver the bad news. Pale and shaken, Joseph and the other leaders conferred until almost two o'clock in the morning. They finally agreed that they had no choice in the matter; their horses were at the Tongue River, and they had no other transportation or winter supplies. Their fervent hope was that Miles would fulfill the peace accord and send them to the Lapwai reservation in the spring.[56]

Federal officials who outranked Colonel Miles had made the decision about where to imprison the Nimiipuu and their allies. Generals William T. Sherman, Philip H. Sheridan, and Oliver O.

Howard were among those who chose to abrogate Miles's surrender accord. Sherman was carrying out his original plans for the prisoners.[57] As he had stated on August 31, he advocated civilian trials and execution for refractory Nimiipuu leaders, and permanent and harsh exile as an example to other Native nations.[58] Sheridan agreed with General John Pope that Fort Riley, Kansas, was best suited for housing the prisoners, but Sherman reiterated his decision to send them to Fort Leavenworth instead.[59] Howard had originally ordered Miles to keep the prisoners at the Tongue River for the winter and to return them to the District of Columbia in the spring.[60] He dismissed the idea of moving the Nimiipuu back to Idaho that autumn because it would require expensive transportation. Within seven months, he would also suggest that the captives be isolated on island reservations in the Puget Sound.[61] While Howard acknowledged the surrender agreement, he insisted that the escapees from the Bear Paw had negated it. On May 18, 1878, he informed General Irwin McDowell that "the terms [of the surrender] were violated by the Indians conniving at White Bird's and followers escape."[62] He denied Joseph's version of the agreement, saying, "The statements with reference to our losses and those of the Indians are all wrong, and Joseph does not tell how his own Indians, White Bird and his followers, who treacherously escaped, after the terms of the surrender had been agreed upon between us at General Miles' battle-field, being permitted by himself, did in fact utterly break and make void the said terms of surrender."[63] Howard erroneously presumed that Chief Joseph controlled Chief White Bird and the other war leaders.

Commissioner Ezra A. Hayt, Secretary of the Interior Carl Schurz, and President Hayes had agreed with the terms of the surrender accord but later withdrew their support. Two months after the surrender, Schurz agreed that the War Department should hold the captives near a convenient supply base until they could be turned over to civilian authorities and banished to the Indian Territory. Hayt subsequently charged that murders of civilians and rapes of white women—charges that the Nimiipuu denied—were cause for the arrest, conviction, and execution of returned leaders.[64] Therefore it was too dangerous to return the Nimiipuu to the northwest. Secretary of War McCrary initially favored lenient treatment of the prisoners and then allowed Schurz and the generals to sway his decision. Colonel Miles tried to honor the peace agreement, but when his efforts failed, he recommended that Nimiipuu leaders and Cheyenne scouts be sent to Washington, D.C. Miles wanted the men to contest further deportations and to understand the federal position. The Nimiipuu could lobby for their return to Idaho, and the Cheyenne scouts would refute deportation of their families to the Indian Territory. Hayt refused Miles's request, declaring that visits to Washington and opportunities to influence federal authorities were privileges earned by submissive American Indians.[65]

Eleven passenger cars and two baggage cars were sent to Bismarck to be used for the transfer, and seventy men from Companies B and G of the First Infantry, commanded by Captain Robert E. Johnston, were assigned to deliver the prisoners to Fort Leavenworth.[66] Lieutenant Hugh T. Reed was designated as Johnston's aide. Acting Assistant Surgeon Redd would continue to Fort Leavenworth in charge of the wounded prisoners. The Great Northern Railroad provided rundown passenger cars for the prisoners and a much-used superintendent's car fitted with sleeping and living quarters for the officers. The prisoners and soldiers would sit facing each other in day cars with no sleeping facilities. Each car contained minimal drinking facilities and a single open lavatory that emptied directly onto the tracks. The Great Northern did not usually run after dark, so special arrangements were made to allow the train to travel through the night.[67]

Chief Joseph's favorite horse had caused quite a commotion in Bismarck, where local horsemen recognized the animal's superior qualities. Joseph had been allowed to keep the horse with him from the Tongue River, and he had ridden it at the head of the procession through Bismarck. But when he asked to take the animal with him to Fort Leavenworth, the army denied his request, even though horses regularly traveled in baggage cars.

Joseph could not afford the fodder and costs to ship the horse to Kansas, so he had to sell it; Johnston and Reed were also forced to sell their horses. Joseph's horse brought its disgruntled owner $35 in cash, while Reed's buyer absconded into the Black Hills without paying for his horse and saddle. A bidding war then broke out for Joseph's horse, but the bids were too low and the new owner canceled the sale. The horse was so popular that a Bismarck newspaperman remarked, "There are millions in Joseph's ponies, if they only multiply like grasshoppers."[68] The army and the Indian Bureau regularly disposed of American Indians' horses in Bismarck, where more than four hundred horses from the Standing Rock reservation had been auctioned off that spring and summer for less than $20 a head.[69] The Nimiipuu's horses were top-quality animals and were prized by the Crows, Northern Cheyennes, Bannocks, and Sioux, who were paid with captured horses for their service as army scouts.[70]

The Nimiipuu and their allies would have preferred to winter in Bismarck, where they were treated well and experienced few restraints. "Here is timber to keep my people warm; and (pointing to the Mississippi River,) there flows the water to give us drink," Chief Joseph told a reporter from the *Saint Paul and Minneapolis Pioneer Press*.[71] The captives visited every store in the little frontier town, where their business was welcomed. One thing the prisoners did not do in Bismarck was drink alcohol; they were remembered by the merchants as sober, decent people. One prisoner even spent an afternoon in a local saloon watching a card game until a gunfight erupted. The observer remained seated on his stool as bullets flew and people ducked for cover. After things calmed down, someone asked him why he had not moved. Modeling several new holes in his blanket, the man raised his arm and displayed the other bullet holes in his shirt. Bullets that do not hit you do not hurt you, was the prisoner's advice to the crowd.[72]

On another occasion, the owner of Whalen's Flour and Feed Store in Bismarck lost a sale to a detainee who wanted to buy a sack of flour. After addressing the man in sign language for more than twenty minutes, the merchant was stunned when the

Numiipuu man finally spoke to him in English. "How do you sell flour in this country?" asked the customer, to which the merchant stuttered, "B-b-b-by the sack," as the man turned and left the store.[73]

The preparations completed, it was time for the transfer to Fort Leavenworth. With tears running down his cheeks, Chief Joseph was forced to tell the bewildered captives to pack their gear and prepare to board the train. Ignoring the prisoners' cries of distress, the quartermasters issued two days' rations of hardtack and four days' rations of beef to the heads of families and provided other special rations for the military personnel and prisoners who would be making the trip. The captives were provided with coffee, and women cooked the beef ration before boarding, because there were no cooking facilities on the train. The Nimiipuu tried to maintain a healthy diet throughout their captivity and purchased fresh foods whenever possible, but fresh vegetables and dairy products were not included in the rations for the transfer to Fort Leavenworth. The beef, canned beans, and other items would be replenished along the way. Within the year, the War Department billed the Indian Bureau for rations issued to the prisoners at Fort Keogh (Cantonment on the Tongue River), Fort Buford, Fort Abraham Lincoln, and St. Paul.[74]

Preparations for leaving Bismarck on Friday, November 23, continued in a flurry of activity. By late afternoon, the captives had loaded most of the drunken troopers and their equipment on the train, and seventeen of Colonel Miles's Cheyenne scouts were also aboard. The scouts, who were members of Two Moons' Band, were deported to join other Cheyennes in the Indian Territory. The prisoners loaded their own gear and baggage, and then they boarded the cars. Ralph Armstrong, an orphan who survived the deportations, remembered being treated like cattle on the trains. When Chief Joseph finally stood alone on the rear platform of the train, a working girl known as the "Belle of Bismarck" rushed up the steps and kissed the startled chief goodbye. A distraught Joseph then moved inside the car, where he sat near an upraised window nodding slowly to the waving bystanders.[75]

The train traveled east on the Northern Pacific tracks through Jamestown, Dakota Territory, and Moorhead and Brainerd, Minnesota, and on to the Northern Pacific junction west of Duluth and south to St. Paul.[76] At Jamestown, Captain Johnston, Lieutenant Reed, and Dr. Redd took Chief Joseph and several other captives out to supper. Because the officers had to provide their own meals, they opted to dine at a café about a hundred yards from the railway depot. After enjoying a meal served on semiformal place settings, the men returned to the train. As the train began to gather speed, cries of "Joseph! Joseph!" erupted from the back car, and the train was brought to a halt. Looking back, the officers saw Joseph running toward them down the center of the tracks, dropping loaves of bread from his blanket. Gasping for breath, Joseph explained that he had seen the bread in a bakery window and had stopped to buy some for his wife and others who had not had supper.[77]

Telegraphers announced the train to stations along the line, and crowds met the prisoners at every stop. At Brainerd, the interpreter showed Chief Joseph around the station, and eager men and women lined up to shake hands with Joseph and other members of the group. Crowds of prisoners abandoned the train at each stop to find fresh drinking water or to relieve themselves. The captives could not force themselves to use the open toilets as the tracks flashed by beneath them.

By five o'clock in the afternoon, thousands of people were waiting for the train at St. Paul. Delayed by an accident to one of the baggage cars, it did not arrive at the St. Paul and Pacific Railroad depot until eight o'clock. Crowds lined the railroad levee as the train stopped at the foot of Jackson and Sibley streets, and Chief Joseph launched a long career of savvy public relations with the United States. He stood on the rear platform of the train, wearing his usual attire and a black, ribbon-trimmed felt hat, shaking hands until his aching arm forced him to stop. Meanwhile, quartermasters struggled through the crowds to replenish the rations, and then the train was moved to the Milwaukee and St. Paul Railroad yard at Mendota. There the baggage cars were attached to another train, and the captives from five of the coaches transferred themselves to five Milwaukee and St. Paul cars. Three hours later, both trains left for Fort Leavenworth.[78]

When women were not tending to children, feeding their families, or trying to rest, they did needlework. One day, Reed stopped to admire a pair of leather gauntlets that Chief Joseph's wife was making. The next day, Joseph went to the officer's car and gave Reed the gauntlets. After reaching Fort Leavenworth, Reed went into town and bought Mrs. Joseph a silk shawl that he presented to Joseph and his wife.[79] Joseph appreciated Reed's interest and made the appropriate response to ensure cordial relations between the prisoners and their captors.

The first detailed census of the prisoners was finally ordered at St. Paul. Dated November 24, 1877, it records that the army held 431 Nimiipuu and Palus prisoners: 79 men, 178 women, and 174 children. Another census taken December 4 at Fort Leavenworth indicated that there were 418 prisoners in military custody: 87 men, 184 women, and 147 children. When adjusted for age and gender, this census, which General Pope guaranteed was the first accurate count of the prisoners, records the loss of thirteen children between November 23 and December 4. The census also included three babies born on the train between Bismarck and St. Paul.[80]

The prison train continued south from St. Paul on the Chicago, Milwaukee, and St. Paul line, traveling through Austin, Minnesota, and then on into Iowa. It stopped every forty miles or so to take on fuel and water. The prisoners were soiled and tired, and the wounded men were not doing well. Three prisoners had died during the trip. The train reached Mason City, Iowa, on Sunday morning, where it stopped for about half an hour. Crowds had gathered at the depot, but by now Chief Joseph was morose and unresponsive. The local dignitaries were disappointed because they did not have time to replicate the Bismarck luncheon. They did, however, give Joseph a few cigars and offer the Nimiipuu their best wishes.[81] The train then continued south to Marshalltown and from there to the junction of the Chicago, Rock Island, and Pacific Railroad, where it was once again met by excited crowds. Headed west on the Chicago, Rock Island, and Pacific tracks, the train passed through Kellogg, Des Moines, and Council Bluffs, Iowa, and rolled on into Omaha, Nebraska. It switched to the Kansas City and St. Joseph tracks at Omaha and then ran south along the east bank of the Missouri River to Perrin, Missouri, before turning west to Fort Leavenworth. After all the changing of tracks, the baggage train was separated from the passenger train and did not reach Fort Leavenworth with the prisoners.[82]

The army officers were not pleased with the parlor car accommodations, and the passenger cars were dreadful. The lack of decent sanitary facilities and fresh water, the constant tourist interruptions, and the circus-like atmosphere violated personal space and limited recuperative opportunities. In addition, the close proximity of the Cheyenne scouts and the soldiers concerned the captives. Lieutenant Reed went through the cars once a day, and Dr. Redd was occupied with the sick and wounded prisoners. Traveling railroad freight agent J. W. Crippen joined the train at St. Paul to help Johnston.

The nightmarish nature of the trip to Fort Leavenworth was barely acknowledged by federal authorities, except for a memorandum that Captain Johnston sent to Crippen, in which he extended to the railroad his "sincere thanks for the very satisfactory manner in which they have transported my command in charge of the Nez Perces Indians (prisoners of war), over their roads. To manage a train of such magnitude for so many days, filled with savages wholly unaccustomed to traveling by rail, without an accident, certainly speaks in high terms of the competence and efficiency of their officers."[83]

Captain Johnston, who was stationed at Standing Rock and at the Brulé Agency after Colonel Custer's defeat, could have been more considerate of the captives, although Chief Joseph never complained about him in public.[84] Lieutenant Reed and Johnston returned to Yankton, Dakota Territory, from Fort Leavenworth, but the Nimiipuu were there to stay.

CHAPTER 4

Survival and Military Jurisdiction at Fort Leavenworth

Early in the morning of Sunday, November 25, 1877, word reached Fort Leavenworth that the prison train was on its way to the fort. Townsfolk, tourists, and army officers waited as a temporary village of canvas tents was set up about a mile upriver from the garrison.[1] Ambulances and hospital tents were readied to receive twenty-five wounded warriors, and Acting Assistant Surgeon A. I. Comfort was sent to the camp from Fort Wallace, Kansas.[2] Before long, another telegram advised that the train would not arrive until one o'clock Monday morning—but the morning came and went with no train.[3] Stalled for fourteen hours behind a derailed freight train near Perrin, Missouri, the prison train did not arrive until five o'clock Monday evening, November 26. Military men and their wives, newspapermen, and tourists watched the twin-engine train come through the cut near the post arsenal. Within minutes, Captain Robert E. Johnston, Lieutenant Hugh T. Reed, Dr. R. G. Redd, Superintendent Walker of the Chicago, Rock Island, and Pacific Railroad, and the soldiers descended from the cars.

For the Nimiipuu, that evening marked the start of eight months of confinement at Fort Leavenworth, although General

Philip Sheridan did not receive official notice of their arrival until the next day.[4] General John Pope refused to comment on how long they would be staying, telling a reporter that the Nimiipuu were there for the time being. The prisoners were transferred to the Leavenworth command, and the Cheyenne scouts were sent on to the Cheyenne and Arapaho Agency at Darlington, Indian Territory, without their Nimiipuu horses.[5]

Captain Johnston reported to Captain George M. Randall, while Captain Joseph T. Haskell ordered troopers to clear a path for the prisoners. Then Chief Joseph and another man stepped down from the train. Joseph was alert, with a sense of strength and movement, and his attire reflected his stature. His hat was striped in brilliant green and black, and wrapped around his shoulders and above his bright blue silk breech clout and green leggings was a multihued blanket. His beaded belt, pouch, and moccasins were "elegantly worked," and over his left arm he carried a gray wolf's skin tied at the feet with eagle feathers. The rest of the passengers left the train after Joseph. For the most part, the men were bareheaded and wrapped in brightly striped blankets; several wore face paint.[6]

Entranced by the ankle bells and brightly colored clothing worn by some of the younger women, *Leavenworth Times* reporter N. P. Perry assured his readers that the prisoners were tidy and well-dressed. Even so, his vision was blurred by romanticism, gas lamps, and the winter twilight. Although Perry became a staunch supporter of the Nimiipuu, he tended to idealize or ignore the women and to concentrate on the chiefs and men. The prisoners had tried to stay clean, but they were soiled and haggard after their difficult journey.[7] The railroad cars contained no bathing or laundry facilities, and the prisoners' extra clothing, if they had any, was on the baggage cars that would not arrive at the fort for another four days.[8] Perry tried to interview Chief Joseph and a male companion but was put off, the companion saying, "Me not talk much English." After trying again in French, Perry just watched and took notes as Joseph and several other leaders tried to organize the weary travelers.[9]

Speaking through the interpreter, Johnston ordered Chief Joseph to gather everyone near the wood storage depot west of the train. Joseph moved quietly to the desired position, where he explained orders to the other headmen and leaders as he received them. The tired travelers gathered around their leaders; silent men avoided eye contact with the tourists and soldiers, and the women collected their families. The seriously injured warriors were carried to the ambulances, and most of the women, children, and the elderly were placed in wagons for the trip to the tent village.[10] Joseph and other able-bodied men were offered rides but chose to walk, pointing out that the wagons were needed by others.[11] Late in the night, more than four hundred prisoners were finally fed army rations and settled on hay-and-ticking bed sacks in the army tents.

The prisoners remained in the temporary village until a permanent camp was established on the infield inside the oval racetrack east of the military prison. Located on the Missouri River bottomlands, the camp area was popular with tourists and soldiers, who normally gathered there to watch the horse races.[12] Unlike Fort Riley, however, where barracks and other facilities were available for the prisoners, the camp at Fort Leavenworth was uncomfortable and unhealthy.[13] General Sheridan had canceled plans to house the prisoners at Fort Riley because it was cheaper to warehouse them at Fort Leavenworth, which also was closer to the Indian Territory and Indian Bureau jurisdiction.[14] To Chief Joseph's disgust, the prisoners' water was drawn from the dirty Missouri River.[15] Human waste was deposited in thirty-foot-long latrines or "straddle trenches" that were riddled with feces, flies, and odors. The old fort was honeycombed with latrine trenches, and covering them with ashes and earth did little to prevent dysentery, typhoid, or injuries.[16] Many of the captives had arrived with no warm clothing, so within the month—and after the Indian Bureau agreed to pay for them—the army issued them surplus Civil War garments.[17]

Within two weeks, tepees replaced the small canvas tents, but the large hospital tents remained in place. Chief Joseph and his family lived in a wood-floored army tent. Innumerable tepees and buffalo hides had been lost or destroyed during the conflict, and most of the surviving dwellings were patched with government-issued canvas. Several of the tepees held comfortable furs and blankets, but many contained nothing; hay was issued to those lodges for bedding. Some of the old tepees displayed painted pictorials. Women complained that canvas repairs were not suitable for the tepees, but there were no replacement buffalo or beef hides. Five months later, the main camp consisted of forty-eight leaking canvas-and-hide lodges that offered negligible protection from the heavy spring rains. Cast-iron stoves warmed the tents, and hardwood fires heated the tepees, where the prisoners piled cords of stove wood around the exterior perimeters for insulation. Troopers and prisoners cleaned the camp every day, but tourists hindered camp management, and their visits were soon restricted to Wednesday and Sunday afternoons.[18]

The prisoners were issued army rations consisting of butchered beef, salt pork, hardtack, beans, flour, coffee, sugar, salt, and tobacco. Each person received an average of eleven pounds of uncooked bone-in beef and about seven pounds of flour per week. Salt pork and hardtack were limited to about one pound per person per month. Moderate portions of soap and salt were issued, and green coffee was restricted to about half a pound per person per week. Women dried or smoked the beef on outdoor racks or in special lodges and prepared the beans and flour, although baking powder and soda were not available. No fresh vegetables were provided.

Payment for the rations caused friction between two federal agencies. The War Department billed the Interior Department for the rations, and then authorities disagreed about which unit would absorb the expense. The War Department wanted the Indian Bureau to cover the costs, and the Indian Bureau tried to avoid the debt. If War Department appropriations fed Indian prisoners, the army paid the bill; after those funds were depleted, the Indian Bureau asked Congress for the money. The War Department spent $14,164.63 for the prisoners' rations at Fort Leavenworth, which amounted to $0.24 per meal, but the escalating costs would eventually move the army to relinquish control of the captives. After remanding the exiles to the Indian Bureau in July 1878, the War Department billed the Interior Department $20,225.29 for rations issued to the captives in fiscal year 1877–78. Ration bills from the next year indicate that Nimiipuu captives were held at Forts Benton and Shaw, Montana; Fort Snelling, Minnesota; Fort Lapwai, Idaho; Pendleton, Oregon; Vancouver Barracks, Washington Territory; and Alcatraz Island, California.[19]

The War Department and the Department of the Interior also disputed the expenses associated with the prisoners' health care. Dr. Comfort was paid $100 per month, plus fuel, living quarters, and one daily ration-in-kind. The surgeon general refused to absorb Comfort's salary and $246.29 for the prisoners' medications and charged the costs back to the War Department. In the meantime, the War Department covered the expenses for the troop of ten men, one sergeant, and one officer assigned to the Indian camp. Among the items bought for the camp were tent barracks, cord wood, two cavalry horses and their feed and gear, cast-iron stoves, thousands of feet of pine lumber, more than three thousand yards of canvas, and tent hardware. The horses were purchased for the lieutenant and sergeant, and the canvas and hospital tents and other materials were used for the captives. The prisoners and their guards burned 141 cords of hardwood from December 1877 through February 1878, although the weather that winter was mostly wet and cloudy, with no severe snowstorms to disable the camp.[20]

Dr. Redd remained at Fort Leavenworth long enough to settle the injured warriors in the Indian camp field hospital and then turned their care over to Dr. Comfort. Comfort started duty with minimal supplies, including bottles of whiskey and sherry and more than twenty-seven dozen assorted bandages. When those were gone, he drew medications and supplies from the post's medical stores each month. Two of Comfort's first patients were "Joe" and another man who had been shot through the hips at the Bear's Paw. Joe's wound had left him with a shattered shoulder and an arm that should have been amputated. By December 4, the man who had been shot through the hips was dying. George Washington and another woman had tuberculosis, and children were suffering from bacterial disorders, constipation, polluted water, and conditions exacerbated by the relocation.[21] Two of the injured warriors treated by Comfort were Fog Blanket (Tom-chich-kim) and Wahnistas Aswetesk. Shot several times during the war, the elderly Wahnistas Aswetesk survived his wounds only to succumb to malaria while in prison. Fog Blanket survived his injuries and captivity, although he was left with a permanent quiver. Another elderly man, Waptastamana (Blacktail Eagle), died soon after reaching the camp. All of the warriors bore signs of earlier injuries, such as scars from bullet wounds, long cuts, jagged surgical scars, missing fingers, or facial scars.[22]

During their first three months at the fort, the prisoners were treated for war wounds and injuries, childhood illnesses, coughs and colds, bronchitis, tuberculosis, digestive and bacterial disorders, bronchial infections, pneumonia, and arthritis. More than sixteen hundred surgical bandages were applied during that ninety-day period. December and the first weeks of January were devoted to treating war wounds and setting broken bones. Casts and splints were made of plaster, red flannel, gutta-percha cloth, and other agents. Dr. Comfort relied heavily on opiates and painkillers, laxatives, belladonna, chloroform, ether, and ergot. Following a common medical practice, he prepared elixirs, tonics, and cough syrups with whiskey, wine, or alcohol. He also administered black tea as a stimulant, and in April and May, when malaria posed a new health hazard, he treated the infection with small doses of quinine.[23]

Prisoners suffered from a variety of medical maladies while at the fort. Some of the captives may have been exposed to tuberculosis before the war, because it was diagnosed at Lapwai in 1871 and continued to spread there through 1879.[24] It also was possible that they contracted the infection during deportation, although Washington was exhibiting severe symptoms only eight days after reaching Leavenworth. Pale, feeble, and hollow-voiced, Washington was confined to his bed except when conducting *wéset* services. He died from tuberculosis on June 8, 1878. The other infected woman had passed away sometime before May 1878.[25] Malaria caused the greatest loss of life at Fort Leavenworth, although it did not become a problem until spring, when mosquitoes appeared. Dr. Comfort had failed to order adequate supplies of quinine-based medications, and the prisoners did not know that quinine was available over the counter in Leavenworth. By the time the captives were relocated to Baxter Springs, Kansas, in July 1878, the epidemic was full-blown, and Comfort still did not have enough quinine to treat more than four hundred people. The prisoners learned to rely on quinine during the first malarial episode, and thereafter, they accepted the preparation when it was available.[26]

Nimiipuu practitioners also conducted essential treatments and ceremonies to help the sick and injured. Feathers around the Neck (Wap-tas-wa-hiekt, Frank Thompson) held healing ceremonies for Chief Joseph's infant daughter in May 1878. Suffering from a high fever, the baby was attended by a *tiwet* (medicine person or doctor), drummers and singers, two practitioner assistants, and her father. Guards kept curious onlookers away as the requisite chants, ceremonies, and drums continued for hours. The baby was treated with burnt herbs, formulaic songs, and ceremonies in a closed lodge while the sounds of the ceremonies reverberated throughout the camp.[27] The child died sometime before July 21, 1878.

Chief Joseph and a local man named H. H. Gregg later testified that twenty-one prisoners died at Fort Leavenworth, but the demographics are difficult to reconstruct.[28] The War Department was not required to keep individual ration records, census data, or lists of deceased prisoners, and recent attempts by specialists to locate the old cemetery using archival records and remote sensing devices have been unsuccessful.[29] Theft is another possible reason why the remains at Fort Leavenworth have not been found. Dr. Comfort, Dr. George N. Hopkins, and other army physicians regularly reopened American Indian graves, sending the disinterred corpses and grave goods to the Army Medical Museum (AMM). Comfort unearthed Ponca remains and associated funerary items from the Ponca Agency in Nebraska and sent them to the Peabody Museum of Archaeology and Ethnology and the Smithsonian Institution.[30] Although repatriation data does not show that Comfort submitted Nimiipuu remains to the AMM, his earlier activities make it likely. The AMM and the National Museum of Natural History were interested in Nimiipuu cadavers and accepted skeletal remains removed from the Bear's Paw, the Big Hole, and Lapwai between 1869 and 1894.[31] At the urging of phrenologists, politicians, physicians, and the surgeon general, skulls were collected in an effort to prove that American Indians were inferior to other races. Based on the notion of Caucasian racial superiority and flawed methodologies, the experiments relegated American Indians to the lowest rungs of the evolutionary ladder. The surgeon general also collected American Indian craniums, skeletal remains, and personal items to advance research on head wounds, battlefield trauma, and American Indian lifestyles.[32]

By May 8, 1878, a small graveyard surrounded by six-foot-tall peeled saplings held the remains of five of the detainees: the "great warrior" known as The Man Who Had Eyes Like a Crane or The Man with Silver Eyes, who had died in February from wounds received at the Bear's Paw; the woman who had died from tuberculosis; and three young children who had died from unidentified causes. Burials after May 8 included Washington, Chief Joseph's baby daughter, and David Williams's younger brother.[33]

Tourists were fascinated by the northwesterners, although at first the prisoners were nervous and preoccupied. To non-Natives, they were a living tableau of the far western frontier that was now within walking distance of Leavenworth. Tourists from Leavenworth and Kansas City flocked to the Indian camp, where they saw fabled ceremonies and dances, met the rising media star Chief Joseph and other "chiefs," intruded into tepees, and went everywhere in the camp. The tourist invasion began as soon as the prisoners arrived at the fort, and the captives gradually grew used to their presence. The prisoners advanced their situation when they could, and otherwise endured the tourists. Their reactions helped cement the peace so essential for their survival. When a group of women went home to Leavenworth and sent back several outfits of baby clothing for Joseph's daughter, he thanked the donors as the child was dressed and shown off by her happy mother. The speeches and pleased reactions were reported in the *Leavenworth Times,* making it clear to readers that American Indians who dressed their babies in western clothing and said "thank you" were becoming "civilized" and harmless. On another occasion, Joseph accepted a handsome pipe and tobacco pouch from a Leavenworth businessman who was visiting the camp. Joseph lit the pipe, inhaled a few times, and passed it around to the assembled "chiefs."[34] He apparently teased one of the young men in the party about being single, and the other men enjoyed a laugh. The reporter's article emphasized the chief's good humor and gracious manners to reassure Leavenworth that the prisoners were harmless. And Joseph soon promised the Reverend Samuel N. D. Martin, "We will never fight again."[35] The Nimiipuu were pledged to peace and made certain that their captors, the tourists, and other influential visitors understood their intentions.

Within days of their arrival, on Sunday, December 9, 1877, the Nimiipuu conducted winter ceremonials, which drew more than five thousand tourists to the prison camp, many of whom lined up to meet Chief Joseph. Appearing more careworn with each new group of chief-seekers, Joseph shook hands until he was tired; then, leaving someone to continue shaking hands in his place, he slipped into the officer of the guards' tent for a rest. Joseph and the stand-ins accommodated everyone who wished to meet an American Indian chief. Another Sunday, damp weather drove most of the tourists away, except for reporter Perry and a crowd who had gathered in Joseph's tent. Perry inspected the village and then worked his way through the crowded lodge, where Joseph, his wife, and the baby were seated facing two other "chiefs" and a woman. After watching Perry take notes, Joseph signaled that he would write; he then gifted the surprised reporter with his autograph. Pointing to his written name, "Young Joseph," Joseph smilingly demonstrated that he was not untutored in American ways. Once again, when the story and a facsimile of Joseph's signature appeared in the *Leavenworth Times,* readers understood that the Nimiipuu were not as "wild" as they had expected. Local entrepreneurs also capitalized on Joseph's presence, sending him complimentary tickets to performances, concerts, and other activities. The chief always attracted a crowd, while women and girls gathered together in the camp to make beaded jewelry and souvenirs to sell to the tourists. Men and boys wedged nickels into notched sticks, then shot them out with their bows and arrows, keeping the coins offered by the tourists.[36]

Although they had lost most of their personal possessions during the war, the prisoners had preserved the ornate regalia necessary for their ceremonials. At home, Nimiipuu celebrants normally gathered in sedentary winter villages for guardian spirit or vision quest dances. Winter ceremonials often went on for days, weeks, or months as spirit dances, individual dances, initiation dances, novice dances, audience dances, initiate feasts, and weather dances were held. Dances united people with their spirit guardians and gave practitioners opportunities to reaffirm their powers within the community. People hosting the ceremonials distributed gifts and feasted dance participants, while practitioners wore ceremonial clothing and displayed symbols linked to their spirit guardians.

A large hospital tent housed the Fort Leavenworth winter ceremonials, which continued for days after the initial ceremonies on December 9. The ailing Washington sponsored the ceremonials, which involved at least 150 congregants. Men and women sat along the tent walls chanting a refrain as people continued to enter the tent. The air was filled with measured and musical chants, as three men stroked small tom-tom-like drums with sticks. The leader strode to the center of the tent, where he spoke and rang a hand-bell; the gathering then sang a response. Participants slowly waved single- or multi-feathered plumes. After the first set of songs, several men rose and testified. Their testimonies were followed by soft, lingering cries as the participants held their right hands skyward. A woman rose and spoke quietly to the leader, who repeated her comments to the congregation in a ringing voice. Another chant and a long dance then followed, and the services continued into the night.[37] When General Oliver O. Howard heard of the activities, he knew at once that the crowds had witnessed non-Christian ceremonials. Howard's religious intolerance and Christian bias was never more evident than when he described Nimiipuu ceremonials as "pernicious doctrines" that were designed to keep fanaticism alive among the nontreaty bands.[38]

Ceremonials the next Sunday included an honoring song for Captain Charles S. Ilsley. An experienced western cavalry officer, Ilsley demonstrated an understanding of the occasion when he addressed the celebrants and acknowledged their goodwill. Senior warriors and their wives were conspicuous at the services held in preparation for the ceremonies scheduled for the following Friday. The Friday celebration included a "war dance" and memorial for a man killed at the Bear's Paw, whose name was not released to the press, but who may have been Chief Joseph's brother Chief Ollokot. Clad in splendid regalia, Joseph was the predominant participant throughout the services. The dead man was honored as a hero, a great warrior, and a person of significance. Several borrowed cavalry horses were garlanded in finery, and an adult grandson of a tribal ancestor rode Ilsley's black cavalry charger. The horses were adorned with strings of bells, beadwork regalia, and animal skins, and sacred eagle feathers fluttered from their tails. Followed by the piercing cries of the women, horses and riders formed a procession around the camp. When Joseph spoke, he guaranteed Ilsley that their intentions toward the Americans were peaceful. He also expressed the hope that when he returned to his country, everyone would understand that he had told the truth.[39] He then presented Ilsley with a handsome buffalo robe, and the dances continued late into the night.

The next day Chief Joseph, Dick Johnson, Yellow Bear, Húsus Kute, Kool-kool-Sneany, Jim Horn, Yellow Bull, and Old Yellow Wolf submitted an affidavit to the War Department requesting that the prisoners be returned to the northwest. Captain George M. Randall completed the document, and Ad Chapman interpreted and witnessed the proceedings.[40] Randall provided the format and legal advice, although the prisoners influenced only the first item because the others ran counter to their interests. That first item demanded that they be returned to their country in the northwest. In the second item, the Indian Bureau requested that a group of Nimiipuu men be sent to the Indian Territory to choose a reservation so that the Canadian refugees could be sent there with the other prisoners.[41] From a historical standpoint, Chapman's translations of the affidavit are problematical because he often lied, and the third and fourth items of the affidavit were of personal benefit to him. He asked to travel to Saskatchewan to bring Chief White Bird and the Canadian refugees back to Fort Leavenworth, and then to go to Idaho to bring the rest of the non-treaty bands to Kansas. The fourth item of the affidavit asked that the prisoners' "friend" Chapman remain with the expatriates. This seems suspicious, because the patriot bands hated Chapman for fighting against them during the war and for stealing their belongings. While many of the captives lived in abject poverty, Chapman's tent was filled with valuable Nimiipuu arts and crafts, including White Bird's wolfskin cap and a pipe that had belonged to Joseph's grandfather Wah-La-Mut-Ki.

The government did not send Chapman to Saskatchewan or Idaho, but he retained his federal employment. General William T. Sherman denied the petition and ordered that Randall be reprimanded for his involvement in the matter.[42] Like many other Americans, Sherman considered the Nimiipuu, Paluses, and Cayuses to have forfeited their sovereign right to influence their destinies. Not long after filing the affidavit, Chief Joseph and the other leaders told Martin that they no longer trusted any white men. The prisoners were suspicious and uncomfortable around the minister as Joseph (through the interpreter) asked, "When will the white chiefs learn to speak the truth?"[43]

The captives made the most of every opportunity to clarify their history and to record their presence. Immediately after their arrival, Chief Joseph created a visual record on a tree trunk. After scraping and peeling the bark down to white wood, he painted a set of complex hieroglyphic characters that retold their history. A row of tepees filled the bottom of the image, and drawings of horses, wolves, birds, dogs, and humans above the tepees marked the interconnectedness of all creatures. The message was clear to the prisoners who gazed at the picture and to everyone else who visited the camp.

In the meantime, the exiles were eager to prove their long history of excellent relationships with the United States. John Red Wolf, an elder son of old Chief Red Wolf, carried with him confirmation of his family's service to the United States. When asked for proof of his past, Red Wolf brought out a leather pouch filled with old letters. Carefully opening the bag, he produced passes dated up to 1856 guaranteeing that the senior Chief Red Wolf was a friend of the United States and should be treated accordingly. A letter dated 1855 was addressed to Chief Red Wolf by Indian Superintendent Joel Palmer. Palmer certified a copy of another letter to Chief Red Wolf by Governor Joseph Lane of the Oregon Territory dated November 8, 1849. Lane assured Red Wolf of his continued high regard for the chief and acknowledged Chief Red Wolf's offer to apprehend the men who had killed Marcus and Narcissa Whitman at Waiilatpu Mission in November 1849. Palmer explained that Chief Red Wolf had been instrumental in the capture of the eight Cayuses who committed the murders.[44] The letters did nothing to gain the prisoners' release, but they offered newspaper readers a different view of Nimiipuu history. Reporter Perry was increasingly convinced that the younger Red Wolf and his father were certifiably the white man's friends.

The Nimiipuu tried to restore some semblance of normalcy to their lives at Fort Leavenworth. Unencumbered by restrictive

Indian Bureau policies, the military authorities did not limit ceremonial or domestic activities, and the prisoners reestablished normal practices as quickly as possible, including the sweat baths that were so vital to their health and well-being. A large sweat lodge, like those common to winter villages, was built a few feet from the Missouri River. The prisoners dug a deep hole and covered it with a rounded earthen roof, leaving an opening to the east. The sweathouse was seven or eight feet in diameter, about three and a half feet tall, and two feet deep. Water was poured into a hole just inside the lodge, and heated rocks from a nearby fire were rolled into the water. Participants entered the lodge in single file and remained in the steam until they were sweating profusely; they then leapt outside and plunged into the Missouri River. Bathing was a daily occurrence, and although segregated sweat lodges were customary at the larger winter villages, the Fort Leavenworth sweat lodge was used in rotation by both sexes. Several of the men told reporter Perry that the sweat bath was "much good" for American Indians.[45]

The prisoners also brought popular games to the camp, including arrow games, ball games, and children's games. Some of the camp children were expert top-spinners and defeated boys from Leavenworth in top-spinning competitions. Tops were started and kept spinning with a whip until the child with the whip grew tired; the last contestant to strike the top won the game. The prisoners also played a ball game similar to lacrosse or shinny. Games were organized soon after arrival at the fort, and were played near the prison village. The participants used bats made from curved wood that resembled large spoons, and a ball made of deer's hair and buckskin. The ball could not be lifted, thrown, or touched with the hands, only kicked or hit with the bat. Most of the ball games were normally played by one sex or the other, but at Leavenworth the sexes sometimes played against each other.[46]

News that more prisoners were expected was always exciting. In late December, there were rumors that another group of men would soon be arriving at the fort. Op-has (Charley Joseph) quietly joined the camp from his cell in the Fort Leavenworth guardhouse. Deported to Fort Leavenworth before the other prisoners, Op-has was released to Joseph, who identified him as a respected warrior. Op-has moved in with Joseph's family and served as their interpreter. He stood guard at their healing ceremonies, and translated for tourists later on at the Quapaw Agency. Another man, referred to as "Charley," was the man who had gotten off the train with Joseph when they arrived at Leavenworth. The hatless, muscular man wrapped in a bright striped blanket who issued orders and deflected Perry's inquiries was probably Yellow Bull. Yellow Bull was "second-in-command," and he was Joseph's almost constant companion throughout their captivity.[47]

Sup-poon-mas and John Fur Cap arrived at Fort Leavenworth on December 6, 1877, and moved right into the prison camp. Several sources warned that Sup-poon-mas was dangerous because he had been convicted of first-degree murder in the killing of a white man years earlier and had been sentenced to hang by the Walla Walla Federal Court in April 1863; the ruling was later overturned, and the charges were dismissed. A member of Chief Big Thunder's band, Sup-poon-mas had killed the man in self-defense while trying to retrieve his stolen telescope. Chief Big Thunder had accepted responsibility for the teenager and refused to release him to federal authorities after James Lawyer and his brother convinced the boy to surrender. The first trial was a farce; Sup-poon-mas was not allowed to testify in his own defense and was not present when the verdict was announced, and the jury left the box and conversed with spectators during the testimony. And when the jurors asked Judge James E. Wyche whether they could convict Sup-poon-mas of the lesser charge of manslaughter, they were instructed to find him either guilty of first degree murder or innocent. Consequently, the verdict was murder in the first degree, and the hanging was set for November 20, 1863. Unhappy with Wyche's instructions, jury foreman James M. Thurmond signed a deposition to that effect, and attorneys Frank Dugan, Leander Homes, and W. G. Langford appealed the case to the Washington Territorial Supreme Court. Sup-poon-mas remained in jail for sixteen months while the Supreme Court heard the case. The verdict was overturned, and a new trial was then scheduled for October 1864 in the Walla Walla Federal Court. No evidence against Sup-poon-mas had been presented during the first trial; he was convicted solely on James Lawyer's testimony. When Lawyer refused to testify at the second trial, the case was dismissed, and Sup-poon-mas was released from jail. Howard's aide Charles E. S. Wood confirmed that the boy Sup-poon-mas and the adult male of the same name and reputation who was deported to Fort Leavenworth were the same person.[48] Sup-poon-mas and Fur Cap settled into the prison camp, where Sup-poon-mas spent quite a bit of time with Joseph.

Women feared a different fate at Fort Leavenworth. It was a dangerous place for them; soldiers and military prisoners outnumbered them seven to one, and authorities rarely prosecuted non-Native men for sexual assaults committed against American Indian women.[49] The camp was also located dangerously close to the U.S. military prison, where inmates often worked outside the prison compound. Prison breaks were common as violent offenders and other fugitives fled in a hail of bullets, and American Indian women were commonly subjected to sexual assaults and soldier violence.[50] During a visit to Washington, D.C., several months later, Chief Joseph warned Congress that American soldiers had sexually assaulted the captive women.[51] Three years later, the women finally told Indian agent William Whiting about the rapes. They also spoke of soldiers stealing their buffalo robes, blankets, personal effects and artifacts, and government supplies. The women received no response to their complaints until the Reverend Archie Lawyer (who was Nimiipuu) came from Idaho. Following Joseph's lead, Lawyer included the sexual assault testimonies in a memorandum presented to the president and to Congress in 1881.[52] The rapes resulted in physical and psychological injuries, unwanted pregnancies, and sexually transmitted diseases. Mothers, grandmothers, and *tiwets* tended to physical and emotional injuries, while Dr. Comfort treated the growing number of cases of venereal disease.[53] Rapes and sexual assaults of American Indian women by soldiers were common in the American West.[54] The post–Civil War military condoned sexual violence against and the killing of Native women. Used as a tool of war, rape intimidated women, families, and societies in an effort to weaken further resistance.[55]

Sexual assaults on Nimiipuu women were not limited to the prison camp. In 1878, government scout and Nimiipuu interpreter Captain George (Miyapkáwit) was returning to Lapwai from Saskatchewan with his daughter, who had escaped with the Canadian refugees. A group of white men shot Captain George and left him for dead near Carroll, Montana, then kidnapped and assaulted his daughter. George managed to drag himself to a Crow camp near the Flathead Agency, and Indian agent Peter Ronan set out to find the girl. Ronan followed the rapists to Benton, Montana, where George's daughter either was released or managed to escape to her family in Idaho.[56] The exiles feared soldiers as sexual predators long after their return to the Washington Territory in 1885.[57]

While the Nimiipuu faced many atrocities at Fort Leavenworth, they were also introduced to the advancing technologies of the age there. Advances in photography, telegraphy, the telephone, the press, and the phonograph were employed to impress them with white America's scientific superiority. But the Nimiipuu responded with composure, aware of the importance of the new technologies.

Chief Joseph understood the possibilities that photography offered, and he engaged the technology, using the images taken of him at Fort Keogh and Bismarck to reassure his family that he was still alive. He sent a photograph of himself to his daughter Kap Kap Pon Mi in Saskatchewan, who had been separated from him during the war. After Kap Kap Pon Mi ran away from Saskatchewan and returned to Lapwai, she showed her father's photograph to an army officer as proof that she was Joseph's daughter.[58] The media-savvy Joseph cherished photographs of his friends and family and posed for many more photographs over the next twenty-five years. And when Chief Ollokot's photograph was shown to his female cousins after the war, they held it and wept for the young man who had been killed at the Bear's Paw.[59]

The army had tried to overawe the prisoners with the telegraph during the train trip from Bismarck. When officers told Chief Joseph that white men could speak across the wires, Joseph requested proof. He asked them to use it to arrange for a white woman to meet the train at the next stop, carrying a glass of water. She was to say Joseph's name and hand him the glass. The delivery went as planned, and Lieutenant Reed considered Joseph suitably impressed.[60] Reed may have assumed that the prisoners were not familiar with the telegraph before that demonstration, but the Nimiipuu did have previous knowledge of the technology. In August 1877, they had torn down telegraph lines, interrupted General Howard's communications, and stopped traffic near Dry Creek Station, Idaho.[61] Joseph also correctly attributed American successes during the conflict to the advantages offered by the advanced communications.[62] After the war, the Nimiipuu woman named In-who-lise told her husband that the Nimiipuu understood that white men were able to communicate with each other over the "click clack."[63] Seven months later, when the Nimiipuu were shown the telephone, Joseph questioned its efficacy as well, until Colonel Daniel R. Anthony walked in the door as he had promised to do during a phone call.[64] Joseph was then satisfied that the instrument operated as promoted.

Another time, during a daylong visit to Leavenworth, Sup-poon-mas, Yellow Bear, Cool Cool Steh-mikt, and Ad Chapman saw the available technology firsthand. Stepping down from a horse-drawn vehicle, the men first entered the *Leavenworth Times* building, where they were treated to a scientific tour de force. Printers laid out the newspaper in the composing room, then set up and printed a special pressrun while the fascinated visitors watched the steam-powered press. Cigars were smoked all around after the pressrun, and the visitors then moved on to a Delaware Street salon for a demonstration of the Edison voice recorder. Edison had demonstrated his "improved phonograph" to Congress two months earlier, and now the American Philological

Society wanted to use it to record American Indian languages, so as to "preserve the exact pronunciation" of nations that might be "dying out."[65] Phonographer F. M. Sergeant had set up a display for the gathering, the rest of whom were already seated when the Nimiipuu visitors arrived. Cautious at first, Joseph, Sup-poon-mas, Yellow Bear, and Cool Cool Steh-mikt were soon comfortably seated with the other spectators near the recorder. The party included Colonel Anthony, James McGonigle, R. H. Hershfield and his daughter, Frank T. Lynch, and reporter N. P. Perry. To Sergeant's surprise, the visitors ignored the first recordings, which were in English. Then Sergeant asked Chief Joseph to record in Nimiputimít. "We are here looking at the white people, who are your friends; we like the city and its people; we will return tonight,"[66] Joseph said through Chapman. Excited by the sound of Joseph's voice, Sup-poon-mas recorded next, saying in hesitant English, "Now I see you my friend, I see you all now very good. I like you all right."[67] Yellow Bear and Cool Cool Steh-mikt spoke next in Nimiputímt, saying that they had enjoyed the visit and would return later in the evening. Hershfield's daughter recorded, the phonographer made more tests, and then Sergeant asked Joseph to sing into the recorder. "I have seen enough to satisfy me that this is a wonderful thing," Joseph said in Nimiputimít as he declined the invitation.[68]

The visitors spent the rest of the afternoon investigating several businesses and Weaver and Small's mercantile store, then enjoyed an ice cream treat at a local emporium. They all returned to the *Leavenworth Times* office at six o'clock, and Sup-poon-mas spoke with Colonel Anthony on the telephone. Then the visitors presented their hosts with a special surprise. Quietly arranging themselves, the men rose to their feet and turned to face their hosts, and Chief Joseph spoke through the interpreter. Restating their friendly intentions, Joseph thanked everyone for their support and pledged his continued dedication to the truth. He then gave Perry a beautiful carved pipe, explaining that it represented peace and was the most valuable gift they could offer.[69] Perry acknowledged the favorable articles he had published about the prisoners and reaffirmed his friendly intentions and those of the *Times,* and the men shook hands. Everyone sat down and smoked for a while, then went to Anthony's home to join another group of guests. They listened to the piano and a female vocalist for another half an hour, and then Joseph asked to speak. As everyone rose to their feet and Chapman interpreted, Joseph reiterated their friendly intentions, saying, "He who takes care of our spirits will make us take care of each other. I hope you have the same feeling. We all think the same."[70] Anthony assured the diplomats that decent folks wished them well and held Joseph in high regard. The gift pipe was lit and passed around, and then the Nimiipuu dined at the St. James Hotel. The next day, a feature article in the *Leavenworth Times* confirmed that the Nimiipuu had experienced the telephone and were the first American Indians to have recorded their voices.[71] The visitors probably took strips of embossed tinfoil with them as souvenirs, because the first Edison recordings were impressed on sheets of tinfoil that did not survive the recordings.[72] The diplomacy practiced that day was critical to the prisoners' survival.

Yellow Bull, Húsus Kute, and Es-pow-yes (Light in the Mountain) earned their own share of diplomatic renown during a trip to Saskatchewan. Authorities on both sides of the international border wanted Chief White Bird and the Nimiipuu refugees returned from Canada.[73] Nimiipuu survivor Henry Tabador told army officers that the Sioux were mistreating the Nimiipuu, and when General John Gibbon heard that the Canadian refugees wanted to come home, he informed General Sheridan that they would return under a general amnesty, with the promise of no armed resistance. Sheridan directed the matter to the Interior Department, where it was rejected by Commissioner Ezra Hayt.[74] Within months, however, an attempt to lure the Nimiipuu exiles back to the United States was set in motion.[75]

Fascinated with American Indians, the press flooded the American public with ideas about the ongoing negotiations. One article mentioned Chief Joseph's mythical offer to send himself and the exiled warriors to Saskatchewan to attack Sitting Bull.

The War Department would be spared further Indian wars, and soldiers could be released for more important duties.[76] Trying to quell such rumors and ease Plains Indians' concerns about how the prisoners at Fort Leavenworth were being treated, the army and the Indian Bureau sanctioned a diplomatic mission. They would send some of the prisoners to Saskatchewan to reassure their friends and relatives who had fled there that all was well in Kansas, and that the refugees should return with them to Fort Leavenworth. General Alfred H. Terry organized the mission and then ordered the return of the Canadian Nimiipuu to Fort Buford and their transshipment to Fort Leavenworth.[77]

Three prisoners were selected as delegates for the mission: Yellow Bull, who was related by marriage to Chief White Bird; his uncle Es-pow-yes, an influential war leader and buffalo hunter; and the Palus leader and orator Húsus Kute. Es-pow-yes brought a special viewpoint to the mission; he had argued against surrender and wanted to hold out for more stringent and explicit post-conflict agreements. He was also convinced that General Howard intended to hang the war chiefs and war leaders.[78] Yellow Bull and Es-pow-yes had both lost sons during the war, and all three of the men had been with the exiles every step of the way from the Bear Paw.[79] They were exceptionally well qualified for the mission, and contrary to federal assumptions, they took their own agenda to the meetings, with the understanding that the Canadian refugees would make their own decisions. White Bird already knew about the illnesses and conditions in Kansas, and Nimiipuu governance did not permit Chief Joseph to dictate orders to him. Diplomatic courtesy required that the men give White Bird pertinent information so that the Canadian refugees could decide for themselves.

Five months after the journey into exile, the diplomats began the bittersweet transmigration. It was a difficult time to leave Fort Leavenworth, because their families were suffering from malaria, there was no news of a return to Idaho, and the women in the camp were in fear of the soldiers. In their prime middle years and at the height of their physical powers, the three men probably felt mixed emotions as they traveled west. Seeing the peaks that overlooked the Bear Paw battlefield in Montana, they remembered their fallen comrades and the disastrous surrender. On the train to Bismarck, standing on the deck of a steamboat from Bismarck to Fort Benton, or driving a team across northern Montana, the men understood their mission. The emissaries were taking information to White Bird from Joseph, and they wanted news of their friends and families. Joseph was worried about his daughter, and one of the diplomats was planning to bring his own son back to Fort Leavenworth.

Accompanied by frontiersman Ben Clark, the ambassadors left Fort Leavenworth on April 30, 1878. They met Colonel Miles's aide Lieutenant George M. Baird at Fort Buford and arrived at Fort Benton, Montana, on June 9. Two days later, they ferried across the Missouri River and left for Fort Walsh, Saskatchewan, home of the North West Mounted Police (NWMP). Delayed two days by flooding along the Milk River, the party arrived at Fort Walsh a week later. Baird explained their mission, and three days later, Lieutenant Colonel Acheson G. Irvine and Lieutenant Colonel James F. MacLeod of the NWMP arrived at Fort Walsh. MacLeod reaffirmed that the Canadian authorities wanted the Nimiipuu to leave the dominion, although they would use diplomacy instead of violence to effect the change. Baird applied for permission to visit the Nimiipuu camp but was denied because the Sioux were highly suspicious of Americans.[80]

Four days later, the diplomats, a detachment of North West Mounted Police, and Lieutenant Colonel Irvine started for the Nimiipuu camp near Sitting Bull's encampment. Duncan McDonald, who was related to Chiefs Looking Glass and White Bird, joined the party as the interpreter, and the embassy proceeded to the Sioux camps. White Bird's camp was found near a large Sioux encampment in the Sandy Hills, where it took three days to convince him, Never Hunts (Took ka lickt se ma), and six other men to return to Fort Walsh. The combined group arrived at Fort Walsh on the evening of June 30. The conferences began the next morning and continued through July 2. Baird presented a false federal position that mirrored the abrogated Bear Paw surrender agreement, promising that Chief Joseph expected the refugees to come to Fort Leavenworth. He also threatened that if they did not go to Fort Leavenworth, the other captives would not be returned to Idaho. Canadian authorities seconded Baird, and the meeting adjourned, leaving the delegates from Fort Leavenworth, McDonald, and the eight Canadian refugees alone to discuss Baird's proposals.

Baird's fabrications were dissected as the diplomats explained the realities of the situation. Chief Joseph had sent no message telling Chief White Bird to come to Fort Leavenworth; he had merely reaffirmed their right to make their own decisions. Joseph's only promise was that they would be welcomed if they came to Fort Leavenworth. The next day, Baird added a codicil to his libelous offer, threatening that if the refugees returned to Idaho individually, they would be hunted down and arrested. White Bird denied that he had sent any messages to the Americans about poor treatment and said that the refugees had no interest in returning to the United States under the present conditions. And none of the escaped Nimiipuu spoke for him. White Bird then established the parameters for their peaceful return: Joseph's band must be returned to Idaho in accordance with the surrender agreement, and then the Canadian refugees would return to Idaho. White Bird also pointed out that there was no reason for them to go to Fort Leavenworth because they were already much closer to Idaho and would meet Joseph's band there. They further understood the situation at Fort Leavenworth and knew that they would share the sad fate of the other exiles if they went there. The diplomats left Fort Walsh on July 3, along with the son whose father had hoped to bring him back. They arrived at Fort Benton on July 5, and four days later they boarded a steamboat for Bismarck. They then took the train from Bismarck to St. Joseph, Missouri, and on to Baxter Springs, Kansas, walking from there into the Indian Territory, where the other prisoners had been moved in their absence. The Canadian refugees remained in Saskatchewan, where they received regular letters from Joseph's band telling them who had died.[81]

Whatever freedoms or semblance of normalcy the Nimiipuu were afforded did not last long. They were caught in a web of power-conscious politicians, generals, and civilians who rarely included them in decision-making processes. They were ignored during discussions about their relocation, which were almost constant until their transfer to the Indian Territory in July 1878. The secretary of the interior, the secretary of war, the commissioner of Indian affairs, Generals Howard, Sheridan, Sherman, and McDowell, and the Nimiipuu schoolteacher and former government scout James Reuben all recommended permanent expulsion to the Indian Territory. Secretary of the Interior Carl Schurz and Sheridan advocated permanent removal, and Howard and Reuben wanted the Nimiipuu incorporated into the defeated Modoc community. Sherman and Sheridan also wanted the Indian Bureau to relieve the War Department of their supervision and expense. The secretary of war agreed to move the prisoners to the Indian Territory if the Indian Bureau would cover the cost, and Howard opposed their return to Idaho, fearing that it would be misinterpreted as a reward for aberrant behavior. Commissioner of Indian Affairs Hayt agreed to the deportation and suggested that any recalcitrant Nimiipuu throughout the West should also be banished to the Indian Territory.[82]

Alfred B. Meacham, editor of the activist journal *The Council Fire,* and Lapwai Indian agent John B. Monteith entered the dialogue after Congress appropriated $20,000 for removal of the Fort Leavenworth prisoners to the Indian Territory on May 8, 1878. A proponent of President Ulysses Grant's peace policy, Meacham recommended that the Nimiipuu serve as a test case for it. According to Meacham, the Nimiipuu could be forced to farm and become Christians in the Indian Territory. Caught between the War Department's struggle to regain control of the Indian Bureau and Grant's peace policy, they would demonstrate the efficacy of continued civilian control of the Bureau. Meacham's summary of the situation was a chilling indictment of civilization programs directed at American Indians. He even admitted that there should never have been a peace accord with the Nimiipuu, because American Indians did not understand provisos or agreements. As a prisoner of war controlled by the government, Chief Joseph must go to the Indian Territory, where he would be undisturbed. Then Meacham called Joseph a religious bigot who must appreciate that his values obstructed his civilization. The Nimiipuu should build homes, farm and log, respect Americans, become self-supporting, and accept Christianity. In addition, religious zealots should not be employed as Indian agents, so that the Nimiipuu could be governed by fair but firm moderate Christians, such as the Quakers. Meacham felt that if all of those conditions were met, the exiles would become self-supporting, reconstructed Christians. If the conditions were not met, they would become wards of an Indian Bureau welfare state.[83]

The Indian Appropriation Act was ratified May 9, 1878, and when the $20,000 became available July 1, the Indian Bureau began planning to evict the Fort Leavenworth prisoners to the Indian Territory. The Nimiipuu, Paluses, and Cayuses would join the tide of Native nations being shifted around by the Bureau. The Cheyenne scouts' families had been sent to Darlington, Indian Territory, in December 1877, after the main body of Northern Cheyennes had been relocated there in April of that year.[84] Victims of land speculators, federal lies, and swindles, the Poncas were shipped from Nebraska to the Quapaw Agency, and then moved to the Indian Territory south of Arkansas City, Kansas, on July 21, 1878. In that same month, the Nimiipuu who had been at Fort Leavenworth since the previous November were moved once again, this time to the Quapaw Agency in the Indian Territory.[85]

Charley Moses and Chief Joseph, seated; unidentified man and Yellow Bear, standing, ca. 1877. National Anthropological Archives, Suitland, Maryland, Inv. #01604002.

Jackson at Fort Keogh, Montana, 1877. National Anthropological Archives, Suitland, Maryland, Inv. #09951000.

Nez Perce boys at Fort Keogh, Montana, 1877. National Anthropological Archives, Suitland, Maryland, Inv. #09951100.

Chief Joseph at Fort Keogh, Montana, 1877. National Anthropological Archives, Suitland, Maryland, Inv. #06668900.

Chief Joseph at Bismarck, Dakota Territory, November 1877. Photograph attributed to D. F. Barry. Denver Public Library, Western History Collection, Denver, Colorado, B-428.

Nez Perce men deported to the Indian Territory. Photograph by T. G. N. Anderton, Fort Walsh, Saskatchewan. Glenbow Archives, Calgary, Alberta, NA-936-33.

Nez Perce men deported to the Indian Territory. Northwest Museum of Arts and Culture/Eastern Washington State Historical Society, Spokane, Washington, L94-7.148.

The Nez Perce prisoners at Fort Leavenworth, Kansas. From *Frank Leslie's Illustrated Newspaper,* February 23, 1878. From the author's collection.

Unidentified man, Chief Joseph, Alfred B. Meacham, Yellow Bull, and Arthur I. Chapman in Washington, D.C., winter 1878–79. L. V. McWhorter Photograph Collection, Washington State University Libraries, Pullman, Washington, 70-0252.

Charley Moses (Sup-poon-mas) in Arkansas City, Kans., ca. 1880–85. L. V. McWhorter Photograph Collection, Washington State University Libraries, Pullman, Washington, PC85, Box 2, Folder 18.

Chief Joseph in Arkansas City, Kansas, ca. 1880–85. L. V. McWhorter Photograph Collection, Washington State University Libraries, Pullman, Washington, H82-052.

Mary (Nez Perce), ca. 1879–85. Photograph by Hezekiah Beck. Kansas State Historical Society, Topeka, Kansas, E99W5.IM*001.

Unidentified woman and child (Nez Perce), ca. 1879–85. Photograph by Hezekiah Beck. Kansas State Historical Society, Topeka, Kansas, E99W5F2*001.

CHAPTER 5

LIFE IN THE *EEIKISH PAH*, THE HOT PLACE

Sent by the Indian Bureau to supervise the Nimiipuu's move to the Quapaw Agency in the Indian Territory, Inspector John McNeil was appalled by conditions at Fort Leavenworth, where more than two hundred Nimiipuu, Cayuses, and Paluses lay ill. Extreme heat and humidity, inadequate housing, limited medications, and filthy sanitary conditions plagued the prisoners. By the time McNeil arrived in July, the captives were suffering unremitting malarial infections transmitted by the mosquitoes that infested the river bottoms. The relationship between mosquitoes and malaria was not yet understood; scientists in those days thought that the disease was caused by swampy areas, dampness, and heat instead of the insects that thrive in those conditions. Armed with a gallon of cinchona (quinine) syrup, a few ounces of sulfate of quinia, and various cough syrups, Dr. Comfort could not control an epidemic that affected nearly half of the prisoners, including most of the women and children.[1]

A correspondent sent to the camp by the Indian rights journal *The Council Fire* was stunned by the neglect and the lack of medical care provided to the captives. The reporter also complained that no census or ration lists were being kept, and no attempts had been made to enumerate or identify the prisoners. Indian rights activist Helen Hunt Jackson and the journalist in their respective writings compared the captives to the emaciated soldiers imprisoned at the infamous Civil War prison at Andersonville, Georgia.[2] Aside from Chief Joseph and some of the other captives, no one knew exactly how many prisoners remained at Fort Leavenworth. The Indian Bureau understood that 200 captives were alive on July 9 but soon changed that estimate to 433. Two weeks later, Ad Chapman estimated that 410 people had been transferred to the Quapaw Agency in the Indian Territory, a number that had been predicted by General John Pope on May 6, 1878. Pope counted 83 adult men, 184 adult females, and 144 children, or 411 prisoners.

Dr. Comfort was assigned to accompany the train, and after five days of preparations, McNeil and Quapaw Indian agent Hiram Jones decided that the prisoners were ready to travel. Captain George M. Randall offered compassionate aid to the expatriates, assigning troopers to help dismantle the camp and to take the captives to the fort's railroad switch. Moved to the switch on July 20, the prisoners waited in the heat and humidity until the next afternoon; several women, including Joseph's wife, collapsed from the heat. Sidetracked because the army was shipping troops to the western frontiers, the prison train could not load until the troop movements were complete.[3]

The prisoners did not know where they were going when the Missouri River, Fort Scott, and Gulf Railroad train left Fort Leavenworth at four o'clock on July 21. Exile to the Indian Territory had been threatened as punishment during the prewar councils, and now the threats were becoming reality. The passenger cars were packed with more than forty adults and twenty-five to thirty children, most of them suffering from malaria and the oppressive heat. Conditions in the cars were lethal as the train moved through Kansas City, Olathe, Fort Scott, and Oswego, Kansas. Dirt and cinders added to the captives' distress, and the unhappy expatriates refused to tolerate any tourists when the train stopped to take on water. In a move to cut costs, Inspector McNeil had substituted a baggage car for one of the passenger cars and crammed more people together in the cars. Six baggage cars held the prisoners' belongings, tents, and other equipment furnished by the War Department. The Indian Bureau paid $2,065 to move the prisoners to Baxter Springs, saving $1,500 after constant reminders to economize. The $20,000 federal appropriation was intended to support relocation and all costs applicable to the prisoners for the next year.[4]

Three and a half hours after leaving Leavenworth, the train pulled into Baxter Springs, the final stop before the Indian Territory. General Pope had refused to assign troopers to accompany the train, so the prisoners unloaded the cars late into the night. A temporary camp was set up near the Baxter Springs depot, and Dr. Comfort worked throughout the night caring for the ailing travelers.[5] Comfort volunteered to travel on to the Quapaw Agency with the prisoners but was ordered back to Leavenworth the next morning. Two children had died in transit, and three more died after reaching Baxter Springs. All five of the children were buried near the Baxter Springs depot, but their graves and corpses soon yielded to hungry hogs.[6]

To further economize, Inspector McNeil and Agent Jones had planned to walk everyone from Baxter Springs to the Quapaw Agency. McNeil was forced to revamp his plans when he realized that many of the prisoners were too sick to walk. Jones hired forty wagons, teams, and teamsters and six Modoc drivers from the Quapaw Agency. The teamsters and prisoners loaded the wagons, and then the sick, the women, the children, and the elderly sat on the loads. The tent poles all had to be left at Baxter Springs because they would not fit on the overloaded wagons. Able-bodied captives walked beside the wagons or rode when they were overcome by heat and flies. The cheerless little wagon train left for Quapaw the evening of July 22, accompanied by dogs and a saddle horse that Chief Joseph may have acquired at Fort Leavenworth.[7] Camp was made that night on the Modoc reservation at the Quapaw Agency.

Situated in an oak grove, the prisoners' new camp was surrounded by rolling prairies and grasslands. The grove sloped down to a clear, spring-fed creek, and the Spring River flowed a few miles away. August was hot and humid, but by October, bright days framed in autumnal colors turned into clear, crisp nights. No accommodations had awaited the exiles at their destination, although a carpenter and assistant had been hired to build cabins. They could not, however, construct sixty units before winter, and although Jones had intended to have the male prisoners help build the cabins, illness and heat put an end to that plan. The prisoners knew nothing about frigid prairie winters, and they had no way of knowing that this winter would be an exceptionally difficult one. By the first of January, deep snow, sleet, and driving winds brutalized the shabby canvas lodges.

Few homes were ever prepared for the prisoners at Quapaw, and temporary shelters or tents were inadequate for the climate. Lumber-grade trees for home building had already been logged off, and the Nimiipuu were too late to harvest the blackberries and wild plums that grew along the creek banks and in the woodlands.[8] The bucolic setting where meadowlarks, quail, and prairie fowl fluttered above the windswept prairies was never a maximal location for hundreds of sick and injured people.

The preparations that had been made for more than four hundred detainees at Quapaw were abysmal, and because fiscal-year budgets had been approved before the Indian Bureau assumed control of the captives, no money had been earmarked for their care. Chief Clerk William Leeds of the Indian Bureau, Commissioner Ezra Hayt, and Agent Jones cobbled together various supply agreements funded by the $20,000 appropriation. However, beef, flour, and corn were expensive, and their quality was questionable because of a limited market. When faced with an emergency, the Indian Bureau purchased whatever was available regardless of quality. Supplies and medicines destined for the Quapaw Agency were scheduled for shipment early in the new fiscal year, and contracts provided cattle in monthly increments assigned to particular Native nations. A herd of 233 cattle designated for the

Poncas was left for the Nimiipuu when the Poncas moved west. The half-starved animals supplied less than the requisite one and a half pounds of beef per capita per day, so the Bureau ordered 75,000 pounds of beef from local rancher Calvin Hood, who agreed to supply cattle that would yield at least 50 percent edible beef. By late November, however, beef issues were poor and irregular, so the army was called in to prevent starvation. Captain Randall was sent from Fort Leavenworth to purchase and distribute beef to the prison camps. During their year at Quapaw, the Nimiipuu, Palus, and Cayuse prisoners rarely received the promised quantity of beef. Standard weekly rations included three pounds of gross-weight beef, half a pound of flour, half a pound of corn, corn meal, or hardtack, beans, coffee, sugar, salt, soap, and a little tobacco. During winters when animals were thin or difficult to obtain, beef contractors often could not fulfill their obligations. Hood found himself in that situation in February and March 1879, and Jones was forced to purchase scrawny local beef.[9]

Fresh vegetables were not included in the rations, so the prisoners took advantage of other opportunities. They purchased fresh corn, tomatoes, and other produce from the Modocs and traded coffee beans and sugar for eggs, turnips, and other vegetables. Kansas farmers, in cahoots with Hiram Jones and his son, who took kickbacks on everything, brought loads of fresh vegetables and molasses to trade for government-issued coffee beans and sugar. Women and older men gathered at the farmers' wagons to trade away government rations. The women also went from door to door, selling or trading rations or ribbon yard goods for additional food. Embarrassed by a *New York Times* article about the Kansas farmers and the Nimiipuu traders, Commissioner Hayt telegraphed Agent Jones to stop the practice at once. Hayt promised to supply vegetables, but dried corn on the cob, bolted cornmeal, and shelled corn were the only vegetable substitutes shipped by the Indian Bureau.[10]

Transferring their skills from the northwest to the Indian Territory, most of the male prisoners spent their time hunting or fishing. Big game, such as buffalo and antelope, had already been hunted out, but prairie chickens, quail, and deer were plentiful. Restricted by soldiers stationed near Quapaw, the prisoners had to remain near the camp and could not hunt big game farther out in the west. They were not allowed to own guns, so the Nimiipuu hunters relied on homemade bows and arrows. Bow makers called up old skills and buried hickory poles in hot coals until they were charred, then scraped away the burned portions to create seasoned bows. Some of the prisoners cut holes in the ice on the frozen Spring River and spearfished. They taught their neighbors how to walk on thin ice, steadying themselves with ten-foot-long poles. Balanced like tightrope walkers, with a pole in each hand and another one between their knees and feet, the men crossed the ice as the poles redistributed their weight. In the summer, the Spring River teemed with suckerfish somewhat similar to the suckerfish in the northwest, and the prisoners fished with hooks they made from suckerfish mouth bones. Chief Joseph and his neighbor Edward Lykins shared Lykins's boat when they fished together on the Spring River, and Joseph borrowed the boat for solitary fishing trips. Contrary to Indian Bureau expectations, the male prisoners showed little interest in farming, mechanics, or logging.[11]

Desperately poor and confined to an area that offered few economic opportunities, the captives adapted old skills to their present environment. When new bark formed on the willow trees in the spring, basket makers made the folded-bark baskets known as *lap'uy.* These sturdy, adaptable baskets were usually made of red cedar, cottonwood, birch, or pine bark by northern plateau or Columbia River groups, but at Quapaw, the women used willow bark and willow reeds found along the Spring River. They stored dried foods in the baskets, sealed them with pitch to carry water, and used them as cooking utensils. To produce the baskets, they made two deep cuts in a tree, freeing a long, rectangular piece of bark. An oval was scored from the middle of the rectangle, and the strip was folded in two. Holes were punched through the bark with bone awls, then the sides were sewn with suckerfish bone needles and strips of bark or willow reed. A small willow limb reinforced the inside rim, and a strip of smooth bark protected the outer rim.[12] The women also made grinding bowls from stones. Hollowing out a round rock, they shaped another rock to fit into the bowl to grind corn and other grains. Accustomed to storing food and clothing in caches or caves, the prisoners discovered an "Old Indian refuge" cave in a bluff on the Spring River south of the Big Knife Ford. Remote and difficult to reach, the cave was used to store the captives' belongings and food supplies. Long after the Nimiipuu, Paluses, and Cayuses left the Quapaw area, Peoria men discovered the cave and the items it contained.[13]

Negligence and staffing problems at the Indian Bureau's New York City warehouse delayed essential shipments to Indian agencies during fiscal year 1879. Quinine and other medications were shipped late in September, six months after malaria had infected nearly 19,000 American Indians.[14] Acknowledging that their mismanagement was costing Native lives, federal bureaucrats promised to do better. "It is feared that many lives have been sacrificed to this delay," said Commissioner E. M. Kingsley, but nothing came of the promises to improve the deliveries.[15] Malaria infected and killed more American Indians in 1878, 1879, and 1880 than any other disease out of the more than 75,000 cases of illness treated by Indian agency physicians each year.[16] Malaria, the lack of quinine, and the neglect at Quapaw caused one of the most concentrated population losses experienced by the Nimiipuu prisoners during their exile. Sixteen people died between July 24 and August 3, another twenty-nine died by October 7, and by the end of June 1879, thirty-four more prisoners were dead. At least twelve children died between February and April 1879, including six youngsters from Yellow Bull's camp, four from the family of Red Grizzly Bear (He-yum-el-pilp), and Daniel Jefferson's little girl. Adjusting for thirty-nine prisoners brought into the camps from the northwest, at least eighty-four prisoners died after removal to Quapaw, including the five children buried at Baxter Springs. By mid-August, 265 people suffering from malaria were still without medications. Commissioners William Stickney and Clinton B. Fisk telegraphed St. Louis for quinine in August, and at times Ad Chapman doled out swigs of the medication from his bottle of quinine.[17] Agent Jones purchased supplemental quantities of quinine and other medicines, but he never ordered enough to properly treat the epidemic.[18]

Another reason for the laissez-faire attitudes about shipping delays to Indian agencies originated with the idea that American Indians were too superstitious to take scientific medicines. Agency physicians and Indian Bureau employees regularly justified their own inadequacies by degrading their Native patients, reporting that they either refused to take western medicines or took them incorrectly. On the other hand, medical records from more than sixty-three Indian agencies show that when medications were effective, American Indians routinely adopted them.[19]

Nimiipuu practitioners also tried to combat malaria and other ailments. One curing ritual performed in early October involved female singers and a male *tiwet.* Lying on a bed made of skins in the center of a closed lodge, the patient was attended by a row of seated women drumming with special sticks on rows of cured hickory poles. The women drummed and sang synchronized chants as the male practitioner introduced his vocals into their melodies. Seated at the foot of the patient's bed, the doctor sometimes chanted in tune with the women or sang a separate note over their voices. One elderly neighbor woman chased a group of tourists away from the curing lodge, while similar drumming and singing resonated from another lodge in the camp. As the tourists continued to snoop around the camp, Old Clark (Daytime Smoker) crawled out of his lodge to greet the guests. Thin and nearly blinded by eye infections, the twisted old man spoke to the tourists and gently touched their clothing. The tourists discounted Clark's efforts to say hello and made snide comments about his illegitimacy and supposed relationship to the famed explorer William Clark. Well known to influential westerners and the Nimiipuu as Clark's child, the red-headed son of the national hero is buried in an unidentified grave in the Indian Territory.[20] Chief Joseph was not in camp that day, so Jones introduced the sightseers to Yellow Bull. Yellow Bull appeared healthy, but his fevered wife lay in their lodge on fur pallets. She was apparently incapacitated for some time, and within the year, Yellow Bull was living with his widowed sister.[21]

Other treatments also remained popular. One older woman spent a chilly March day enjoying a hot water bath. Rising early, she went to a spot near the creek downstream from the main camp where a bathing hole about three feet around and four feet deep had been prepared. Water was funneled from the creek into the bath. The woman built a fire and placed limestone rocks in it to heat them. Using a forked stick, she raked the hot rocks into the bath, then submerged herself in the hot water. After soaking for fifteen or twenty minutes, she leapt into the cold creek. She repeated the process until the bathing rocks cooled. The old curing rituals and hot water baths augmented the ministrations of the agency physician.[22]

Dr. F. B. Culver was employed by the Indian Bureau to treat all of the Indian camps served by the Quapaw Agency. As was usual at Indian agencies, the doctor's patients were located in distant locales, which he visited in all kinds of weather. In January 1879, the ride in from the camps during a snowstorm left Culver bedridden with pneumonia and unable to continue his practice. Many people were sick in the camps, but the Nimiipuu and other patients at Quapaw were left without a physician during the winter of 1878–79 until Culver's replacement arrived. Dr. H. E. Coleman from Seneca took over on March 11 and worked without a day off until his employment was terminated by Agent Jones in May. Although the Modocs, Nimiipuu, Paluses, and Cayuses preferred Coleman as their physician, Jones replaced him with a friend from Illinois, Dr. W. W. Johnston. Coleman felt that twenty years of practice in the area, his Civil War service, and his experience in treating American Indians qualified him more than someone who had no experience with American Indians or the local diseases. Dr. Coleman's petition to accompany the Nimiipuu, Palus, and Cayuse wagon train on their western migration in 1879 was accepted, and by all accounts, the prisoners wanted him to remain with them.[23]

By midwinter, the prisoners were suffering from coughs and bronchitis, tuberculosis, arthritis or rheumatism, constipation, and psychological disorders. While their leaders struggled with federal officials, some of the exiles withdrew from outside contact. They were deeply affected by the lack of predictability in their lives, and the lingering effects of depression and shock exacerbated the loss of control.[24] Adult males tended to secret themselves in their lodges when Agent Jones or other outsiders were in the camp. Chief Joseph and Yellow Bull also exhibited symptoms of severe stress and depression. Yellow Bull could be uncharacteristically caustic with strangers, and Joseph was sometimes apprehensive and morose. On one of Alfred B. Meacham's visits to Quapaw, Joseph was upset with Meacham's justifications for their removal and expressed concern about the wretched food, the inadequate medical attention, and the lack of housing.[25] The Nimiipuu were sickly and dejected after so many deaths that summer and fall, and the prison camps were often silent except for the sounds of mourning that marked another death.[26]

So many deaths in such a short time caused the prisoners to modify their customary burial practices, even though mortuary practices remained intact. Common burial practices included earth inhumation, stone and stick burials, low-lying shed burials, cairn and talus slope burials, and modified platform burials. During the first months at Quapaw, corpses were wrapped and sewn into deerskins or blankets after several days of mourning. Faces were painted, bodies were dressed in their finest clothing, and then the corpses were wedged in tree forks or tied to tree branches. When hollow trees were available, the deceased were sealed within them. Before long, however, complaints about the burials caused Jones to order the exiles to bury their dead like other reservation residents, using coffins made from hollowed-out logs. The underground burials were concentrated in an area north of the Spring River. Platform and tree burials resumed after the prisoners were moved to the Ponca Agency, until they were replaced by the use of coffins made of pine boards. One special interment spot was located along the junction of Deer

Creek and the Salt River, where corpses wrapped and sewn into blankets were tied in low-hanging tree branches. Settlers remembered this burial grove for its macabre appearance and unique odor, but they did not want the graveyard disturbed. Nature eventually took its course, and the skeletal remains lay undisturbed along the creek. Long after the prisoners were gone from the Indian Territory, floods carried piles of bones onto the banks of the Salt Fork River. The Nimiipuu burials were documented by witnesses, who did not confuse them with Ponca burials. Customary burial practices were environmentally adaptable, and the Nimiipuu had employed modified platform burials in their old homelands as late as 1806.[27] Altered burial practices were common in American Indian communities suffering from catastrophic illnesses; the Mandans, Hidatsas, and Gros Ventres died so rapidly during the smallpox epidemic of 1837 that they could not even bury their dead.[28]

Sixty-three lodges situated in an oak forest grove on about twenty acres accommodated the captives' family and band arrangements. When newcomers arrived in the camp, they moved in with relatives, or families established their own lodges. Widows lived with relatives, banded together, or lived alone. Thirty-four women headed fourteen households that cared for ten boys and eight girls in July 1878. By June 1879, thirty-eight women in twenty-four lodges were caring for nineteen boys and thirteen girls. Five women in At-ko-koo's camp died during fiscal year 1879, and the orphaned children were moved into another family situation. Twenty-two households headed by men accommodated several adult males and more than one adult female. Plural marriages did not increase, and over the next three years, only three or four non-Christian families continued polygamous relationships. Adult males rarely lived alone, although many more women than men died. Because so many young adult males did not survive the war, few younger men were evident in the camps until the Canadian escapees were sent to the Indian Territory. In July 1878, three lodges contained no children, and within the year, seven more families were childless. Census lists prepared between July 1878 and June 1879 note that at least fifteen adult males, fifty-seven adult females, and twelve children died during this period, although the actual rate of decline was higher because stillbirths, newborn deaths, and spontaneous abortions were not recorded. Orphaned infants starved to death after their mothers died because cow's milk was not available, and unless someone bought milk or infant foods in Baxter Springs, the babies perished.[29]

The Indian Bureau did not record age-specific data, the names of the children, or the names of most of the women. Federal law required only that the names of heads of families receiving rations be recorded, along with the number of rations issued to each family. Census data was recorded on the weekly ration-issue inventories, which tallied the number of adult males and females, girls, and boys remaining in each family. In early July 1878, families ranged in size from three to twelve people, with an average size of five or six people. Within the year, the number of large families decreased, the number of small families increased, and the mean family size remained between four and six people. A year later, the mean family size was between four and five people, while larger families continued to decline.[30]

When Mark Williams and James Reuben, both of whom were Nimiipuu, began keeping the ration census lists, they reordered them to reflect community affiliations, inserted names by family affiliation, and brought continuity to the records. Reuben also struggled with meaningful English-language translations, as he indicated to Professor R. L. Packard during the winter of 1880–81. Packard was interested in sacred or religious information, which Reuben refused to share, but he did explain Nimiipuu names, their meanings, and, in effect, their English translations. Reuben mentioned the names of two men who were on his mind at the time, Hoofs around the Neck (Hoof Necklace, Pe-ya-wa-hickt) and Eyes around the Neck (Seelo Wahyakt). He told Packard how vision quest names were acquired and explained that these names signified a special dream in which "a wolf or bird of prey appeared to the watcher with those trophies of the hunt."[31]

Samuel Fleming was a recent Christian convert, and Seelo Wahyakt was a young warrior deported to the Indian Territory with Yellow Wolf who found prison camp life extremely difficult. Packard was interested in the folkloric value of the names as Reuben brought the professor's interests into the realm of daily life.[32] Reuben's phonetic spellings and typeset lists, and the order that he and Williams brought to the agency records remain essential historical resources.[33] More importantly, Reuben's English-language phonetic spellings, assigned translations, and English-based names serve as historical markers. When the first census of the Chief Joseph's Colville exiles was prepared after their return to Washington on June 30, 1885, without James Reuben, it indicated that the Nimiipuu had not abandoned their old names. They thought of themselves by those names and not by the assigned names and translations devised by Reuben.[34] Lists of warriors' and survivors' names dictated by Chief Joseph and others, ration census lists, correspondence, school records, and almost all of the federal records are based on Reuben's English-language phonetics and assigned English names.

Problems with restrictive federal policies, bureaucrats, and a felonious Indian agent plagued the prisoners at Quapaw. No longer viewed as romanticized tourist attractions, the Nimiipuu were objects to be "broken, tamed, or civilized" like their neighbors, the Modocs. The Modocs supposedly exemplified the ultimate federal power because they tended small farms and gardens, supported themselves, wore civilized clothing, sent their children to school, attended church, and caused no trouble. They were also encouraged to tell the newcomers about their reconstruction and to recant their war with the United States. As Meacham told the secretary of the interior, Quaker missionaries Asa and Emeline Tuttle and Quaker Indian agent Jones, accompanied by his friend Ad Chapman, were the right people to "tame, break, civilize" the Nimiipuu and to lead them and their "wild urchins" to civilization.[35] Another lesson that was not lost on the exiles was that although their war chiefs and leaders had been killed in the war, the Modoc war leaders and chiefs were executed *after* their war with the United States. The poverty and population decline suffered by the Modocs in the Indian Territory was a prelude to the Nimiipuu experience, although it was glossed over in the federal narrative.

Now that the Indian Bureau controlled the prisoners, they were subjected to a host of civilian bureaucrats. Secretary of the Interior Carl Schurz, a German immigrant, touted civilization programs for American Indians. A former freedom fighter in the Rhineland, Schurz had migrated to the United States, served as ambassador to Spain, commanded a Union Army troop in the Civil War, and was elected to the Senate from Missouri.[36] Appointed secretary of the interior by President Rutherford B. Hayes, Schurz regretted broken American Indian treaties and blamed the transgressions and the Indian wars on the army and frontiersmen. Schurz also justified the Indian Bureau as basically honest in its management of American Indian affairs, and he encouraged rapid development of schools to separate American Indian children from their parents.[37] Helen Hunt Jackson, however, accused Schurz of murder. She and other historians held him responsible for the deportation of the Northern Cheyennes, for the war with the Nimiipuu, for stealing the Poncas' lands, and for the Utes' forced relocation and subsequent land swindles. Schurz was the "most adroit liar I ever knew," commented Jackson.[38] Schurz insisted that the Nimiipuu, Palus, and Cayuse prisoners must become agriculturists who valued separatism and western education and respected the American political structure. He admitted that he found Chief Joseph and other able but "wild" American Indian leaders to be limited in their ability to plan for the future. Schurz preferred Native leaders who had been bludgeoned into nationalistic views of the future, such as the Utes' Chief Ouray. He lauded Ouray as a man of "comprehensive vision, of large views," who appreciated the future and the necessary measures and assimilation required to protect American Indians from extinction.[39] Schurz did not mention the 11 million acres that the United States had recently taken from the Utes in what he considered the "most humane way possible to induce them to accept our conclusions."[40]

When wealthy New Jersey businessman Ezra Hayt took office as commissioner of Indian affairs in 1877, he was condescending and authoritarian, demanding that the Nimiipuu, Paluses, and Cayuses accept the Indian Territory as their permanent home. Despite Chief Joseph's repeated requests to visit Washington, D.C., Hayt kept Joseph away from important federal officials as much as possible.[41]

One of the worst officials encountered by the Nimiipuu in their exile was Hiram Jones, the Indian agent, who was a Quaker hired under President Ulysses Grant's peace policy. Jones stole supplies and medications intended for American Indians and accepted substandard supplies, services, and beef on government contracts, then kept a share of the extra profits. He awarded no-bid building contracts and allowed traders and local businessmen to inflate prices of goods sold to American Indians by 200 to 300 percent, then collected 10 percent of the gross sales. He faked bills, receipts, and payments for goods never received. Jones also allowed illegal timber cutting on the Ottawa reservation and was a firm believer in nepotism. He made life miserable for the prisoners at Quapaw. The refugees often went hungry or were fed spoiled rations and suffered without needed medications. The Indian Bureau overlooked Jones's activities for a long time before the Nimiipuu, Paluses, and Cayuses were moved to his jurisdiction, because Jones could be relied on to "break or tame" American Indians.[42] And when complaints were lodged against Jones, he blamed fiscal-year limitations, shipping irregularities, or the drying up or natural shrinkage of supplies. Jones certified at one point that the only shortages with respect to Nimiipuu supplies were 3,402 pounds of soap and 2,112 pounds of dried beans.[43] It is improbable that four hundred hungry people wasted a ton of beans, and that women who traded everything would have allowed a ton and a half of soap to disappear. When Jones's career began to crumble, he generated certificates of loss and affidavits and tried to cover his tracks.[44] Entangled in a power struggle with Jones, Ad Chapman claimed that Jones had shorted the Nimiipuu more than 5,000 pounds of beef in one week. The week after the complaint, Jones fired Chapman; Hayt, however, reversed the decision, telling Jones that if anyone left the agency, it would be Jones himself. Chapman carried the feud to his friend Meacham at *The Council Fire*, where he warned that Jones was threatening Nimiipuu who refused to become Quakers with banishment farther south into the Indian Territory. Jones also promised that refugees who accepted the Quaker faith would be returned to Idaho.[45]

The situation at the Quapaw Agency was indefensible. The prisoners were squatting on the Modocs' land, using their timber and tent poles, and there was no suitable agricultural ground.[46] The camp had to be moved because people were living in their own filth, and game disappeared. Chief Joseph and other leaders pressed Jones and the Indian Bureau for a resolution to the problems; they wanted to go home. In return, the Indian Bureau tried to force the exiles to accept permanent residency on the Quapaw reservation. Hayt's office admonished Joseph to cooperate with Commissioners Stickney and Fisk, who were coming to Quapaw to select a permanent home for them. Consequently, when Stickney and Fisk held preparatory meetings with Joseph and the other leaders, they were amazed that the exiles remained focused on returning to the northwest. Joseph reiterated the army's show of bad faith and negation of the surrender agreement and presented the commissioners with a copy of Colonel Nelson Miles's official surrender document dated December 27, 1877. The report left no doubt about Miles's intentions, but the commissioners denied responsibility for subsequent decisions made by the War Department. They felt that the War Department had done the best it could and that the exiles needed to make the best of the situation. After that, Joseph refused to join the officials on their property-seeking trip and would not attend the council with Miami and Peoria leaders. The authorities selected 7,000 acres, formalized an agreement with the Miamis and Peorias for the property, and told Jones to move the prisoners.[47]

Commissioners Stickney and Fisk called on Chief Joseph before leaving, but Joseph refused their advances. They finally dictated a letter to him extolling the beautiful, fertile, and well-watered lands they had chosen for the prisoners' home. They also guaranteed Joseph a house that was already on the property and assured him that everyone else would soon have good homes as well. Stickney and Fisk urged Joseph to lead his people along peaceful paths, picturing happy, industrious farmers who would send their children to school and attend Christian churches. Agent Jones, they added, would move them as soon as possible, and the government would provide everything.[48] The exiles ignored the powerful bureaucrats, and a month later, Commissioner Hayt refused Joseph's second request to come to Washington, D.C.; Hayt was coming to Quapaw in mid-October and would meet with him then.

In the meantime, a congressional committee conducted hearings at Seneca, Missouri, to determine American Indians' preferences for Indian Bureau affiliation and to solicit complaints about Jones. The committee was concerned about Jones's mismanagement of the Quapaw Agency and his treatment of the Nimiipuu. Previous complaints about Jones had been ignored because the agent was firmly entrenched in the Indian Bureau. On October 7, a local businessman and farmer named H. H. Gregg testified to the thefts, neglect, check-cashing schemes, and numerous other crimes committed by Jones, who managed finances and affairs for nine tribal communities and was responsible for at least fifteen hundred people. Chief Joseph was asked only for demographic information, so he offered no comments about Jones. Gregg and rancher George D. Morrow laid out the case against the agent, to which Jones responded by saying that he had done only what his superintendent did or what was necessary. Morrow testified to the agent's fraudulent dealings with local cattlemen as he told of one cattle dealer who had warned Morrow that Jones had to be "tickled" with bribes. Morrow bid one herd of cattle so low that he could not pay the bribe, and then Jones bought the same herd through someone else for a higher price that included the "tickle." The committee interviewed Modocs, Nimiipuu, members of the Five Tribes (Creeks, Choctaws, Cherokees, Chickasaws, and Seminoles), and other Native nations and continued on to Omaha, Wyoming, Utah, and California. Six weeks later, when another Senate committee visited the prison camp, Joseph testified that the Modocs had warned them that Agent Jones was a thief. By mid-November, Jones was stealing at least half of their provisions, and the Nimiipuu were without food two or three days each week.[49]

When no action was forthcoming as a result of these hearings and two earlier investigations, Gregg and a group of concerned citizens refused to participate in another Indian Bureau cover-up. They hounded the Bureau about Jones and harassed Hayt with their complaints. Gregg, D. S. Finn, Z. P. Cogswell, Morrow, and five other men were determined that the Bureau would rectify the situation at Quapaw and accused Hayt of negligence.[50] Some of the complaints against Jones were initiated by men who wanted improved access to government contracts and by other men who held contracts they wished to improve. Gregg, however, did not hold or bid on Indian Bureau contracts.[51] Chapman added his voice to the anti-Jones sentiment, complaining that even John McNeil, the Indian inspector, was protecting Jones. Chapman also used the issue to assure Meacham of his good intentions, saying that he would fight until Jones left the Indian service or until he himself was forced to quit. Secretary Schurz stepped in, and on July 23, 1879, he confirmed that Special Agent James M. Haworth was going to fire Jones. "A mountain is bearing down on this man," Gregg warned in the *Baxter Times*.[52]

While senators and congressmen were unearthing horrific tales of Jones's abuses and criminal activities, Secretary Schurz was pressing for permanent relocation of the prisoners in the Indian Territory. Public opinion favored the refugees, however, and the

Bureau was forced to respond to those pressures. Influential East Coast religious groups such as the Friends (Orthodox Quakers) reported on conditions in the press, to the secretary of the interior, and to Congress. Chief Joseph refused to acknowledge Agent Jones's authority and circumvented him whenever possible, lobbying Commissioner Hayt directly. Colonel Miles complained about the abrogation of the surrender agreement and the subsequent mistreatment of the prisoners by the Indian Bureau. Acting Commissioner of Indian Affairs Leeds and Hayt asked Schurz to petition the War Department for copies of the surrender agreement. The Indian Bureau was not prepared to deal with prisoners who understood their rights, demanded fair treatment, and continually cited a surrender agreement they had not seen. Civilian officials also had to admit that they had ignored Joseph's version of the war and its origins. In the meantime, the prisoners remained at the center of the debate over which federal entity should control the Indian Bureau. While Commissioner Hayt was at Quapaw trying to force another removal agreement with Chief Joseph and Húsus Kute, Leeds acknowledged that the Bureau was stymied. "We are having many difficulties with the captive Nez Perces," he said, admitting that nothing could convince the prisoners to accept permanent placement at Quapaw.[53]

Meanwhile, Commissioner Hayt was facing other problems in the Indian Territory. Chief Joseph and a council of leaders and headmen had notified Hayt that the location selected for them by Commissioners Stickney and Fisk was a disaster. The land would not support farming, subsurface water was nonexistent, and timber was scarce. Two wells recently drilled on the property had yielded no water, and the captives would perish if sent there. They also rejected Hayt's comparisons of them to successful Modoc farmers who labored under similar conditions. Commissioners Hayt and Kingsley visited the proposed Quapaw location and saved face by arguing that it was too close to the corrupt merchants and whiskey traders of Baxter Springs, Kansas, and Seneca, Missouri; saloonkeepers in the two towns targeted

American Indians, and an increase in alcoholism was accompanied by concomitant increases in violent crime, homicides, and domestic violence.[54]

Secretary Schurz agreed with Commissioner Hayt's assessment of the situation and the prisoners' demands, and Chief Joseph, Húsus Kute, Hayt, and Kingsley set out on a 250-mile odyssey to locate a more suitable property. Joseph and Húsus Kute considered moving to the Ponca reservation after the tour but did not guarantee that they would accept the new reservation or remain in the Indian Territory. Joseph was deeply concerned, fearing that the exiles and their descendants would face a dismal future anywhere in the Indian Territory. Hayt returned to Washington, D.C., with Joseph's promise to consider the move, after warning Joseph that settlers would retaliate against the Nimiipuu if they were returned to Idaho. Hayt assured Schurz that Joseph would agree to the relocation when he had finally abandoned all hope of returning to the northwest.[55] Hayt continued to press Joseph for a decision, and in the meantime, the Nimiipuu tried to go over his head to President Hayes.

By January, Agent Jones was still trying to force the expatriates to yield to his authority when they were exploited at their most vulnerable point. Joseph refused to sign the quarterly ration list on January 8, 1879, and Jones threatened to discontinue the rations, even though Hayt had failed to tell Joseph that he must sign the ration reports. Joseph wanted that point clarified before he signed anything. Húsus Kute and Yellow Bear stepped in and urged several other men to sign the reports to continue the rations, allowing Joseph time to deal with the problem. Húsus Kute, Yellow Bear, Jim Horn, Jim Nat (Kool Kool Sub-im), Three Eagles (Met-tat-wap-tas), Hohats Sumpkin, Seelo Wahyakt, and John Fur Cap signed for the rations while Jones waited for instructions from Hayt, and the rations continued. Jones threatened Joseph again on February 26, this time saying that Joseph himself must sign the ration lists. As soon as Jones left the prison camp, Joseph, Yellow Bull, and the other men who had signed the reports hurried to the notary's office in Seneca. They did not take Reuben with them because his role in the war was still too fresh in their minds.[56] They found the notary at the hotel with Chapman, and Joseph dictated a letter to Hayt, explaining that they were temporarily dependent on the rations and would starve without them. Jones, he continued, had tried to force him to sign the ration sheet without an approved interpreter. Hayt was out of the office, and the acting commissioner of Indian affairs instructed Jones that the rations must not stop. The situation was still volatile when Jones was fired later in the spring and a temporary agent was assigned to the agency. The army stepped in again at that time, and Captain George Towle distributed rations to the camps.

Hayt was absent from his office much of that spring, preparing for his own trial for corporate fraud; he was eventually acquitted on a technicality. Chief Clerk Leeds resigned, and his replacement, E. M. Brooks, made many of the decisions that affected the prisoners. Protected by a federal statute that limited Indian agents' administrative crimes to misdemeanors, Jones was fired and left the agency. In defiance of the Indian Bureau, he took many of the agency records with him. The temporary agent and the Bureau tried to retrieve the records, but paychecks to American Indian employees were delayed, and the agency remained in a state of flux.[57]

Other problems surfaced when a group of warriors who had been deported from Fort Lapwai arrived at the prison camp. Captain Charles A. Dempsey delivered fourteen of the battle-hardened veterans to the Quapaw reservation on December 14 or 15. These men had not joined the surrender, and they resented the outcome of the conflict. Many of them were single and had lost families or friends in the war, or their wives remained in Idaho. The few younger warriors in the camp before their arrival were living quietly with families and friends. Family men such as Tom Hill, Sup-poon-mas, John Fur Cap, Dick Johnson, and Little Man Chief had settled into the camp, although they held differing opinions about the conflict and surrender.[58] The new group of unattached warriors refused to cooperate with Chief

Joseph, Yellow Bull, or the other leaders and brought alcohol into the community. Like many other combatants, they were not reconciled to the surrender, and their transition to camp life was difficult. The incoming prisoners also joined a camp that was governed by peace leaders trying to establish new protocols; the war chiefs who could have influenced the young men were either dead or in Canada. Interviewed by a reporter from the *Omaha Herald*, one veteran who had come to the camps earlier blamed Joseph for the surrender and captivity. Fur Cap spoke in the Crow language and signed to an army officer that even the women in his band had wanted to fight instead of surrender, and fifty years after the war, Many Wounds (Sam Lott) still resented the surrender and avoided Joseph. Captured army scouts also caused problems, including Skou-cum-Joe, who insisted that he must return to Montana. Skou-cum-Joe, who had been adopted as a Crow, complained bitterly about being in the prison camp, claiming that he had served in the army against the nontreaty bands. Worried that the turmoil was driving the camp beyond his control, Joseph asked Commissioner Hayt to remove the disruptive men, but they remained where they were.[59]

Bored, dismounted, and penniless, the prisoners introduced horse racing and gambling to their neighbors. To Agent Jones's disgust, the Nimiipuu gambled, raced, and traded for horses with Modocs, Ottawas, Miamis, Eastern Shawnees, Wyandottes, Senecas, and Citizen Potawatomies. Guy Jennison, who was an Ottawa, remembered the gambling and the fun of the races that he attended as a child. Another elderly gentleman recalled exciting horse races between the Nimiipuu and Modocs and authorities who had no patience with the gambling. Racing fever swept the reservation at the same time that Agent Jones banned Green Corn Dances, Sun Dances, and Long House ceremonies and tried to put an end to non-Christian ceremonials. Boys practiced sneaking and stalking, shot pennies and dimes from slotted sticks, and listened to stories of the past. Young men painted the parts in their hair with red, donned beaded leggings and moccasins, and displayed their jewelry and regalia. Seated near their fires, elders spoke of Nimiipuu heritage and histories.[60]

Women patched, mended, made, and remade clothing, and they traded unwanted government issue-items, including some of the goods they had been given in January and February. Hundreds of yards of indigo cloth, balmoral skirts, and black pants and jackets had been purchased by the Indian Bureau and sent to the camps. The women either remade the balmoral skirts or traded them, because they were designed to be worn with corsets. Caddo and Wichita ladies wore the skirts as dresses because the tiny waists were better suited as necklines. The black pants and jackets were intended for the men and boys, and the indigo yard goods were to be used for clothing or bedding. The Indian Bureau usually supplied heavy duck for tepee repairs and other fabrics that were suitable for bedding, clothing, and mattress ticking. The Bureau also purchased variegated blanket coats for distribution to American Indian men, like those that Chief Joseph and Yellow Bull wore to Washington, D.C.[61]

Christianity, education, agriculture, and a sedentary lifestyle were key federal objectives for the prisoners. However, when Presbyterian minister Samuel N. D. Martin, army chaplain Andrew D. Mitchell, and a Presbyterian minister from Leavenworth approached the exiles at Fort Leavenworth, their overtures were rejected. Deeply involved in winter ceremonials, the captives were not interested in Christianity or any offers that promoted other agendas. A former teacher and part-time minister at Lapwai, Martin had planned a ten-day mission to the camp. He would infuse the adult captives with the New Testament and Christian doctrine and appeal to the children with biblical lore and stories. When Martin interviewed the unenthusiastic Chief Joseph, Joseph refused to accept a copy of the Book of Matthew printed in Nimiputimít. When he was pressured to take it, he made it clear that many of the captives blamed the Presbyterians for interfering with Nimiipuu spiritual practices, politics, and values. Martin also spoke with the prisoners who had studied Christian doctrine before the war and were not participating in the winter ceremonials. They remembered him, even if they were not interested in his present activities. The Reverend John C. Lowrie of the Presbyterian Board of Foreign Missions had another worry: "We fear these Nez Perce are Romanist and that a priest is with them."[62] Although some of the Nimiipuu who had supported the war were Catholics, there was not a priest living in the prison camp.

Three Nimiipuu Christians were relocated to the Indian Territory from Lapwai to accelerate the introduction of Christianity and other federal programs. Reuben, the Reverend Archie Lawyer, and Mark Williams left Lapwai for the Indian Territory on November 8, 1878, arriving in Baxter Springs on December 6, 1878. Lawyer brought with him several bags of gold dust and his mother's double buffalo hide tepee for church services and council meetings; Reuben left a considerable amount of personal property behind in Idaho.[63] Initially hired as the new interpreter, to replace Chapman, Reuben was instead appointed as the schoolteacher. Lawyer and Williams were licentiate Presbyterian pastors, although Lawyer had been hired to be the schoolteacher, and Williams was assigned as assistant agency farmer. The changes in appointments were confusing; Commissioner Hayt expected Reuben to replace Chapman, but Agent Jones presumed that Reuben had been hired as the teacher.[64] Regardless of the confusion, federal officials wanted the men to start a school, establish a Christian church, and persuade the prisoners to remain in the Indian Territory. Deeply divided by the war with the exiles, the three young men had supported the treaties, the war, and the federal relationship. Related to Chief Joseph by marriage, Reuben had served as an army scout and participated in combat against the nontreaty bands. He also supported the war and permanent removal of the nontreaty bands to the Indian Territory, and served as a government interpreter.[65] Son of treaty chief Lawyer and one of missionary Sue McBeth's ministerial students, Archie Lawyer needed a pastorate and more experience before he could be ordained as a Presbyterian minister. Williams was the son of Elder Billy Williams and was another of McBeth's ministerial students.[66]

The men all had friends or family in the camp, although there were mixed reactions to their arrival. The young warrior Yellow Wolf resented Reuben, recalling his combat against the nontreaty bands during the war and his postwar arrogance. He also accused Reuben of favoring federal edicts and of slanting interpretations to deflect blame onto the prisoners; he further disliked Reuben's Christian doctrines and interference with non-Christian ceremonials. Several of Reuben's subsequent comments and activities indicate that Yellow Wolf's criticisms may have been well founded. Reuben inserted his own comments into a letter supposedly dictated by Chief Joseph to General Oliver O. Howard, taking on Joseph's voice in order to guarantee Howard's support for his own pro-Christian agendas. According to Reuben, Joseph apologized to Howard for the war, saying, "I remember the councils we had at Lapwai, Idaho. You and I could have agreed if it had not been for other Indians. I regret those days. I now see that you were talking to me right." Reuben was one of those "other Indians" and was preparing Howard for Joseph's next apology when he supposedly said, "I know religion is good. It makes all feel kind toward each other. I want you to know now I am going to be a Christian man, so I want you to make known my wishes to all ministers in the West."[67] Joseph had no reason to apologize to Howard, and through various interpreters over the next six years, he demanded Howard's attention to the Bear Paw surrender agreement. Although Joseph attended several Christian services at Oakland, he did not become a Christian; Presbyterian ministers complained that he would not join the church.[68] Joseph certainly told Howard that "religion is good," because he was dedicated to the *wéset* faith and became a Sun Dance participant and supporter in the Indian Territory. In a final attempt to lobby for Howard's approval, Reuben closed the letter, "Yours truly, Nez Perce Chief Joseph," a term that Joseph never applied to himself. And then Reuben signed Joseph's name to the letter, which was not necessary because Joseph signed his own documents.[69] Howard's supercilious reply congratulated Joseph on becoming a "real" Christian, denied responsibility for the broken surrender agreement, and advised Joseph to make the best of the Indian Territory:

> I feel sorry that so many have sickened and died. I know how like children the living ones desire to see the hills and mountains where they were born. But now the soil contains the remains of those who have died, the soil where you are. Can you not make good farms and have good schools there in the Indian Territory? If you can get your people well to work, and make a garden of the land which the Government has assigned you, and if you can say to the children, "Go to school, and grow up contented and happy and industrious," you Joseph, will show yourself a truly great man, and your people can never be blotted out.[70]

Howard added that he looked forward to his visit with Reuben, who was supposed to be in the northwest at the time.

Some of the other federal officials and Agent Jones favored Reuben for his pro-government stance and claimed that Chief Joseph had shunned Reuben, Lawyer, and Williams for some time after their arrival in the Indian Territory.[71] According to a newspaper reporter who spoke with Joseph soon after the surrender, however, Joseph felt no great personal animosity toward Reuben; the men held differing opinions, but the war was in the past.[72] By the time Reuben returned to the northwest in 1883, the two men seem to have reconciled most of their differences, although Joseph remained cautious about Reuben's translations.

Conditions at the Quapaw prison camp were abysmal when Lawyer, Williams, and Reuben learned that they had been brought to the Indian Territory under false pretenses. Promised decent government wages, the men complained that their salaries were less than half those paid to non-Native men. They had also been told that the prisoners had agreed to permanent residency in the Indian Territory, so they were surprised to learn that the captives had no intention of staying there. The men were also treated shabbily by Indian Bureau employees who assigned them menial jobs as interpreters, as teachers in a nonexistent school, and as an assistant farmer in a program that had no equipment. They had paid their own train fares on the promise of federal repayment and then had to beg Commissioner Stickney to intercede with Commissioner Hayt to reimburse them for those fares. They also wanted their share of the funds generated by the treaties of 1855 and 1863 forwarded to them at Quapaw, although federal law denied treaty payments and annuities to hostile Indians and to the captives.[73]

Their financial situation precarious, the young men were forced to board at the agent's home and to purchase their food, clothing, and other supplies on credit. Lawyer and Williams were paid before Reuben, who received no money until the following October because of the disparities in his job description. Agent Jones had listed Reuben as a teacher on the payroll records that he sent to the Indian Bureau, while Commissioner Hayt understood that he had been hired as the interpreter. When the men were all finally paid, their salaries were more than doubled to equal those of the non-Native employees.[74]

While Reuben gradually replaced Chapman as interpreter, he and Williams witnessed affidavits and ration issues and assumed responsibility for keeping the ration records. Williams also worked with the farmer and cattle herder, and the three men forged ties with other American Indian teachers and missionaries. There was no church at the camp, so by February, several of the blanket-clad exiles were attending services at the Wyandotte Quaker Mission along with Lawyer, Williams, and Reuben. The visitors addressed the Friends meeting, describing their mistreatment and the terrible conditions at the prison camp. After agreeing to visit the mission again, they asked the congregants for their help and prayers. The Nimiipuu did go back to the mission, although they did not adopt the Quaker faith.[75]

As Reuben, Lawyer, and Williams joined in the life of the camp, they began to alter their impressions of the prisoners' situation. They did not actively promote the return of the prisoners to Idaho until after their relocation to the Ponca Agency, but they did argue for better conditions. While taking part in training institutes for mission teachers, Reuben and Williams lectured on the terrible conditions in the prison camp. They also participated in the institutes as educators. Lawyer recommended suitable opening exercises for Indian schools; Reuben discussed the importance of American Indian parents to the educational processes, and he and Williams lectured about teaching techniques that were suited to American Indian children. The men also participated in training exercises for mathematics and other subjects.[76]

Archie Lawyer conducted Christian services in his extra-large lodge before a Presbyterian church was formed. According to Chief Lawyer's great-granddaughter Mylie Lawyer, the Christian prisoners gathered there for services, and everyone who visited spoke of the mountains and rivers of home.[77] Lawyer, Reuben, and Williams remained at the Quapaw Agency until summer 1879, when they traveled west with the exiles to the Ponca Agency.

The treatment of the Nimiipuu by the local community at Quapaw differed greatly from what they had experienced at Leavenworth. Unlike reporter N. P. Perry from the *Leavenworth Times* and Colonel Daniel R. Anthony of Leavenworth, newspapermen in Baxter Springs and the surrounding area offered few opportunities for Chief Joseph or other American Indians. Letters and comments continued to be sent to the *Leavenworth Times,* but few members of the local press were particularly interested in the prisoners. When Joseph and his interpreter visited newspaper offices, editors mentioned their visits. Stopping at the *Baxter Springs Times* on his return from the Ponca Agency in October 1878, Joseph reported that the location was about as good as anything in the Indian Territory. Steeped in the romanticism of the Noble Savage, the *Empire City Echo* billed Joseph as the "noblest Red Man of them all" when he pointed out that the prisoners did not approve of the land selected for them at Quapaw.[78] Ad Chapman told the *Empire City Echo* that the Indian Bureau was probably going to send the exiles to the Dakota Territory, while J. F. McDowell warned tourists to hold on to their scalps when visiting the Nimiipuu or Modocs. McDowell also misstated the terms of the agreement under which the Nimiipuu, Paluses, and Cayuses moved to the Ponca Agency in 1879, saying that they had ceded 4,800 acres of their Idaho homelands in exchange for the new reservation at the Ponca Agency.[79]

Local newspapers printed items concerning the Nimiipuu from larger newspapers, interviewed federal employees, and welcomed correspondence from missionaries. Most local newsmen objectified the Nimiipuu and other American Indians while expressing little real concern for their welfare. One of the few people who were actively concerned for the prisoners, H. H. Gregg argued his objections to Agent Jones with N. D. Ingraham, vice president of the Kansas State Historical Society, in the *Baxter Springs Times.* Gregg advocated removal of the agent, but Ingraham, claiming Indian Bureau support for Jones, determined that he should remain in office.[80] Chief Joseph's visits to Baxter Springs were newsworthy vignettes, especially when he stayed at the local hotel. Those visits to the Planter's House have led local historians to accuse Joseph of being drunk in the hotel bar; however, Joseph's nemesis Kate McBeth and his friend Indian trader Joe Sherburne guaranteed that Joseph never used alcohol.[81] According to McBeth, "Joseph had one good thing about him. He was a temperance man," and Sherburne recalled that when he knew Joseph in the Indian Territory, "he was not using liquor, he never drank at all."[82]

The Nimiipuu, Paluses, and Cayuses also experienced the post–Civil War racism of the Old South while at Quapaw. Tourists made pests of themselves at the prison camp, where they degraded the Nimiipuu, Paluses, and Cayuses as racially inferior people who were destined to vanish from the American landscape. They gawked at the captives and then blamed the victims for their miserable condition. When Op-has accepted a quarter, he was reviled in the *New York Times.* Snubbed as a beggar and a joke for explaining the sad circumstances in the camp, Op-has was likened to a corrupt American senator accepting millions of dollars in Crédit Mobilier stock. The tourists also warned that unless diseases killed the prisoners, they would become liars, thieves, and vagrants. "These captive Nez Perces with their haughtiness, their wretched, sordid life, their sulky scora, and ignoble grasping for petty advantage, are fair examples of the peculiar traits of a fading race," said the visitors. The Nimiipuu had become vanishing Americans for twenty-five cents.[83]

Another visitor to the prison camps was Baxter Springs merchant Bob Sands, who denigrated American Indian women as "squaws" and preferred the "white woman" missionary Emeline Tuttle. Sands scorned Native men as the last of the "Noble Red Man" or "dusky braves" and displayed his arrogance as he barged into Chief Joseph's tent. "They have only been here about 10 months and a great many are still in their blankets. They are a motley crew. We drove into their camp and after some length of time by motions and gesticulations, I got an old squaw to understand I wanted to see Chief Jo. She pointed out a tall tent or wigwam and on driving up was met by two tall braves in red paint and fancy clothes, jewelry, etc. I very reluctantly shook them by the hand."[84] Inside the tent, Sands interrupted Joseph and about twenty men who were probably discussing the move to the Ponca Agency, although to Sands it seemed an odd gathering. As he bragged to his wife, "After surveying the mystic group I retired—or withdrew—and drove about the camp taking items."[85] At least Sands understood that Joseph, although polite, did not welcome the interruption. Sands presumably sold the stolen items in his store.

An eighteen-year-old Modoc boy named Shepaliva was murdered at Seneca, Missouri, the last week the prisoners were at Quapaw, a crime that further clarifies the racism that was directed at American Indians. Furious that Shepaliva had spent $1.50 with one of his competitors, Seneca merchant John Albert accused the teenager of cheating him out of a pair of boots. Shepaliva protested, calling Albert a liar and declaring that he always paid his debts. Albert grabbed the boy and slapped his face. After running across the street to get his gun, and egged on by his brother's screams of "Shoot the damn little son of a bitch," Albert chased Shepaliva behind another store.[86] He shot the unarmed boy twice in the back, then circled around the store and shot him two more times. Shepaliva died at the scene. The justice of the peace released Albert the next day after setting his bond at $1,000. The prosecuting attorney was a fellow Confederate veteran and personal friend of Albert's and handpicked a grand jury that refused to indict Albert. Jury members even offered bets before the hearing that there would be no indictment. Special Agent Haworth, Secretary of the Interior Schurz, and Commissioner Hayt tried to involve the U.S. attorney in the matter and to get the case moved to another court. Meanwhile, Modoc leaders Bogus Charley and Steamboat Frank rode into Seneca with Haworth to meet with worried townsfolk. Frustrated by the lack of legal support, the Modocs borrowed guns and ammunition, then returned them and waited for local authorities to take action against Albert.[87] They were warned that the prosecuting attorney and the law would not prosecute white men for crimes against people of color, and federal officials were also told to stay out of the case because the state of Missouri viewed federal involvement as a violation of their state's rights.[88]

Federal plans to warehouse the prisoners on the Quapaw reservation had fallen apart. Poor planning, neglect, criminal agents, inept federal authorities, racism, disease, starvation, and substandard living conditions had to be addressed. And in addition to everything else, the Quapaw Strip was about to be opened for non-Native settlement; a tide of white emigrants was expected on the reservation, and local people were encouraging the new business coming to Baxter Springs.[89]

CHAPTER 6

Peace Chiefs and Diplomats

Caught in a web of revolving bureaucracies, the Nimiipuu and their allies tried to establish predictable relationships with federal officials even as constant shifts in authority limited their opportunities. During their incarceration, the Nimiipuu, Paluses, and Cayuses endured four presidents, five commissioners of Indian affairs, eight Indian agents, and various agency superintendents. Chief Joseph tried to establish a receptive relationship with President Rutherford B. Hayes soon after moving to Quapaw, but Hayes was more interested in the Poncas.[1] President James A. Garfield complained about corruption and mismanagement in the Indian Bureau, but he was assassinated and replaced by Chester Arthur in September 1881. President Arthur proposed no innovations in American Indian policy and supported allotment and extension of state and territorial laws to American Indian reservations.[2] "Their tribal days are over," said Arthur. "It is now for their best interests to conform their manner of life to the new order of things."[3] Grover Cleveland was the first Democrat to be elected president after the Civil War, and during his first term of office, 1885–89, he revived the spoils system, factional bias, and nepotism in the Indian Bureau.[4] Federal Indian policy remained fairly constant despite the changes and focused on placing American Indians on reservations, providing food to prevent resistance, and allowing the exercise of almost dictatorial authority by Indian agents. Federal policies also mandated that American Indians become self-supporting, receive a formal education, and accept conversion to Christianity.[5]

Commissioners of Indian affairs exercised extreme power over the lives of American Indians. The five men who held the position while the Nimiipuu were in captivity included men who had little interest in or experience with American Indians, men who should have been in prison, and men who focused on bureaucratic structures and administrations. John Q. Smith was dismissed from office ten days before the surrender at the Bear Paw and bequeathed to the Indian Bureau a legacy of corruption.[6] He was replaced by wealthy New York businessman Ezra Hayt, who had already been discharged from the Board of Indian Commissioners by President Ulysses S. Grant. President Hayes brought Hayt back to the Indian Bureau to support the building blocks of his American Indian policy. In Hayt's first and second annual reports, he insisted that federal "civilization" programs would render American Indians harmless. The programs advocated a legal code for reservations and an American Indian police force controlled by non-Native officers.[7] Hayt also proposed that reservations be divided up into individual allotments, and he reinforced the emphasis on agriculture and self-support. Common schools and industrial and compulsory education were to be extended to reservations, where Christian teachers and missionaries could regain lost opportunities. Christianity would replace so-called American Indian religious practices, and rations and clothing would be issued in exchange for labor, regardless of treaties or agreements. Hayt would place all American Indians on consolidated reservations in an effort reminiscent of the Indian Removal Act of 1830 and California's attempts to purge American Indians from that state to the Indian Territory in 1852.[8] He planned to eliminate twenty-five reservations, close eleven Indian agencies, and return more than 17.6 million acres of American Indian land to the public domain.[9] Hayt extended these policies to the Nimiipuu, Palus, and Cayuse exiles even though on February 27, 1879, Congress banned additional American Indian relocations to the Indian Territory, with a few minor exceptions.[10] He also denounced nepotism in the Indian Bureau and then appointed his son as secretary and disbursing officer to an important federal commission.[11] Hayt was discharged by President Hayes after twenty-eight months in office.

President Hayes appointed his friend Rowland Trowbridge as Hayt's replacement. Trowbridge was considered to be an honest businessman who could have reorganized the Indian Bureau, but ill health restricted his activities, and he resigned within the year. Trowbridge supported the abolition of polygamous marriages, replaced tribal punishments with systemic legal recourse, raised the pay and status of American Indian police, and increased livestock production on reservations.[12] Hiram Price, another successful businessman and politician, replaced Trowbridge on May 6, 1881. Determined to continue American Indian "civilization" programs, Price encouraged the eradication of Native languages and a reduction in Indian Bureau costs. He promoted American Indian self-support and moral reforms, and like Hayt he was an advocate of the idea of allotment in severalty, which would confirm American Indians as individual property owners. Instructed by Secretary of the Interior Henry Teller, Price established Courts of Indian Offenses at Indian agencies and increased enrollments in the Indian police force. He also pursued cooperation with Christian clergymen, Indian reform movements, and political action groups, although he exhibited a limited understanding of American Indians and Native nations. The commissioner supported independent American Indians who owned land or raised livestock. Price retired voluntarily on March 26, 1885.[13]

John D. C. Atkins replaced Price as commissioner of Indian affairs in 1885. A Confederate army general and representative to the Confederate Congress during the Civil War, Atkins expedited the allotment of reservation land, promoted assimilation, industrial, mechanical, and agricultural education programs, and backed the removal of American Indians who refused allotment to small, consolidated reservations. Atkins resigned June 14, 1888, to run for the United States Senate.[14]

American Indians were rarely consulted when agents were appointed, transferred, or retired. Indian agents were not yet included in the civil service system and were subject to few educational or experiential requirements. When religious organizations held sway over the Indian Bureau during President Grant's administration, they engineered the appointment of favored missionaries and others as Indian agents. As religious influences faded, the president, the secretary of the interior, and the commissioner of Indian affairs began to make their own appointments. Indian agents were also transferred between agencies when money was tight at the Indian Bureau or during departmental reorganizations. Dr. Dolphus Dunn and other physicians held joint appointments as physicians and superintendents at the Oakland Subagency in the Indian Territory as a measure of economy. When Hiram Jones was fired at the Quapaw Agency, he was temporarily replaced by Dr. W. W. Johnston, who was soon succeeded by Special Indian Agent James Haworth.

William Whiteman was the agent in charge of the refugees at the Ponca Agency until he was forced to retire because of his involvement in a murder. In March 1879, as the Nimiipuu, Paluses, and Cayuses were considering relocation to the Ponca Agency, Chief Standing Bear and a small band of Poncas who were seeking to return to their Nebraska homelands were arrested in Omaha. Following a horrific journey and detention, Standing Bear sued for a writ of habeas corpus in the Omaha Federal Court. On May 12, Judge Elmer Dundy handed down his landmark decision in *United States ex rel. Standing Bear v. George Crook,* ruling that "an Indian is a person" and that the government had no right to hold the Poncas. In June, the Nimiipuu, Paluses, and Cayuses were moved to the Ponca Agency, where they wondered whether Dundy's decision would apply to them. On October 31, Agent Whiteman ordered the arrest of Standing Bear's brother Big Snake, who had been visiting local Indian agencies for several months without a permit. Having been taken into custody for exercising the freedoms granted in the Dundy decision, Big Snake was detained in Whiteman's office. He was unarmed and insisted that he could not be arrested without due cause. Troopers stormed the office, and as Big Snake struggled to his feet, he was smashed in the face with a rifle butt and shot in the head.[15]

There are several different versions of how Big Snake died. The official story as concocted by the Indian Bureau was that he was killed by an army corporal. Another account implicated Whiteman in the murder, although he carefully shifted the blame to the corporal. Trader Joe Sherburne, who was in Whiteman's office that day, thought that one of the troopers had killed Big Snake. Interpreter Joseph Esaw testified to a Senate investigating committee that it was impossible to identify the shooter, in spite of the committee's efforts to bully him into blaming the corporal. And a Ponca policeman who was in the office that day recalled that it was Whiteman who shot Big Snake.[16] Some combination of the stories likely explains the killing, although Esaw's testimony supports the policeman's version of the murder. Whiteman was also accused of fiscal malfeasance; after a visit to Washington, D.C., the charges of fraud were dismissed, and he retired.[17] Commissioner Hayt tried to have the Standing Bear writ dismissed, and the Indian Bureau refused to recognize the freedoms affirmed under the decision because the case had not been reviewed by the Supreme Court.[18] Rumors flew on the reservation after the killing, and it was suggested that the Nimiipuu, the Poncas, and a group of dissident Northern Cheyennes might be planning a breakout. Aware of the discontent caused by the murder, Whiteman relied on the Nimiipuu police for assurance that no outbreak was at hand.[19]

A succession of political appointees replaced Whiteman at the Ponca Agency, including Thomas J. Jordan, Lewellyn Woodin, and John W. Scott. Dr. Dunn was appointed superintendent and physician at the Oakland Subagency, the eventual home of the refugees at the Ponca Agency. As superintendent, he was responsible for the general administration of the agency and for supervision of the two non-Native farmers, the American Indian schoolteacher, the interpreter, the herder, and four laborers. Dunn's performance as a physician was inadequate, his clerical work was woeful, and his administrative abilities were nonexistent. "The Nez Perces dislike him and Joseph and others complained to me of his inability to assist them in any way," Agent Woodin complained to Commissioner Price.[20]

By November 1877, the winds of freedom were being fanned in the western Indian Territory. The Nimiipuu, Paluses, and Cayuses arrived at Fort Leavenworth while Standing Bear, Big Snake, and other Poncas were in Washington, D.C., seeking redress for their removal to the Quapaw Agency and the theft of their Nebraska reservation. The Poncas had suffered disastrous population losses from malaria and neglect at the Quapaw Agency and continued to die from the disease at the western Indian Territory reservation. Meanwhile, hundreds of Northern Cheyennes died after being deported to Darlington, Indian Territory. Nearly two thousand Cheyennes and Arapahos seeking treatment for malaria at the Darlington Agency were turned away in 1878; the agency's annual supply of quinine had been depleted in only ten days. Cheyenne leaders Dull Knife and Little Wolf then led a group of runaways to their northern homes as their battles with the army and the rising tide of public sympathy became known to the Nimiipuu, Paluses, and Cayuses.[21] In the midst of the tumult, Chief Joseph and Húsus Kute attended a meeting with Chief White Eagle and other Ponca leaders and a federal commission in August 1878. The Poncas spoke about their removal from Nebraska to Quapaw, about the deaths at Quapaw, and about their health problems at the new reservation. Húsus Kute and Joseph also visited an Osage council and attended a meeting with the Kaws before they returned to the Quapaw reservation.[22] Joseph and Húsus Kute relied on the information from these meetings as they contemplated their relocation to the same area.

About a month after the Cheyenne escape and three months before Standing Bear and the Poncas fled the Indian Territory, Chief Joseph testified to a congressional investigating committee in Seneca, Missouri. He set the tone for a sophisticated understanding of American Indian civil rights and civic duties. Questioned about his preferences for control of the Indian Bureau, Joseph replied that he favored neither civilians nor the military. "I think both of them could be set aside," he said.[23] When asked for his policy recommendations, Joseph said that one set of laws should govern all people, non-Native and American Indian alike. American Indians should be able to enjoy their liberty and the freedom to be self-supporting, and they would accept the responsibilities to obey and support a system of laws applicable to everyone. "Liberty is good and great," said Joseph as he rejected the government's authority to hold American Indian prisoners.[24] He had reiterated this position to Commissioners Hayt and Kingsley and repeated his promise that American Indians understood the statutes and laws and would abide by decisions that were mandated by fair and inclusive tribunals.[25]

Chief Joseph and other American Indian leaders insisted on proper diplomatic etiquette in their dealings with federal officials. A high-ranking Indian Bureau official accompanied Commissioner Hayt to the Indian Territory in August 1878, and Joseph insisted that the Palus leader Húsus Kute join him in a similar capacity. Húsus Kute, Joseph, Commissioners Hayt and Kingsley, and an interpreter spent nearly a week examining properties in Kansas and the Indian Territory. A preferential location was finally selected from the 6-million-acre Cherokee Outlet, although Joseph and Húsus Kute would not agree to move without further community conferences.[26] The new location consisted of more than 90,000 fertile, well-watered acres, in contrast to the 7,000 acres of arid scrubland that had been selected for them at the Quapaw reservation by the government.

A national debate ensued in an effort to clarify title to the Wallowa Valley, the legality of the exchange of the Idaho properties for the new Indian Territory location, and the expatriates' rights. Admitting that the expatriates had never relinquished title to their old homelands by treaty or agreement, Commissioner Hayt wanted the government to gain clear title to the northwestern properties. Hayt acknowledged that this title would be a valuable advantage to settlers, and he recommended that a reasonable payment be made to Chief Joseph's band.[27] But Joseph still desired access to eastern power brokers, and Alfred B. Meacham made arrangements for him and Yellow Bull to travel east with interpreter Ad Chapman. Meanwhile, James Reuben, who had recently arrived at Quapaw from Lapwai, was angry because Joseph would not take him to Washington as their interpreter.[28] The delegates traveled by train from Baxter Springs north to Omaha, then on to Washington, D.C., where they arrived on January 13, 1879.[29] They met President Hayes, attended the Board of Indian Commissioners' annual Missionary Board meeting, and addressed a special meeting of congressmen, senators, diplomats, and Indian reform activists at Lincoln Hall.[30]

Chief Joseph, Yellow Bull, and Chapman attended the president's annual White House reception on January 14, 1879, the day after their arrival. Clothed in beaded and embroidered regalia and blanket coats, Joseph and Yellow Bull joined Washington elites at eight o'clock that night for the opening of the White House social season. Crystal chandeliers and candelabra lit the Blue and East rooms, where fires blazed under flower-laden mantels, and the U.S. Marine Corps Band played selections of classical and dance music. Joining the tuxedo-clad men and evening-gowned women, Joseph and Yellow Bull moved through the Blue Room receiving line. Webb Hayes presented the men to his father the president, and then they were introduced to First Lady Lucy Webb Hayes. What Joseph and President Hayes said to each other remained between them, although Joseph undoubtedly made the most of his moment with the president. Then Joseph and Yellow Bull circulated around the East Room and moved into the conservatory with the other celebrants. Whether stationed on the carpets of the East Room or strolling among the giant banana palms and tropical plants in the conservatory, the Nimiipuu men were the hit of the evening. Surrounded by satin-gowned ladies exclaiming over their regalia and clothing, Joseph responded to the charming women as he and Yellow Bull spoke with community and government leaders. By all accounts, the Nimiipuu diplomats enjoyed the evening.[31] No wine or alcohol was served, and the Hayeses never allowed dancing, so everyone enjoyed coffee and light refreshments. At ten o'clock the band played "Home Sweet Home," and President and Mrs. Hayes bade their guests farewell in the East Room.[32]

The next day, the chairman of the Missionary Board conference, Sewall S. Cutting, invited Chief Joseph and Yellow Bull to their evening meeting at the Interior Department. When they arrived, Meacham was addressing about thirty religious leaders and their staffs, cabinet members, and diplomats on the question of military versus civilian control of the Indian Bureau. He paused while the guests took their seats. The attending group of American Indian dignitaries included Joseph, Yellow Bull, six Colorado Utes, and two Cherokee and Creek executives. Like Joseph, the Utes were protesting a disastrous agency consolidation and removal to a diminished reservation, and the Cherokee and Creek leaders were concerned about issues affecting the territorial status of their nations. Meacham finished speaking, and Cutting introduced Joseph and Yellow Bull by recalling their first meeting in Idaho, when Joseph had tearfully lobbied the council against being forced onto the reservation. Quaker missionary Benjamin Tatam invited Joseph to address the Society of Friends (Quakers) in New York, and then Joseph spoke. In a brief but cordial speech with Chapman interpreting, Joseph reiterated his position on equality and freedom for American Indians and non-Natives. He then introduced Yellow Bull, saying that his childhood friend understood his heart and his honorable intentions. Joseph assured the assembly that, like them, he was growing more knowledgeable with experience and maturity. Then he extended an invitation to attend the Lincoln Hall event at which he would be giving a longer speech on January 17.[33]

Two nights later, Chief Joseph led fourteen American Indians into Lincoln Hall to enthusiastic and continued applause. The event was intended to give the Natives a chance to address their concerns and reiterate their rights. It was also a promotional event for Meacham's Indian rights journal, *The Council Fire.* More than eight hundred attendees paid the twenty-five-cent admission. Yellow Bull and Joseph wore Navajo blanket coats decorated with furs and feathers, shirts and decorated leggings, and decorated moccasins. The Ute leaders wore red face paint, blankets, and full regalia. They were joined by William Ross, William P. Adair, and other Cherokee, Chickasaw, and Choctaw leaders. Ad Chapman and a Cherokee Indian agent joined the party on the speaker's platform, although neither man was asked to address the meeting. Joseph spoke for almost two hours while Chapman interpreted, replicating the cadences and timing of the speech.[34]

Joseph started slowly. He poured and drank a glass of water, cleared his throat, crossed his hands, and began to recite the litany of the Nez Perce treaties. High-pitched and strained at first, his voice deepened as he gained confidence in his audience. Speaking Nimiputímt augmented with the graceful movements of sign language, Joseph shared memories of his father. He spoke of his father's love and his steadfast refusal to sell their homeland, then continued with a cogent review of Nimiipuu history. Joseph, who had previewed his speech at an earlier press conference, talked of the treaties and their violation by non-Native people. He described the war, the surrender agreement, and the prisoners' subsequent deportations to one place after another, ever farther from home. Joseph also recalled a few humorous stories for the spellbound audience. He told of sending a group of young men on a horse raid, suggesting that the men had only traded their skinny, worn-out horses for fat, fit animals. The audience joined the charismatic young chief in a moment of laughter. Joseph evoked another round of merriment when he told of the men who stole General Oliver O. Howard's herd of mules, reminding the audience that not everything had gone Howard's way during the war. He asked the government to treat the Nimiipuu as equals, to give them the chance to become self-supporting again and to live as free people. He also suggested that if they could not go to their homes in Idaho or Oregon, they should be returned to the Bitterroot Valley in Montana. An edited version of his speech was soon published in the *North American Review* and several other journals, although Chapman and others criticized the editors for adding to or reorganizing the chief's presentation. Several reporters who attended the event remarked on Joseph's unique style of speaking and understood the complex nature of his message, which elicited cries of distress from the enthralled audience.[35] Joseph closed his two-hour oratory with an unadorned, eloquent statement: "This is my story and here I am."[36] Dr. Cora Bland then recited her poem "Nez Perces Joseph," and the Cherokee delegates talked about the problems facing their nations. One of the Ute men then spoke briefly, and the evening ended.[37]

General Howard responded to Chief Joseph's message after reading reprints of it in the *Army and Navy Journal.* Howard felt that the lecture was a bit *of ex parte* dialogue and avoided the romanticism accorded Joseph by the popular press. Echoing his letter to Joseph dated July 20, 1880, Howard disputed the critical tone of the speech, justified his conduct of the war, and defended federal policies and the shattered surrender agreement. He accused Joseph of gross historical distortions and discounted his training as an oral historian. Howard also denied any culpability in the war and blamed indigenous religious practitioners for the non-Christian viewpoints that he considered central to the conflict. The general did not, however, take Joseph to task about the mules.[38]

Twenty-four years after his first visit to the White House, Chief Joseph joined President and Mrs. Theodore Roosevelt in the Blue Room on February 12, 1903, where he again lobbied generals, admirals, and congressmen for Nimiipuu rights.[39] He repeated the positions he expressed at Lincoln Hall many times before his death in 1904.

Surprisingly, just before Chief Joseph and Yellow Bull left Washington on the evening of January 31, 1879, they signed an agreement giving up all claim to their lands in the Idaho Territory or elsewhere. In return, Joseph's band would receive four townships in the Indian Territory as their permanent home, and $250,000 invested in United States bonds, payable at 4 percent interest per year. The United States agreed to absorb the purchase price of the Indian Territory property and to pay removal expenses to the new reservation in what is now Kay County, Oklahoma.[40] Commissioner Hayt supported the proposition and implemented arrangements to pay the Cherokees for the land located on the Cherokee Outlet.

Like the accord that Commissioner Hayt had hammered out with the Tabaguache, Yampa, Grand River, and Uintah Utes two weeks earlier on January 14, the Nimiipuu agreement was not ratified by Congress, and the cessions and exchanges did not become law.[41] Because the agreement was not ratified, it remains a historical anomaly that may reflect Chief Joseph's state of mind on that particular day. Joseph and Yellow Bull had just spent two weeks vigorously campaigning for their return to the northwest or to the Bitterroot Valley. They wanted better living conditions in the Indian Territory, but they did not intend to commit the group to permanent residence there. Furthermore, their continued efforts to return to their northwestern homes, especially to the Wallowa Valley, were relentless. The federal government coveted clear title to millions of acres of lands owned by Native nations during this era and forced many other American Indians into agreements they did not fully understand.[42]

The signatures on the agreement are suspect because they were recorded by the same man, who signed himself as "Young Josep[h]" and then signed "Yellonce Yellon." The name Yellonce Yellon does not resemble any English or Nimiputímt spelling of Yellow Bull's name, and Chapman knew this.[43] Consequently, the signature or a clarifying mark as Yellow Bull would have reflected a clearer understanding of English names and concepts. Chief Joseph's signature is misspelled, and there is no corrected spelling inserted in the document, indicating again that the language and intent of the agreement were unclear. Joseph did tend to sign his name in this manner, yet neither man's name is spelled correctly next to his signature or anywhere else in the agreement. They are referred to as the "First and Second Principal Chiefs" of Chief Joseph's band, and in the rush to prepare the document, they were never clearly or legally defined.[44] The timing of the transaction is also suspect because the agreement was formulated just hours before Joseph and Yellow Bull left Washington.

Most importantly, the document contains no specific mention of the Wallowa Valley in Oregon, the ancestral home of the Joseph's band. Only the general term "or elsewhere" inserted by federal authorities could have encompassed the Wallowa Valley, and that English-language term was arguably meaningless to Joseph or Yellow Bull at that moment.[45] Then again, Joseph may have preferred that the Wallowa Valley remain separate from the agreement as it was read to him.[46] Chapman's sincerity as an interpreter and his ill health may also have affected the translation and a full understanding of the agreement. The interpreter was a favorite with federal authorities and could have purposely misinterpreted the document, although there is no proof of this. Chapman admitted that he was so ill before, during, and after the trip that there were times he "thought I wold shurly [*sic*] kick the bucket."[47]

There are other problems with the agreement, including the assumption that Chief Joseph and Yellow Bull were legally responsible for all of the detainees. Húsus Kute and the other Palus were not members of the Joseph's band, and neither were the fragments of the Looking Glass and White Bird bands who were living in the prison camps. Strictly speaking, Joseph and Yellow Bull could not determine their property rights. Neither did Joseph have the right to sell, assign, or trade properties on the Lapwai reservation; the other properties at Salmon River and the Imnaha Valley, Idaho, were already lost to the Nimiipuu. When Congress refused to ratify the agreement, any consideration of the legalities or understandings it contained was null and void. Congress continued to make annual appropriations to maintain the Nimiipuu and to cover the cost of their relocation to the Ponca Agency.[48]

Chief Joseph and Yellow Bull returned to the Indian Territory, where they continued to influence pubic opinion and policymakers. Joseph did not, however, return to Washington, D.C., three months later, as was suggested by historian Merrill D. Beal. He was at the Quapaw reservation dealing with intrusive tourists.[49] Like Joseph, Yellow Bull was focused on freedom and the recognition of American Indians' civil rights. Four months after their relocation to the Ponca Agency, Yellow Bull, his brother Red Elk (Wa-wook-ya-el-pilp), and Yellow Bear were guests at the Cowley County Fair on October 8, 1879. President Hayes had declined an invitation to attend the fair, although the governor and hundreds of tourists from Wichita and other Kansas towns arrived by train. Invited by the fair managers to address the crowd, Yellow Bull, Red Elk, and Yellow Bear were seated on the speaker's platform with Governor John P. St. John. After St. John's speech, Yellow Bull spoke through Chapman, saying that he was pleased to meet everyone, and that even though he had "fought the whites" the previous summer, he "wanted them to know now that he knew how to make friends. The Great Spirit made this world for them all to stand on, and he wanted to live like one people, under one roof, with one law to govern them all. He knew that the people were friendly towards him because they did not run away from him as though they were mad."[50] This was exactly what the governor and everyone else was wanting to hear; they hoped that the civilizing effects of Yellow Bull's speech would spread to other Native nations. After that, the visitors toured the fair, where they enjoyed the cattle and horse exhibits, found a variegated rug that Yellow Bull thought would make a good saddle blanket, and pointed out a cured dogskin.[51] Yellow Bull lobbied for recognition of the Nimiipuu's civil rights for the rest of his life, testifying to Congress more than thirty years later that he still expected those rights to be recognized.[52] The Fair Board was advised to include another delegation of American Indians on the platform the following year.[53]

Chief Joseph's presentation at Lincoln Hall had successfully spurred public interest in the extension of the Fourteenth Amendment right of habeas corpus and other liberties to American Indians. By March *The Council Fire* reported widespread interest in the refugees' situation. In addition, the prisoners were aware of the Standing Bear decision and paid close attention as attorneys and activists tried to take their case to the Supreme Court.[54] Back east, however, the Friends (Quakers) had failed to raise $4,000 for attorneys' fees, and the case did not go forward.[55] Chief Standing Bear followed Joseph back to Washington, D.C., and spent several months in the fall and winter of 1879 and 1880 campaigning for American Indian civil rights. Although federal commissions and officials investigated both cases, neither the Ponca nor the Nimiipuu complaints reached the Supreme Court. Ten months after the trip to Washington, a disheartened Joseph met with Meacham at the Oakland Indian Territory reservation. Through his interpreter, he said, "You come to see me as a man upon his deathbed. The Great Spirit Chief above has left me and my people to our fate. The white men forget us, and death comes almost every day for some of my people. He will come for all of us. A few months more and we will be in the ground. We are a doomed people."[56]

Joseph and the other leaders maximized every occasion to influence their release and recognition of their civil rights. When General Nelson Miles and Commissioner William Stickney visited the Indian Territory in January 1881, Joseph told them that he held the government responsible for the failure of the surrender accord.[57] Indian trader Sherburne was in the office that day and recalled that Joseph held Miles personally liable for the fact that the agreement had not been implemented. Joseph reminded Miles that he had promised that the expatriates would be returned to the Idaho reservation, and that punishment was to have been exacted after their return to Idaho. Miles defended the position, saying that he did not have the authority to force government compliance, while Joseph insisted that anyone who had the power to make such an agreement should have the power to enforce it.[58] He and the attendant prisoner delegation urged the president, his god, and the white people who worshipped that god to have mercy on them. They were dying and desperately needed to go home, as Miles had promised that they could.[59] Miles could not disagree, and he and Stickney returned to Washington, D.C. A letter from Miles to President Hayes dated January 19, 1881, attested to the horrible conditions in the prison camp and asked the president to authorize the prisoners' return to Idaho, as had been promised at the Bear Paw. Miles also reminded Hayes that there had been no investigation to determine responsibilities for the war, and he admitted that the prisoners would accept equitable punishment if they were sent home. Appealing to Hayes as a politician and humanitarian, Miles reminded the president that the war had taken place during his tenure in office. Miles reviewed the letter with Secretary of the Interior Carl Schurz before submitting it to the president, and Schurz agreed with Miles's recommendations up to a point. President Hayes and Schurz readily acknowledged the problems, although they wanted Miles to conduct a further investigation of the matter after he assumed command of the Department of the Columbia.[60]

While the secretary of the interior, the secretary of war, and the other generals were shuffling papers and dragging their feet, a frustrated General Miles asked Indian rights activist Helen Hunt Jackson for help.[61] Jackson insisted that Hayes had promised Miles that he would take a proactive stance in the matter, regardless of the fact that Miles had waited for the president's reply.[62] On May 8, 1881, Jackson asked Senator Henry L. Dawes to determine whether any federal action was forthcoming or whether Miles's request was bogged down in the bureaucracy.[63] In the meantime, Miles assumed command of the Department of the Columbia and was in a position to protect settlers or the prisoners if they were moved back to the northwest.[64]

In 1882, Commissioner Price made several surprising admissions about the expatriates, the surrender, and their condition.

He conceded that the prisoners were refusing to give up their incessant desire to return to the northwest. According to Price, "It has been hoped that the advantages of the location selected for this band of Nez Perces in the Indian Territory would . . . engender in them a spirit of enterprise and emulation, which after a few years would make them comparatively contented with their new home. This hope, however, has not been realized . . . yet [as] each year passes numerous petitions and urgent requests come from them praying to be returned to their old home and relatives."[65] Price then questioned the surrender agreement and justified the mismanagement of the prisoners: "They persistently claim that when they surrendered to General Miles it was with the express stipulation that they should be sent back to Idaho. Whether this alleged stipulation be true or not, it is a fact that their unfortunate location near Fort Leavenworth, when in charge of the military, and the influences of the climate where they are now located in the Indian Territory, have caused much sickness among them."[66] Price acknowledged the continued efforts of certain army officers to fulfill the surrender agreement, then closed with the following: "In view of all the facts, I am constrained to believe that the remnant of this tribe should be returned to Idaho, if possible, early next spring."[67]

The unhappy Nimiipuu, Paluses, and Cayuses remained in the Indian Territory while General Miles prepared to investigate the situation in Idaho.[68] And when Archie Lawyer introduced Chief Joseph to the Reverend George L. Spining at the Oakland Cemetery in the fall of 1883, Joseph asked the minister to remind President Arthur that the captives continued to die in the Indian Territory. Spining recalled that as he sat on his horse watching the men tour the cemetery, "Chief Joseph pointed to the graves and said to tell the Great Father in Washington maybe his heart will be touched."[69]

American Indian leaders such as Chief Joseph and Standing Bear were essential to the promotion of Indian rights in the dawning era of activism and reform movements. They leapt the chasms of language, distance, religious beliefs, and political, cultural, and societal differences. They learned to manipulate the media, they understood the importance of new political relationships, and they remained focused on their rights. They traveled to Washington, Boston, New York, and Philadelphia to motivate the rising tide of Indian rights activists. They waged a never-ending struggle to establish predictable relationships with ever-changing federal officials. Joseph, Yellow Bull, and Standing Bear were among the many western American Indian leaders who willingly followed their politically savvy Cherokee, Choctaw, Chickasaw, and Creek compatriots to the halls of Congress. But the wheels of freedom turned too slowly. Regardless of the abrogation of their civil liberties and property rights and their determination to go home, the Nimiipuu, Palus, and Cayuse prisoners were moved to the Ponca Agency south of Arkansas City, Kansas.

CHAPTER 7

Removal to the Oakland Subagency

New Lives, Demographics, and Changing Intertribal Relationships

The Nimiipuu, Paluses, and Cayuses met with Inspector James M. Haworth on April 23 and 24, 1879, to decide whether the entire group would move west to the Oakland Subagency of the Ponca Indian Agency. During two three-hour council meetings held on successive afternoons, the prisoners expressed their aversion to moving farther west in the Indian Territory. Joseph was deeply concerned about living where so many Poncas had died or were sick. Other council participants were confused and did not understand the arrangements and promises that Joseph had made in Washington, D.C. Joseph explained that he hoped that Generals Benjamin F. Butler and Nelson Miles and the forty senators and congressmen he had met in Washington would keep their promises. They had promised to allow the Nimiipuu to return to the northwest, and Miles had pledged a speedier relocation if their health continued to deteriorate. Needing time to confer with the group, Joseph asked for an adjournment, and the council disbanded until the next afternoon. Haworth felt that Joseph wanted to avoid problems with the government, although he seemed certain that the prisoners would agree to relocate. The group of Paluses led by Húsus Kute, however, were opposed to the move, and the differences between the factions intensified during the discussions.[1]

Húsus Kute and his followers did not agree with Chief Joseph when he finally expressed a willingness to go west in the Indian Territory. They did not want to move to the Ponca Agency; they preferred to remain at Quapaw. Highly intelligent and somewhat influenced by Archie Lawyer and James Reuben, Húsus Kute believed some of the rumors that were directed at the exiles. It was said that if the band cooperated with Agent Hiram Jones and caused no trouble, they would be sent directly home from Quapaw. The band had remained near the Quapaw Agency and worried that they should stay there if the rest of the group moved to the Ponca Agency. As usual, the leading men addressed the council, saying that they all expected Colonel Miles to honor the Bear Paw surrender agreement. The speeches grew more impassioned when Haworth warned that the government would not separate the group. If one person moved to Ponca, they all moved. Haworth had already notified the council that they should cooperate with the federal authorities and continue to work out their problems after the move. Late in the afternoon of the 24th, the council agreed to relocate to the Ponca Agency, and Haworth credited the interpreters and his own actions for bringing order to the dissenting factions. He failed to realize that Joseph, Húsus Kute, Yellow Bull, and the leaders and community members must have spent the night in intense discussions. After that, they were ready to announce their decision following the speeches and deliberations at the second council: they would move west together.[2]

Bureau employees made preliminary plans throughout April for the move. American Indian relocations were always problematic. Delays at the Indian Bureau were never-ending, and funding depended on congressional appropriations that were often late or tied to the new fiscal year, which began July 1. Weather and illness caused special problems, as had happened with the Poncas' relocation to the Indian Territory in the summer of 1877. Plagued by tuberculosis, malaria, and other illnesses, the Ponca migrants were struck by a tornado near Milford, Nebraska. Wagons and animals were destroyed, several people were blown away, and one child was killed. And in an attempt to avoid the heat and malaria of summer, the Pawnees were removed to the Indian Territory in the dead of winter, when traveling was also hazardous.[3] Telegrams between wagon trains and Indian Bureau administrators took more than twenty-four hours, and when there was no telegraph available, couriers galloped to the nearest telegraph office. The constant turnover of officials in the Indian Bureau also delayed processes and responses. A steady stream of written reports and information produced during and after removals itemized the horrors of relocation but did little to alleviate conditions or stop the deportations.

Preparations for the Nimiipuu migration shifted into high gear after the second council meeting. Inspector Haworth organized the wagon train, Dr. H. E. Coleman was assigned as the accompanying physician, and Ad Chapman was hired as the wagon train master.[4] Haworth ordered enough beef and rations for twenty days, even though the move was scheduled to take only half that long. Orders were issued to purchase forty mules or broodmares to be issued to the prisoners. The Indian Bureau supplied shovels, picks, heavy chains, axle grease, lariats, extra water buckets, and several kegs of muleshoes, horseshoes, hoof picks, and toe caulks.[5] Chains secured doubletrees to wagons, and grease kept wagon wheels turning. Lariats were rigged for extra pulling power. Horses and mules frequently lost shoes on the rough trails, and caulks added to the shoes worked like studs to give the animals extra traction. Hoof picks were essential for removing debris that had become packed in hooves, which could cripple the horses and mules. Toolboxes, special wrenches, and other mechanical items were carried on each wagon. While waiting for delivery of twenty wagons, bows, and covers, Haworth arranged to lease additional teams and wagons. He also made arrangements to feed and pasture all of the horses and mules along the route for ten cents a head. In the meantime, the prisoners readied the camps for the move. By May 6, they were growing restless; they wanted to travel before the harsh summer heat set in.[6]

Reuben, Lawyer, and Mark Williams would accompany the wagon train as federal employees, although they had not been paid since coming to the Indian Territory. Agency carpenter Francis King, an Ottawa, was hired as a teamster instructor and aide, and supplemental wagons were borrowed from the Modocs.[7] Inspector Haworth advertised in local newspapers to purchase forty sound broodmares or mules that were between four and seven years old, were broke to work, and stood under fifteen and a half hands tall. His budget allowed $5,000 to buy horses or mules and provided another $3,600 to lease thirty six-mule teams. Haworth, as always, paid a significant personal performance bond before spending government funds.[8] Between May 23 and June 8, Haworth bought forty mares and two mules. When the twenty wagons ordered for the Nimiipuu failed to arrive, he found them "blockaded" in the Kansas City freight yards. He also discovered that the Indian Bureau had confused the original order and marked the wagons for the Modocs, leaving only two wagons for the Nimiipuu, Paluses, and Cayuses.[9] Haworth corrected the problem, and the wagons were finally issued to the exiles, in addition to the four wagons and mules that had already been allotted to them at Quapaw. Once the wagons were assembled and driven to Oakland, they were branded with "ID"—the old Indian Department brand, which was still used by the Indian Bureau.[10]

Purchasing, inspecting, and preparing the horses and mules for the trip took most of one week. Haworth was required to submit inspection certificates for the animals with the invoices to the Government Accounting Office, so he hired William Julian of Olathe, Kansas, and asked General John Pope to detail Captain George Towle to help with the inspections. Julian was paid $5 a day plus his expenses, and the horses cost the Indian Bureau about $65 a head.[11] The men did an outstanding job of selecting the animals, which were the first good horses assigned to the prisoners since the Bear Paw. "I guess Joseph felt more himself than at any time since his surrender," Haworth said after Joseph had inspected and approved the horses.[12] Mares in estrus were bred, and then all of the horses were branded and shod. The mares were stabled in town while preparations for the move went forward in the camps. Haworth and the prisoners worried about the delays, fearing the heat, horseflies, and the flooding expected along local rivers.[13]

By June 6, the stage was set for the westward migration just as many of the prisoners were succumbing to another outbreak of malaria and the intense summer heat. Lawyer and Reuben, who were being paid to help with the wagon train, also came down with malaria as preparations were made for the westward trek. Forced to revamp his plans because people were too ill to walk all the way to the Ponca Agency, Inspector Haworth added more wagons and teams to the train.[14]

Dr. Coleman provided his own team and wagon, which was loaded with medical supplies and camp gear. He received $2.50 a day for the wagon and horses and was paid $100 a month for his medical services.[15] Experienced in the harsh realities of wartime medicine, the veteran Civil War surgeon was probably the best man to operate the mobile clinic.

The day before leaving Quapaw, the freshly shod horses and mules were brought together with the wagons and their new owners. The animals were harnessed and hitched to the wagons, and teamster school began. Because few of the men had driven teams before, they received instructions in working a two-horse or four-horse hitch.[16] They also learned the mechanics necessary to operate the wagons and how to keep the wheels and hubs greased. Most of the new teamsters learned rapidly, although some of them needed a few days to get the hang of things. Haworth issued rations and supplies for the trip, while the prisoners dismantled the camp. Lawyer, Reuben, and Williams received $75 advances against their unpaid salaries, and Chapman received a $100 advance. Because the Bureau had defaulted on the Quapaw Agency payroll for the fiscal quarter after Hiram Jones was fired, Haworth borrowed the money on a personal note to fund the advances. As federal employees, Reuben, Williams, and Lawyer drew rations for the trip, and those costs were deducted from their salaries.[17] Haworth and the other federal employees provided their own supplies, meals, and transportation. The federal statute requiring American Indian men to earn the value of their rations was suspended between April 20 and June 16, 1879; the government absorbed the cost of feeding the Nimiipuu, Palus, and Cayuse men during the trip.[18]

Extra teams and wagons were leased from A. I. Woolard and Son of Baxter Springs, who provided thirty additional two-horse teams instead of the six-mule teams. In all, sixty-four wagons and Dr. Coleman's ambulance were required for the move. Before leaving, the supplemental teamsters driving Woolard's teams were lined up and warned that cursing or vulgar behavior would not be allowed, and drunkenness or improper behavior would lead to their immediate dismissal. Any discharged teamster would forfeit his wages. Woolard also demanded that the drivers obey orders and behave, or they need not bother to load up. Francis King and Thomas Stanley helped with the loading, checked all the wagons and harnesses, and supervised as the axles and hubs were greased. They also inspected the wagons every night, trying to prevent problems while on the march. Five days later, the new teamsters no longer needed as much help, so Stanley returned to Baxter Springs.[19]

After much adjusting and balancing of loads, sixty-five wagons set off for the West on June 6, 1879. First camp was made at Tar Springs, about eight miles north of the starting point. The wagons were on the move again at five o'clock the next morning. They crossed the Neosho River and camped that afternoon on the west bank of the river near Chetopa, Labette County, Kansas. The wagon train left at four o'clock the next morning so as to pass through town before everyone was awake. The Poncas had held a big dance there the year before during their westward move, and people in Chetopa still feared that the regalia and face paint threatened a war dance.[20]

The wagon train usually traveled across Kansas just north of the Indian Territory border. In an attempt to reduce travel during the hottest part of the day, the wagons normally started by four or five o'clock in the morning, then proceeded until lunch and stopped in the early afternoon. The group camped on Snow Creek on June 9, then passed through Coffeyville, Kansas, on June 10 and camped near Fawn Creek in Chautauqua County, Kansas. Two mules were reshod at Coffeyville, and several wagons were repaired. One elderly woman died from malaria and exhaustion after making camp at Fawn Creek and was buried there at sundown. A young girl living on a nearby ranch recalled the funeral. Fifty years later, the migrants' grieving cries still echoed in Florence Richmond's memories. A rainstorm blew in just before dark, but the mud did not slow travel the next day.[21]

Awakened at three o'clock the next morning, the refugees started extra-early in order to take advantage of the cooler weather. They traveled through Caneyville and crossed the Caney River, then went through the little hamlet of Peru, Kansas, and were in camp by two o'clock in the afternoon. The terrain roughened, and for the next few days, the wagon train traveled over harsh country. The teams struggled over high hills on bad roads, and the wagons made difficult crossings at Grouse Creek and Silver Creek. Chief Joseph and the men cleared roads and performed other necessary maintenance, using the shovels and picks from the supply wagon to fill in holes and washouts. On June 11, the refugees camped on the Big Caney River near Cedarvale, where several horses wandered away. The wagon train moved on after the strays were rounded up, and the next camp was made following a complex crossing at Silver Creek. One mare was crippled by a snag and was left behind at Silver Creek after the most difficult day of the trip. The wagon train usually covered about twenty miles a day.[22]

Wearing a combination of western and Nimiipuu clothing and a hat decorated with a long feather, Chief Joseph rode at the head of the wagon train as it entered Arkansas City, Kansas, on June 13. The travelers were filthy and exhausted as the wagons stopped in Arkansas City, where townsfolk asked the prisoners to demonstrate their bows and arrows. Several men and boys shot dimes from perforated sticks, gaining a little hard cash in the process. Meanwhile, Inspector Haworth sent a messenger to

William Whiteman at the Ponca Agency to alert him that they would be arriving the next day. Haworth asked Whiteman to meet the refugees with beef, medicine, and other supplies, but Whiteman had received no other notice of their arrival. Commissioner Ezra Hayt was often slow in replying to Haworth's telegrams, and he had neglected to make arrangements at the Ponca Agency for the detainees. Whiteman could supply enough rations for only seven days, and he had no quinine. Although the ambulance was well stocked with pain medications, Dr. Coleman had brought along only a few ounces of quinine-based medications, and he had run out before the migrants reached Arkansas City. He had other palliatives, but they were not effective against malaria.[23] There apparently had been a misunderstanding between Haworth, who reported before the trip that only "several of the Indians are sick," and Coleman, who ordered the medicines.[24] Haworth had underestimated the number of prisoners who were infected with malaria, and consequently, Coleman had not ordered sufficient medications to control the epidemic. Once again, moving the prisoners at the height of malaria season was a deadly mistake.

However, the stop at Arkansas City marked the beginning of new opportunities for the Nimiipuu, Paluses, and Cayuses and their return to the northwest. Cowley County was more progressive than eastern Kansas and southern Missouri, and people there were more accepting of American Indians' participation in economic and social structures. Wagon trains of migrant American Indians were also a common sight, because Pawnees, Otoes, Missourias, Kaws (Kanzas), Northern Cheyennes, Poncas, and others often passed through borderland Kansas. Thousands of American Indians from the western Indian Territory also spent their money in south-central Kansas.[25] Pawnee cavalcades passed through settler communities on the way to their annual buffalo hunts, and when they enlisted as army scouts in 1876, railroad cars of war-ready Pawnees stopped in Kansas on their way to fight the Sioux.[26] Ranchers and local businessmen relied on lucrative Indian Bureau contracts for beef, supplies, and shipping. Businessmen regularly fulfilled Bureau contracts for millions of pounds of flour and beef; mill owner A. A. Newman sold the Indian Bureau more than $50,000 worth of flour in 1879. In addition, government contracts meant that farmers and ranchers would have to live in peace with the Natives in order to produce their crops and livestock.[27] Peaceful and prosperous relationships were also essential to the Nimiipuu, Paluses, and Cayuses who were moving into the area.

Local ranchers and cattle brokers sold nearly 10 million pounds of beef to the Indian Bureau every year, which was delivered on the hoof to nearby Indian agencies. These contracts were worth ten times more than the beef contracts for the Quapaw Agency.[28] Independent teamsters running wagon trains down to the army at Fort Sill in the Indian Territory were often accompanied by a herd of cattle destined for the Kiowa and Comanche Agency. One local freighter held a contract to haul 1.5 million pounds of freight to Fort Sill and other locations in the western Indian Territory. Another contractor delivered the mail to the Pawnee Agency from Independence, Kansas, and freighters moved cattle hides and buffalo robes to the railroad from the Indian agencies. Other lucrative deals included a railroad car of agricultural equipment for the Ponca Agency and builders' contracts to supply the lumber for homes and infrastructure there. The Arkansas City and Southern Express Company ran twice-weekly stagecoach service from Arkansas City to Willow Springs, the Ponca Agency, and east to Okmulgee.[29] The Indian Bureau was good for business, and Arkansas City entrepreneurs welcomed Native nations to the area. Merchants also kept track of annuity payments to American Indians and appreciated the attendant fiscal opportunities.[30]

American Indians were important participants in the social life of Cowley County. When Costello's Double Circus and Zoological Aggregation came to Arkansas City, acrobats and wild animals entertained the audience while enterprising Kaws and Pawnees sold the crowds handmade bows and arrows. Pawnee men who had joined Buffalo Bill's Wild West Show or the Pawnee Bill Wild West Show always made news when they came through town.[31]

American Indian dancers were welcome on the streets of Cowley County. Robert Hudson, Jr., recalled the dancers who were invited to Winfield, Kansas, where city folks participated in the social dances. "I still remember, with pleasure, learning the peculiar shuffling steps and joining in the festivities," said Hudson.[32] Local merchants sometimes roasted a beef to serve to their American Indian customers at events such as Independence Day celebrations. Whether in town or down in the Indian Territory at Fort Sill, Independence Day included entertainment and horse races between locals, soldiers, and American Indians. Prostitution and the liquor trade existed along the border with the Indian Territory, although both activities were vigorously prosecuted.[33] One of the greatest differences between Baxter Springs and Arkansas City was that law enforcement and the judiciary in the latter supported the Nimiipuu, Paluses, and Cayuses.

On that first day at Arkansas City, the Nimiipuu, Paluses, and Cayuses met several men who would become important to them, including Haworth's friend Cyrus M. Scott. Known throughout the Indian Territory because of his unique position in Kansas state and borderland politics, the young newspaperman and entrepreneur also spied on American Indians as a special agent for Governor John P. St. John and the Kansas Militia. Like everyone else, Haworth knew about Scott's illegal activities when he accepted his offer to guide the wagon train to the Ponca Agency. Scott joined the procession early on the morning of June 14 to begin his extraordinary acquaintance with the Nimiipuu, Paluses, and Cayuses.[34] Scott was well connected throughout Cowley County, and his relationships with newspapermen, businessmen, and ranchers would translate into access to local power structures for the expatriates. In contrast, some of his friends, such as Nathan Hughes of the *Arkansas City Traveler,* supported other agendas for American Indians that could have harmed the Nimiipuu and their allies. Hughes promoted the release of the Indian Territory to non-Native settlement and individual allotment of reservations in severalty. He also proposed that all American Indian treaties be abrogated and that the federal court with jurisdiction over the Indian Territory be relocated from Fort Smith to Arkansas City.[35] Fortunately, Hughes did not remain at the *Arkansas City Traveler* too long after the Nimiipuu arrived at their new agency, and Scott made certain that the editors who replaced Hughes were supportive of the captives. The exiles would make the most of every new opportunity, but first they had to complete the journey to the new reservation.

The teamsters paid careful attention to the two-ton load limit when crossing the old bridge over the Arkansas River at Arkansas City. Heavily damaged by floods in 1877, the south end of the bridge could not reliably support even one horse and buggy, as Joe Sherburne learned when his carriage horse fell through the bridge.[36] After crossing the dangerous span, the wagon train traveled southwest and camped on the headwaters of Shallato Creek. Following Chief Joseph and Scott, the exiles left camp at four o'clock the next morning, traveling south along the road between Bodock Creek and Duck Creek to reach the mouth of the Chikaskia River about three o'clock in the afternoon.[37]

Gathered on the east bank of the Chikaskia River after the twenty-six-mile trip from Arkansas City, the teamsters prepared for another difficult crossing. Teams were double-hitched, and women, children, and old folks piled into the wagons, many of them too sick to walk or swim. Braying mules and crying babies added to the commotion as animals and men prepared to ford the river. With the sun beating down and the horseflies biting, the teamsters cracked their whips and urged the four-horse hitches toward the water. The exhausted captives clung to the sides of the jolting wagons as the excited horses leaned into their harnesses, some straining to move ahead, others balking or trying to turn back. The lead teams plunged down the bank into the river, where the overloaded wagons quickly became stuck in the sand. Men waded in to help, and Chief Joseph, the only exile riding a horse, rode into the water to meet every wagon. He attached his lariat to each wagon tongue and to his saddle horn, then he and the other men pulled the straining lead teams up the west bank. Teamsters unhitched their teams on the far bank and rode them back across the river, where they were rotated with fresh lead teams to pull another wagon across.[38]

Sherburne never forgot that afternoon in the timber, and he never forgot Chief Joseph. "He was certainly a fine specimen of a man," he said. "I can see him now as he looked then, riding a big fine horse."[39] Sherburne also noted that as far as the prisoners were concerned, Joseph was the man in charge of the wagon train. As their leader, Joseph was expected to be instrumental in helping the refugees to their destination. He repaired roads, helped load and unload the wagons, and was involved in all of the details of the trip.[40]

Although Haworth, Hughes, and Sherburne did not mention the other men by name, Hughes reported that Chief Joseph was "helped by his men," who certainly included Yellow Bull, Húsus Kute, Yellow Bear, Yellow Head, Jim Horn, Sup-poon-mas, and Es-pow-yes.[41] At least six people rode in each wagon on top of the toolboxes, tepee covers, household goods, and supplies. Large families, including Húsus Kute's group of nine and E-ya-lo-kaun's and Hohats Sumpkin's families of ten, divided the extra passengers among their relatives.[42] Smaller families such as Daniel Jefferson's, which included two women, pooled with other small families, and extra passengers rode with Dr. Coleman.[43] Teamsters took turns driving the twenty-four wagons assigned to the Nimiipuu, while the able-bodied men walked, repaired roads and trails, and helped care for the horses and mules. Healthy women walked as far as they could, while older women, younger children, and sick people remained in the wagons. Of the eighty-one families that made the trip, thirty-three widows and single women, including Its-ca-tite (Ips-ket-tit, Susan), To-sa-im (Emma Ruth), Hoo-ko (Hair), Tam-mooks, Ho-pope, and Pie-wa-we-e-ma, rode in the hired wagons with their children.[44] Ho-pope and two other adult women cared for one small boy, while the widow Hum-lats traveled alone. Elderly couples, such as At-tas-poo (Abraham Wentforth) and his wife and Red Grizzly Bear and his dependents, traveled in Woolard's wagons, because the agents issued teams and wagons to men they considered important or productive.[45] Joseph and Yellow Bull often shared a wagon, although Joseph soon drove a horse and buggy around the Indian Territory. Other teamsters who received wagons for that trip most likely included Frank Buzzard (Al-lul-ta-ka-nin), Sup-poon-mas, Yellow Head, Powder Horn Owl (Kool-kools-mul-mul), Feathers around the Neck, John Hill, and Red Elk.[46]

The Chikaskia crossing took several hours. Hughes, Sherburne, and Whiteman watched the wagons move into camp near the junction of the Chikaskia and Salt Fork rivers. Sherburne and Hughes eventually drove off to the Ponca Agency with Whiteman, while the prisoners finished the crossing. Guaranteed their salaries and horse feed for the seven-day return, Woolard and the hired teams, borrowed wagons, and drivers left for Baxter Springs. Haworth remanded control of the refugees to Whiteman, and then he too returned to Baxter Springs.[47] Haworth testified that the trip was conducted speedily and safely, within federal budget constraints. The refugees traveled more than 177 miles in nine days, and their wagons required extensive repairs by the end of the trip.[48]

Haworth's account and subsequent Indian Bureau records detail the route and business of the wagon train and praise the non-Native men who were involved in the trip. Many of the details would have been lost had Sherburne and the newspapermen not documented the event. They acknowledged Nimiipuu contributions to survival and recorded the heat, filth, and exhaustion suffered by the refugees. They also accorded the Nimiipuu, Paluses, and Cayuses a measure of humanity that was absent from the official records.

The second fatality of the trip occurred as the refugees established their new camp. A young man who had been ailing before leaving Baxter Springs died that evening after the wagons crossed the river. According to the ration census list for the period through April 1879, 390 Nimiipuu, Paluses, and Cayuses started out with the wagon train. By the end of August, 370 of the prisoners remained alive at the new agency.[49] Twenty people died between April and August 1879, in addition to the two people who had passed away during the relocation. The losses mirrored the fatalities endured at the Quapaw Agency between July and October of the previous year.

Dr. Coleman remained with the prisoners until he was released from duty on June 25, and Ponca Agency physician Henry J. Minthorn then assumed medical responsibility for them. The doctor's office was about fifteen miles away from the Oakland Subagency, and because of the distance, Minthorn visited the Oakland camps only twice a week. Most of the newcomers were suffering from malaria. Worried about the public's increasing interest in the captives' health, Indian Bureau officials justified the relocation by announcing that the malaria epidemic had ended soon after the prisoners reached the new agency. This was untrue; malaria abated with the arrival of cold weather and the end of mosquito season, not because of a new location or federal largess. Every year, federal physicians reported heavy caseloads of malarial infections at all of the Indian agencies in the western Indian Territory. Doctors at seven local Indian agencies treated more than 13,000 cases of malaria during fiscal year 1879 and about 8,000 cases the following year.[50] Also common to the area were respiratory and bronchial infections, tuberculosis, eye infections, and poisonous snakebites. Many of the elderly exiles already exhibited the terminal symptoms of tuberculosis, and at least five of those patients died during the winter of 1879–80.[51]

Venereal disease was epidemic among the western Indian Territory populations, and within the year, the number of cases of syphilis and gonorrhea treated at the Cheyenne and Arapaho Agency, among the Kiowas, Comanches, and Wichitas, and among the Pawnees increased by 200, 300, and 400 percent, respectively. Medical statistics at the Ponca Agency indicate that venereal diseases were increasing there, too, although detailed records note that the Nimiipuu, Paluses, and Cayuses suffered comparatively few venereal infections. By 1880, venereal diseases were still raging out of control at the Arapaho and Cheyenne Agency.[52] They continued to affect the Cheyennes, Arapahos, Kiowas, Comanches, and Wichitas throughout 1884, although the Nimiipuu, Paluses, and Cayuses suffered only one case of congenital syphilis and three cases of gonorrhea, indicating that their contacts with their neighbors did not tend to be sexual.[53]

When Dr. Cora Bland visited the refugees in September, she attributed the deaths of the prisoners to "nostalgia" or homesickness. Ignoring the long-term effects of malaria, she blamed the victims and the medicine men for their failing health.[54] The refugees were indeed homesick, but their poor physical condition was a result of residual malarial infections. Like other physicians of the time, Bland had no knowledge of psychosomatic disorders such as depression and problems related to stress. Between 1881 and 1882, there were four suicides among the expatriates. Three people, including the Christian convert John Bull, had committed suicide by June 30, 1881, and one more person killed himself the next year. Bull, who believed that the government had held them in the Indian Territory so that the climate would kill them, shot himself in the stomach while digging a grave for a recently deceased friend. The Nimiipuu, Palus, and Cayuse population in the Indian Territory dropped to 322 during this period.[55]

The Nimiipuu, Paluses, and Cayuses were surrounded by larger, more powerful Native nations at their new reservation. The Osage reservation bordered the agency on the east, with the Otoe and Pawnee reservations to the south. The Sac and Fox reservation was about 65 miles southwest, and it was 100 miles to the Cheyenne and Arapaho reservation. About 75 miles from there was the Kiowa, Comanche, and Wichita reservation.[56] More than 12,000 American Indians surrounded the Oakland Subagency, including at least 900 Northern Cheyennes who had been deported to the Cheyenne and Arapaho Agency at Darlington, Indian Territory. General Pope warned that the Northern Cheyennes were mounted, armed, and angry, and that they posed a danger to unarmed American Indians in the Indian Territory.[57] Faced with hunger, malaria, and no medications, Chief Dull Knife, Little Wolf, and 353 Northern Cheyennes had run away from the Indian Territory the night of September 9, 1878. The Cheyenne and Arapaho Agency was in a state of turmoil, and some of the

Northern Cheyennes remaining in the Indian Territory were focused on their return to the Dakotas.[58] Many of the nearby Northern Cheyennes had scouted against the exiles during the war, and any trouble would have had disastrous consequences for the new arrivals. The Nimiipuu, Paluses, and Cayuses owned only a few hidden pistols and rifles and their bows and arrows, plus forty-eight horses and mules, which afforded little defense against an attack.[59] The situation grew increasingly volatile as hunger and illness plagued the Northern Cheyennes. In addition, there were not enough federal troops in the area to protect other American Indians. The Poncas were also wary of the Northern Cheyennes, who had attacked them in their old homelands.[60] The Indian Bureau understood the problem but did not offer the Nimiipuu, Paluses, and Cayuses any extra protection.

Understandably cautious in their relationships with the Northern Cheyennes, the Oakland refugees made peace with their old adversaries. Then, to counterbalance their powerless position, they coordinated their activities with the governor's spy, Cyrus M. Scott. While the Nimiipuu participated in social and spiritual activities such as Sun Dances with the Cheyennes and Arapahos, Yellow Bull guaranteed the peace; he reported their activities to Scott. The governor could call out the state militia or the army if the exiles required protection from refractory Northern Cheyennes, and order was essential to their survival. Scott joined the Nimiipuu, Paluses, and Cayuses on their visits to the Cheyennes and other Native nations until he resigned from the governor's service in December 1882. Without resorting to violence, Chief Joseph, Yellow Bull, and the other Sun Dance participants allowed Scott to benefit from their activities with the Northern Cheyennes.[61] In return, Scott guaranteed the exiles ready access to local newspapermen and provided a conduit to the governor if they needed help.

During their incarceration at Oakland, Chief Joseph, Yellow Bull, and the other refugees took advantage of a supportive Kansas press that was promoted by Scott. Scott also facilitated other opportunities for the detainees to express their objectives and requirements, such as when he arranged for Yellow Bull to speak at the Cowley County Fair. In addition, Scott was an active proponent of leasing the Oakland reservation when the detainees sought that opportunity.

The prisoners moved to their new reservation at the Oakland Subagency just as federal troops were evicting a colony of illegal Cherokee settlers from the property. During the spring of 1879, Colonel James Bell had settled the colony on the right bank of the Chikaskia River without permission from the Cherokee nation. Bell's cattle and the rest of their belongings were removed from the reservation with the stipulation that if they returned, their wagons would be burned and their livestock impounded. The Oakland Subagency was located on the Cherokee Strip, and although the Nimiipuu, Paluses, and Cayuses occupied the reservation, the Indian Bureau did not gain title to the property until mid-July 1883.[62]

Six weeks after their first weary stop at Arkansas City, the Nimiipuu, Paluses, and Cayuses signaled their will to survive when they participated in a train of twenty wagons hauling supplies from Wichita, Kansas, to Oakland. Two weeks later, twenty-three Oakland teams and wagons were on the road again, hauling lumber and provisions from Arkansas City to Oakland. The refugees were clean and appeared healthier, and when given the chance, they employed their new skills to provide for themselves and their families. Chief Joseph, who was much admired in borderland Kansas for his expertise in selecting superior horses, led the freight trains on his "very fine" horse.[63]

CHAPTER 8

Life at the Oakland Subagency

Challenges and Change

Many new challenges faced the prisoners at the Oakland Subagency. The lack of infrastructure was exacerbated by a cycle of droughts and winter storms that began in 1879. Installations at the supervising Ponca Agency were fairly complete, but hundreds of Poncas were still living without adequate housing, and no housing awaited the Nimiipuu, Paluses, and Cayuses at Oakland. The Ponca Agency facilities included a new eight-room home for the agent and a network of buildings that were needed for administration of the agencies, including shops and outbuildings, a schoolhouse, a sawmill, and an ice house. However, homebuilding for the Poncas always lagged behind current needs, and the Indian Bureau never reconciled the lack of suitable housing at Oakland.[1] The only structure the exiles found at Oakland was a commissary building where rations and agricultural supplies were stored. Even after the massive relocations of American Indians earlier in the century, the Indian Bureau had no planning commission, no relocation specialists or social workers, and no corps of relocation engineers. Special Indian agents or inspectors moved people to reservations where supportive infrastructure was either nonexistent or barely under construction.

Reservation housing was rarely appropriate, and regardless of agreements, treaty provisions, or congressional appropriations that stated otherwise, the Indian Bureau expected American Indians to build their own homes. Indian traders built their facilities and Joe Sherburne assembled his Ponca Agency store, boarding stable, and corrals the year before the Nimiipuu came to Oakland. The trading post was essential to the agency and offered a commercial outlet for the expanded customer base that the Nimiipuu, Paluses, and Cayuses brought to the reservation. Sherburne accommodated as many of the prisoners' needs as they could afford to pay or barter for, and the trading post became a popular gathering place for Chief Joseph and the other captives.[2] Apartments in the agency schools housed the teachers, and other agency employees were provided with small homes or commuted from the Ponca Agency or Arkansas City.

Within weeks of their arrival at Oakland, Nimiipuu, Palus, and Cayuse men had broken sod for farming, cut stove wood, and hauled logs to the Ponca Agency sawmill. But that first winter, they lived in rotting canvas tepees while stoves, furnishings, and other items intended for the proposed log homes remained in government warehouses.[3] The old twenty-horsepower sawmill was eventually moved from Ponca to the Chikaskia River, and thereafter the Nimiipuu, Paluses, and Cayuses processed between 100,000 and 184,000 feet of lumber every year. Four one-room box houses intended for Chief Joseph and three other leaders were built during 1880; however, the homes were unheated, and Joseph insisted that they were uninhabitable. Agent William Whiting promised everyone that they would have houses by winter, but there were only seventeen houses ready for occupancy the following August. Supervised by the agency machinist, Nimiipuu, Palus, and Cayuse apprentices milled and cut hundreds of feet of lumber and shingles every day. The agency carpenter and four Nimiipuu assistants also built a stable and covered the sawmill; but nearly all of the new lumber had been stored outside and was warped and ruined. Most of the families spent another winter in the dilapidated tepees, and when temperatures reached

110° F in the summer, the available cabins were abandoned in favor of the ventilated tepees or brush arbors.[4]

Spring and summer were devoted to farming, and house building was scheduled for later in the year. During the fall and winter of 1882, nineteen homes were built and occupied, but seventy families remained homeless. Thirty-seven houses were built the next year, but only eighteen of them were occupied by the following summer. Fifty-five box or log homes were occupied by fall 1884, but three of these dwellings had no heat or furnishings. Wood cooking stoves and furniture were finally delivered to the families in early spring 1884, after the temperature dropped to –20° F.[5]

A cycle of summer droughts and freezing winters began in 1879, just before the exiles arrived at Oakland. The early spring rains moved in on schedule that year; farmers were able to plow new acreage in the pliable prairie sod, and Cheyennes, Arapahos, Kiowas, Wichitas, Comanches, Osages, Kaws, and Poncas all planted their usual gardens and crops. The earliest plantings did well, but unusually heavy rains later in the spring washed seeds and crops away. Second plantings were sown as the rains ended, but then the heat and wind began. As the sod and soil dried up, it became almost impossible to break ground or plant replacement crops. Decimated by the heat and searing winds, crop yields plummeted and pastures dried up. The Nimiipuu, Paluses, and Cayuses arrived too late that summer to plant crops or gardens, although they began limited sod-breaking operations.[6] The following winter was not unusually severe in an area that was commonly buffeted by winter storms and freezing rain and hail. None of the Indian agencies in the western Indian Territory reported serious problems that winter, but the Nimiipuu, Paluses, and Cayuses remained in their old tepees.[7]

The next four summers settled into a pattern of recurring drought. Small crops and gardens dried up, and the soil hardened, making plowing difficult and sod-breaking nearly impossible. Crop yields were low. Prairie fires burned off two thousand acres near the Ponca Agency, while other pastures dried out or went up in flames. Wells went dry at the Pawnee Agency, and American Indian stockmen moved their operations along local creeks.[8] Early spring rains that encouraged gardens and vegetables were followed by blazing heat and high winds. Crops that matured later in the summer, such as field corn and spring wheat, were susceptible to the drought, although winter wheat usually produced an adequate crop. Planted in the fall and watered by snow and early rains, the wheat was harvested in the early summer before the droughts intensified.[9] Nimiipuu gardeners made the most of the early rains, producing small plots of sweet corn and vegetables, and in 1880 they ordered enough winter wheat seeds to plant one hundred acres. Sudden July rains saved the late corn that year, although the rain did not last.[10]

The winter of 1880–81 was especially cold and snowy. By spring, agency cattle were thin but still alive; thousands of other cattle had perished on the Cherokee Strip near Oakland. Nimiipuu farmers planted winter wheat that fall and harvested it before the drought and prairie fires of the next summer.[11] The winter of 1882–83 was so cold that the Oakland children were unable to attend school, but that was merely a prelude to the disastrous winter of 1883–84. Early December 1883 was fairly moderate, but by the end of the month, the temperature was –6° F, and the Arkansas River was frozen over the dam at Arkansas City. By January 6, the river ice was a foot thick, and for the next two months, the Indian Territory was crippled by one of the worst winters in memory. January brought freezing rain, ice storms, and falling temperatures, and in February the temperature dropped to –20° F, remaining well below zero throughout the month. Tens of thousands of cattle perished across the Indian Territory. Nimiipuu apprentices repaired farm implements inside the machine shop, and Nimiipuu men tended the agency cattle herd, but everything else came to a halt. Spring thaws and heavy July rains flooded the Arkansas and Walnut rivers. The cycle of summer droughts ended that year with an excessively wet spring. The winter of 1884–85 was another terror, with subzero temperatures, dangerous storms, and record livestock losses.[12]

Despite the weather, the impoverished Nimiipuu, Cayuses, and Paluses positioned themselves wherever they could within the local economy. One of the few regular sources of income at Oakland was government freighting. On March 1, 1877, American Indians gained the exclusive right to almost all Indian Bureau shipping. The Act of 1877 ensured Native teamsters' participation in federal programs designed to promote labor and financial independence. Indian Bureau freight contracts exceeding $2,000 were reserved for private contractors, but all other shipping was left to American Indians. The Indian Bureau provided freight wagons and harnesses, which were paid for by the teamsters, and American Indians supplied the teams, the manpower, and any other needed materials. Chief Joseph and the other prisoners embraced the freighting business as they managed their own earnings, teams, and efforts. The teamsters signed up to haul loads at the agency office and were paid with checks drawn on local banks.[13]

Within the first sixty days of their arrival, the Oakland prisoners hauled more than 100,000 pounds of household goods, farm equipment, and other supplies from Wichita, Kansas, to Oakland. Over the next six years, they also cut and hauled thousands of feet of logs and lumber, hundreds of cords of wood, and thousands of rods of wooden fencing. For the Oakland teamsters, freighting payments originated in federal appropriations and contracts that paid them $0.65 per hundredweight for the round trip from Oakland to Wichita. Teamsters included Chief Joseph, Yellow Bull, Yellow Head, Húsus Kute, Frank Buzzard, Powder Horn Owl, Sup-poon-mas, and Feathers around the Neck. The Oakland teamsters joined hundreds of wagons owned and driven by American Indians that lined up in Arkansas City and Winfield, Kansas, to pick up Indian Bureau contracts. Business was brisk in June and July, when existing contracts were fulfilled and new contracts were opened for delivery. More than 120 tons of flour was loaded onto American Indians' wagons during the third week of July 1880 at Arkansas City; on one busy Saturday, eighty-seven wagons driven by American Indian teamsters loaded and left Searing's flour mill. Loading continued twenty-four hours a day through Sunday and Monday, because more wagons were due in from the Indian Territory on Tuesday. The Oakland teamsters joined long lines of wagons driven by Osage, Pawnee, Cheyenne, Arapaho, Kiowa, and Comanche teamsters who had come into Arkansas City that week. At least three hundred teams driven by American Indians hauled freight during the summer of 1881 from Arkansas City into the Indian Territory, and in June, A. A. Newman of Arkansas City secured new contacts to supply another 1.4 million pounds of flour to Indian agencies. The Nimiipuu, Palus, and Cayuse teamsters moved about 50,000 pounds of flour every year, hauled wheat seeds packed in 150-pound osnaburg sacks, and transported all of the supplies coming into Oakland from the railroad depot at Arkansas City.[14]

Most of the Oakland freight wagons were manufactured by the Jackson Wagon Works. Pulled by two-horse or four-horse hitches, they could support a 2,000-pound load. The wagons featured reinforced axles, spring seats, bows, and covers and cost individual teamsters about $50 each. The teamsters paid around $20 for each set of heavy-duty double harnesses, although they did not have to pay for lighter-weight farming harnesses. Crated wagon parts were shipped by rail to Wichita, Kansas City, or Arkansas City, where the wagons were assembled by local mechanics before being picked up by the teamsters.[15]

The Oakland teamsters also used their new skills to help their neighbors. When William Aiman and a group of non-Native freighters wrecked a wagon on the frozen Spring River near Yellow Bull's camp after one of their horses went down on the ice, crippling itself and tearing the tongue off of the wagon it was pulling, Yellow Bull directed the rescue effort from the opposite bank. He ordered several younger Nimiipuu men to prepare a trail on the ice. Using blankets and hides, the men spread sand on the ice and up the bank, then helped the injured horse off the frozen river. The other horses were untangled and led to solid ground, and the wagon was pushed along the sand and up the bank. Long after dark, Yellow Bull invited the exhausted Aiman and his friends to spend the night at his camp. His widowed sister gave Aiman her bed in their cabin and spent the night in her tepee.[16]

The Nimiipuu, Paluses, and Cayuses exploited available resources to complement their subsistence strategies. In 1879, wild turkeys, black-tailed deer, antelope, and small game were still plentiful near Oakland. The buffalo herds were located about two hundred miles to the west, and a herd of thirty elk ranged within forty miles of the Cheyenne and Arapaho Agency at Darlington. The Oakland prisoners were allowed to hunt with bows and arrows and to travel around the Indian Territory, but they were not permitted to go west to the buffalo grounds. Because the prisoners were banned from owning firearms, anyone with a shotgun or rifle was important to them.[17] Aiman liked Yellow Bull and loved to hunt, so he shot turkeys and other game for Yellow Bull's family; Yellow Bull and his sister always gave Aiman something of theirs in return for his help. Yellow Bull appreciated Aiman's efforts and offered to adopt him. The food and friendship were so important that he may have been trying to formalize the relationship. But the young man misunderstood the nature of the adoption and declined the honor. The Indian Bureau demanded that the nearly 17,000 American Indians in the area subsist on wild fowl and game whenever possible, and non-Natives also mounted massive hunting parties and expeditions into the area.[18] It became increasingly difficult to exist on wild game because of the constant pressures exerted on the game by the hunters. Between 1879 and 1885, game birds and animals gradually disappeared from the western Indian Territory.

The Oakland women maximized their participation in the borderland economies of Arkansas City and Winfield. The women were known for their fine needlework, leather gloves, moccasins, beadwork, and other arts. By 1881, they commanded the leather glove trade in Arkansas City, manufacturing and selling more than 1,000 pairs of gloves. Two years later they accelerated production and sold more than 3,600 pairs of gloves and moccasins, earning $2,455.00.[19] Plain buckskin gloves sold for about $0.75 a pair; gloves to which the women had added artwork were popular with cowboys and ranchers and brought a higher price. Chief Joseph and Yellow Bull were a familiar sight as they drove into Arkansas City to deliver their wives' products to local merchants. Many of the women also worked their way into the local credit economy. At Joe Sherburne's trading post, they enjoyed a reputation as reliable debtors. Nevertheless, the leather goods market was not always a reliable source of income, and widows who had no horses or supportive families were especially vulnerable to market conditions. If no cattlemen were in town or if local stores were overstocked with leather goods, Oakland widows who had walked into town to sell their products returned home to their hungry, weeping children empty-handed. James Reuben bought a few Cheyenne horses that he shared with the poorest widows for transportation, but that did not solve the problems of supply and demand.[20]

People who knew the Nimiipuu, Palus, and Cayuse women recalled them as intelligent, attractive, and hardworking. They were regarded as extraordinarily hygienic and almost unfailingly friendly. Wearing ankle-length ribbon dresses and silk headscarves, the women wound strips of red, yellow, and navy blue strouding around their legs. They wore moccasins with six-inch tops that tied over the strouding.[21] Most of the women wore long shawls and seemed to favor the color red. Adjusting to the prairie sun, the women welcomed a shipment of Kansas sunbonnets. Some of the women preferred manufactured hosiery, such as the Nimiipuu woman who tried to buy a pair of long red stockings at Eli Youngheim's Mammoth Clothing House in Winfield. The shopper struggled to make Youngheim understand that she did not want the short red socks he was insisting that she purchase; instead she wanted long red hosiery. After a frustrating half-hour, she finally lifted her skirts and showed him just how long the stockings ought to be. Then she dropped her skirts and walked out of the store as the other customers observed Youngheim's astonished response. Caught off guard by the demonstration, Youngheim and his clerk needed time to collect their sensibilities.[22]

Clothing and hairstyles changed as the Nimiipuu, Paluses, and Cayuses who joined the Presbyterian church adopted western attire and cut their hair as a mark of their faith. Even Chief Joseph understood the political implications of western clothing; he often donned a suit when conferring with government authorities or attending Presbyterian functions. Large black Stetson-like hats and striped blankets remained popular with the men, although Christian converts adopted more conservative headwear. Many men wore feathers in their hatbands or attached to their hats that signified a personal or sacred affiliation. Non-Christian men wore their long hair loose or in braids, while male Christians demonstrated their Presbyterian affiliation by cutting their hair. Christian men no longer wore feathered or shell ornaments; they adopted silk neckerchiefs. Non-Christian men retained their customary regalia. Yellow Bear gave away his war shirt sometime after he joined the Presbyterian church, while other men burned their traditional clothing. Christian women wore western-style dresses they made from calico, checkered government-issue cloth, or wool. Some of the ladies wore their hair in two braids, and others double-looped their braids. Women wore shell earrings and jewelry and retained their headscarves, although the Christians among them gave up the larger earrings and ornaments. Christian women learned to crochet collars for their new dresses, and all of the women made or purchased trade-cloth shirts for their sons and husbands.[23]

Memorializing their presence in the Indian Territory, the prisoners visited the bustling little Kansas border towns, where they patronized photographers' studios and were pursued by local newspapermen. Chief Joseph posed with people such as Reuben and Cyrus M. Scott; Mary, Wolf Head, Captain Jack (She-wa-tas-hai-hai), and an unidentified woman and her child posed for Winfield photographer Hezekiah Beck. Joseph and Sup-poon-mas must have had their photographs taken sometime after they joined the Sun Dances, because Sup-poon-mas displayed his Sun Dance mirror for his portrait. When the Nimiipuu, Paluses, and Cayuses went to Winfield or Arkansas City, newspapermen eagerly recorded their visits. Reuben spent time in Winfield with the agency physician and attended seminars and meetings. Yellow Bull was a frequent and favored visitor to Arkansas City and learned to speak English in addition to the other American Indian languages, Chinook Jargon, and sign language that he already knew. Old-timers around Arkansas City remembered Yellow Bull for his rapid mastery of the English language, which enabled him to travel without an interpreter. When the Reverend and Mrs. Archie Lawyer, their baby, Joseph's wife, and other members of the Oakland Presbyterian Church visited Winfield for a few days in August 1881, the editor of the *Winfield Courant* was pleased to record the occasion.[24] Joseph, Yellow Bull, Reuben, and Lawyer dropped into local newspapers to discuss their plans and activities with receptive editors and reporters as a way to gain media support for their return to the northwest.

Cattle and rations were the lifeblood of the Oakland Subagency. After the cattle were weighed and branded at the Ponca Agency and driven to Oakland, a non-Native butcher slaughtered the weekly issues of ration beef. The Ponca agent issued the butcher a government horse, rifle, and cartridges. The butcher shot the cattle in the Oakland corrals, where the carcasses were quartered and taken to the meat house before being distributed to ration ticket holders. The unused cartridges were then tallied for a report to the Indian Bureau, after which they and the rifle were returned to a locked case in the agent's office. Hides from the Oakland slaughter cattle sold for $.07 a pound when delivered to Arkansas City, although Sherburne paid the women up to $5 for moderate- to good-quality cured hides.[25] The captives also sold some of their cattle hides to dealers who came to the reservation. One dealer paid $10 to a Nimiipuu seller who had agreed to deliver a load of hides to an Arkansas City butcher, where he was to be paid another $40. In the meantime, the hide dealer collected the money from the butcher and skipped town. The seller lost the hides and the money, and a local boy hired to return the hide buyer's horse to Winfield lost a dollar when the horse turned out to be a rental animal.[26]

As the captives were establishing themselves at Oakland, the Indian Bureau ordered that all ration beef was to be issued as carcasses. The officials then kept more than $100,000 worth of slaughtered beef hides that should have accrued to American Indians. The Bureau paid the agency herders from the extra income, and if more hides were produced than were required for the salaries, the extras could be allocated to the Nimiipuu, Paluses, and Cayuses. When cattle were in good condition, the butcher slaughtered three animals a week at Oakland, or about $450 worth of hides a year, which covered the herders' salaries. The Oakland prisoners advocated that the policy be rescinded, requesting that they receive all of the slaughtered beef hides, which they considered to be part of the animals that the federal government had agreed to provide them. Indian agent Lewellyn Woodin tried to convince the Bureau to absorb the herders' salaries, but the budget was not adjusted for the funds. Thereafter, the Oakland women traded finished leather products to Sherburne for more hides.[27]

Rations provided the only semi-reliable food at Oakland, although they were allocated according to a sliding scale based on agents' and farmers' reports on the prisoners' crops. Rations were intended to supplement farm and garden production, but in fiscal years 1879 and 1880, the prisoners were considered incapable of self-support and the government provided 100 percent of their support. They arrived too late to plant crops in 1879 and did not have enough acres of sod turned by 1880 to raise substantial crops. In fiscal years 1881 and 1882, the Indian Bureau provided about 65 percent of their required subsistence, and by 1884 the provisions had been adjusted to 75 percent of need. The reductions were based on optimistic farm and garden yields and population figures established by the agent. When rations were reduced to reflect these figures, the exiles were limited to a four-day supply issued once a week. Standard weekly rations were calculated at about seven ounces of bacon, four ounces of coffee, seven ounces of sugar, two to four pounds of flour, and seven pounds of beef per person. The amount of flour was inadequate for hardworking people and was increased to four pounds per week in 1881.[28]

The Indian Bureau hired a farmer to break two hundred acres of sod for the Nimiipuu's use in 1879, and the next year the prisoners plowed another one hundred acres.[29] During their first summer at Oakland, the Nimiipuu also harvested and stored about seventy-five tons of hay, a job that was probably accomplished by the women. Agent Whiteman disliked men who refused to farm and did not take into consideration the pride and determination that the women dedicated to their farms and gardens. Women were integral to the Oakland farms, where they threshed the wheat with their horses. Working in pairs as they had done in Idaho, the women made a skin sled and moved the heads of wheat into a hide-floored threshing pit, where they rode their horses around on the wheat to separate out the grain.[30] By 1884, the Oakland residents had broken 330 acres of sod but tilled only 137 acres in small farms and gardens. Not every acre was suited to farming, and seeds ordered by the Indian Bureau often arrived too late to plant for maximum yields. In addition, the farmers struggled with cattle that damaged and destroyed their crops and gardens, like the trespassing animals that ruined Crow Blanket's (Ko-koh-tsis-kum) hay crop in 1881. Droughts also limited farmable acreage, and by 1884, rumors that the prisoners would be leaving had lessened their interest in farming.[31]

Despite the dry summers, the families managed to raise respectable home gardens. They raised root crops of Early Rose potatoes, carrots, and turnips, and their field crops included "Indian corn," sweet corn, red and green beans, and peas. Pumpkins, watermelons, and muskmelons also produced substantial yields under their care, and several families raised popcorn. Crops were well cared for, although the yields did not impress the Indian agents, who expected surplus market production regardless of the droughts. Seed orders were placed in January, and Chief Joseph and other leaders requested fruit trees and grapevine stock in

1880. When seed orders were delayed or the Indian Bureau sent the wrong seeds, the prisoners purchased seeds as well as other garden items from Sherburne.[32]

Yellow Bull and about one-third of the group moved away from the main Oakland camp soon after their arrival. They requested seeds, cows, pigs, domestic fowl, and farm equipment from the Indian Bureau. By 1882, the Oakland farmers were harvesting more than 2,500 bushels of wheat, corn, and vegetables and putting up more than 600 tons of winter silage. Húsus Kute's crops impressed the Board of Indian Commissioners in fall 1883, although that year the detainees produced only 1,900 bushels of wheat, corn, and other vegetables. Women dug and lined underground caches where they stored potatoes, onions, and melons. Meanwhile, the captives marketed their surplus produce; the 8,500 melons produced in 1883 were sold in Arkansas City and to Indian traders, agency employees, and other American Indians.[33]

Agents stopped referring to the Numiipuu as lazy when they saw how hard the prisoners worked on their farms and gardens, at various jobs around the reservation, and at the agency. Production records were maintained only for male heads of families, however, and tended to ignore the women's efforts. Red Elk and the women in his family raised more than 50 bushels of turnips and potatoes and sold $100 worth of garden vegetables in 1880 despite the drought.[34] Like the other women, Chief Joseph's and Op-has's wives tended large flocks of chickens, gardened, farmed, and marketed their gloves and moccasins.[35] Jay Gould (Kool-kool-tick-lih-kin) and his wife worked together raising wheat, corn, potatoes, melons, chickens, cows, and calves, and Mrs. Gould sold her handmade crafts and moccasins. In 1882 and 1883, the Oakland women tended nearly 3,000 domestic fowl in flocks of from 75 to 100 birds, and kept one or two pigs per family. In four years, the Oakland men cut and hauled enough wooden fencing to enclose 510 acres, which was divided into small farms and gardens.[36]

Physical danger was inherent to labor-intensive occupations such as farming and logging. The sawmill, however, was the most hazardous working environment. Loose clothing, unprotected walkways, exposed saw pits, and shafts turning 150 revolutions per minute were especially dangerous. One Pawnee man got caught in the agency sawmill and was crushed to death before it could be shut down, while at Oakland the physician treated thirty-seven wounds and injuries probably related to the mill. The high wound and injury count is unique to fiscal year 1882, reflecting an increase in heavy labor performed by untrained workers. Assisted by Reuben and Henry Rivers, Dr. Henry J. Minthorn amputated one man's arm, probably as the result of an accident at the mill. The unidentified patient recovered from the ether-assisted surgery at the Ponca Agency. Lame John smashed his ankle at the Oakland sawmill, and Black Trail died from a suppurated shoulder wound exacerbated by heavy labor at the mill. Black Trail had been shot through the shoulder at the Big Hole, and his collarbone never did heal properly, although he survived until hard work and infection caused his death at Oakland.[37]

Horses were an integral part of life at Oakland. The mares and mules that had been issued for the wagon train, however, could not support the required volume of work. The expatriates needed at least twenty more teams of mules or horses, a dozen teams of oxen, and twenty additional wagons and harnesses. Agent Whiting requested the animals and equipment from the Indian Bureau, and in October 1881, twenty-four brood mares and fifteen wagons and sets of harness were delivered to Oakland. The Bureau did not provide the oxen that were needed for logging and heavy hauling, and the mares and lightweight wagons broke down from the heavy work. The mares were American horses, and although the prisoners liked the animals, they required more care than Indian horses. They needed winter shelter and special feed and grooming, and the families had not raised enough corn to feed the additional animals over the winter. The Indian Bureau bought 700 bushels of corn for the horses in January 1881, but after that, the prisoners had to produce the extra grain. Unfortunately, few of the new mares were pregnant, and only three foals were delivered that year. By 1882, the captives owned 200 horses, although the size of the herd fluctuated with the droughts and winters. By 1884, 189 horses and ten mules were on hand.[38]

Federal employees failed to record the inventive ways in which the Nimiipuu rebuilt their horse herds and did not include Indian horses and strays in their official reports. Although the captives did not participate in the local horse-raiding economy, they did round up stray horses that had been lost by ranchers or left behind by cattle drovers, or that had wandered away from cowboy camps. Trying to locate the owners of strays took time and caused unnecessary work for the exiles. They reported lost horses and mules to the Cowley County sheriff and to the Kansas newspapers, then fed and cared for the animals until their owners could come to retrieve them. Unclaimed horses were added to the captives' herds.

Yellow Head lost a sizable herd of horses during the war, which he rebuilt by bartering and collecting unwanted animals in the Indian Territory. He was also a talented veterinarian who rescued a cowpony with a broken leg just as a weeping cowboy was about to shoot it. Yellow Head offered to treat the animal, and the grateful cowboy gave him the favored horse. Rigging a special rope sling in a tree, Yellow Head suspended the horse in the sling. He stabilized the leg and treated the animal every day for months. The following summer, when the cowboy came through on another cattle drive, Yellow Head sold the healthy horse to the delighted man for $10. Many years after the prisoners returned to Idaho, Yellow Head shared this story with his grandson Lynus Walker. Mr. Walker also remembered that when his grandfather was old and preparing to die, he had his bed placed in the pasture with his horses. After Yellow Head's death, several of his horses died for no apparent reason "as he took them with him."[39]

The Nimiipuu had enjoyed a history with cattle long before the exiles were moved to the Indian Territory. By the mid- to late 1850s, they were superb open-range cattlemen in their old homelands. Many Nimiipuu purchased cattle from or exchanged them with the first white settlers in the area, and they subsequently expanded their purchases south into Mount Shasta, California.[40] The stockmen rotated their herds between summer and winter ranges and participated in local bovine economies by trading and selling cattle. The conflict in 1877 cost the nontreaty bands enormous numbers of cattle and dairy cows as settlers stole their livestock and the army confiscated their herds. Consequently, the ninety-six two-year-old heifers and four bulls distributed to the Oakland detainees on July 20, 1880, were a source of great pleasure. The government was finally beginning to fulfill its promises to supply them with breeding stock.[41]

The new bulls and heifers were apportioned to the families and then pastured with the herd of slaughter and agency animals. They were branded with the Indian Bureau's "ID" as well as with distinctive brands designed by the individual owners. Branding prevented theft or the fraudulent sale of animals to the men who prowled American Indian reservations trying to buy or steal Indian cattle. Most of the heifers in the stock herd were not bred, and only nine calves were born the next year. The Indian Bureau furnished additional breeding stock for the prisoners in 1883, and the size of the cattle herd fluctuated between 193 and 320 animals by late summer 1884. In addition to the 22 cattle that died during the winter, Oakland cattle were lost to an epidemic of Texas tick fever that swept through the Indian Territory in 1880 and 1882, brought in by the more than 100,000 cattle that were trespassing on the Cherokee, Choctaw, Chickasaw, Creek, Seminole, Osage, and Pawnee reservations. There were no effective treatments for the disease, and thousands of animals died. Despite Indian Bureau complaints to local and federal officials, impounded herds, and Indian policemen's attempts to keep the cattle off the reservations, infected cattle inundated the Indian Territory and Oakland. A "dead line" quarantine zone established by cattlemen in Kansas placed the Oakland livestock in even greater peril. The quarantine zone pushed Texas herds farther into the Indian Territory and across the Oakland reservation for longer periods of time. The Indian Bureau tried to limit the Texas cattle to specific trails, but a shortage of federal law enforcement officers allowed infected herds to overwhelm Oakland and the other reservations.[42]

Thefts of reservation cattle were epidemic by 1879, and it was not unusual for rustlers to steal cattle from the herds at Oakland. In 1881, John T. Bennett stole eleven head and drove them to his ranch or sold them to butcher J. S. Hazzard in Wellington, Kansas. Hazzard, who had acquired stolen cattle from Bennett before, bought seven of the Oakland cattle and butchered four of them. However, Bennett had been seen cutting the cattle out of the Oakland herd, and the herder and several of the Oakland men had followed him, while others rode for the agent and the sheriff. Chief Joseph, At-tas-poo, the non-Native herder John Gooch, Tsis-koop (Ticklish, Adelia Emeline), Cloud Blanket, Swift Runner (Tel-ho-wich), Tom Hill, Sup-poon-mas, Cayuse (Eaw-se-cath Sa-cum), and Wolf Head hurried into Wellington to identify their stolen animals. Reuben rode with them as their interpreter. Sheriff Joe Thralls responded to their complaints and jailed Bennett in Wellington. In a jailhouse interview, Bennett asked Hazzard to run the brands on the live cattle and suggested that he smudge the brands on the butchered animals' hides. But Hazzard turned state's evidence against Bennett and was not charged with the crime. Bennett posted bail of $1,000 and promised to return to Fort Smith, Arkansas, for trial. Chief Joseph, At-tas-poo, Cayuse, Sup-poon-mas, and Hazzard testified before the grand jury in the federal district court, and Bennett was charged with larceny. In the meantime, Bennett had jumped bail and returned to Lebanon, Indiana. Judge Isaac Parker issued a warrant for his arrest, but the case became inactive after several failed attempts to locate him. This all happened between August and November 1881, and Agent Thomas J. Jordan was still asking Parker to extradite Bennett from Indiana the following June. Jordan wanted the rustler tried as a deterrent to other cattle thieves, who were usually sentenced to thirty days in jail and fined $1,000. After serving their sentence, the felons signed a pauper's oath and either left the Indian Territory or went back to rustling cattle. Bennett was never tried, but the Oakland cattlemen recovered three of the hides and seven of their cattle.[43]

The captives' problems were growing worse, as Lieutenant Tom Hill complained to the commissioner of Indian affairs on June 4, 1881. "The whites are driving and running their cattle across this land, running our stock and we have no protection, no peace," he wrote.[44] This was Hill's third letter to the commissioner, reminding him that they still had no wells at Oakland, many families had no teams or wagons, and the tools and implements sent to them were only "loaned to us for a little time and we must return them."[45] And of course, Hill reminded the commissioner that the prisoners had no roots in the Indian Territory. "Would you like to improve land that was not yours?" he asked.

By 1883, poverty, weather, and the many other problems inspired the small-scale Oakland ranchers to contemplate leasing the reservation to non-Native ranchers. The captives could not afford to buy livestock, and the government had not supplied enough cattle to stock 90,000 acres. Rube Houghton's first offer to lease Oakland for $1,000 a year was denied by the secretary of the interior on April 7, 1883. Houghton, who was already pasturing cattle along Bodock Creek without a lease, increased his offer, and on February 9, 1884, fifty-four Nimiipuu, Palus, and Cayuse men met at Oakland to discuss it. Nearly overwhelmed by the herds of cattle pastured at Oakland by ranchers who were paying them nothing, the group agreed to accept Houghton's offer of $2,000 a year to lease Oakland for cattle grazing. Most of the adult males at Oakland, including Wolf Head, Captain Jack, Crow Blanket, Five Times Over (Pa-ko-lee-ka-sat), Frank Buzzard, and Goose over the Mountain (We-ya-wes), attended the meeting. The council selected Chief Joseph, Yellow Bull, Yellow Bear, and Húsus Kute to enact the lease. In contrast to the grazing leases for the Ponca reservation, the Oakland stockmen insisted that their lease be drawn up before a constituted legal authority. Accordingly, thirteen days later, the four-man executive committee completed the Oakland lease in the Winfield District Court. Lieutenant Hill and Lawyer both served as interpreters, to check each other's translations, and Lawyer verified the written document. Fifteen sections of timber and all of the small fenced farms maintained by the exiles were exempt from the 75,000-acre lease. Lease payments would be due at Oakland on the first of July and December in $1,000 cash installments. Lease monies were to be apportioned among all the Oakland captives, with per capita payments made directly to heads of families.[46] The first payment was made on July 1, 1884, but the December installment was delayed because of Senate investigations into the Indian Territory leases. Sherburne, Houghton, and Scott were competing with former Indian inspector William J. Pollock, Standard Oil, British cattle barons, power brokers from the Chicago livestock market, and other corporate giants for the leases. Indian Territory grazing leases were in universal demand, as was exemplified by Secretary of War Robert T. Lincoln's requests for preferential leases to his friends.[47]

Responding to complaints about the leases, the president and attorney general questioned the leasing of more than 11 million acres held by American Indians in the western Indian Territory. The Kansas ranchers and Indian traders had signed their leases before national bids for the properties could be advertised. A Senate committee eventually determined that the rent paid by Sherburne, Houghton, and others might have been higher if national bids had been entertained, but the Oakland lease was allowed to stand. Scott eventually leased 5,043 acres from the Cherokees, Sherburne leased 50,000 acres from the Poncas, and Houghton leased Oakland. Houghton agreed to leave all of his improvements on the leasehold and guaranteed not to use more timber or stones than was necessary to build fifty miles of fencing. Chief Joseph, Yellow Bull, Húsus Kute, and Yellow Bear appeared before Judge Elisha S. Torrance of the 13th District Court in Winfield, where the Oakland lease was recorded on February 22, 1884. By March 12, Houghton had 2,500 cattle on the range and was planning to have 4,000 pastured there by the end of the summer. Within the first six months of 1884, all of the reservations associated with the Ponca Agency were leased to non-Native cattlemen.[48]

Houghton's lease provided the Nimiipuu with a small but reliable source of income and helped to keep unwanted livestock off the reservation.

The detainees opted to rely on formal legal processes soon after their arrival at Oakland. Because crimes committed on Indian reservations by non-Natives were federal offenses, the prisoners became familiar with the federal courts. The year before Bennett stole their cattle, Sup-poon-mas, Wolf Head, and James Reuben testified in the Leavenworth Federal Court. They identified the cattle hides stolen earlier by the vagrant hide buyer and testified against George Manson, a local tailor who had sold whiskey to Sup-poon-mas. After Sup-poon-mas testified that Manson had sold him the alcohol, Manson confessed and was fined $25 and court costs.[49] The hide buyer was gone, but it was important that the Nimiipuu had addressed the issue as participants in the legal system.

Civil order in the prison camps was a problem, as Chief Joseph had already suggested. One response by the Indian Bureau to problems on the reservations was to establish an American Indian police force. Two years later, forty agencies employed more than eight hundred American Indian officers. Their duties included arresting and removing intruders and evicting rustlers and outlaws from reservations. The Indian police also served as scouts, guarded shipments of annuity goods and monies, and assisted with ration issues. They protected agency property and buildings, served as truant officers, and tried to keep whiskey traders off the reservations. Indian police also deterred or made arrests for disorderly conduct, drunkenness, and domestic violence. They served as couriers and messengers and as middlemen who explained and implemented changing legal concepts to reservation communities. Police lieutenants and noncommissioned officers wore uniforms consisting of dark blue jackets and pants, dark blue kersey vests, and silk neckerchiefs; privates were recognized by their sky blue kersey pants. Policemen were paid between $5 and $8 per month, an appallingly low salary that was only about one-third of the teamsters' salaries and less than half of other agency salaries.[50]

Chief Joseph seems to have supported the Indian police at Oakland, although there was some friction between them and the Nimiipuu. Yellow Wolf joined the prison camp in the turbulent aftermath of the war and blamed Christian converts for problems caused by the police. Fifty-five years later, he was still unhappy as he recalled that Lieutenant Hill had shot his friend Henry Tabador. Yellow Wolf felt that Hill had exceeded his authority and had misinterpreted his federal mandate. Reuben and Tabador were also at odds over Reuben's participation in the war and his propensity to favor federal edicts when Tabador was evicted from an agency meeting. In the aftermath of that meeting, Hill shot Tabador. Although the wound was not serious, Tabador died later when his cap-and-ball pistol misfired.[51] No one mentioned that Joseph resented or resisted the police or that he did not maintain cordial relations with the men on the force.

Shifting federal and communal expectations caused frequent changes in the Oakland police force. The six-man force consisted of one lieutenant, one sergeant, and four privates. Tom Hill served as the lieutenant for several years, until he was replaced by Thomas Peters (Wat-u-sa-kaun). Agent Jordan made several important changes in the police force during the month of July 1881, which may have been related to religious biases. Crow Blanket was fired and replaced by Peter Platter (Kal-la-tose) on July 4, and Dick Johnson replaced Frank Earth Blanket (Wa-tas-tsis-kum) on July 10. Jordan apparently entertained a different vision for the Indian police, because the day after he fired Earth Blanket, he also fired and replaced five Ponca policemen. The Ponca Sun Dances had recently ended, and Crow Blanket and Earth Blanket had participated in several Sun Dances and the Oakland Independence Day celebration. Platter was a recent Christian convert, whereas Crow Blanket and Earth Blanket had not converted. The Oakland superintendent, James S. Woodward, fired Lieutenant Peters in January 1884, charging that he was lazy and inattentive to duty. Agent John Scott commented that the lieutenant was an excellent employee, although he spoke little English. Peters was angry and embarrassed over losing his job and accused Hill of influencing the decision. Yellow Bear, Húsus Kute, and Thomas Lindsley petitioned the commissioner of Indian affairs to modify the decision, arguing that Peters had been fired because he favored Christians. Agent Scott supported Hill, asserting that he had been caught in the middle of the conflict through no fault of his own. Scott could have vetoed Woodward's decision to fire Peters, but he did not. No written regulations required that Indian policemen speak English, yet Peters appears to have lost his job for that reason.[52]

Earth Blanket did not respond well to camp life after he was fired from the police force. He kept a few cattle, Sun Danced with Chief Joseph and Yellow Bull, and joined Lame John, Eagle Blanket (Tip-la-la-na-tsis-kun), John Andrews (Tip-yal-la-nat-kekt), and Daniel Jefferson at the Oakland lease meeting on February 9, 1884. Six months later, however, he was arrested for domestic violence against his wife (she suffered a broken arm) and the rape of a fifteen-year-old Nimiipuu girl. The girl's parents asked Agent Scott to incarcerate Earth Blanket, and the former policeman was arrested. He was held in the Otoe Agency jail for two weeks, where the agent furnished a jailer and provisions for both men until distance, costs, and community leaders convinced him to reassign the prisoner. A deeply remorseful Earth Blanket was released to Hill and other leaders, who guaranteed his future conduct to agent Scott. The men must have exacted a severe punishment from Earth Blanket, because Nimiipuu social constructs did not tolerate rape, and the offense was aggressively punished by public flogging or permanent exile. Earth Blanket returned with Hill to Oakland, where Scott hoped that he would cause no more trouble.[53]

Federal agents implemented another official program at Oakland in February 1885, when Agent Scott selected three men to serve as judges on the Court of Indian Offenses. Yellow Bear, Red Wolf (Him-in-sl-pilp), and Jay Gould were given the appointments. Following federal guidelines, Scott chose men whom he considered to be "intelligent and progressive"; he did not select judges from the police force or from among the other community leaders.[54] Established as petty tribunals, the courts adjudicated misdemeanors, such as drunkenness, polygamy, and theft. Non-Christians, women, and men who maintained polygamous marriages were not eligible to serve on the court. The Court of Indian Offenses convened several times a month to settle matters brought before it by the agent, and penalties usually involved fines, although the judges could order incarceration. There were no standardized penalties for offenses, and the judges' decisions could be discarded in favor of a court with legal standing or review by the commissioner of Indian affairs. Judgments were also subject to the agent's review, reflecting another attempt to assert federal law on reservations.[55] The three Oakland judges were progressives who belonged to the Oakland Presbyterian Church and sent their children to boarding schools at the Chilocco Indian Industrial School and Carlisle Indian Industrial School in Pennsylvania. Chief Joseph was not eligible to serve on the court because of his religious affiliation and marital status. Joseph maintained his polygamous marital obligations until his wife Tom-ma-al-wa-win-mai left his camp and established her own home. The Indian police and the court also allowed Joseph the time to advance the extensive intertribal relationships that he developed in the Indian Territory.

National holidays offered opportunities for American Indians to incorporate old celebrations into their changing circumstances. At the Independence Day festivities at Fort Reno, Natives and soldiers gathered for horse races, skill-based contests, and beef barbecues. On July 4, 1880, Joe Sherburne entertained the Ponca Agency with fireworks and festivities, while the Oakland Christian prisoners celebrated with a day of prayer. On the next July 4, Nimiipuu, Cheyenne, Arapaho, Pawnee, and Kaw celebrants attended the fireworks and enjoyed the picnics and barbecue in Arkansas City. Another big celebration was held at Oakland, where most of the exiles gathered for an event that combined their old summer solstice ceremonies with new practices. The older summer celebrations included modifications introduced by Euro-American fur traders, and the new ceremonies accommodated

Presbyterian doctrine and the national holiday. The Oakland celebration brought the community, agency employees, and other friends together for a special day. Days of preparation went into the event as the Oakland women, accompanied by Mrs. Minthorn and Mrs. Hank Nelson, prepared a grand feast. Celebrations of first foods customarily included salmon and other foods indigenous to the northwest, but this feast was adjusted to the Indian Territory. Instead of salmon and elk, the celebrants enjoyed local fish and game, and early garden fruits and vegetables replaced wild blueberries and kous or camas roots. Water was also sacred to the ceremonies, although the local water was an inadequate substitute for the waters of the old homeland.[56]

Like the old fur trader celebrations, the summer celebration began before dawn with gunshots and other noisy demonstrations, and lasted well into the night. Lieutenant Hill, Earth Blanket, and the Indian policemen were mounted up and on their way to the picnic grounds by eight o'clock in the morning. Later in the morning, the Nimiipuu, Paluses, and Cayuses gathered at the picnic area, where a large brush arbor sheltered picnic tables spread with neat white cloths. Schoolgirls modeled new dresses made for them by Mrs. Minthorn and Mrs. Nelson, while the other celebrants wore western-style clothing or donned their customary regalia. The Nimiipuu, Paluses, and Cayuses formed two long lines standing about twenty feet apart. One line consisted of groups led by Chief Joseph and Yellow Bull, while the other included the bands led by Húsus Kute and Yellow Bear. Joseph stepped forward to welcome the day and greet the community, and then Yellow Bear spoke in the same manner. Hill translated English-language speeches, mentioning the "Star-Spangled Banner" waving at the head of the lines. The Reverend Archie Lawyer was the last to speak, as he offered a Christian blessing. Then the lines of exiles shook hands with each other until everyone had exchanged greetings. After that, the crowd gathered under the arbor around the feast-laden tables. Lawyer asked another blessing, and the meal was served. Lawyer offered another prayer after the banquet, and a quiet afternoon of visiting and social exchanges carried over into the evening. The agent presented a fireworks display after dark for the children, and then groups of adults carrying lanterns went from home to home, singing old songs and Christian hymns in Nimiputimít. When the prisoners were finally returned to the northwest, they brought the shared celebration with them back to Lapwai.[57]

Ill health continued to plague the prisoners at Oakland, even though the Indian Bureau had trumpeted their improved health as an excuse for the move. The heat and mosquitoes sustained the cycle of malaria, declining birth rates, and heavy mortality. Once again, a long move during malaria season caused an inordinate number of deaths. Forty-six people died between April 1879 and June 1880, and the Oakland population fell to 344. Dr. Cora Bland visited Oakland from Washington, D.C., in September 1879, and found the people still coping with malaria, psychological disorders, and what was probably puerperal fever. Startled by a cry from a nearby lodge, Bland questioned Chief Joseph about the lament. Excusing himself, the chief explained that the wail was a woman's death song. He allowed Bland to join him in the lodge, where the young woman was being attended by other women and a medicine man. Inserting herself in the process, Bland diagnosed the woman's ailment as heat prostration. She accused the medicine man of negligence and misdiagnosis, not realizing that she was in a maternity lodge, where the woman had just given birth. Bland knew almost nothing about bacteria, and antibiotics were nonexistent, so she treated the woman with ice, cold compresses, and liquid ozone while complaining that the medicine man was defeatist and useless. Bland blotted ozone on the woman's nostrils, then applied artificial respiration to force the substance into her lungs. The patient was also dosed with other stimulants, despite the medicine man's continuing insistence that she would not live. Bland thought the woman was improved the next morning, in spite of the medicine man, who continued to insist that the young mother could not survive.[58]

Chief Joseph spent most of the month of August 1880 confined to his bed, as his wife nursed him through a bout of malaria.[59]

Twenty-one prisoners had died by June 30, 1880, and forty-nine more deaths were reported between June 1881 and May 1885. Three people completed suicide in 1881, followed by another in 1882, and a fifth suicide occurred before the prisoners left in May 1885. This death was one of three suicides recorded at all Indian agencies that year, as the Pine Ridge agent warned that it was not uncommon for American Indians to take their own lives on reservations.[60] The Cheyennes and Arapahos were experiencing epidemic venereal diseases and malaria, and tuberculosis was rampant at Pine Ridge, where the other suicides occurred. At the Yankton Agency, a deadly combination of malaria, tuberculosis, and other epidemic diseases caused forty-four deaths, plus one suicide. The number of completed suicides remained fairly constant at between two and six per year, at agencies faced with multiple social and medical problems.[61] Sadly, the number of Nimiipuu suicides was within the norm for American Indian reservations.

By 1885, the average family at Oakland consisted of two to three persons, and seven men and nine women lived alone. Only one family contained six members, and one other family supported five people. Chief Joseph's family consisted of himself and one other person; his wife To-ma-al-wa-win-mai (Magdallenia) lived by herself. Yellow Bull's family now consisted of him and his son, who attended the Chilocco Indian Industrial School. Húsus Kute lived alone after his ailing wife left the Indian Territory with Archie Lawyer in 1884. Billy, Samuel Fleming, Nat Wentforth, Crow Blanket, Long Yellow Nose, and John Fur Cap were among the bachelors, widowers, or divorced men. Red Elk had died in February 1884. By the end of 1885, at least thirty-one families had experienced at least one death. Six families lost two members, and Rope (Ka-moo) lost four family members. Ten children under the age of five died in fiscal year 1885, and twenty-six births were recorded between 1881 and 1884. (The number of births in 1885 was not recorded.) By June 1882, the prison camps contained 90 men, 156 women, 54 boys, and 3 girls.[62] Two years later, in June 1884, only three children born since 1881 remained alive; ten children under the age of five died during fiscal year 1885.[63] There were at least fourteen infants alive in late May 1885, and twenty widows, nine orphans, and two older men returned to Idaho in 1883 with James Reuben.[64] Three Eagles, Jim Nat (Kil Kil Chuslum), and Amelia Young returned to Lapwai with James Reuben, leaving their dependents William Bull, Susan, and Alice to return to Colville with Chief Joseph. James Hayes left a woman named Mollie behind in camp while he boarded at the Chilocco Industrial Indian School, and Adelia Emeline (Tsiskoops) lost a dependent before leaving for Colville in 1885.[65]

Avoiding malaria was impossible, and the effects of the disease compromised the prisoners' health and immune systems. Epidemic at all of the neighboring Indian agencies, malaria infected more than 9,700 Cheyennes, Arapahos, Kiowas, Comanches, Wichitas, Osages, and Poncas by 1879.[66] More than 70 percent of the Oakland captives were suffering from lung diseases and the chronic effects of malaria by June of that year. Every Oakland prisoner was treated for malaria at least three times between 1879 and 1885, and the disease caused stillbirths and premature births of fetuses ranging from one to three months from maturity. The Modocs experienced the same rate of infant mortality as the Nimiipuu, complaining that none of their children born in 1884 survived infancy. Malaria accelerates population decline, degrades population regeneration, and is particularly harmful to women and children. The disease also causes miscarriages, reductions in fecundity and potency, and anemia. More Nimiipuu women and children than men died in captivity.[67] Between 1878 and 1880, 23 families lost 33 members, and by May 1885, 52 families had lost 127 members, while other families disappeared.[68] Malaria was the primary cause of death, although other disorders and ailments added to the prisoners' discomforts and demise.

By the end of August 1879, more than 500 patients at the Ponca Agency were suffering from respiratory ailments, including the Oakland residents.[69] Bronchitis, asthma, and whooping cough compounded other afflictions affecting the prisoners. Women rarely sought help for gynecological problems or childbirth. Several people required treatment for gunshot wounds, including

Hooper, who had been shot by Lieutenant Tom Hill. Under the influence of alcohol, Hooper had fired four shots from a Colt revolver at Hill, who was trying to arrest him. Hooper's shots went wild, and Hill winged Hooper in the hip with his carbine.[70] Broken bones were not common, and only one person required treatment for frostbite during the winter of 1881–82. Five prisoners suffered from syphilis, and two congenitally infected infants were born in 1884 and 1885. By 1885, two Oakland prisoners were infected with primary or first-stage syphilis. In contrast to the epidemics of syphilis and gonorrhea affecting nearby agencies, venereal diseases did not spread into the general Oakland population. Tuberculosis and scrofula (lymphatic tuberculosis) infected nineteen elderly prisoners, who eventually returned to the reservations at Lapwai and Colville, where both forms of tuberculosis had been present before the prisoners were relocated.[71] The Oakland children were also exposed to tuberculosis at the Carlisle Indian Industrial School, and at the Forest Grove Indian and Industrial Training School in Oregon. Tuberculosis took the lives of Ellen Rebecca (Price) and Mary Wilson at Forest Grove, and of Samuel Johns, Rebecca Littlewolf, and Luke Phillips at Carlisle.[72]

The threat of smallpox was a deadly reality, and many of the prisoners had not yet been vaccinated when they arrived at Oakland.[73] Dr. Minthorn administered smallpox vaccinations in 1881, although as often happened with bovine-based vaccines, some of the prisoners suffered severe reactions, and several died after the treatments.[74] Smallpox infected other agencies in the area as well; an outbreak occurred at the Kaw Agency in 1878, and spread to the Osages in 1882. The disease could have spread to Oakland, and vaccinations were necessary at the Ponca Agency again in 1882.[75] Smallpox is deadly in unprotected populations, and vaccinations dramatically increase the chances of group survival. Dysentery and diarrhea were chronic conditions at Oakland, although they caused no fatalities except when combined with diphtheria or influenza. Diphtheria caused several deaths in 1884, and epidemics of influenza in 1881 and 1883 infected almost everyone at Oakland. By 1885, anemia and chronic liver failure also infected a few of the prisoners.

At least 124 people died between April 1879 and May 21, 1885, at which point census records indicate that the surviving Oakland population had plummeted to 266. There were 268 Nimiipuu, Paluses, and Cayuses delivered to Idaho and Washington Territory in May 1885.[76]

Captain Jack (She-was-tis-ha-hai), ca. 1879–85. Photograph (*carte de visite*) by Hezekiah Beck. Donald D. and Elizabeth M. Dickinson Research Center, National Cowboy & Western Heritage Museum, Oklahoma City, Oklahoma, 2004.015.2.

Wolf Head, ca. 1879–85. Photograph (*carte de visite*) by Hezekiah Beck. Donald C. and Elizabeth M. Dickinson Research Center, National Cowboy & Western Heritage Museum, Oklahoma City, Oklahoma, 2004.015.3.

Side view of original Sherburne Indian trading post, Ponca Reservation, ca. 1877. K. Ross Toole Archives and Special Collections, Maureen and Mike Mansfield Library, the University of Montana Libraries, Missoula, Montana, accession 2006-01.

Students at the Carlisle Indian School. Standing, Jesse Paul, Charlie Wolf, and Samuel Johns; seated, Dollie Gould and Rebecca Littlewolf. National Anthropological Archives, Suitland, Maryland, Inv. #06859600.

Harriet Mary at the Carlisle Indian School, ca. 1880–86. National Anthropological Archives, Suitland, Maryland, Inv. #06817700.

James Reuben, Mark Williams, Archie Lawyer, and John B. Monteith, ca. 1878. Courtesy of the National Park Service, Nez Perce National Historical Park, NEPE-H1-0179.

Carter, Rob Minthorn, John Hayes, Albert Johnson, and John Minthorn. Courtesy of the National Park Service, Nez Perce National Historical Park, NEPE-HI-0531.

Levi Jonas. From Juliet Axtell, *Gospel Hymns in the Nez Perce Language* (1897). Manuscripts, Archives, and Special Collections, Washington State University Libraries, Pullman, Wash., BV510.N4 A9.

James Horn Grant (Tewiispelu) in Lapwai, Idaho, ca. 1890. Courtesy of Veronica Mae McCormack Taylor and the Lapwai United Methodist Church.

Yellow Bear and wife in Mount Idaho, Idaho, ca. 1890. L. V. McWhorter Photograph Collection, Washington State University Libraries, Pullman, Wash., PC85, Box 2, Folder 17.

"The Transfer of the Nez Perces": Boarding the train at Arkansas City. From *Frank Leslie's Illustrated Newspaper*, June 20, 1885. From the author's collection.

James McLaughlin and Chief Joseph, standing; interpreter Rabain, Peo Peo Tholekt, and Phillip Andrews, seated. From the *Sunday Oregonian*, June 24, 1900. Courtesy of the National Park Service, Nez Perce National Historical Park, NEPE-HI-0517.

CHAPTER 9

Federal Indian Schools and Nimiipuu, Palus, and Cayuse Students

Shortly after the Nimiipuu, Palus, and Cayuse prisoners reached Fort Leavenworth, they were targeted by the burgeoning American Indian boarding school movement. Hoping to capitalize on the celebrity of the Nimiipuu resistance, General Samuel C. Armstrong tried to relocate some of the prisoners from Fort Leavenworth to his school for African American students, the Hampton Normal and Agricultural Institute in Hampton, Virginia. Armstrong predicted that an industrial education and exposure to the English language and to men of good character would enable him to "break" any American Indian to "right ideals and good discipline."[1] He initially proposed to keep 150 Nimiipuu prisoners at Hampton for three years. Armstrong appealed directly to President Rutherford B. Hayes and the chairman of the House Committee on Indian Affairs for their support, but he soon abandoned the idea because of a lack of federal funding and interest. By the next spring, however, his desire to gain control of the prisoners resurfaced when Lieutenant Richard Henry Pratt suggested to federal authorities that the younger male Nimiipuu, Palus, and Cayuse prisoners be sent to Hampton, where they could be instructed in "civilized" ways.[2]

On May 29, 1878, Lieutenant Pratt received permission from Secretary of War George W. McCrary to take fifty of the younger men from the Fort Leavenworth prison camp to the Hampton Institute.[3] He requested only fifty of the men because, he said, "The preponderance of women, aged, and disabled persons among the adults, and the absence of the active young men is discouraging."[4] In June 1878, Pratt went to Fort Leavenworth, where hundreds of the detainees were suffering from the heat and malaria.[5] General John Pope had approved Pratt's proposal, but Pratt had second thoughts when he realized that he would not be able to keep the men under lock and key at Hampton. The prisoners would need to be subdued before they could be appropriately receptive to the schooling that Pratt had in mind for them, so he decided that they should first spend some time in a provisional prison camp, to be set up in a remote southern seacoast area, perhaps at St. Augustine or Fort Wood. There, he believed, "They would daily see the strength of government and the civilized world in the passing. This would make them feel their own insignificance and they could be led to hope for fellowship with us."[6] Once he had gained control of the men, he planned to move those who were compliant to Hampton, with any who remained assertive to be sent to an undisclosed location to become farmers. McCrary, Pope, and Pratt understood that the men would continue to face serious health hazards in the malarial swamps of the South. "Numbers would probably die," Pratt told McCrary, "but no more, I think, than if sent to the Indian Territory."[7] Pratt may have had high hopes for his plan, but it was rejected by Chief Joseph and the prisoners, and Pratt was forced to postpone his recruitment of the Nimiipuu.

In February 1880, James Reuben, the former assistant schoolteacher from Lapwai, started a day school at the Oakland Subagency.[8] Of the seventy school-aged youngsters on the reservation, seventeen boys and eighteen girls attended Reuben's school until the July 1880 recess. On average, twenty students attended school five days a week that first year, depending on the distance they had to travel, their health, and whether they had warm clothing to wear.[9] Malaria kept many children out of school the first year, and absences in subsequent years always increased during malaria season. Federal issues of clothing usually arrived late in the year, causing some students to miss classes because of cold weather. When enrollments at the Oakland school increased, federal agents requested that a combination school and church be built there. Instead, agency carpenters constructed a shop building that could do double duty as a school. Measuring thirty-six by twenty-four feet, it was uninsulated and had an open ceiling.[10]

The shop building was desperately cold in the winter, and hunger and illness also challenged the children. "We have no school house," Lieutenant Tom Hill complained. "Our children go here to school in this carpenter shop."[11] But Reuben and the children were making do, as Indian inspector William J. Pollock remarked after visiting the school in May 1881: "Fifty four of the young people attend school in the carpenter shop, and they have the more regular attendance, and best conducted Indian agency day-school I ever saw."[12] Pollock did not, however, observe the school in the winter. In August 1884, after many of the youngsters had walked two to three miles to school each day for several years, it was finally suggested that the school be restructured as a modified day or boarding school. In addition, Agent John Scott felt that the children should be given at least a midday meal. However, the lunches never materialized. Instead, the children volunteered to plant and tend a school vegetable garden to supplement their lunches, "when they happen to have one."[13] The Indian Bureau spent $350 in fiscal year 1880 and $800 in fiscal year 1881 to support the school, but it never provided food or uniforms for the students.[14]

A foundation was built for a proper school, but the building was delayed by purchasing and funding problems. Lumber and materials were delivered and stored at Oakland before the construction stopped. Classes continued in the shop building, and in 1884 the Indian Bureau officially abandoned the new school. The materials were transferred to other agencies, and the prisoners gradually lost interest in having a new school as word circulated through the camps that they would be returning to the northwest.[15]

The school at Oakland experienced its greatest achievements and tragedies during Reuben's tenure as teacher. Everyone who visited the school praised the students; they were intelligent and well-behaved, and they were learning to read and recite in English. They also performed difficult arithmetic and blackboard exercises and sang for their visitors.[16] Reuben and the assistant teacher taught drawing, world geography, arithmetic, spelling, and English grammar and employed Bibles and gospel hymnals to teach reading and music. Reuben taught geography using a large map of the United States and another global map, on which he must have pointed out the Nimiipuu homelands to the children.[17] And since council and community meetings, church services, and many other events took place in the combination shop-school building, runaways must have used the maps to mark their paths home.

Attendance at the Oakland school averaged between forty-four and fifty-eight pupils per day during the 1881–82 and 1883–84 school years. Under Reuben's guidance, more boys than girls attended school, and as students dropped out, others enrolled. Reuben's records detail the students' attendance and illnesses, extended absences, and the deaths of three youngsters. George W. Red Wolf (George W. Wolf) dropped out of school in the middle of September 1882 during malaria season. The ailing boy returned for a few weeks in November and again in December, but his participation was interrupted by long periods of illness. He struggled to stay in school and returned again in January, but he then dropped out for the final time, dying on February 9, 1883. Walter Benjamin passed away the third week of October 1882 after a brief absence from school, and Eliza Moses (He-yo-wa-pat-kekt) died on May 7, 1883, following a long illness. Other students, including Levi Jonas, Johnny Simon, Silas Samuel, and Elias Davis, suffered lengthy bouts of illness during 1882 and 1883 but managed to return to school. John Andrews enrolled in the Oakland school in February 1883, but as warm weather and the incidence of malaria increased, his attendance declined, and he quit school as a result of illness the first week of May.[18] Attendance usually peaked before malaria struck the camps in the spring and summer.

Attendance also declined during the unusually harsh winters of 1883–84 and 1884–85. Commissioner Hiram Price insisted that the students must go to school even when daytime temperatures were well below zero.[19] Price was disconnected from the realities of the Indian Territory, and Agent Scott begged his understanding. Scott insisted that the "little fellows" could not walk for miles out on the prairies in the subzero temperatures. Responding to complaints from the Indian Bureau, Scott finally stopped issuing rations as a way to put pressure on families whose children were not attending school, although mandatory American Indian education was not legalized until 1892.[20]

After the first year, school began in September and continued through the next spring. The first term was only five months long; thereafter, the school term vacillated between eight and ten months. Reuben selected Rosie Martha, who was Cayuse, as his assistant teacher, and Mrs. Hank Nelson was the school matron. Fourteen-year-old Rosie Martha supported herself and her blind mother, Sa-caw-ta-she, on her assistant's salary of $15 per month. Sa-caw-ta-she had been stranded in the Indian Territory with her daughter after her Nimiipuu warrior husband was killed in the war. Aware of the financial difficulties facing the girl and her mother, Agent Thomas J. Jordan granted the young assistant teacher a paid vacation for the summer recess of July and August 1881. Mrs. Rose Price preserved Reuben's school records, in which many of the entries appear to be in her handwriting. Assistant teachers Amelia Young (Pe-wa-ya-ta-lee-ka-sat) and Rosie Martha took attendance and kept track of students who were ill or who dropped out of school. Mrs. Nelson, who was also the cleaning lady and monitor, taught sewing and cooking classes and helped with the younger children.[21] She was rumored to have supplied the ingredients for the cooking classes from her home and garden.

The students attended the Oakland school until they returned to the northwest or were transferred to other schools. Reuben recruited students from the camps, and older students enrolled and remained in the school because of the education he offered. The teacher also circulated through the camps, recording ration issues and serving as the first deacon of the Oakland Presbyterian Church. Any of these activities could have influenced James Hayes, Charles Bear, and Philip Walker to enroll in the school within days of each other and to attend classes on most of the same days. Hayes was about twenty years old, Bear was about eighteen, and Walker was a young adult. All three of them quit school before Reuben returned to Idaho in May 1883. Kate Malone, the daughter of the non-Native sawmill mechanic, attended the Oakland school during October and November 1881, but she withdrew on the last day of November. Reuben's school also attracted young adults or teenagers who were responsible for dependents or small families. Levi Jonas, Amelia Young, Rosie Martha, Jeanette Rachel (Nots-no), Lydia Joanna, Delia Mary, Eliza Moses, and Woman Riding (Ta-ma-ya-to-wa-son-mai, Carrie Schutt) attended even while taking on adult responsibilities as their parents or guardians died. The older students may also have gone to school because they were forced to by the agent or by the Indian police.[22]

Reuben was the first teacher to send students from Oakland to the new experimental American Indian boarding school that Pratt opened in Carlisle, Pennsylvania, in 1879. Having convinced the federal authorities to allow him to use the Carlisle army barracks for his school, Pratt recruited children first from the Rosebud and Pine Ridge reservations and then from the Pawnees, Kiowas, Sacs and Foxes, and Poncas and from Oakland. Pratt visited the Indian Territory in the fall of 1879 and arranged for four Nimiipuu children to attend Carlisle. Harriet Mary, Jesse Paul, Luke Phillips, and Samuel Johns arrived at the

Carlisle Indian Industrial School on February 20, 1880, and James Porter was sent from Oakland to join them on May 27, 1882. After that, no more Oakland students were sent to Carlisle until after Reuben had left the Indian Territory in 1883. He may have sent a few pupils to the Ponca Indian Industrial School, but he did not send any students to the new Chilocco Indian Industrial School south of Arkansas City in the Indian Territory.[23]

Reuben had come to the Indian Territory under difficult circumstances. Having left his wife at Lapwai, he struggled with irregular pay and debilitating illnesses, and was widely disliked because of his politics and his involvement in the war. Reuben soon reassessed the consequences of the war and the lives of the Oakland prisoners. Hired initially as the interpreter and then as the teacher at Oakland, he spent many hours with Chief Joseph and the other leaders creating lists of names. The men dictated the names of all the warriors they remembered from the war and created a census of the dead and injured from each battle. Through Reuben, they drafted an important document that they did not want lost to history.[24] By June 1882, Chief Joseph and the men had provided Reuben with hundreds of names. They had also noted the elderly men, recorded the deaths and injuries of women and children, and memorialized where people were injured, captured, or killed during the war. At the end of the dictation, Reuben began to write his "History of the Nez Perce War of 1877."[25] The incomplete story reflected his yearning for the rivers and mountains of the beautiful northwest. In spite of his politics, James Reuben did not castigate the prisoners whose names he recorded for posterity. He did, however, urge conversion to Christianity and acceptance of non-Native life styles, and he was praised by Indian agents for his interference with the old "superstitious" religious practices. Reuben also continued to worry about his influence at Oakland in the wake of his return to Idaho in 1883. He sent letters to James Haworth after he left, asking the Indian inspector for information: "I want you to tell me all the news. Is there any school at Oakland Agency, and if so, who is the teacher? Do you ever go there? How do the Nez Perces get along without me?"[26]

When Reuben left Oakland in 1883, Agent Lewellyn Woodin suggested that Luke Phillips be returned from the Carlisle Indian Industrial School to become the Oakland teacher. Woodin intended to pay Phillips about one-third of Reuben's salary, but he shelved that plan and hired a non-Native English-speaking teacher instead. The only federal complaint directed at Reuben was that he taught several classes and singing lessons in Nimiputimít, and federal officials wanted an English-only speaker in the classroom. Consequently, twenty-four-year-old Carrie Shults was hired as the teacher, and the widowed Annie Shults was employed as matron and assistant teacher for the 1884–85 school year.[27] The Shultses had come to Oakland from Illinois to assist Sadie E. Pickering, who had taught there with Reuben since 1881. Carrie was popular at Oakland, where even Lieutenant Tom Hill studied English grammar and penmanship as a day student. Hill, who had taught himself to speak and write English, attended the school at Oakland in addition to his regular duties at the agency. "Now my friend I wish you let me go to school every day," Hill told Hiram Price. "I like to learn and get smart like white man. Every time when somebody, anybody want to talk to superintendent, I come quick from schoolhouse about two minutes."[28] About the younger Shults, Hill said, "Now good teacher all boys and girls make smart. All love teacher, nice good teacher, work, good all time for Indians."[29] Hill was not alone in his praise of her. When Woman Riding chose an English name, she adopted the name Carrie Schutt.[30] Hill was eager to advance his new skills and hoped to continue his education at the Forest Grove Indian School in Oregon after the prisoners returned to the northwest.[31]

Carrie and Anna Shults eventually transferred to the Otoe School, but Pickering remained at Oakland until the school closed in May 1885. The teachers were paid $600 a year, and the matron's salary was $300. But class sizes and attendance declined after Reuben's departure. Adjusting for nine orphans that Reuben took to Idaho and seventeen students who were transferred to the Chilocco Indian Industrial School, the average daily attendance dropped to twenty-two. Pickering operated the school on a nine-month school year and spent less than $25 a year on supplies and fuel.[32]

In response to federal directives to transfer advanced students to other federal schools, Pickering sent a second group of Oakland students to the Carlisle Indian Industrial School on October 13, 1883.[33] Rebecca Littlewolf, Dollie Gould, Charlie Wolf (Charlie Williams), and another boy were sent east with Mr. A. O. Standing and a group of Cheyenne and Arapaho students. Pickering and Shults also directed the first students from Oakland to the Chilocco Indian Industrial School. Sup-poon-mas delivered three boys to Chilocco in mid-February 1884, and within the year, sixteen Oakland students were enrolled there.[34] One additional Oakland student transferred to Chilocco, while several of the first girls dropped out and were replaced by boys.[35] James Haworth, the former special Indian agent who was now the U.S. Indian school inspector, oversaw the recruitment of the first Chilocco students from the Indian Territory and delivered them to the school. Winter weather caused serious problems as wagonloads of Cheyenne, Arapaho, Wichita, Comanche, and Pawnee students struggled through the blizzards of 1884 to reach Chilocco.[36] The school also paid agency teamsters such as Sup-poon-mas to transport students from the Indian agencies.[37]

Among the Oakland students who enrolled at Chilocco were Harrison and Josiah Red Wolf, Alice Lawrence, Lilly Moses, Lilly Newman, Charles Bear, Thomas Gould, Jimmie and Jacob Snow, Silas Samuel, Stephen Julius (Ip-pits-ke-tit), Frank Jackson, Isaac Lawrence (Ke-ko-she-im), Eddie Johnson, Harry Anderson (Ko-she-she-man), James Hayes, and Cornelius Baldwin (He-we-lee-ka-sat). Jackson was a double orphan, having lost both of his parents, and the mothers of the Red Wolf boys, Charles Bear, and Thomas Gould were deceased. James Hayes was the oldest of the group and had left a woman named Mollie Hayes (At-we-ya-we-non-mai) at Oakland. Baldwin was sickly when sent to Chilocco and died soon after his return to the northwest in May 1885.[38]

James Hayes attended the Oakland school before he was transferred to the Chilocco Indian Industrial School. Like most of the Oakland survivors, he raised a family and built a successful career after leaving the Indian Territory. After returning to Lapwai in 1885, he became an ordained Presbyterian minister. He served as an intertribal evangelist to the Fort Hall Shoshones and Bannocks, the Shivwits at Fort George, Utah, and the Makahs at Neah Bay in Washington Territory, and also ministered to his Idaho pastorate. Hayes rarely used an interpreter; he preached and sang in Nimiputímt and accompanied himself in fluent sign language. Known as the "man who loved children," he was a gifted raconteur at evening campfires, where he entertained his traveling companions with Nimiipuu lore. Hayes was awarded a doctorate of divinity from Whitworth College two years before his death in 1926.[39] Gould advanced to the rank of sergeant of his Chilocco cadet company, where he earned $60 a year before leaving the school in May 1885. Like the cadet corps at Carlisle, the Chilocco cadet corps was intended to instill military discipline in male students. Cadets were often young men marked with leadership potential who supervised the squads of students assigned to work in the school farms and gardens. Thomas Gould and Charles Bear had been at Chilocco less than three months when they were advanced to the rank of cadet sergeant, although Bear resigned after thirty days.[40]

Unlike the Oakland school, the Chilocco Indian Industrial School was a boarding school that promised male students an industrial and mechanical education, meals, and housing. Many of the school's first students were disappointed, however, because no industrial or mechanical trades were actually taught. Instead, the students were put to work farming, digging sewers, or setting fences, or they were assigned to the bakery, the carpenter's shop, or the paint shop. The first Chilocco students built the school's outbuildings and agricultural facilities. Girls learned to sew and majored in the other "domestic arts," such as cleaning and cooking, as they too worked for the school. In groups of thirty, the students attended blocks of classes taught by three non-Native women that lasted all morning or afternoon. Classes were conducted in the English language; teacher Emma De Knight favored a highly organized atmosphere, with squads of students assigned to clean the blackboards and classroom.[41] The teachers taught English, mathematics, and other subjects, although the efficacy of the education remains in doubt. Two matrons, a doctor, a nurse, seamstresses, cooks, disciplinarians, and other staff members managed the first Chilocco students, who lived in crowded dormitories in the school building.[42]

Christian education was mandatory, and everyone attended Sunday services and Sunday school classes that rotated among local ministers. Students were not allowed to leave the school until the summer recess, but lonely children often hitched a ride home with passing American Indian wagon trains. Students were accepted on "the Carlisle Plan," a contract guaranteeing that they would remain at the school for thirty-six months. Parents were promised that their children would be returned to them after three years, although Indian agents and school administrators tried to circumvent the agreements so as to keep them there longer. The Oakland students were accepted at the Chilocco school without the three-year proviso because it was understood that they would be returning to Idaho in the near future. The first few months that Chilocco was open, chiefs and families visited the school, and tepees and family camps were a common sight on the campus. But so were wild cowboy camps that attracted alcohol, racing, and gamblers from out in the Indian Territory. When Dr. Henry J. Minthorn returned from the Forest Grove Indian School to supervise Chilocco in November 1884, he was frustrated to discover that some of the parents expected to stay inside the school building with their children during cold weather.

A rapid turnover in superintendents reflected some of the problems at the new school. W. J. Hadley, Minthorn, and John B. Riley served as superintendent in 1884, 1885, and 1886, respectively. They complained of similar problems and lacked a sense of cohesiveness and vision for the institution. After seven months at Chilocco, Minthorn could see no value or plan to the school or to the education it offered American Indian students. Reported to have been a "man of indomitable will," Minthorn also disapproved of contact between students and their families and other American Indians, believing that it countermanded the civilizing influences being exerted by his faculty and staff. The superintendency of the school was seen as an appropriate post for professional men who were advancing their Indian Bureau careers or as a second career for a former agency physician such as Minthorn.[43]

The first Chilocco students spent much of their time working on the school's buildings or farm, and their classroom experiences suffered both from overwork and from poorly coordinated pedagogies. They also endured scanty meals and severe discipline. Nevertheless, when recruiters from Chilocco visited Idaho in 1903, five Nimiipuu students transferred to the school. Nimiipuu students, some of whom were related to the Oakland prisoners, continued to attend Chilocco through the first decades of the twentieth century.[44]

By the time Captain Pratt recruited the Oakland students to his Carlisle Indian Industrial School in Pennsylvania, he was clear about his mission for the school. "I hold in common with many others, that the only good Indian is a dead one," Pratt said at a meeting in Philadelphia's Association Hall. "But," he continued, "I believe in killing the Indian and saving the man."[45] Pratt's vision encompassed Christian conversion, eradication of indigenous languages, and reeducation on the public school and industrial training models. He intended to create farmers, blue-collar workers, and domestic servants to replace the "barbarian" hordes of American Indians. One of the Oakland children, Harriet Mary, was in the group of American Indian students who heard Pratt deliver that speech. They also listened to Amos Cloud Shield, William Big Snake (who was Ponca), Reuben Swift Bear (who was Sioux), and a Creek boy enrolled in the Dickinson College preparatory program, who were touted as exemplars for Pratt's experimental education program. Before delivering their speeches in support of Pratt's project, the students had visited the Philadelphia Zoo, Girard College, and the Institution for the Deaf and Dumb, where Indian agents asked to send children with special needs. Harriet Mary was the daughter of the nontreaty leader Sum-kain; her mother, Mary, had stayed at the Oakland prison camp with Harriet's younger sisters. The Carlisle students were inculcated with Pratt's racist anti-Indian ideologies, although they sometimes dropped the façade of internal colonization. Eighteen months after the Association Hall event, Harriet Mary told her teacher that she would prefer working as a domestic servant on a Pennsylvania farm to living at Carlisle.[46] Meanwhile, parents at Oakland were concerned about the type of education their children were receiving at the school. Húsus Kute, for example, wondered why his son was not spending more time in the classroom.[47]

On May 2, 1883, the parents of Luke Phillips, Samuel Johns, Jesse Paul, and Harriet Mary asked to have their children returned to Oakland. The children had been at Carlisle for three years, as had been agreed to when they were initially taken there. Agent Woodin and Captain Pratt pressed the families to leave the young people in Pennsylvania. Harriet Mary's mother was particularly insistent that her daughter be brought to her at Oakland, because she and her other daughters were returning to Lapwai with James Reuben. The Oakland parents resisted Woodin's arguments, citing the agreement that guaranteed their children's return. Woodin assured Pratt that he would revisit the parents to change their minds, and by July he had convinced the parents of Jesse Paul, Luke Phillips, and Samuel Johns to leave them at Carlisle. Meanwhile, Harriet Mary's mother and her sisters Delia and Anna (Annie) had returned to Lapwai as planned. After that, the Oakland agent told Pratt to keep Harriet Mary at Carlisle. Since her mother was already at Lapwai, Woodin hoped that other family members would be able to persuade Mary to leave her daughter in Pennsylvania. Harriet Mary's thirteen-year-old sister Delia was sent to the Forest Grove Indian School in Oregon, and Anna enrolled at the Carlisle Indian Industrial School in Pennsylvania in 1891.[48]

Harriet Mary and Jesse Paul eventually returned to Idaho, but Luke Phillips and Samuel Johns remained at Carlisle. While at Carlisle, Harriet Mary worked for the Potter family in Bellefonte, Centre County, Pennsylvania, as an outing student. Outing students lived with families in the communities around Carlisle. Pratt believed that the practical experience gained by working and living in American homes would help train American Indian students in "civilized" living. Boys were expected to learn to farm, and girls were to learn the "domestic arts." Outing students were paid a small wage, and in many instances they were treated well and learned to care for their temporary families. Other children did not fare so well and were literally treated like slave labor.

As the Potters' live-in domestic helper, Harriet Mary lit the morning fires, did the laundry, milked the cow twice a day, and was the "busiest girl."[49] Although she was lonely at first, she did not want to go back to Carlisle, where she was often angry and unhappy. Seven years later, she wrote to her former teacher from her home in Idaho, expressing her gratitude to the Carlisle School for teaching her to read and write. Like so many students who experienced the intense anti-Indian propaganda at Carlisle, Harriet Mary seemed discontented in Idaho. She felt that she was locked in the dark with people she no longer understood. A year later, she took a job with Alice Fletcher, an anthropologist who had been hired to manage the allotment of the Lapwai reservation. While there, she married another Carlisle graduate, James Stuart. Harriet Mary and her husband maintained a lifelong interest in justice for the nontreaty bands.[50]

Luke Phillips never returned to his family. About thirteen years old when he arrived at Carlisle, Phillips served as the president of the Young Men's Christian Association (YMCA), was active in various school organizations, and compiled an impressive service record at the school. Librarian for the boys' library, he also served as a noncommissioned officer in a Carlisle cadet company and worked at the summer camp. He loved the camp and a cabin he affectionately called "The Campbell's Hump."[51] Phillips internalized the school's anti-Indian propaganda, although he gradually expressed qualified resistance to the concepts. Thirty-four months after arriving at Carlisle, Phillips addressed the New York County Teachers' Institute. He trumpeted non-Native accomplishments and declared that "blanket" Indians must learn to labor and live like white people. Three years later, however, he sounded a tenuous note of resistance in a letter he sent to the *Morning Star.* He recognized the stolen lands and broken treaties that had caused the war, he wrote, but feared going directly to federal authorities, saying that it was not his place to speak to the government. Phillips died of tuberculosis on January 10, 1888, and is buried in the Carlisle Indian cemetery.[52]

Samuel Johns and Jesse Paul also remained at Carlisle. Johns, who had arrived at the school with Phillips, was active at the summer camp and in many other school activities. Johns was another victim of the tuberculosis epidemic at the school; he died on February 11, 1888, a month after Phillips. Johns and Rebecca Littlewolf, who also died at Carlisle, are both buried in the Carlisle Indian cemetery.

By 1880, tuberculosis was epidemic among the students at Carlisle, a situation that was exacerbated by the dormitory-style living conditions. Even though tuberculosis was also spreading at Oakland, the Nimiipuu students exhibited no symptoms until they had been at Carlisle for several years. In his first annual report to the Interior Department, Captain Pratt falsely stated that the school had not been affected by any epidemics. Maintaining that four students' deaths had been caused by heredity or chronic illnesses, he insisted that the children had arrived at Carlisle infected with tuberculosis contracted from their parents or families. Pratt blamed the victims for their illnesses, accusing them of genetic or hereditary weakness. He did not mention the sixty-two new cases of the disease that were flaming through the student population. By 1888, the tuberculosis epidemic had killed a total of twenty-one students. The students at Carlisle also suffered from malaria and other optic, respiratory, and digestive disorders. Mumps infected most of the students in late 1884 and early 1885 but caused no deaths. Six students died from tuberculosis that year, and thirty-six others were sent home because of failing health or "mental weakness."[53] Pratt and the heads of other Indian schools returned terminally ill children to their reservations to avoid including their deaths in school statistics.

Charlie Wolf and Jesse Paul returned to Lapwai and in 1888 were employed by a local surveyor. Paul made a hammer that was part of the Carlisle Indian Industrial School display in the Senate Indian Committee room. The youngster was good at mechanical drawing and completed a diagram and plan for a telephone in philosophy class.[54] Paul's great-grandson and namesake, Jesse Paul, recalls that his great-grandfather received that name at Carlisle. The boy's name was "Ka kun nee," and "his father was Seven Days Whipping [who] died in Oklahoma 'The Hot Place.'"[55] The elder Paul became a successful rancher who raised a large family and built a progressive ranch where he farmed two hundred acres of prime Idaho farmland. He held the mortgages of many non-Native farmers and was respected for his financial acumen and managerial abilities.[56]

The last of the Oakland students had returned to Idaho from Carlisle by August 1889, and no more Nimiipuu students attended the school until 1891. During that year, nine girls and five boys came to Carlisle from Lapwai, and six more boys and five girls followed them the next year. One boy returned to Idaho, and the Carlisle population stabilized at twenty-four Nimiipuu students.[57]

CHAPTER 10

Communities of Faith in the Indian Territory

The relocation to Oakland and the increased freedom of movement enabled the Nimiipuu, Paluses, and Cayuses to expand their spiritual boundaries. Some of the prisoners practiced the old *wéset* faith with its attendant ceremonials or participated in older heliocentric celebrations. Other exiles formed a dynamic new Christian community, and still others blended old and new beliefs or discarded older practices for new doctrines. Celebrations of the *wéset* faith remained constant, but they were held in private more often now, because the Quaker agent at Quapaw had tried to abolish the ceremonials, even though they did not attract crowds of tourists to Oakland as they had done at Fort Leavenworth. The grave markers at the Oakland cemetery served as a poignant reminder of the prisoners' shared experiences and spiritual traditions. Christian and non-Christian graves occupied the same windswept cemetery, where *wéset* burials were marked with bells tied to long poles. Chief Joseph often sat on his horse near the graveyard, quietly contemplating the sounds of the little bells.[1]

Soon after reaching Oakland, the prisoners encountered the familiar old spiritual tradition of the Sun Dance. The Nimiipuu had joined early-nineteenth-century heliocentric dances held near Walla Walla, Washington Territory, and knew other Sun Dances from Montana and their travels out on the plains.[2] The Walla Walla dances had gradually given way to other non-Christian ceremonials or to Christianity, although Otis Halfmoon's grandfather Sol Webb and other elderly men sang the old Sun Dance songs well into the twentieth century.[3] The Canadian refugees had watched the Sioux Sun Dances in Saskatchewan. The Sun Dances in the Indian Territory, sometimes called "medicine dances" by the press, were open to the public and attracted hundreds of American Indians and other interested observers. Newspapers in Kansas and across the Indian Territory advertised and reported on the events. Enthralled by the Sun Dances, Cyrus M. Scott and Joe Sherburne often attended, although they did not take an active part in the ceremonies themselves. Scott also attended Sun Dances with the Nimiipuu, Paluses, and Cayuses in his capacity as Governor John P. St. John's spy.

The prisoners arrived at Oakland too late in the summer of 1879 to attend the Poncas' Sun Dance, but they still found ways to express their faith. Because they were preparing for the winter with so many people suffering from malaria, they also did not take part in any of the other Sun Dances that were held that year. The next summer, however, twenty-one Nimiipuu, Paluses, and Cayuses joined the Indian Territory Sun Dances.

The first Sun Dance attended by the Oakland prisoners was the Ponca Sun Dance held the last week of May 1880. Conducted in a large tent-like enclosure, the ceremonials involved one tall center pole and fifty smaller poles.[4] Banners and strips of calico waved from the poles as fifty-one men joined the dance, seeking spiritual power and divine guidance through sacrifice and personal pain. Painted and stripped to the waist, the men held amulets made of beaver skins or grass and small hand mirrors. To the accompaniment of drums, singing, and eagle bone whistles, each man had the skin on his back pierced with a sharp object, and a pin attached to a thong was then inserted through the wound. One end of a rope was attached to the pin, and the other end was tied to a pole, leaving the man suspended. The men blew their eagle bone whistles until the attaching pins tore loose from their flesh; their sacrifice was then complete. Individual males celebrated their sacrifices by donating a horse to the tribe, while women and girls gathered inside the tent to encourage the supplicants. A group of women pierced their arms, although they danced and prayed without being suspended from the poles. Several muscular men took the rites a step further when they connected their sacrificial ropes to horses. Food had been withheld from the animals for several days before the Sun Dance, and they were eager to reach the hay that was now scattered at the far end of the tent. Using the ropes attached to their backs, the men dragged the reluctant horses around the enclosure, away from the hay, until the pins tore through their flesh, the horses were freed, and their sacrifices were completed. The Sun Dance participants fasted and took no fluids during the ceremonies, which lasted from Wednesday night through Saturday. During special evening ceremonies, parents presented babies to have their ears pierced.[5]

The Poncas remained active Sun Dancers throughout 1884, even though the Indian agent had banned such ceremonies under the auspices of the Religious Crimes Code of 1883. Too late to halt the dances in 1884, the new agent was determined that they would not be held in subsequent years. A group of Ponca chiefs argued that earlier agents had ignored the dances, although Agent John W. Scott had threatened military intervention to halt further ceremonies.[6]

Two weeks after the Ponca Sun Dance, the Nimiipuu, Paluses, and Cayuses joined the Arapaho Sun Dances held at the Darlington Agency. The Arapaho dances were celebrated several times a year, in a cycle that began in June and resumed at the winter solstice. Although Indian agent Daniel B. Dyer felt that hundreds of American Indians were wasting their time at the dances, he did not put a stop to the ceremonies.[7] Chief Joseph and Yellow Bull led the first group of Sun Dancers, which included Joseph's wife, Yellow Bull's sisters, and Co-co-clum, Red Elk,

Tim-sus-sle-wit (Rosebush), Tis-ca (Skunk), Wolf Head, and Sup-poon-mas. Accompanied by an interpreter—a Pawnee man named Joseph Esaw—the group left Oakland after the summer crops were planted. The first group remained at Darlington for two weeks, and a second troupe from Oakland took part in the Arapaho and Cheyenne Sun Dances later in the year. That party was led by Húsus Kute, who was joined by Three Eagles, Thomas Peters, Red Wolf, Crow Blanket, Captain Jack, John Fur Cap, Johnson (Los-tso-kas-tin), Yellow Bear, and Daniel Jefferson.[8]

Joseph and Yellow Bull and their wives and sisters also traveled to the January 1881 Cheyenne and Arapaho ceremonials. They were joined by a group of men who would attend the Sun Dances with them for the next few years. Those men included Co-co-clum, Red Elk, Tim-sus-sle-wit, Tis-ca, Wolf Head, Sup-poon-mas, Feathers around the Neck, Es-pow-yes, and several others.[9] Having made peace with the Nimiipuu, Paluses, and Cayuses, the Cheyennes honored seventeen of the Nimiipuu attendants, including Henry Rivers and Yellow Head, with a special dance and feast during their June 1881 Sun Dance.[10] Christian Nimiipuu, including James Reuben, Lieutenant Tom Hill of the Oakland Indian police, and Jay Gould, joined Earth Blanket, Mat Whitfield (Em-mo-tah), Ow-hi (Benjamin Grant, a Yakama man), and Cyrus M. Scott for the June 1882 Cheyenne and Arapaho Sun Dances.[11] Reuben probably attended as the interpreter; Hill may have been there in his official capacity, but he also may have attended to take part in the ceremonies. Combining the Sun Dances with other spiritual practices was not unusual; Hill, Húsus Kute, Yellow Bear, and Red Wolf attended despite having recently joined the Oakland Presbyterian Church.[12] Many of the Nimiipuu, Paluses, and Cayuses crossed spiritual boundaries in their search for divine guidance or power to ease their captivity.[13]

At the same time, the Kiowas were experiencing a diminished cycle of Sun Dances. Their ceremonials required buffalo sacrifices, and the buffalo were disappearing. The Kiowa Sun Dance ceremony was held in 1881, but it had to be delayed from June, the month in which it was usually celebrated, until August, when one old buffalo bull was found. The following summer, no buffalo appeared in response to a Kiowa medicine man's call to the buffalo, so the 1882 dance could not be held.[14] In 1883, Chief Joseph and forty Nimiipuu, Paluses, and Cayuses joined one of the last Kiowa, Apache, and Wichita Sun Dances. They danced with the Kiowas and Apaches at Semat P'a, then joined the Kiowa ceremonials held north of Rainy Mountain Creek.[15] The Kiowas and Cayuses had known each other in western Montana and dimly recalled the Nimiipuu as the "people who cut the hair round across the forehead."[16] The Sun Dance enabled them to rekindle that historical relationship. Kiowa calendars that record special events memorialize the 1883 ceremonial as the Nez Perce Sun Dance, and privately owned Kiowa calendars still recognize the year as the Nimiipuu Sun Dance.[17] The old Anko calendar features a man at the Sun Dance pole who is cutting his hair in the Nimiipuu style, while the Set-t'an calendar shows a man near the medicine lodge wearing the haircut and striped blanket favored by the Nimiipuu.[18]

Some of the Nimiipuu, Palus, and Cayuse celebrants joined the Sun Dances as full participants. Others limited their involvement to certain aspects of the ceremonies. Piercing and sacrifice required fasting and a time of preparatory prayer, which precluded ad hoc involvement in the ceremonies. They did participate in Sun Dance horse giveaways, an activity that presumed that the recipients were fully involved in the event. Giveaways involved the transfer of power and prestige and often required some type of reciprocal activity. The Nimiipuu, Paluses, and Cayuses received twenty-seven horses at the Arapaho Sun Dance in 1882, although they did not sacrifice there before going on to other Sun Dances. They arrived at the Kiowa dances in 1883 too late to take part in the giveaways, but they were actively invested in the ceremonials.[19] In cases of extreme poverty, Nimiipuu recipients traded or sold songs or stories in exchange for ceremonial participation.[20] The Kiowas did not practice self-sacrifice at their Sun Dances. Unlike the Cheyennes, they regarded any bloodshed during the ceremonies as an "evil omen" that marked an immediate end to the dances.[21] That may be one reason why the Oakland dancers took part in the Kiowa dances.

The Sun Dances were not a replacement for ceremonials that celebrated the *wéset* faith. However, the winter celebration at Oakland was not reported to the press or recorded in government records. The Quaker agent at Quapaw had tried to end the ceremonials, but they did not attract crowds of tourists to Oakland as they had done at Fort Leavenworth. Nevertheless, some of the older students at Oakland—including the famous young warrior Phillip Walker, Charles Bear, future chief David Williams, and John Anderson (Nick-yas-ko-hem)—took time out to attend the celebrations before returning to school.[22] Chief Joseph sometimes attended services at the Oakland Presbyterian Church, although he never became a Christian. Joseph practiced his *wéset* faith and shared other spiritual observations to ensure the prisoners' survival. And in a further effort to ensure divine guidance, the Nimiipuu, Paluses, and Cayuses incorporated some aspects of the Sun Dances into their devotional services at Oakland. Húsus Kute and Christian Sun Dancers erected pole and brush arbors for their Sunday services at Oakland, where Christians and non-Christians worshipped together under the arbors.[23]

Intertribal ceremonials also introduced the Nimiipuu, Paluses, and Cayuses to new regalia and music that they later took with them back to the northwest. For example, Albert Johnson and some of the other young men adopted bone hair-pipe breastplate ornaments from the Poncas. Joe Sherburne had recently introduced the ornaments, which were made from beef leg bones, at his Ponca trading post, and when the Oakland dancers saw their neighbors wearing them, Johnson and the others adapted the ornaments to their own use. Other intertribal celebrants adopted buckskin dance songs that were incorporated into the lexicon of Nimiipuu performance art. The Nimiipuu did not adopt the bone hair-pipe ornaments from some unidentified Plains tribe, as posited by anthropologist Herbert Spinden; they brought them home from the Indian Territory. Rob Minthorn and Johnson wore the bone hair-pipe breastplates with their *wéset* regalia after their return to the northwest, and the buckskin songs can still be heard in the 1911 Nez Perce Musical Archive recordings.[24]

There were also Christians in the prison camps, despite the insistence of Lapwai agent John B. Monteith and Presbyterian missionary Kate McBeth that no Presbyterian Nimiipuu had supported the resistance. Otis Halfmoon, whose Catholic relative was incarcerated at Fort Vancouver, agrees that Catholic and Presbyterian Nimiipuu fought and went into exile alongside their non-Christian relations, because family was more important than politics or theology. Even the *wéset* holy man George Washington admitted that he was a Catholic. Halfmoon also concurs that Christian detainees used a wall of silence to hide from federal officials in the prison camps.[25] They were afraid of the authorities and non-Native Christians, including the Reverend Samuel N. D. Martin and Andrew D. Mitchell, the army chaplain at Fort Leavenworth.[26] By the time the prisoners reached Oakland, they had expressed their individual religious preferences to Archie Lawyer, James Reuben, or Mark Williams. Some came forward to reveal their old Christian beliefs and affiliations, such as the elderly blind man Amos Bear, who testified at an Oakland church meeting that he had been baptized as a Presbyterian forty years earlier in Idaho.[27] Other Nimiipuu Christians repeated the Lord's Prayer and sang old hymns learned before the war, in English or Nimiputímt.[28]

By 1879, Williams, Lawyer, and Reuben had stepped up their efforts to establish a Presbyterian church at Oakland. As licentiate Presbyterian pastors, Williams and Lawyer could not administer communion, perform marriages, or accept new church members. Limited by illness, bureaucratic indifference, and abysmal conditions, they ministered primarily to the temporal needs of the prisoners at Quapaw. That changed at Oakland after several influential prisoners joined with Lawyer and the agent to ask local Presbyterians to help them establish a church on the reservation. Lawyer, Williams, and Reuben laid the foundations of faith for the Oakland Presbyterian Church.[29] Lawyer and his wife Dollie then went back to Idaho for his ordination, returning to Oakland in the summer of 1881.[30] When Lawyer was asked by the Nimiipuu parishioners to lead the Oakland church, his transfer was commissioned by the Presbyterian Board of Foreign Missions.[31]

The Oakland Presbyterian Church was organized October 21, 1880, during services conducted at the agency. Because there was no church building, the Reverend S. B. Fleming, D. P. Marshall, and James Reuben conducted the first official service in an unfurnished building. Runners were sent to farms and family camps, and on the day of the service, 125 Nimiipuu, Palus, and Cayuse celebrants filled the yard and building. Dozens of children sat on the floor in front of Marshall and the agency physician, Dr. Henry J. Minthorn. Women sat in orderly rows on the floor behind the children, surrounded by the seated men. Hymns were sung in Nimiputímt, and the congregation recited the Lord's Prayer. Fleming directed questions of faith to the congregation through Reuben, who acted as an interpreter for the service, and fifty-nine communicants came forward for baptism and acceptance into the church. Most of them asked the pastors and Minthorn to help them choose English names, which were acknowledged that day. Then the tearful communicants, ranging in age from fifteen to more than forty years old, accepted baptism and communion. Chief Joseph refused to participate in the first service, although he attended the next service in February. Joseph may have been uninterested in the event, or he may have been recovering from a month-long bout of malaria that he suffered in late August.[32]

Fleming and Marshall returned to Oakland in February and held services in the twenty-by-forty-foot building that was serving as a temporary school. The building was only partially furnished, but it was adequately heated by a wood-burning stove. Sunday services began at 10:30 in the morning, and this time Chief Joseph, clad in a suit and shirt, occupied a chair in the front row. He refused to join the church, however, despite the non-Native preacher's efforts to "bring him to the Cross."[33] Lieutenant Tom Hill stood just inside the doorway, and to his left were Húsus

Kute, Three Eagles, Jim Horn, Yellow Bull, and Yellow Bear. Yellow Bear and his wife and daughter were among the first converts.[34] Most of the new Christians and a few of the non-converts wore western-style clothing; others attended the services in their usual attire of leggings, shirts, and blankets or camp dresses. Children were outfitted like their parents, and many of the women carried babies laced in cradleboards. Gospel hymns and crying babies sounded in the little building, as thirty-eight more Nimiipuu were baptized and accepted into the church.[35]

Several communicants gave emotional testimonials before being baptized by Fleming. Lieutenant Hill stepped forward to confess his evil past and expressed the peace and joy he felt toward all men. He shared the hope that his sins were forgiven and that he was "saved through Jesus Christ."[36] Jim Nat was wracked with sobs before his testimony; other Nimiipuu also made emotional confessions of old sins and new faith. Húsus Kute rejected his untutored old faith, saying that the Gospel and the spirit of Jesus Christ had brought him from the "darkness to the light."[37] Public testimonials, "the place of weeping," and explicit confessions were common bridges between the old spirituality and the new religion.[38] Services were discontinued between 1:00 and 2:30 that afternoon for dinner, after which the congregation reconvened to choose three ruling elders. Jim Horn, Jim Nat, and Red Wolf were elected. Reuben was to serve as deacon. Elders were usually chosen for their family ties and respected positions in the community, and they often were former tribal leaders. Either they or the deacon conducted services in the pastor's absence, and they were responsible for their own moral behaviors and those of church members. Elders also determined who remained in the church and under what conditions former members should be allowed to return. Adultery, violating the Sabbath, imbibing alcohol, patronizing old faith healers, and gambling were among the behaviors that were moderated by the elders.[39]

The Oakland Presbyterian Church was formally constituted with 93 members. More than 20 people made public confessions, and the new Christians indulged in a moment of silent prayer before taking the Lord's Supper.[40] The congregation numbered 124 by August, and under Lawyer's guidance, the church included 150 Nimiipuu by September. By 1883, the Presbyterian General Assembly recorded 127 members of the Oakland church.[41] Many years later, Jim Horn remembered how sad the new Christians felt as the men and boys sacrificed their long hair to mark their new faith.[42]

Lawyer was back in full swing as pastor of the Oakland church by June 22, 1881, when he preached a dynamic sermon that was praised by Fleming. Shortly thereafter, he assumed full charge of the church, and the non-Native pastors discontinued their evangelizing efforts. Lawyer also delivered a short speech and said the Christian blessings at the Oakland Independence Day celebration that summer. Lawyer, Dollie, and their babies lived in a tent or with another family until the congregation proudly raised $45 to build them a home. The house was completed by carpenter Hank Nelson and two Nimiipuu assistants, who worked on it in their spare time, and the family moved in toward the end of August.

Although Lawyer was occupied with his ministerial duties, he also became an effective political activist during his second stay at Oakland. He encouraged non-Native Presbyterians to support the prisoners' return to the northwest, and he authored a letter that headlined a congressional memorial. Speaking as the voice of the Oakland congregation, Lawyer reminded Congress of the many deaths and the abrogation of the Bear Paw surrender agreement. He said that the members of his congregation had "expressed in our tears and sorrow" their legal rights and their desperate desire to go home. Lawyer addressed Kansas Baptist meetings and congregations and joined Reuben in fundraising and political activities at Methodist Episcopal and other Kansas churches. His services and sermons were popular and well attended, and Indian agents and other federal authorities praised him for his professional and political activities.[43] In late January 1884, Lawyer traveled to Washington, D.C., to lobby Congress and religious groups to accelerate the prisoners' return to their homelands. He went back to Oakland with the Interior Department's promise that a return to Idaho was in the immediate future.[44]

Deacon Reuben conducted services during Lawyer's absence.[45] The elders, the deacon, or Lawyer also conducted evening prayer meetings and two prayer meetings on Sundays. When the Nimiipuu, Paluses, and Cayuses entertained visiting Christians from other reservations, they often held joint prayer meetings. When visiting other reservations, the Oakland Christians exchanged prayer meetings with their friends and neighbors.[46] Christians and non-Christians often worshipped together at the Oakland services without rancor or difficulty.[47] Although Chief Joseph and Yellow Bull had not converted, they often attended Christian services at Oakland. Of the known Sun Dancers, eleven eventually returned to Lapwai with the Christians, and nine non-Christian Sun Dancers went to Colville, Washington Territory, with Chief Joseph.[48] Even Reuben accompanied the Sun Dancers without any apparent problems. The Reverend Archie Lawyer's granddaughter Mylie Lawyer recalls that Joseph participated in services conducted by Lawyer in the Indian Territory. Ms. Lawyer also remembers that Joseph and Archie lobbied members of the Kansas Presbytery to garner support for their return to the northwest.[49] Regardless of religious affiliation, all of the Oakland internees were interested in the Presbyterians' efforts to facilitate the captives' release from the Indian Territory. Neither the Oakland congregation nor Joseph wanted a church constructed at Oakland; they preferred to focus on their return to the northwest.[50]

The Lawyers took part in a variety of social events in the Indian Territory. Along with Mr. and Mrs. Húsus Kute, James Reuben, several Ponca chiefs, Indian agents, and about seventy other guests, they attended Dr. and Mrs. Minthorn's tenth anniversary party at the Ponca Agency. Dinner was served in the agent's house, and then everyone strolled around the lawn, visited with friends and acquaintances, and took part in the hilarity attendant to a tin wedding anniversary.[51] Dollie, or Delia, was Archie Lawyer's second wife, whom he had married in the Indian Territory after losing his first wife and infant son Willie in an accident on the Clearwater River in Idaho.[52] Dollie may have been related to Húsus Kute, because when she and Lawyer returned to Lapwai in July 1884, they took Mrs. Húsus Kute home with them. She was frail and suffering from tuberculosis, and they hoped that the cooler climate in Idaho would save her life.[53] Mylie Lawyer did not know whether Dollie was in fact related to Húsus Kute, but the families were certainly close friends, and taking Mrs. Húsus Kute home sounds like something that a man would have done for his mother-in-law.[54] Dollie suffered from malaria, and she and Archie buried at least three of their children at Oakland, where he performed the funerals.[55]

Archie Lawyer's return to Lapwai placed him in an awkward position with the Presbyterian missionaries Sue and Kate McBeth. As females, the sisters were not eligible for ordination, so it was difficult for them when their former pupil returned from the Indian Territory at the leading edge of his career. Lawyer enjoyed the power and support of the male-dominated Presbyterian hierarchy and of many Nimiipuu families. The McBeth sisters were condescending and controlling. They expected to pick up their relationship with Lawyer where it had left off in 1878, but their former student had moved beyond them. Kate McBeth accused Lawyer of heathen activities, regressive "Coyote medicine," and doctrinal arrogance, as she pointed out her preference for more malleable Nimiipuu ministers, naming her personal favorites. For his part, Lawyer exercised privileges in the male-dominated hierarchy of the Presbyterian church that were not extended to the women. In the face of complaints by the McBeth sisters, Lawyer declared himself, saying, "before God I know myself. I am alright and I am a Christian."[56] Kate McBeth did not approve of the man that Lawyer had become in the Indian Territory; the experience in the camps had changed him (and everyone else). Unfortunately, she was blind to Lawyer's growth and could not fathom his experiences. She detested the war and disapproved of Chief Joseph, and she rejected every expression of faith except her own type of Christianity. She ignored or resented Lawyer's responsibilities at Oakland and sidetracked his career away from Lapwai.

Within three months of Archie Lawyer's return to Idaho, he was assigned to evangelize at the Crow Mission, then sent to Umatilla, and on to Fort Spokane in Montana.

The young pastor had ministered to a dynamic, diverse group of Oakland Christians who helped to mold him as a man. Kate McBeth would never enjoy the responsibilities, authority, or opportunities that were extended to Lawyer. Neither would she experience the devastation at the Quapaw and Oakland prison camps. She resented Lawyer's inherent understanding of Nimiipuu culture, of the *wéset* faith, and of Christianity. Lawyer parted with Kate McBeth and the First Presbyterian Church at Lapwai in 1890 when he established the Second Presbyterian Church.[57] Not surprisingly, many of the prison camp survivors joined him at the new church. The split may have been inevitable, because only those who had experienced the prison camps could understand the importance of Christianity, the *wéset* faith, and the Sun Dances to their survival.

CHAPTER 11

INTERACTIONS AND LIFE IN THE INDIAN TERRITORY

Daily life at Oakland involved a complex variety of government and other relationships. Five Indian agents stationed at the Ponca Agency between June 1879 and May 1885 supervised the Oakland Subagency. William Whiting replaced Whiteman until June 1881, when Civil War veteran Thomas J. Jordan was appointed Ponca agent. Jordan remained in office until August 1882, when the Pawnee, Ponca, and Otoe agencies were combined, and Lewellyn Woodin then took his place at the consolidated agency.[1] Woodin was soon accused of mismanagement and fraud, although Commissioner Hiram Price cleared him of any wrongdoing, and the interpreter who levied the charges was vilified as a rumormonger. Woodin resigned from the Indian Bureau, however, and John W. Scott was appointed to replace him in January 1884.[2]

All of the Ponca agents and Bureau employees supported the federal "civilization" policies of education, Christian conversion, and agricultural development for the Oakland prisoners. Whiting, an advocate of American Indian education, sent the first Oakland children to the Carlisle Indian Industrial School in Pennsylvania, promoted the Oakland school, and was involved with the Ponca Indian Industrial School. He also recognized the importance of involving the community in the educational processes, however, and included Chief Joseph and other community members in special school events. Jordan did not change established education policies, and he supported advanced teacher's training for James Reuben.[3] Woodin promoted the enrollment of the children at Carlisle and then denied requests from parents to return their children to Oakland.[4] Scott supported sending Oakland schoolchildren to the new Chilocco Indian Industrial School and replaced Reuben with an English-speaking non-Native teacher at the Oakland school.[5]

All of the Indian agents supported Christian conversion for the prisoners, even though they differed in their attitudes toward non-Christian ceremonials. Whiting readily permitted the Nimiipuu, Cayuses, and Paluses to attend Sun Dances, but at the same time he considered conversion to Christianity to be a critical step in the "civilization" of the prisoners and invited local Presbyterians to help organize the Oakland church. Jordan also encouraged the Presbyterians, and he too did not stop the Nimiipuu, Paluses, and Cayuses from joining the Sun Dances.[6] He did, however, praise the Christians and favor them in his reports. He considered the Christian Nimiipuu to be "truly religious" people who "kept the Sabbath Day holy," and encouraged those who adopted white men's dress and "as far as possible, the habits of white men."[7] Woodin continued to issue permits for the Oakland residents to visit Sun Dances, and he did not try to recapture prisoners who ran away under cover of the ceremonials.[8] Scott, however, threatened military intervention to stop the Sun Dances; he was adamant that Christianity would be the only religion on the reservation. He also supported the Oakland Christians and demanded that they be included in negotiations leading to the prisoners' release.[9]

All of the agents promoted agriculture, livestock ranching, and hard work for American Indians. Whiting did not approve of idleness and considered working Indians and projects-in-progress as a mark of the prisoners' development.[10] American Indians' willingness to build and live in houses was an indicator of civilization for Jordan, who also viewed those who labored in their gardens and on farms as evidence of successful Indian Bureau policies. Like many other Indian agents who used their position to find employment for their families, Jordan hired his son as Oakland's farmer, then moved him to the Ponca Agency when there were complaints that the boy was no help at Oakland.[11] Although Woodin felt that building houses was suitable labor for the prisoners, he was somewhat sanguine about their agricultural production. He recorded exaggerated garden and crop productions that reduced the prisoners' weekly rations. Woodin expected the Nimiipuu, Paluses, and Cayuses to continue their rapid advances toward "civilization" and self-support.[12] He also categorized the prisoners according to their labors and religious preferences. Only the "better element among them," said Woodin, "is rapidly becoming civilized."[13] A proponent of leasing Indian Territory reservations to enterprising non-Natives, Scott also promoted gender-biased domestic training and what he saw as suitable behaviors for American Indian females.[14] Jordan was somewhat less biased toward women. Woodin was not especially supportive of the Oakland women, but he did recognize that the federal policy of withholding the hides of ration cattle would limit the women's economic activities.[15] Like a number of the other Indian agents, Whiting knew little about Nimiipuu culture or history. When the first heifers and bulls were issued to Oakland as breeding stock, he was amazed to discover that the captives were superb, "natural" cattlemen. Whiting failed to ask the captives how they knew so much about cattle; to him, they were simply better cattlemen than "any other Indians I ever saw."[16]

The Ponca agents and Oakland administrators were all similarly organized in their administrative practices, although Jordan and Scott experienced notable problems with the Oakland Indian police. They replaced key members of the force, despite evidence that other agency employees had erred in their judgments of the policemen.[17] The agents had the authority to rescind unfair terminations but ignored those responsibilities.[18] Jordan was at least concerned that Indian policemen should be reimbursed for using their own horses and wagons when hauling government freight.[19]

The Indian agents were an odd mix of humanists and imperialists who varied in the amount of compassionate aid they provided to the prisoners. Whiting searched the prison camps for people who had been lost from Idaho families, and then did not send them home. When he located Cayuse prisoners in the camps whose worried families had specifically asked him to search for them, he admitted their dependent positions but kept them in the Indian Territory.[20] Whiting did acknowledge the lack of decent food and petitioned the Indian Bureau for increased rations for the hardworking Nimiipuu, Palus, Cayuse, and Ponca men. He also forced a non-Native rancher to pay for the hay crop that his cattle had ruined on Crow Blanket's farm.[21] Jordan supported Reuben's plans to take a group of widows and orphans home to Idaho because it would save the government money. Families and friends at Lapwai would absorb the refugees, and the agency would no longer have to feed them. Woodin also encouraged the return of the widows and orphans to the northwest, although he blamed the victims for their poverty and intra-group neglect. At least he expected the Indian Bureau to pay for their trip home.[22] To his credit, Jordan tried to suppress cattle rustling at Oakland and went out of his way to facilitate equitable judicial processes.[23]

Most of the agents were more enduring than blatantly xenophobic, although none of them took innovative action to improve life in the prison camps. They relied on civilians, religious groups, the captives themselves, and other supporters to lobby for the prisoners' release. The agents often recorded staggering death tolls, diseases, and other troubles in the camps while distancing themselves from the problems. Woodin remarked that while malaria was killing so many Oakland prisoners and his imported horses, he was taking quinine "almost as regularly as I take my meals"; the prisoners, however, never had enough of the medication.[24] The agents urged federal attention to certain problems and often couched their requests in popular terms, such as the notion of the Vanishing American. "They will soon be extinct," Jordan warned, "if something isn't done."[25] Woodin echoed the sentiment: "Their fate is inevitable; they are doomed and must become extinct like all Indians."[26]

Indian Bureau salaries were low, and budget restrictions, personal preferences, and presidential choices all contributed to the turnover in federal employees. Agency employees were subject to few hiring guidelines and rarely met more than minimal experiential requirements. Dr. Henry J. Minthorn, who was recruited from Arkansas City to be the Ponca Agency physician in 1879, was an anomaly in the Indian medical service. A graduate of two reputable universities, he was more highly educated than most other Indian Bureau physicians. Minthorn moved to the Ponca Agency in November 1879. He spent two days a week at Oakland until the Indian Bureau transferred him there full-time.[27] Minthorn was initially assigned as both the Oakland farmer and the agency physician, but his medical caseload eventually excluded his other duties. By May 1880, a former commissary clerk at the Ponca Agency had been promoted to the post of Oakland superintendent, and Minthorn was able to devote his time to health care. An active proponent of full-service medical care, he was popular with the Nimiipuu, Paluses, and Cayuses. He was also well connected to mainline America; he was Herbert Hoover's uncle and foster father. Like many other prominent Americans, Minthorn used the Indian Bureau to build a second career after his Civil War service.[28]

Dr. Dolphus Dunn was assigned to Oakland as the physician and superintendent after Minthorn, but within months of his arrival, Chief Joseph and the other prisoners demanded that another physician be assigned to the agency, insisting that Dunn was doing them no good in either of his intended capacities. Although the captives had no official input into federal hiring decisions, they asserted themselves whenever possible. Physicians were assigned multiple duty at small agencies as a cost-cutting measure by the Indian Bureau. Agency physicians were paid less than $1,200 a year, but their salaries drained agency resources. In response to the complaints, Dunn was transferred to the Pawnee

Agency, and Dr. James S. Woodward was transferred to Oakland. Agent Woodin did not like Woodward and moved him to Oakland so that he would see less of him. Dr. Woodward did not get along with the Oakland policemen and fired Lieutenant Thomas Peters. Several of the Christian policemen insisted that Peters had been fired unfairly, and they petitioned the secretary of the interior for Woodward's removal, insisting that he had neglected his duties. Almost overwhelmed with administrative work, Woodward may indeed have abandoned his medical duties, or he may have stumbled into a community dispute that he failed to investigate before making an ill-advised decision.[29] Surprisingly, once the doctor was out of Woodin's immediate presence at Oakland, the agent reported that the young physician was doing an excellent job.[30] Within the year, however, Agent Scott assigned Woodward to cover three agencies: Oakland, Ponca, and Otoe.[31] In the meantime, agency carpenter Hank Nelson was appointed Oakland superintendent.

Nelson was an experienced Indian Bureau hand who had worked at the Wichita and Ponca agencies before moving to Oakland. Well known in Arkansas City and Cowley County, he and his wife were familiar with most of the Indian agents in the western Indian Territory. Nelson was also acquainted with many of the Oakland prisoners, to whom he taught carpentry and the building trades in addition to his other duties. Nelson was a sociable man who seemed to enjoy the company of the Nimiipuu, Palus, and Cayuse prisoners. He was also a tough individual who had survived some hair-raising accidents. Thrown from a speeding wagon as he tried to stop a runaway team at the Wichita Agency, Nelson walked around with his arm in a sling for a while. After he transferred to the Ponca Agency, he was shot during a hunting accident. Although his injuries were serious, Nelson survived the accident, and clerk John Gooch eventually recovered from nearly killing his friend.[32]

Mrs. Nelson was one of the reasons that Hank Nelson was given a full-time job at Oakland. The agent and the prisoners wanted her to remain at the agency. An early Kansas settler, Mrs.

Nelson volunteered hundreds of hours helping the women make patterns and sew school clothing, and she also lent a hand when they were learning to bake with wood-burning stoves. She taught the women the frontier arts of cabin housekeeping, helped them find and arrange new furnishings, and provided them with a much-needed support system. After she was hired as the school matron and the Oakland field matron, she maintained her rigorous schedule for a salary that rarely exceeded $300 a year.[33] One of a small group of women who paved the way for the Indian Health Service nurse corps, Mrs. Nelson provided indispensable services to the destitute women, even though her duties were never clearly defined. She seemed to be the perfect field matron: middle-aged, wise, loving, and willing to work like an ox. She was also a pioneer of the Motherhood in America movement, which considered women morally, mentally, and physically suited to raise and train children as they advanced a love of humanity and home economics. Indian Bureau field matrons represented the feminine side of the "civilization" of the American Indian: women helping women were seen as agents of change. Regardless of their ethnicity, field matrons were expected to help American Indian women learn to "shoulder the white woman's burden." They were not meant to serve as social workers or nurses, although women such as Mrs. Nelson went out of their way to make a difference in the lives of other women.[34]

Dr. Woodward left Oakland in the spring of 1884, apparently worn out from trying to serve three agencies. He was replaced by the middle-aged and discontented Dr. W. H. Rouse, who was there only a few months before he asked the commissioner of Indian affairs to transfer him to a wealthier agency. Furious that Rouse had gone over his head, Agent Scott would not approve his request. Rouse argued that he was an experienced physician who deserved either a better salary or a transfer to the more affluent Indian school system. He also understood that the prisoners would be leaving the Indian Territory, and he was seeking a secure position in a better climate. Rouse apparently neglected his duties while he was at Oakland, and according to Lieutenant

Tom Hill, he was not popular. Hill was upset that Rouse would not support his requests to continue his education in Oregon. Rouse's transfer was not forthcoming, and he resigned from Oakland the next spring, leaving the camps without a physician. The Indian Bureau hurriedly reassigned a physician from the Otoe Agency, although by then the prisoners were only a month away from leaving.[35]

The captives' lives at Oakland involved regular interaction with federal employees, their families, and trader Joe Sherburne. Three months after meeting Chief Joseph and the wagon train crossing the Chikaskia River, Sherburne brought his bride to the agency. The couple lived in an apartment at the end of the trading post and enjoyed an active social life while maintaining good relationships with the Nimiipuu, Paluses, and Cayuses. They sponsored special events and parties for American Indian children at the agencies served by their trading post.[36] Sherburne's memories of Joseph, Sup-poon-mas, and the other prisoners remained vivid fifty years later as he responded to historian Lucullus McWhorter's inquiries about the Indian Territory. Sherburne remembered Joseph and other Nimiipuu, and when McWhorter asked him about his photographs of Joseph and Sup-poon-mas and for more information about the prisoners, Sherburne recalled,

> I think, he [Chief Joseph] was a very even dispositioned man. Nothing surly about him, neither was he overly the other way, but I think he was a fine man in every other way. In disposition, physique, and every way. They [the photographs] were taken at a little town at that time, Arkansas City . . . this is a perfect picture of Chief Joseph as I knew him. They were very dear people to me . . . and I remember Yellow Bull very well, and Yellow Bear, and Charley Joe [Op-has], Charley Moses, and Tom Hill. I could have had a record of all you would like to know. But in those days we had no idea of how much we would want anything of this kind. So we said nothing only the little we carried in our minds. I am so interested in anything of Joseph and his people. They were very dear people to me and your

letter brings back so much of interest for it makes me live over some of the time in those days.[37]

Unlike the traders at Quapaw, Sherburne provided an honest marketplace for the Oakland residents. As the exiles learned to trust him, the women sold or traded some of their crafts at his trading post. They also purchased necessities there, paying for them with the dwindling supply of precious gold dust they had carried with them in tiny pouches since the war. When the gold ran out, they established credit accounts at the trading post. Nevertheless, after so many federal lies and their dealings with dishonest merchants at Quapaw, the prisoners insisted that Sherburne keep no written records of their transactions. Relying on his honesty and their memories, they always paid their accounts in full and on time.[38] The Nimiipuu, Paluses, and Cayuses were intimately involved in the daily life of the trading post and the agency. They went in and out of the agency office, picked up supplies at the commissary, and brought repair jobs to the blacksmith and carpenter. They also called on the agency doctor, attended social events, and became acquainted with the children of the agency staff. Chief Joseph, Three Eagles, Red Wolf, Jim Horn, Yellow Bull, Red Elk, Lieutenant Hill, and John Hill all heard young Katie Whiting play the organ at the Ponca Indian Industrial School dedication. Seven months later, as a grieving community dealt with the teenager's terminal illness, reservation residents called at the family home to express their sorrow for the dying girl.[39]

With the exception of the Indian agents, most of the federal employees and Indian traders at Ponca and Oakland had known each other before joining the Indian Bureau. Joe Sherburne, Cyrus M. Scott, Rube Houghton, James M. Haworth, and Indian inspector William J. Pollock formed extensive business ties in the Indian Territory and at Arkansas City or Winfield, Kansas. Scott introduced Sherburne to the Cheyennes, Arapahos, Caddos, Kechi, Wacos, Delawares, Kiowas, Comanches, and Wichitas during a trip through the Indian Territory in January 1877.[40] They scouted out information about the Indian agencies, and Sherburne evaluated opportunities for Indian agency business.[41] Scott and Sherburne also liked Haworth, a Civil War veteran who became the new agent at the Kiowa, Comanche, and Wichita Agency and served on the influential Sioux Commission in 1878. Haworth was subsequently appointed as an Indian Bureau inspector, and in June 1879 he managed the relocation of the Nimiipuu, Paluses, and Cayuses to the Ponca Agency. He also replaced Hiram Jones as the agent at Quapaw and later managed the Sac and Fox Agency in the Indian Territory. He was a member of the federal commission that investigated Big Snake's murder, and he was the superintendent of Indian schools when the first Oakland children were recruited for the Chilocco Indian Industrial School.[42]

Sherburne and Houghton had traded and sold common interests in drugstores and other ventures in Arkansas City before Sherburne began buying hides on American Indian reservations. The men also shared an interest in cattle ranching on the reservations; Sherburne leased the Ponca reservation, and Houghton leased the Oakland reservation. Houghton moved his family to their ranch on the Oakland lease, but three months after the Nimiipuu, Paluses, and Cayuses returned to the northwest, the Houghtons moved back to Arkansas City.[43] Houghton retained his interests in the Oakland leasehold, however, and the year after the refugees went back to the northwest, he shipped twenty-three carloads of cattle from Oakland to St. Louis.[44]

Business declined at the Ponca Agency after the Nimiipuu, Paluses, and Cayuses left the Indian Territory, and President Grover Cleveland's new Democratic administration took away the trading licenses that were held by Republicans. The president's administrators sold traders' permits, cheated licensed traders out of their purchase fees, and permitted theft and graft at Indian agencies. When it came time for Sherburne to renew his license, he thought that he was protected from Cleveland's henchmen. The Poncas submitted a petition to the Bureau asking that Sherburne be allowed to remain as the agency trader, but it and Sherburne's renewal application were both ignored. Commissioner John D. C. Atkins, a former Confederate army general, awarded the trading licenses to his southern friends and former Confederate sympathizers.[45] When Sherburne's license expired, the Ponca trading permit was transferred to a Missouri man, whom the Poncas did not like. Sherburne was given ninety days to remove his property from the agency; he moved his family back to Arkansas City on March 6, 1886. Two weeks later, he sawed his house into quarters, loaded the sections onto heavy-duty hayracks, and moved it across the prairie to Arkansas City.[46]

Sherburne paid the $1,700 Ponca grass lease and then gathered his cattle off the lease at the end of the term. The next spring, he sold the lease and forty miles of walnut post and barbed-wire fences and equipment to George Miller, founder of the 101 Ranch.[47] The Senate Committee on Indian Affairs investigated the loss of traders' licenses at the Sac and Fox, Kaw, Pawnee, Cheyenne and Arapaho, Ponca, and Oakland agencies, but the damage had been done. Although Sherburne did not face complete financial ruin, he lost his accounts receivable, more than 5,000 bushels of corn, his stock, and the trading post.[48] Sherburne remained in Arkansas City, where he continued to conduct limited trading operations and supplied contract beef to Indian agencies. In 1895, he moved his family to Montana, where he built another successful Indian trading business.[49]

Sherburne was one of only a few people from the Indian Territory whom any of the prisoners looked up after their return to the northwest. When Tom Hill called on Sherburne at his home in Browning, Montana, forty years later, the men did not recognize each other. Sherburne signed to Hill, and Hill told him in English who he was, and the old acquaintances then had a good visit. A few years later, Sherburne was grateful they had met again before Hill's death.[50]

One federal employee who was roundly disliked by the prisoners was interpreter Ad Chapman. Interpreters were essential to Native nations; they translated agreements and conversations, served as intermediaries, and shared the complexities of life on the reservation. However, the Nimiipuu detested Chapman, who had served as an army scout and volunteer militiaman against them in the war and was then hired as their interpreter and agency farmer. Chapman interfered with the prisoners' lives, argued with the Indian agents, and ingratiated himself with federal bureaucrats. He was a violent man who used his position to brutalize and intimidate the prisoners, and he represented the dominant society, which brought prewar animosity and dissension into the prison camp. The Nimiipuu viewed him as a braggart, thief, and murderer who had stolen their cattle, land, and property, and who had killed Coyote with Flints and Wolf Head.[51] Thomas Beal, Yellow Wolf, and Arthur Simon also identified Chapman as a horse thief.[52] And in one violent episode, Chapman tried to kill two Nimiipuu children who had raided his watermelon patch. He beat the boys with a whip, tied their hands behind their backs, bound their feet, and tossed them into a corral with untamed horses. He then whipped and lashed the animals, trying to make them trample the boys as they leapt over them.[53]

Chapman was also a bigamist and sexual predator who was avoided by the Nimiipuu, Palus, and Cayuse women in the Indian Territory. He had been married to a Umatilla woman, with whom he fathered five children, and the Nimiipuu had tolerated his presence in Idaho because of the family.[54] Sometime before the war, Chapman gave his wife a few ponies and sent her and several of their children back to the Umatilla reservation.[55] He fathered a stillborn child with a young Blackfoot woman named Maggie, whose mother lived near Kamiah, Idaho.[56] He then continued his sexual predations in the Indian Territory, where he seduced and impregnated a young Modoc girl. When the prisoners finally drove him away, he left the girl and their child to be cared for by the Modocs. Chapman eventually married a white woman and called himself "Colonel" Chapman, a self-aggrandizing title that had not been awarded to him by the volunteer militia or the Indian Bureau.[57]

Chapman's military service during the war and his reprehensible conduct should have been enough to disqualify him from federal employment, but General Oliver O. Howard and the other authorities ignored his checkered past because he spoke Nimiputímt and worked to curry their favor. Supported by Alfred B. Meacham and some of the other officials, Chapman was promoted as a man of good heart, a straight shooter, and a reliable friend to the prisoners. Meacham even insisted to Chief Joseph that Chapman was his friend, then sent Chapman to deliver a message designed to humiliate Joseph and intimidate the prisoners. Through Chapman, Meacham told Joseph that his *wéset* faith and religious leaders had misled him, and that he must give up all hope of going home. Meacham also recommended Chapman as the right man to force the prisoners into federal compliance.[58]

Chapman lied about his authority and assumed unofficial power over the prisoners. After hanging Yellow Bear by his thumbs for supposedly drinking alcohol, he bragged that he ruled the Nimiipuu with an iron fist. He claimed that another man's badly scarred face was the result of a beating or knife wound that he had inflicted before the war.[59] In a self-serving scheme, Chapman bilked the refugees out of their cash with false promises to take them home to the northwest. When he was found out by Agent Hiram Jones, he took Chief Joseph, Yellow Bull, Es-pow-yes, and four other men to a notary public in Seneca, Missouri, to dictate an exculpatory letter to Commissioner Hiram Price. Chapman tried to portray himself as a kindly, generous person who had the prisoners' best interests at heart. He insisted that he should not have to pay back the money because the prisoners had given it to him in return for his help.[60] As usual, Chapman involved no second interpreter to clarify the document, and the notary public only spoke English.

Chapman was officially hired as the agency interpreter and was subsequently fired and rehired as the agency farmer. He handed out prescribed medicines from time to time and served as the wagon master on the trip to Ponca, although it was Joseph that the Nimiipuu, Paluses, and Cayuses looked to for leadership and guidance. In a letter to the *Leavenworth Times,*

Chapman emphasized the terrible conditions the prisoners were living in and his heroic efforts to relieve their suffering. He was worried about the poverty in the camp and gave himself credit for purchasing medicines and milk. He capitalized on remarks supposedly made by Joseph and repeated a conversation with the Modoc leader Steamboat Charley. After dropping the names of the two famous American Indians, he revealed his true motive for writing the letter. "My duties are acting agent, hospital steward, Commissary Sergeant, Interpreter, and Superintendent of Farming," he wrote, "and I am looking for an appointment as agent of a life insurance company." Chapman was hoping to find a better job.[61] Yellow Bull hated Chapman, and when the two of them were photographed together along with Joseph during their trip to Washington, D.C., in 1879, Yellow Bull was seen carefully distancing himself from Chapman.

Chapman's self-serving letter was reprinted in the *New York Times* on September 8, and a few days later, ten young men who had recently been deported to the Indian Territory drove him away from the Oakland reservation. Still angry over the war and Chapman's involvement in it, the men chased him across the Salt Fork River and threatened to kill him, after supposedly stealing his horses and those belonging to Dean's ranch. The rancher and Chapman escaped and rode into the Ponca Agency, then on into Arkansas City. When they arrived there and Chapman relayed the news of the "uprising," Agent Scott, Lieutenant Cushman, and eight troopers hurried out to Oakland. Everything was calm on the reservation, and Dean was not missing any horses. Chapman remained out of sight in Arkansas City, complaining that he would never return to Oakland. However, he was back at the agency within three weeks. The situation boiled over again, and this time Chapman left for good, claiming that he had overheard the prisoners plotting to kill him. When Chief Joseph and the other leaders met with Chapman and Agent Whiteman in the office where Big Snake had been murdered, they denied the charges. When Reuben called Chapman a liar, Chapman threatened that Reuben would be the next dead Indian in the room, and Reuben kept quiet. Before the meeting, Joseph had guaranteed the agent that even though the prisoners detested Chapman, they would not kill him.[62]

In the face of the challenges and disruptions at Oakland, Joseph, Tom Hill, and the other survivors took control of their lives and their situations whenever possible. They established friendly relationships with people who treated them fairly, and took an active part in managing personnel or situations that were detrimental to their welfare. Their successful interactions were not, however, intended to keep them in the Indian Territory. In spite of everything, the prisoners remained focused on their return to the northwest.

CHAPTER 12

Leaving the Indian Territory

Although the captives were determined to return to the northwest, they did not want to be forgotten in the Indian Territory. Accordingly, Friday, October 22, 1880, was a special day when the detainees left proof of their existence in the foundation of the Ponca Indian Industrial School. More than two hundred Nimiipuu, Paluses, and Cayuses arrived at the Ponca Agency just after sunrise to join about one hundred Poncas, agency employees, and other guests for a daylong celebration. Clad in western-style clothing or multihued blankets and face paint, the Oakland men were complemented by women wrapped in brightly colored shawls and headscarves. Ponca horsemen swept into the schoolyard in a display of equine athleticism, while Agent William Whiting conducted tours of the new school's foundation. By eleven o'clock, the participants were arranged in front of the speaker's platform, where the chiefs and presenters were seated, and Joseph Esaw and James Reuben stood ready to translate. An Indian pipe was smoked, and the day unfolded with Christian prayers, speeches, and hymns.[1]

A large tin time capsule was brought out, into which the Nimiipuu and Poncas placed sacred or personal artifacts. Jim

Horn and Jay Gould donated war ornaments, including Horn's feather battle ornament and Gould's war bonnet horns. Feathers around the Neck and Alexander Waters (E-yal-lo-ka-win) contributed bear-claw necklaces. Three Eagles, Samuel Fleming, and Chief Joseph offered finger rings, and At-tas-poo, Red Elk, Daniel Jefferson, and John Hill added necklaces or bracelets. Red Wolf included a string of beads, and White Owl donated a shell earring. The Oakland women bequeathed an eagle feather, elk's teeth, and artifacts indicative of their arts and crafts, and Reuben added a letter and a census to the collection. Reuben's letter detailed the Nez Perce treaties, the resistance, and the mistreatment of the nontreaty bands in the Indian Territory. In a comment that reflects his maturation, he also recognized that the deportations and suffering in the Indian Territory were a deadly mistake, as he warned: "But take it in the right light—Nez Perce have been wrongly treated by the Government and it cannot be denied, not Nez Perce only but all other Indian Nations in America."[2]

After the time capsule was plastered into the cornerstone, the Oakland delegation sang a hymn, and Reuben and Lieutenant Tom Hill spoke. Reuben preached of Christian conversion and asked everyone to understand the captives' plight. Hill testified to his boyhood and the events that had sent him to the Indian Territory. Hill, who had recently joined the Presbyterian church, also honored his new Christian friends. The ceremonies ended as the Nimiipuu sang another hymn, and a non-Native minister offered the benediction.[3]

When the school was torn down in 1934 and the time capsule was reopened, the items associated with warfare and males were missing. There had been a great deal of interest in the time capsule when it was created, and an interested buyer had offered $500 for the artifacts within days of the dedication. The warriors' artifacts were already collector's items, and even the elk's teeth were worth about $80 apiece. The time capsule may have been looted before the walls were built, because the brickwork was not finished until December 1881. It may also have happened during demolition of the school in 1934. Whenever it occurred, everything but the women's artifacts and the letter and census were stolen.

The items placed in the time capsule conveyed a sense of history that was reinforced two years later when the exiles dictated the list of warriors and women to Reuben and authorized it for future study. As stated at the end of that document, which is dated June 1, 1882, "The names and the number killed by the soldiers in different battles and the numbers of men engaged at Clearwater battle are given by Chief Joseph and some of his men to the undersigned for future use."[4]

Leaving the Indian Territory was never far from the thoughts of the captives as they explored diverse avenues of release. When Skou-cum Joe asked to be returned to the Crow nation in 1878, the decision was deferred to the War Department. Their investigation determined that Skou-cum-Joe was a renegade from Chief Lawyer's band who had allegedly murdered two of his own people. Investigators also found out that Joe was not an adopted Crow and that he had not served as a sworn army scout. His relocation to the Indian Territory had been an excuse to escape confinement at Fort Custer in Montana. In addition, Chief Old Crow, Skou-cum-Joe's Crow wife, and her relatives did not want Skou-cum-Joe returned to the Crow nation. General Nelson Miles was not overly concerned that the troublemaker continued to be warehoused in the Indian Territory, where he was feared by the other prisoners.[5]

In March 1881, a group of Palus and Cayuse prisoners petitioned the Indian Bureau for their release. The group included Little Man Chief and his wife and child, Cayuse, Dick Johnson and his wife and daughter, Sur-lee-i-haikt, and Sa-caw-ta-she and her daughter. Little Man Chief and his wife were in good health, but Cayuse was alone and unhappy. Johnson and his wife and child were well, but Sur-lee-i-haikt worried constantly about his wife in the northwest. The blind widow of a Nimiipuu warrior, Sa-caw-ta-she was dependent on her teenage daughter and asked to be allowed to go to the Umatilla reservation to join their relatives. Despite General Oliver O. Howard's and Secretary of the Interior Carl Schurz's earlier suggestion that Little Man Chief be returned to the Umatilla Agency, Agent Whiting refused to release the prisoners because of their participation in the resistance. Howard would not set a date for their return, even though he recommended on January 30, 1879, that Little Man Chief be released. The prisoners understood that their return depended on their good behavior and would be considered after things settled down in Idaho. All of these prisoners remained in the Indian Territory until May 1885.[6]

A few of the prisoners hoped that their involvement on the side of the United States or noninvolvement during the war would help with their release. Several months later, a group of citizens from Mt. Idaho lobbied the Indian Bureau for Yellow Bear's release. The group felt that Yellow Bear did not deserve to be imprisoned because he had warned them that war was coming in 1877. Indian Bureau officials considered the matter but kept Yellow Bear and his family in the Indian Territory.[7] Responding to several official inquiries, Commissioner Hiram Price found Jim Horn in the prison camps during January 1882. In spite of his service to the United States in Spotted Eagle's company of army scouts during the Washington-Oregon war of 1855–56, Horn was not released.[8] The teenager John Pinkham (E Lous See La Kat Tset) had been arrested with a group of buffalo hunters and deported to the Indian Territory, where he was located by the Lapwai agent. Agent John B. Monteith arranged for Pinkham's release to Lapwai.[9]

Survival in the Indian Territory was predicated on the prisoners' belief that somehow they would return to the northwest. They paid close attention to every effort to gain their release. However, some of the exiles refused to wait. A group led by John Fur Cap escaped from Oakland under cover of the Sun Dances. Fur Cap, who had been traveling with the Sun Dancers for two years, ran away in August 1882 along with Oto-kea (Pete), Albert Joe (Shaw-we-haa), two women, and one child. Oakland Sun Dancers on their way to the August ceremonials met the fugitives driving a team of Indian horses. Soon thereafter, the escapees abandoned the wagon and made their way home to Idaho with the horses. Albert Joe and his wife had recently separated, and she and their children remained at Oakland. The runaways' absence caused no serious problems, and the agent did not report them missing until the first week of October.[10]

On May 30, 1881, Inspector William J. Pollock submitted requests from Chief Joseph, Yellow Bear, and Lieutenant Hill to the secretary of the interior asking that they be allowed to visit Washington, D.C. The situation at Oakland was terrible, and they wanted to talk to the president. There were no wells at Oakland, and the old people and children were dying. They did not want to remain in the Indian Territory. "Everything here seems temporary," worried Hill. Yellow Bear warned, "Our hearts are broken, it seems we must desist."[11] Living on land that would never belong to them, the hostages were desperate to go home. "Without our land, we are nothing," said Hill.[12] Speaking through the interpreter, Joseph begged for mercy: "I ask nothing for myself, I am poor and feeble. Before long I will sink into this strange country until I die. I have two wishes; to return to my country, and the other to die."[13]

Three months later, the movement to repatriate some of the widows and orphans to Lapwai was gaining momentum. More than one hundred war widows and orphans were living in the camps, and federal officials thought they would receive better care at Lapwai.[14] Dispersal of the widows and orphans dominated federal thinking at the time, and Dr. Henry J. Minthorn came up with a plan for the prisoners' return to the northwest. Widows and orphans could leave as soon as possible, while participants in the war who had not killed or injured civilians could leave in two years if they were self-supporting and paid their way. The rest of the prisoners would remain in the Indian Territory for ten years, until they were self-supporting and could pay their way home. Minthorn's plan was not implemented. Archie Lawyer and James Reuben also argued for the prisoners' release and begged local churches and civic organizations for help.[15]

Reuben's plans to take several of his relatives and friends back to Idaho moved forward when he returned to Idaho in June 1880 to lobby General Howard and influential Presbyterians for their support.[16] Returning to the Indian Territory, Reuben complained to the commissioner of Indian affairs that Agent Lewellyn Woodin was neglecting the widows and orphans. Furious at Reuben's interference, Woodin insisted that the widows and orphans were being treated no worse than anyone else. He blamed the widows for their own troubles, insisting that the other prisoners refused to care for them and that they would not care for themselves. Woodin also admitted that he had not issued wagons, horses, or household items to the destitute widows, who were still living in ramshackle tepees. Instead, he gave the items to men such as Three Eagles, whom he considered to be more productive and deserving of support.[17]

On October 16, 1882, the Lapwai Presbyterians voted to accept thirty-one of the prisoners into the community if Reuben would bring them there. Woodin supported the release, and the next day Reuben told the exiles that they were going home.[18] Three Eagles, Jim Nat, and Amelia Young would go with the group, leaving dependents in the Indian Territory who eventually chose exile with Chief Joseph at Colville in 1885. Reuben's group of migrants consisted of his friends and relatives and several of the poorest widows and orphans.[19] At least seventeen widows and their dependents remained in the prison camps, where they were partially supported by their extended families. Women sold arts and crafts to help pay for their travel, and Reuben's appeals for donations in Kansas were generously supported after the secretary of the interior granted permission for the return.[20]

On May 27, 1883, Reuben closed the school at Oakland and prepared to board the Atchison, Topeka, and Santa Fe train at Arkansas City. He purchased tickets to Kelton, Utah, and arranged for men and saddle horses from Lapwai to meet them there. Then he laid out provisions, trunks, and miscellaneous items before the group boarded the train on May 31. The refugees spent the next six days on the train, changing from the Atchison, Topeka, and

Santa Fe to the Denver and Rio Grande, and finally to the Central Pacific Railroad. They stopped at Garden City, Kansas, went on to Coleridge, Kansas, and breakfasted June 2 in the bustling little town of Pueblo, Colorado. Following coffee and dinner at Canon City, Colorado, the train traveled on through Ogden and then on to Kelton. The travelers breakfasted in several restaurants along the way, although the women prepared their other meals, consisting of hardtack and beans, bacon or beef, and coffee. When they arrived at Kelton on June 5, Reuben received news of their first delay. The horses coming from Lapwai were supposedly too exhausted to continue, and more were being sent in their place.[21] In reality, non-Native settlers had prevented the men and horses from leaving Lapwai. When told of the delay, Reuben leased wagons, teams, and drivers and waited for a detachment of troopers to protect the party between Kelton and Lapwai. The Interior Department and the army arranged the escort, monitoring their progress by telegraph.[22]

The refugees restocked their provisions and necessities, and the little cavalcade left for Boise, Idaho, on June 6. They camped at Emigrant Station, Utah, then crossed the Raft River and proceeded to Rock Springs. From there, they continued north to Alkali Springs and ferried the river at Lower Crossing on June 15. After crossing the Rattlesnake Mountains, the group finally reached Boise on June 19. Teamsters and wagons were sent back to Kelton, while the travelers rested at Boise and the ladies added butter, potatoes, and dried fruits to their camp supplies. Reuben purchased saddles, bridles, and other equipment, and they were on the trail again July 5 on the Lapwai horses. The procession ferried across the Payette River and reached High Valley, Idaho, on July 7, thirty-seven days after leaving Arkansas City. The refugees were exhausted, especially the youngsters. None of the Oakland children were healthy, and everyone was infected with malaria.[23]

By July 7, groups of eager Nimiipuu were waiting at the Lapwai Agency and near the Presbyterian church as a welcoming committee rode out to meet the migrants at Thunder Hill. Reuben had rehearsed a coming-home ceremony, so the travelers did not go back to Lapwai with the committee. Reuben changed into a fresh suit, strapped on a cartridge belt and pistol, and groomed his horse before they reached Lapwai. Following Reuben, the little parade finally approached the agency, where they remained seated on their horses, surrounded by friends and family. Reuben delivered his welcoming speech from the saddle, guiding his horse's head toward his audience. He spoke of the grief and hardship in the prison camps, of the rigors of the trip home, and of the many graves in the Indian Territory. Agent Monteith addressed the group, and then Reuben dismounted and extended his right arm to the crowd. The exiles did the same as hundreds of people wept and mourned for those who had not returned, then shared the joy of coming home. Reuben was repaid for his expenses out of the next Indian Appropriation Bill.[24]

Two weeks later, Lapwai agent Charles Monteith and Reuben took nine of the Oakland children to the Forest Grove Indian and Industrial Training School in Oregon.[25] Levi, Lucy, and Julia Jonas, Rosa Price (Mattie Rosie, Tuck-te-we-ta-la-sha), Ellen Price, Jeanette Rachel, Mary Wilson (Kool-luts-tah), and Delia Parnell (Tuk-tu-lats) were enrolled at the school on July 21, 1883. As agreed, six of the students remained at Forest Grove for thirty-six months. Ellen died sometime during the term, and Wilson died at Forest Grove in 1887 of tuberculosis.[26] Levi graduated in three years, served as Sunday school superintendent of the Kamiah First Presbyterian Church, and helped to assemble a songbook published in the Nimiputimít language.[27] Mattie Rosie preserved Reuben's records, which were rescued many years later from an attic in Modesto, California.[28]

Interested in every effort to support their release, the Nimiipuu, Paluses, and Cayuses back at Oakland watched as Kansas Presbyterians prepared a memorandum to Congress in the fall of 1881.[29] In response to a letter from the Oakland Presbyterian Church and the Reverend Archie Lawyer, a Kansas synod commission had investigated the Nimiipuu's detention and found that they were being "wrongfully held and dishonestly treated."[30]

The Presbyterians also held that the federal government was bound to support the Bear Paw surrender agreement and urged that the survivors be returned to Idaho.[31] By April 1882, the memorandum had been submitted to the president and was enjoying wide support throughout Cowley County, Kansas.[32] When Yellow Bull addressed the Independence Day celebration in Arkansas City that summer, he repeated the federal inequities and the captives' subsequent poor treatment to a receptive audience. Survivors of the prison camps protested their losses and mistreatment for the next three decades.[33]

General Miles tried to convince President James Garfield to honor the surrender agreement, but Garfield's assassination in the fall of 1881 ended that hope. Garfield's widow, however, supported the efforts to release the prisoners.[34] In February 1885, a Nimiipuu student attending the Carlisle Indian Industrial School published an eloquent essay addressing the release. Cautiously countering federal edicts, Luke Phillips blamed the war on non-Native intrusions onto the Idaho reservation. He identified specific incidents of criminal trespass and theft and asked the Bureau to release the prisoners from the abysmal conditions in the Indian Territory. "Let them go home, and say once again, 'My Idaho,'" begged the cadet.[35]

In April 1883, the Nimiipuu, Paluses, and Cayuses also engaged the services of attorney William J. Pollock to advance their release. Pollock, who usually dealt fairly with the prisoners, recommended that they accept title to the Oakland reservation. The property was increasing in value, he said, and would someday provide them with a substantial asset. A general council of Nimiipuu, Paluses, and Cayuses held at Oakland rejected Pollock's suggestion. The prisoners had no desire to remain in the Indian Territory, and nothing would change their minds. Pollock mentioned that some of the men faced criminal trials in Idaho, but the prisoners preferred to go home and face the courts if necessary. They would accept the outcome, whether punishment or acquittal, because they preferred to live freely under a legal system that they hoped would treat them fairly. Pollock appealed their decision to Commissioner Price, saying that he would make the arrangements and help to defray the costs of sending them home if they would be allowed to leave then.[36]

As efforts to relocate the prisoners increased among East Coast philanthropic groups, Indian rights associations, and the Presbyterian church, Dr. George L. Spining addressed a group of Christians at Oakland in late October 1883. Invited by Lawyer, Spining brought a message of Christian brotherhood and sympathy from the Presbyterian General Assembly at Saratoga, New York. He also called for an open discussion as the prisoners spoke of their regrets about the past, their willingness to support the federal government, and their submission to Christian principles and civil law. Spining counseled that the Presbyterian General Assembly did not fault the government and that the Nimiipuu had been treated fairly. Nevertheless, the General Assembly would lay the matter before federal officials in order to promote their relocation to a healthier climate. They would pursue removal to the Idaho reservation only if it would save the government money.[37]

Tensions mounted at Oakland as the prisoners waited to learn whether the Indian Appropriation Act for 1883 would provide for their relocation. Their hopes were dashed when Commissioner Eliphalet Whittlesey visited Oakland in November 1883. Whittlesey, who maintained cordial relations with Lawyer, Reuben, and Húsus Kute, met with a general council on the evening of November 30. He had reported their wishes and conditions to the Senate Committee on Indian Affairs, and Senator Henry L. Dawes had added an amendment to the Indian Appropriation Act providing for their return. Congress, however, had defeated the amendment, and the prisoners were to remain in the Indian Territory for another year.[38] Spirits remained low at Oakland as Lawyer spent the second and third weeks of January 1884 in Washington, D.C. Meeting with a committee of Presbyterian leaders and with federal officials, he urged the exiles' immediate return to the northwest. Lawyer returned to Oakland the first week of February.[39] The prisoners received another blow that week when Yellow Bull's brother Red Elk died at his camp on the Chikaskia River.[40] Red Elk had supported the resistance movement and the peace process, had helped to make peace with the Northern Cheyennes, and had Sun Danced with Chief Joseph and Yellow Bull. He left a teenage son and another dependent at Oakland, where his funeral took place as the prisoners prepared for a major lease meeting on February 9, 1884.

Most of the adult males at Oakland came together for the lease meeting, where they also heard Lawyer's promises of an early release. The first lease payment, due on July 1, would provide every family with badly needed cash.[41] In the midst of the stalled federal efforts to send them home, the men attending the council understood that they could create other opportunities with the increased earnings. Hope for a speedy release permeated Oakland, where everyone was focused on leaving. Reuben returned from Idaho the first week of June 1884, assuring the prisoners that they would be released after harvesting their crops.[42] Lawyer also promised that the Indian Bureau was about to release the prisoners to the northwest. Reuben returned to Idaho after a few weeks, and word then leaked out that only the Christians would be released.[43]

At Oakland, apprehension was fueled by concern about the cemetery. The men hauled logs to the sawmill and milled lumber to build a fence around the graveyard.[44] Reuben continued to pressure the Indian Bureau, and the efforts to influence Washington, D.C., began to bear fruit. Senator Dawes attached a key piece of legislation to the July 1884 Indian Appropriation Act that transferred power regarding disposition of the Oakland detainees to the secretary of the interior. Secretary of the Interior Henry Teller now had the authority to send the prisoners away or to send them home. Between April and June 1884, Senator Dawes and five other United States senators presented more than four thousand signatures to Congress advocating release of the captives. Most of the supporters were from Kansas, Indiana, and New Jersey, although James Garfield's widow sponsored more than five hundred signatures from Ohio.[45]

In the meantime, Archie Lawyer and his wife took Mrs. Húsus Kute home to Lapwai the second week in July 1884, presuming that the rest of the prisoners would be leaving before winter. Both Reuben, who helped to organize Mrs. Húsus Kute's return, and Inspector James Haworth, who shared memories of the beloved woman, worried that she would not survive the trip. The Húsus Kutes sold their livestock to pay her train fare.[46]

Rumors that only Christians would be leaving created a new sense of urgency at Oakland. Agent John W. Scott was furious with Lawyer and Reuben, whom he blamed for interfering with camp life and for upsetting the prisoners. When letters from Dr. Spining, the Reverend Samuel Fleming, and other non-Native Presbyterians fell into Scott's hands, he was forced to deal with the ministers who were promoting the release of the Christians. The ministers asserted that the non-Christians were to be left in the Indian Territory. In a blistering denunciation of the exclusionary efforts, Scott informed Commissioner Price that the non-Christians were equally deserving of his consideration. "If they go, they all go. If any stay, they all stay," Scott warned Price.[47]

A telegram from Price dated September 16, 1884, brought stunning news: he planned to split up the Oakland group and relocate them.[48] Christians would be returned to Lapwai, while those who remained with Chief Joseph would be sent to a reservation at Colville, Washington Territory. A full council meeting was scheduled for September 18, at which Joseph and the leaders were told of the Colville split. Agent Scott tried to explain Colville's location as a selling point, but Price's plans fell on deaf ears. Even though many of the exiles wished to return to Lapwai, they did not consent to having any part of the group sent somewhere else. Joseph then spoke to the council. He did not want to go to Lapwai; he wanted to return to his own country. Failing that, he would consider going to any reservation assigned to him and to all of his people. He did not, however, want to go to a strange land at Colville. Joseph also insisted that they would not move without a firm federal commitment with regard to their destination and a statement of their rights. Joseph argued that he had fought for what he believed was right and that he had been defeated and subsequently punished. He did not want to be branded a "wild" Indian and segregated from his people. The exiles argued that they had been punished enough, and they all wanted to return to their old homes. "If I could," said Joseph through the interpreter, "I would take my heart out and hold it in my hand and let the Great Father and the white people see that there is nothing in it but fond feelings for him and them."[49] The non-Christians felt that they would be "as good as dead" if they were separated from the rest of the group, and the council rejected Price's offer.

Chief Joseph, Yellow Bull, Yellow Bear, and Húsus Kute requested permission to travel to Washington, D.C., to meet with Commissioner Price. They wanted to clarify and solidify the relocation plan with a higher authority. Although Scott supported the idea, nothing came of it. In the interim, the Ponca agent telegraphed Price that the prisoners had rejected the split relocation offer.[50] Years later, Josiah Red Wolf remembered hearing Joseph and his father discussing the Colville split. Joseph understood that he and some of the other men could be hanged if they returned to Idaho.[51] Several of the prisoners who did not attend the council had no knowledge about the split until the train carrying the relocated prisoners arrived at Wallula Junction, Washington Territory, the following year. For Yellow Wolf, that was his first indication of where they were to go. He remembered that their choices were based on religious preference: Christians would go to Lapwai and non-Christians to Colville.[52]

The stalemate dragged on while non-Native Presbyterians petitioned Price and the Indian Bureau with demands in support of the Christians. Price referred Samuel Fleming's latest letter to Scott, who was away from the agency, and Superintendent T. S. Stover submitted their reply to Fleming. The Indian Bureau was furious with Fleming's singular interference on behalf of the Christians and admonished him that the church was ignoring the rights of the non-Christians. He also assured the minister that the Bureau planned to handle the matter without the church's interference. Seven months later, Secretary of the Interior Lucius Q. C. Lamar convinced George Spining to rescind his support of a separation that would have left the non-Christians at Oakland.[53] Lamar asked whether all of the detainees should be allowed to relocate, and Spining finally admitted that plans to relocate both the Christians and non-Christians should take precedence. "I would keep the faith of the Nation with Joseph and his people, four fifths of whom are now women and children, widows and orphans, and would entrust them to the Lord and to General Nelson A. Miles for protection and safe keeping," said Spining.[54]

By November 1884, serious health issues added to the discontent at Oakland. Earlier that year, diphtheria had infected the camps, and now epidemic dysentery, chronic diarrhea, and bronchitis plagued the prisoners. The lingering effects of anemia and malaria had already weakened the population, and in November several people died from dysentery.[55]

Disappointment swept through the reservation again when word reached Oakland that Commissioner Price had denied their immediate release. Agent Scott tried to convince the exiles that it was too late in the season to move them, and that weather would deter any relocation. Their troubles then multiplied when the lease payment due in December was delayed because of the Senate investigations. Once again, Chief Joseph and the other leaders were not allowed to visit Washington, D.C., where a new president, secretary of the interior, and commissioner of Indian affairs would soon take office.[56] The winter of 1884–85 passed in growing anticipation of the promised return to the northwest.

To their credit, most of the prisoners remained calm as they waited to learn whether the Indian Bureau would honor its latest promise.[57] Commissioner Price included $10,000 for their relocation in the January 1885 Indian Appropriation Act and estimated that it would cost that plus other applicable funds. Price warned that it was dangerous for the prisoners to be returned to Idaho because of outstanding criminal indictments and anti-Nimiipuu sentiment. Despite their earlier refusal to be separated, the captives were now considering the Colville split. Those who were not subject to indictment or punishment could be returned to Lapwai, and the rest of the prisoners would be relocated outside of Idaho.[58]

Criminal indictments on the docket of the First Federal District Court of Idaho called for the arrest of Chief Joseph, Yellow Bull, Yellow Head, and eleven other men. Other documents filed with the indictments targeted eighteen "extremely dangerous" men who had participated in the war. The U.S. attorney had attempted to *nolle prosequi* the indictments to clear them from the docket, but angry Idahoans demanded that authorities deliver the men for trial in 1885. By April 8, Joseph seemed somewhat resigned to separation of the bands. When asked what he thought about the Bureau's resolution to divide the group, he said that it would have been preferable to consult the prisoners before making any decisions concerning them. He also held that they had been cheated out of the Wallowa Valley.[59] By May 12, Joseph affirmed their decision to return to the northwest, regardless of the Colville split and the risk of possible indictments or revenge. The new commissioner of Indian affairs, John D. C. Atkins, informed the secretary of the interior that the Christians would return to Lapwai, and that the rest of the group was being sent away because of the outstanding indictments. According to Albert Andrews, many of the prisoners elected to remain with Joseph at Colville.[60]

Idahoans resented any release of the Nimiipuu, Paluses, and Cayuses from the Indian Territory. Several citizens notified Agent Monteith and the commissioner of Indian affairs that there was no room in Idaho or Washington for the expatriates. They threatened that vengeful whites would reignite the war, and unless the army established a permanent post at Lapwai, settlers and expatriates would pose a great danger to each other. They were also concerned that the return would "disturb the good feeling now existing between the whites and the Indians now on the reservation."[61] In other words, the informants were apprehensive about upsetting the balance of power, which had shifted to the non-Native community after 1877. Federal authorities also yielded to pressures applied by western senators and additional threats to take action against the war leaders.[62]

Although most Idahoans blamed Chief Joseph for the war, he was charged with only two crimes, allegedly committed on June 13, 1877. Yellow Bull was charged with the same crimes, and Yellow Head was accused of another killing, on June 14, 1877. Several of the men named in the five original indictments had died during the war or in the Indian Territory. And until Ad Chapman vindictively pointed them and the other "dangerous" men out to General Miles, the people charged in the indictments were difficult to identify. Fictitious names, such as Bowie or Big Bird, rendered the indictments almost incomprehensible; the only persons who were clearly marked were Young Joseph and Yellow Bull.

The U.S. attorney, the attorney general, and other authorities tried to have the charges dropped or to shift decisions regarding the exiles to General Miles. Orders to investigate the indictments and the prisoners' return were finally sent to Miles on June 7, 1881, a month after he had appealed to Indian rights activist Helen Hunt Jackson to help speed up the process. Miles's recommendation the following October was that anyone not charged with a crime should be released to the Lapwai reservation. Miles also clarified the names on the indictments and recommended that the charges be explained to the men. They should have the opportunity to stand trial or agree to stay out of Idaho.[63] Angry Idahoans rebuffed reasonable attempts to resolve the problems. Secretary of the Interior Carl Schurz, President Rutherford B. Hayes, and Secretary of War Robert Lincoln then added a new twist to the debate. They were hesitant to upset the balance of power in the Indian Territory, where the Oakland exiles served as a buffer between non-Native incursions into the Indian Territory and Native nations farther south and west. Schurz, Hayes, and Lincoln feared that their removal would create a vacuum that could be exploited by desperados and land-hungry settlers.[64] Without the opportunity for fair trials, the specifics of the charges against the Nimiipuu were never examined or made public. Furthermore, no non-Natives were tried for wartime activities, or for killing

Nimiipuu, Palus, and Cayuse men, women, or children or stealing their livestock. By the time Miles thought that the way had been cleared for the prisoners' return in 1884, the northwestern newspapers had entered the debate and were arguing against it.

By March, the prisoners were still waiting for a final decision, and by the first of April 1885, more than a few of them were absent from Oakland. As authorities were preparing a removal census, everyone at Oakland understood that several prisoners had run away. Some of the captives did not want to return to the northwest and remained in the Indian Territory. One family occupied Yellow Bull's settlement for a while after the main group left, and within a few years, several of the refugees were farming in Oklahoma. One family moved to Muskogee, Oklahoma, where one of the women became a nurse. She was almost certainly employed as Doris Swayze Bounds's baby nurse in Muskogee by 1906, and there were rumors of other runaways. One survivor's family is still trying to locate information about their ancestor Consuelo, who was also a nurse about that time. Consuelo's Nimiipuu surname was either Yosyós (blue) or Lip Trap (*ilp pilp,* or red). Several families escaped to the northwest, and children disappeared from Indian schools, where they had been apprenticed to leather or shoe repair shops. Other refugees married into the Osage nation, although their elderly descendants retain their Nimiipuu memories.[65]

Long after the homecoming in 1885, Lynus Walker told his family about Yellow Head's return to Idaho. After losing his horses during the war, Yellow Head had worked hard to rebuild his herd. When the release from the Indian Territory was finally determined, he took his horses and returned to Idaho by himself. Not about to lose another herd, he drove his horses by night, then rested and grazed the animals during the day. He followed the North Star until he recognized a familiar mountain, and from there he drove his horses "west into the sunset."[66]

If the Indian Bureau had wanted to pursue the runaways, they could have called in the federal troops that were stationed at the Ponca Agency and at the Chilocco Indian Industrial School. They did not call out the army, however, and the inspector prepared a census of the detainees in mid-May that accounted for 231 of the 266 Oakland prisoners. At that time, the inspector understood that 119 people would return to Lapwai, and 112 would remain in exile at Colville.[67] Relocation personnel admitted that they were responsible for at least 265 people but would relocate only as many as they could find.

Dr. W. H. Faulkner of Washington, D.C., was assigned as the relocation supervisor. He arrived in Arkansas City on May 4, then missed the stagecoach to Ponca, arriving at Oakland on May 6. As ordered, Faulkner agreed to have the exiles on the trail by May 21 and out of Arkansas City on May 22. Agent Scott worried that the prisoners were not prepared to leave, but Faulkner told Scott and Chief Joseph that ready or not, they were leaving Oakland on May 21. The prisoners had not sold their livestock and were still worried about the cemetery and other graves farther out on the reservation. Three graves near Yellow Bull's Crossing and one grave secreted in the Salt Fork bottomlands were isolated and untended. The Oakland cemetery contained about one hundred graves, and a lone western red cedar seedling marked the secret grave. Someone placed stone markers on the graves at Yellow Bull's Crossing before 1892, and the secret grave remained inviolate. Fifty years later, a tall western red cedar stood at the secret grave, and the Native stone markers had been removed from the other two graves.[68] After allotment of the Oakland reservation to the Tonkawas, the cemetery was destroyed and cultivated as farmland.

On May 19 and 20, the prisoners packed their belongings, while most of the missing people reported to the agent. Then 35,000 pounds of gear and personal possessions were loaded onto thirty-four wagons. Scott ordered a ton of hardtack, a ton and a half of beans, 140 pounds of coffee, and 160 pounds of sugar delivered to Arkansas City for the migrants. The travelers owned coffee boilers and cups, and because there was no fresh fruit, Scott hoped they could buy apples along the way. Ponca teamsters were hired to accompany the wagon train to Arkansas

City and to return the teams to the Ponca Agency. On Thursday morning, the children, the sick, and the elderly were placed on the loaded wagons, and the final Nimiipuu, Palus, and Cayuse wagon train left Oakland. Most of the men, and many of the women, plodded along in the rain and mud alongside the wagons. One especially determined woman walked alone in front of the wagon train, leading the way out of the Indian Territory. After a brief stop for lunch, the wagons resumed the march, but by then, about half of the teams were exhausted. Faulkner took some of the wagons with him and reached Arkansas City around midnight, while the other half of the wagon train struggled with the spent teams to reach Arkansas City by daybreak. Faulkner and the men worked all night to guide incoming wagons across the railroad tracks into camp.[69]

The prisoners spent Friday morning drying out and cleaning up and sold several of their horses and some of their personal possessions. A few people shopped around town, but Faulkner had everyone back to the train by ten o'clock in the morning. The prisoners sold a few of their cattle before May 21; the Indian Bureau considered giving the rest of their possessions to the Tonkawas, but the lot was instead sold at auction on June 29, bringing $2,860.50. All of their cattle and miscellaneous items, plus forty-one horses and mules, went through the sale. Two years later, Leg Marrow and Some Left on Top (Ta-mai-yo-tsa-ka-win) received their proceeds from the sale. Chief Joseph received $37.50 for his horse and $15.50 for one cow. Several years later, Joseph's well-worn buggy and harness were also sold.[70]

The title to the Oakland reservation remained in limbo until Scott received the paperwork to clear occupancy of the reservation on May 22. The Nimiipuu, Paluses, and Cayuses did not hold Oakland in fee title, and at a meeting held at the train depot, the leaders signed a quitclaim deed to the reservation. They relinquished to the government all rights, title, and interests in and to the lands.[71] Chief Joseph, Yellow Bull, Yellow Bear, and Húsus Kute signed the deed in return for considerations provided in the Indian Appropriation Act of March 3, 1885.[72] Because the refugees relinquished their rights without legal representation during those hectic final hours, how well the quitclaim deed was understood remains a viable question. Three Eagles testified in 1911 that the prisoners had a different understanding about the disposition of the reservation. According to him, they had agreed to compensation for the Wallowa Valley or, in lieu of that, a substantial cash payment for the Oakland reservation. They also understood that if they gave up the reservation, all of the prisoners would be returned to Lapwai. Three Eagles swore that the Colville split was an abrogation of the final agreement and that the Nimiipuu had never ceded the Wallowa Valley to anyone. In the same testimonial, Yellow Bull confirmed that they had never sold the Wallowa Valley.[73] Yellow Wolf also understood that the government had promised their return to Wallowa once they cleared up the title and occupancy.[74] Nevertheless, the Indian Bureau maintained that in return for the quitclaim deed, the government was to fund the prisoners' care and their return to Colville and Lapwai.

Among the few non-Natives who gathered to bid farewell to the Nimiipuu, Paluses, and Cayuses at the Arkansas City depot were Joe Sherburne and William J. Pollock. The men drove in from the Ponca Agency just to wish Chief Joseph and their other friends a safe journey. Joseph certainly understood the special nature of the gesture, because many of his other acquaintances were not at the depot that morning. As the men said goodbye, Joseph gave Sherburne a pair of rawhide-covered stirrups.[75] For Sherburne, the stirrups were a treasured reminder of Joseph: "I prize them very highly, they being the stirrups that he used on his old saddle through that war campaign with Howard and Miles . . . they were home made stirrups, probably made by his wife, probably of willow wood covered with wet raw hide and allowed to dry which makes them about as solid as iron."[76]

By noon, everyone from Oakland was on the train, and it was waiting for the Winfield Express to clear the tracks. But then Dr. Faulkner refused to allow the Chilocco students to board the train. Even though the students had enrolled at Chilocco with the stipulation that they would return to the northwest with their families, Faulkner was now insisting that they remain at Chilocco for thirty-six months. Anticipating problems with Faulkner, Chilocco superintendent Henry J. Minthorn and his assistant R. O. Munson had decided to deliver the students just before the train left Arkansas City. Meanwhile, Agent Scott had closed the school at Oakland on May 20, and those children were on the train.[77]

Anxious parents and guardians watched from the train as Munson drove up with eleven Chilocco students. Six students—Jacob Snow, Isaac Lawrence, Stephen Julius, Harry Anderson, Cornelius Baldwin, and Lily Moses—were already on board, having left the school before May 1885.[78] Faulkner continued to argue that the students must remain at Chilocco, and tensions mounted as the detainees realized that he meant to keep their youngsters in the Indian Territory. Yellow Bull, Red Wolf, Laura Minthorn (Ip-na-som-wee-san-mai), Dick Johnson, Jay Gould, Edward Newman (Mal-its), and Frank Jackson's guardian were stunned. Faulkner refused to listen to reason as Munson appealed to his ethics, reiterated the federal agreement to return the students with their families, and then appealed to Faulkner as a gentleman. Nothing worked until Munson offered Faulkner a convenient disclaimer: Chief Joseph and the prisoners had kept their bargain to remain at peace, and in return Faulkner should honor the promises made by the "Great Father." Threatened with the president, Faulkner relented and allowed the students to board the train. Nearly frantic with relief, Yellow Bull tearfully thanked Faulkner and the government for allowing the students to leave.[79]

By 1:15, the Winfield Express had gone, everyone was on the train, and the tracks were clear. The engineer pulled the steam whistle, producing one long farewell blast, and 268 emotionally charged Nimiipuu, Paluses, and Cayuses left Kansas. Loaded into emigrant cars, the migrants traveled with their baggage, equipment, and supplies. The only furnishings were backless wooden benches, and people slept on the floors around and under the benches. Women cooked on fires built near the tracks or in rail yards, and water was carried in barrels that were refilled when the train took on water. Traveling in emigrant cars was demanding, although Faulkner asserted that the prisoners were as comfortable as possible. By 9:00 that night, the returnees were at McPherson, Kansas, where the station manager wanted them out of his jurisdiction. Worried that the crowds waiting to see the prisoners would interfere with their transfer to the Union Pacific Railroad, he and Faulkner completed the change of trains as quickly as possible.[80] Nevertheless, it was midnight by the time the train left McPherson, heading west through Salina and Hays, Kansas, and on to Denver, Colorado, and Cheyenne, Wyoming. Daytime temperatures in the cars were blazing hot as the train passed through Laramie, Rock Creek, Medicine Bow, and Rock Springs, Wyoming, then crossed into Utah.[81] From there it continued north, and on May 26 it reached Pocatello, Idaho, where railroad officials created a new problem. Alarmed by non-Natives' negative reactions to the prisoners' return, railroad officials wanted to divide the train. They would divert Chief Joseph and the Colville exiles north to Spokane Falls on the Utah, Northern, and Northern Pacific Railroad and send the Lapwai group via Wallula Junction to Riparia and on to Lewiston. As crowds of unfriendly onlookers gathered around the train, Faulkner telegraphed the Indian Bureau for instructions. Separating the group at Pocatello was not in the railroad's contract.[82]

In the meantime, Major Frank Baldwin delivered General Miles's warning that Chief Joseph and the Colville exiles were in grave danger. Baldwin urged Dr. Faulkner to move the expatriates out of Idaho as quickly as possible, saying that Idahoans intended to hang Joseph and the other men under indictment. The U.S. marshal from Garrison was due at Pocatello on the morning train to arrest Joseph, Yellow Bull, and the other men. Consulting with a worried Joseph, Faulkner waited all night for instructions. Having heard nothing from the Indian Bureau, Faulkner finally wired for additional military protection and, lacking new instructions, ordered the train to leave for Washington Territory. The railroad's contract was revised to terminate with delivery of the entire group to Wallula Junction, and the train left for Washington just after midnight, guarded by Captain Charles A. Dempsey and a company of Third Infantry soldiers. Johnson, Yellow Wolf, Fleming, and Little Man Chief surely recognized Dempsey as the officer who had delivered them to the Indian Territory in December 1878.[83]

The train finally arrived at Wallula Junction, Washington Territory, on May 27, 1885. In contrast to the fifty-day trip into exile, the returnees made it back to the northwest in five days. This time, however, no supportive reporters and eager crowds were there to meet them, and northwestern newspapers ranted against their return to Idaho. Aaron F. Parker, editor of the *Nez Perce News* in Lewiston, Idaho, was a determined anti-Indian opponent, and a citizens' committee was formed in Lewiston to try to stop their return. The *Spokane Review* warned that the "hard looking crowd" of exiles was guarded by a forty-two man squad of U.S. cavalry, and assured readers that Chief Joseph and the Colville exiles were removed from direct contact with non-Native citizens. The *Lewiston Journal* warned that people in Lewiston were extremely anxious about having the Nimiipuu back in the Washington-Idaho area. To be fair, however, that article also said that anyone who understood the Nimiipuu knew they had little to fear from the exiles. Although most local press coverage warned that the returnees posed a danger to business, personal lives, and political conditions in the northwest, other reviewers called for calm. On May 22, the *Walla Walla Weekly Journal and Watchman* reviewed the treaties, the war, and the planned return to the northwest. Citizens and settlers were frightened and requested military reinforcements, even though it was admitted that if war broke out again, it would probably be caused by white-on-Indian violence. The newspaper guaranteed that the Nimiipuu resistance was broken, and the threat of war was no longer a viable complaint. Another popular opinion expressed in Lewiston was that the only good Indian was a dead Indian. The *Morning Oregonian* even went so far as to report that General Miles had not implemented a surrender agreement that ensured the captives' return to the northwest.[84] Bitter about the war and protective of opportunities to gain land and army supply contracts at Fort Lapwai, non-Native people threatened the exiles long after their return from the Indian Territory.

The Colville exiles were separated from the Lapwai returnees at Wallula Junction. Faulkner reported no deaths or accidents when Agent Charles Monteith met the exiles at Wallula with a detachment of soldiers from Fort Walla Walla. The 118-person Lapwai contingent bade farewell to Chief Joseph and the Colville exiles. Sup-poon-mas, Húsus Kute, Op-has, Feathers around the Neck, Red Grizzly Bear, and Phillip Williams said goodbye to old friends and partners who were destined for Colville. Brothers Tom and John Hill were separated; Tom and one dependent left for Lapwai, while John, his wife, and their ten-year-old daughter went to Colville. Tom Hill, who was appointed the captain of the Lapwai police force, did not know that he would soon face indictment for alleged war crimes in Idaho County.[85] Stephen Julius, Tit-een (Having Teeth), Yellow Head, Three Eagles, and Captain Jack divided their basic family units between Lapwai and Colville.[86]

The Lapwai group was scheduled to continue on to Riparia via Grange City on the Walla Walla and Columbia River Railroad. The connecting steamboat failed to make its run, however, and the Lapwai families had to wait at Fort Walla Walla for the next boat. When they finally arrived in Lewiston on June 1, 1885, the exiles were met by men from Lapwai with horses and wagons. Worried that people in Lewiston would misinterpret the presence of too many Nimiipuu men and horses, the Indian agent limited the number of Lapwai men who rode into Lewiston to greet the refugees. The wagons were loaded with the women, children, and elderly and were surrounded by the men and boys riding horses when the returnees left for Lapwai, where they were expected about four o'clock in the afternoon.[87]

More than five hundred people were waiting at Lapwai when word came to gather at the camp meeting grounds near the mouth of Lapwai Creek. The eager reception committee formed a semicircle eight to ten persons deep as the returnees dismounted and formed up along the half-circle. Ceremonies, prayers, speeches, federal authorities, missionary George Deffenbaugh, and civil authorities represented by James Lawyer welcomed the refugees to Lapwai. Elder Solomon offered a prayer of thanksgiving, the Reverend Silas Whitman delivered a short sermon, and James Lawyer spoke. Then Tom Hill responded for the refugees. Choked with emotion, he reviewed their incarceration and spoke of their desperate yearning for home. He thanked the church, the law, and the various leaders who had actuated their return. He assured the Lapwai community that the returnees would live within the law and that they believed in the Christian God. The shaking of hands began, and within the hour, every man, woman, and child had clasped hands with every returnee. A line of happy, expectant people moved along the cordon of returnees as friends and families looked for loved ones. Some families were joyously reunited, even as others lost hope of seeing their missing family members.[88]

The weary travelers camped at the meeting grounds, where everyone gathered for a campfire worship service. Within weeks, eighty of the returnees had joined the Presbyterian churches at Lapwai. Nevertheless, life was not tranquil for the returnees. They lived in fear of continued non-Native threats and punitive actions, and many of the returned Christians burned their feathers and drums and refused to speak to outsiders about the war.[89] Although several of the exiles did not regard their religious affiliation as their only reason for acceptance at Lapwai, George Deffenbaugh clarified his position regarding the nontreaty bands. Deffenbaugh defended the idea of segregating the "un-subdued" bands from the "subdued" Christians in some isolated location. Agent Monteith offered scant comfort to veterans or sympathizers who slipped back in from Canada. When members of Chief White Bird's band quietly returned from Canada, Monteith forced the veterans to submit to personal indignities such as cutting their long hair and complying with his regulations.[90] For Monteith, life at Lapwai revolved around obedient American Indians. "To make him fear you," said Monteith "is to make him respect you."[91]

After a brief but emotional separation at Wallula Junction, Chief Joseph and the Colville outcasts were loaded aboard Northern Pacific Railroad cars. Their train traveled north from Wallula Junction through Pasco and Connell, Washington Territory, and on to Spokane Falls. Dr. Faulkner stayed with the company until they reached Fort Spokane, where the post surgeon assumed responsibility for the ailing exiles. Some of the exiles were blind or frail elderly, and several were suffering from end-stage tuberculosis. One woman was thought to be about one hundred years old, and three women and one man were at least eighty. None of the Colville exiles died during transport, although their medical problems were exacerbated by the relocation and exhaustion.[92]

Chief Joseph's group consisted of 103 adults, 34 school-aged children, and 13 younger children. Thirty-one families were headed by husbands and fathers, three single men were alone or cared for by friends, and two boys and one girl were orphans. Several single males were caring for elderly mothers, grandmothers, one great-grandmother, and one thirty-year-old sister and her two-year-old baby. Six single women were caring for daughters, sons, younger dependents, or each other. Few elderly couples survived the internment, although At-tas-poo and his wife endured the return to Colville. Joseph and Yellow Bull adopted the two male orphans: Willie Andrews was taken into Joseph's family, and Red Elk was cared for by his uncle Yellow Bull.[93]

Supervised by a military escort, the wagon train to Colville was not greeted by any welcoming ceremonies, happy families, or considerate agency officials. Furious that the expatriates had been sent to his agency, Agent Sidney Waters reviled the eastern liberals who had forced the detainees into his jurisdiction. Waters thought that the exiles should have remained in the Indian Territory, and he criticized Indian Bureau policies, the lack of planning, and reductions in his supplies for the Nimiipuu. The army finally stepped in with extra rations when Waters complained that without the provisions, the outcasts would perish. He also notified Washington that without further ration increases and improved planning, the Nimiipuu faced a bleak future at Colville. Not surprisingly, Waters was replaced and left the Colville Agency within three months.[94] The following year, Colville agent Benjamin Moore filed a telling report with the Indian Bureau: "There is very little encouraging here," said Moore, referring to the placement of the Nimiipuu on one-fourth rations until summer 1886, when the military would distribute more food in the Nimiipuu camps.[95] Faced with their desperate need, the Indian Bureau finally agreed to increase the exiles' rations to one-half portions, and then to full portions soon after that. The exiles needed cattle, horses, wagons, and cows, and the Indian Bureau insisted that they farm.

To make matters worse, other agency residents refused to allow the Nimiipuu to settle on their assigned lands. They shared no old customs and relationships and no languages or spiritual beliefs with the Nimiipuu, and the reservation had never been their home territory. After his visit with Chief Joseph several years later, General John Gibbon reported that no open hostilities were expressed against the exiles. Nonetheless, stakes marking Nimiipuu farms disappeared every two or three days, and fences were damaged or torn down. Cattle issued to the Nimiipuu were hamstrung or shot and left to die in their pastures. And shots were fired by an unidentified person near several Nimiipuu men who were out rounding up cattle, although no one was killed. Skolaskin, a San Poil chief, was arrested without due process and deported to Alcatraz Island in 1889, and the incidents affecting the Nimiipuu then stopped. When Skolaskin was returned in 1892 after portions of the reservation were opened to non-Native settlement, he felt betrayed by federal authorities. In all fairness, he denied knowledge of the shootings, the injured cattle, and most of the trouble with the Nimiipuu. The upper band of Spokanes also resented the government's perceived preferential treatment of the Nimiipuu, as they complained to agent Hal J. Cole: "We have always been at peace with the white people, but where is our reward! When Joseph went to war we refused to join him. Now Joseph and his children are given food and clothing, houses, and farming tools, and we get nothing. This is not right."[96]

The first years were difficult for everyone, but over time, the Native nations at Colville established workable relationships. The Indian Bureau eventually issued cattle, clothing, rations, and other necessities to the Nimiipuu, but they remained uncomfortable with a military presence. When a well-meaning Portland-area man tried to donate clothing through General Gibbon, Chief Joseph and the exiles refused the gift. Despite the coming winter, the exiles feared that it was military clothing, and they wanted nothing to do with it. When they understood that the gifts were civilian clothes, Joseph brought the garments to the reservation.[97]

Almost eight years after their deportation to the Indian Territory, the Nimiipuu, Paluses, and Cayuses who had chosen to remain with Joseph at Colville faced continued exile. Their travels had taken them across a significant portion of the United States; they had fulfilled the agreement made at the Bear Paw and remained at peace with the United States. Like the refugees who returned to Lapwai, however, the Colville refugees faced non-Native aggression; Chief Joseph never traveled without guards as people adjusted to the new reservation.

EPILOGUE

The Colville exiles slowly rebuilt their families or re-formed condensed family units. The middle-aged widow Tsis-koop settled at Colville with her twenty-year-old son and younger daughter. To-sa-im, who was about twenty-five years old, formed a childless household with another woman who was forty years old. Sixteen-year-old E-yal-ilp-pilp (Charlie Monckton) lived with his fifty-year-old mother, another middle-aged woman, and one of the few elderly ladies to survive the prison camps, Fox-se-ap-poo, who was reported to be one hundred years old. By 1887, Fox-se-ap-poo was no longer included on the Colville census, and a three-year-old boy had joined the family.[1] Mr. and Mrs. Wolf Head, their teenage son Luke, and their six-year-old son Charlie had gone to Colville, but five years later, Mrs. Wolf Head was dead and the widower was supporting his sons.[2] Húsus Kute relocated to Lapwai and then moved to Colville, where he spent the rest of his life near Chief Joseph.[3] Eighteen-year-old David Williams and his thirty-year-old sister also moved to Colville with Joseph. Within three years, Williams was married and had fathered a daughter, who died in infancy.[4] Most of the deaths in 1891 were due to an influenza epidemic that March.

Age was not a deterrent to parenthood, as several mature couples added to their families. John Hill and Little Man Chief, in their forties and fifties, and their thirty-year-old and thirty-five-year-old wives added baby boys to their families, and a daughter joined Little Man Chief's family within seven years of their arrival at Colville.[5] Other couples, including Crow Blanket and his wife, remained childless. Chief Joseph and his wives arrived at Colville with two daughters aged fifteen and two years.[6] Within a few years, the three adults and the orphaned Willie Andrews were the only family members recorded in Joseph's family.

Many of the Colville exiles practiced their *wéset* faith, but the religious intolerance expressed by General Oliver O. Howard and the Indian Bureau was never forgotten. Even such notables as Edward S. Curtis could not convince Yellow Bull to share details of sacred ceremonials or the old beliefs.[7] Federal prohibitions against American Indian ceremonials were gradually relaxed, and proscriptions against dances and ceremonies were slowly discarded at both Nespelem on the Colville reservation and Lapwai.[8] By 1890, evangelists Archie Lawyer and Silas Whitman had established a Presbyterian church on the Spokane reservation. Even though they did not officially extend their efforts to the Nimiipuu at Colville, there must have been some contact between the groups.[9] Most of the neighboring Coeur d'Alenes, Colvilles, Lakes, and Okanogans were Catholics, and Jesuit priests maintained religious services on those reservations.[10] A few of the Nimiipuu in Chief Joseph's band and several people with Chief Moses on a nearby reservation were Catholics as well. The Jesuits seldom traveled to those distant reservations, so the Catholic Nimiipuu usually made do without formal religious services.[11]

Communications and movements between Colville and Lapwai were not unusual, although the letters and visits usually left the Colville folks feeling unhappy and abandoned.[12] When planning for allotment in severalty of the Lapwai reservation, the Colville Nimiipuu had the choice of taking land at either Colville or Lapwai. Some people accepted allotments at Nespelem; Yellow Bull and his family moved to the Lapwai reservation in May

1891.[13] Most of the Colville Nimiipuu would have preferred to hold their land in common and to continue cyclical hunting and gathering activities, even though federal programs urged individual ownership of property and farming.[14] As participation in the cash economy became more important, the Nimiipuu picked hops in the Yakima Valley and participated in off-reservation roundups, social events, and employment opportunities.[15]

Chief Joseph refused an allotment at Lapwai and never abandoned his efforts to recover the Wallowa Valley. While on a visit to Washington, D.C., in April 1897, he urged the Interior Department to establish a Wallowa Valley reservation. Having been introduced to William "Buffalo Bill" Cody by General Nelson Miles, Joseph traveled to New York City from Washington, D.C., as Cody's guest for President Ulysses S. Grant's reburial ceremonies. While there, he advocated the return of the Wallowa Valley to reporters from the *New York Times.* Joseph, his nephew Ollokot, and their interpreter toured New York City, met the mayor, and attended a Wild West show and circus at Madison Square Garden. Named an official "aide" for Grant's parade, Joseph rode a sorrel mustang next to Cody through the city, responding to the cheering crowds, the blaring bands, and the American extravaganza.[16]

Chief Joseph and a group of Colville Nimiipuu paid their first postwar visit to the Wallowa Valley in August 1899. Appearing at a public meeting with residents of the valley, Joseph expressed their desire to purchase land there for a permanent reservation. After being told that it would not be possible, Joseph returned to Colville, where he continued to lobby the Interior Department for a Wallowa Valley reservation. Joseph, Peo Peo Tholekt, Phillip Andrews, and Indian inspector James McLaughlin returned to the Wallowa Valley in 1900, hoping to make another offer to buy land. Joseph was given a friendly reception but was told this time that a sale was impossible and that he should never return. McLaughlin and Joseph visited Joseph's father's grave while they were there, although it had been desecrated.[17]

Chief Joseph's efforts to seek federal redress did not end with the disappointing trips to Wallowa. He returned to Washington,

D.C., in February 1903 to ask President Theodore Roosevelt to keep settlers from overrunning the Colville reservation. Once again, Joseph and his retinue attended a White House reception, where they met President and Mrs. Roosevelt and joined Washington elites in the familiar Blue Room.[18] The group remained in Washington until late February, then went on to New York City before returning to the West. Following a public speaking tour in Portland and Seattle, Joseph's last public speech was delivered at the Carlisle Indian Industrial School graduation on May 13, 1904. After meeting General Howard at the school, Joseph told the students that he no longer held any animosity toward the general. According to Elizabeth Penny Wilson, a Nimiipuu student who graduated from Carlisle that day, Joseph encouraged American Indian youths to gain an education and reminded them that the war was in the past.[19]

Chief Joseph passed away September 21, 1904, at Nespelem, Washington. History and the agency physician record that he died of a broken heart while seated in front of his tepee fire.[20] The next summer, his compatriots bade their friend a formal farewell at Nespelem. Yellow Bull, Es-pow-yes, Albert Waters, and Professor Edmund S. Meany from the University of Washington delivered the eulogies. Surrounded by the Colville community and Joseph's family, including his younger widow and his nephews Peo Peo Tholekt from Lapwai and Albert Waters, Yellow Bull and Es-pow-yes gave their friend and lifelong companion a proper farewell. Clad in formal regalia, the eloquent old warriors spoke from a dais shaded by a large American flag.[21]

In the decades following Joseph's death, Yellow Bull and the other old warriors and survivors pressed for recognition of their civil rights and restoration of the Wallowa Valley. The valley was never returned; but the legacies continue today, as the struggles for land, language, and peoplehood are still being waged in tribal cultural centers, in the courts and tribal offices, in the press, in boardrooms and classrooms, in the longhouses, and in the historical archives.

Notes

Abbreviations Used in the Notes

AIC	American Indian Correspondence, Presbyterian Historical Society, Philadelphia
ARBIC	*Annual Report, Board of Indian Commissioners to the Secretary of Interior* (Washington, D.C.: United States Government Printing Office)
ARCIA	*Annual Report, Commissioner of Indian Affairs to the Secretary of Interior* (Washington, D.C.: United States Government Printing Office)
ARSW	*Annual Report, Secretary of War* (Washington, D.C.: United States Government Printing Office)
CC	Census, Nez Perces of Joseph's Band, Colville Indian Agency, National Archives and Records Administration, Washington, D.C.
IINP	Issues to Indians, Nez Perces, Oakland, Indian Territory, National Archives and Records Administration, Washington, D.C.
LDNPOA	Letters and Documents concerning Nez Perce Tribal and Individual Indian Affairs, Pawnee, Ponca, Otoe, and Oakland Indian Agency, Indian Territory, Oklahoma Historical Society, Archives Division, Oklahoma City
LDNPQA	Letters and Documents concerning Nez Perce Tribal and Individual Indian Affairs, Quapaw Agency, Indian Territory, Oklahoma Historical Society, Archives Division, Oklahoma City
LROIA	Letters Received, Office of Indian Affairs, National Archives and Records Administration, Washington, D.C.
McW	Lucullus Virgil McWhorter Papers, Washington State University Libraries, Pullman
NARA	National Archives and Records Administration
NPS	Letters Received, Office of Indian Affairs, Quapaw Agency, National Park Service, Lewiston, Idaho

NPWF Nez Perce War File, National Archives and Records Administration, Records of the Attorney General's Office, Washington, D.C.

RG Record Group

Chapter 1

1. Stuart A. Chalfant, "Aboriginal Territory of the Nez Perce," in Chalfant and Ray, *The Nez Perce Indians,* 30–34; Slickpoo and Walker, *Noon Nee-Me-Poo,* 67; Chalfant and Ray, *The Nez Perce Indians,* 300.

2. Holm, Pearson and Chavis, "Peoplehood," 43–68; Flanagan, "The Invalidity of the Nez Perce Treaty," 84–85; Ray, *The Sanpoil and Nespelem,* 28–29, Ray, *Plateau Culture Element Distributions,* 248–50; Chalfant, "Aboriginal Territory of the Nez Perce," 134–35, 138; Marshall, "Nez Perce Groups," 23–24; Slickpoo and Walker, *Noon Nee-Me-Poo,* 61; Pearson and Harrington, "Numipu Winter Villages," 65; Josephy, *The Nez Perce Indians,* 15.

3. Flanagan, "The Invalidity of the Nez Perce Treaty," 75, 78–79; Haines, *The Nez Percés,* 14–15.

4. Josephy, *The Nez Perce Indians,* 27–33; Marshall, "Nez Perce Groups," 37–38; James, *Nez Perce Women in Transition,* 100.

5. Josephy, *The Nez Perce Indians,* 40–41, 43–45, 52, 55, 68–69, 71, 77, 118–19; Flanagan, "The Invalidity of the Nez Perce Treaty," 77.

6. Josephy, *The Nez Perce Indians,* 129–35.

7. Slickpoo and Walker, *Noon Nee-Me-Poo,* 71–72, 164; Chalfant, "Aboriginal Territory of the Nez Perce," 46; Kappler, *Indian Affairs,* 524; Elijah White, "Indian Agent's Report," in U.S. House, *Message from the President of the United States to the Two Houses of Congress, 1843,* 450–62; Heard, *The Far West,* 39; Haines, *The Nez Percés,* 95.

8. White, "Indian Agent's Report," 450–68.

9. Slickpoo and Walker, *Noon Nee-Me-Poo,* 51–54.

10. Josephy, *The Nez Perce Indians,* 231; Haines, *The Nez Percés,* 96, 117.

11. H. H. Spalding, "Laws of the Nez Perces," in U.S. House, *Message from the President of the United States to the Two Houses of Congress, 1843,* 462–68.

12. Heard, *The Far West,* 339; Kappler, *Indian Affairs,* 603–605, 843–48.

13. I. I. Stevens, "Report of Explorations of a Route for the Pacific Railroad," in U.S. House, *Reports of Explorations and Surveys, to Ascertain the Most Practicable and Economical Route for a Railroad from the Mississippi River to the Pacific Ocean,* 91, 146, 148, 34.

14. Pearson, "The Politics of Disease," 351.

15. Minutes of Proceedings of the Commission for Holding Treaties in Washington Territory and the Blackfoot Country, NARA, Washington, D.C., reel 5; Slickpoo and Walker, *Noon Nee-Me-Poo,* 142.

16. Kappler, *Indian Affairs,* 702–706; Flanagan, "The Invalidity of the Nez Perce Treaty," 86.

17. H. C. Wood, *Report Submitted to General Oliver O. Howard,* 22–23; Drury, *Chief Lawyer,* 131; Kappler, *Indian Affairs,* 702–706.

18. Slickpoo and Walker, *Noon Nee-Me-Poo,* 81.

19. Minutes of Proceedings of the Commission for Holding Treaties in Washington Territory and the Blackfoot Country; Kappler, *Indian Affairs,* 524, 694–98, 722–25.

20. Deloria and DeMallie, *Documents of American Indian Diplomacy,* 1333, 1342; Kappler, *Indian Affairs,* 693–95, 843–48.

21. William P. Dole, "Gold on the Nez Perce Reservation," *ARCIA* 1863, 431–32.

22. O'Marr et al., "Before the Indian Claims Commission," 433–35, 438, 441–49; "Reports of the Pierce Gold Strike in 1860," *Idaho Yesterdays* 3, no. 2 (1959): 14–19.

23. Hawley, *History of Idaho,* 100, 103; Blase, "Political History of Idaho Territory," 2.

24. Pierce, "Orofino Gold," 2–5; Hawley, *History of Idaho,* 103.

25. Wells, "Farmers Forgotten."

26. "Welcome to Pierce, Idaho!" http://www.idahoshighway12.com/pages/pierce/prcehwy12.html (accessed June 28, 2002); Hawley, *History of Idaho,* 113; Dole, "Gold on the Nez Perce Reservation," 427, 431–32.

27. McWhorter, *Yellow Wolf,* 43.

28. W. W. Miller, "Reduction of Reservation," *ARCIA* 1861, 176; Deloria and Demallie, *Documents of American Indian Diplomacy,* 1341–42; Slickpoo and Walker, *Noon Nee-Me-Poo,* 147; Chalfant and Ray, *The Nez Perce Indians,* 407–409.

29. Hawley, *History of Idaho,* 8, 209; Haines, *The Nez Percés,* 211; Bird, "Portrait of a Frontier Politician," 8–11.

30. Bird, "Portrait of a Frontier Politician," 8–11; Hawley, *History of Idaho,* 209; Drury, *Chief Lawyer,* 7, note; Blase, "Political History of Idaho Territory," 48, 50, 52.

31. Kappler, *Indian Affairs,* 843–48; Slickpoo and Walker, *Noon Nee-Me-Poo,* 147.

32. Evans, *Voice of the Old Wolf,* 12.

33. O'Marr et al., "Before the Indian Claims Commission," 272, 449; Pearson, "Numipu Land Loss," 42; Shennon and Full, *An Evaluation Study,* 1: 180.

34. William Willard, interview with author, March 24, 2006; A. I. Chapman, letter to the editor, *San Francisco Chronicle,* November 1, 1877.

35. Chief Joseph, "An Indian's View," 417–18, 420.

36. Kappler, *Indian Affairs,* 3, 4, 5, 8, 843–48.

37. McWhorter, *Yellow Wolf,* 29–30.

38. Kappler, *Indian Affairs,* 1024–25.

39. Slickpoo and Walker, *Noon Nee-Me-Poo,* 168–77; Haines, *The Nez Percés,* 212.

40. Flanagan, "The Invalidity of the Nez Perce Treaty," 80; Slickpoo and Walker, *Noon Nee-Me-Poo,* 178–80; Kappler, *Indian Affairs,* 702–706.

41. Ulysses S. Grant, "Executive Orders, Establishing, Enlarging, or Reducing Indian Reservations, Also Restoring Certain Indian Reservations to the Public Domain, from May 14, 1855, to October 29, 1878, Wallowa Valley Reservation, June 9, 1873," *ARBIC* 1878, 269–70; Ulysses S. Grant, "Order to Rescind Wallowa Valley Reservation," June 10, 1875, *ARCIA* 1875, 270; Flanagan, "The Invalidity of the Nez Perce Treaty," 80–81.

42. L. F. Grover, "Communication," July 21, 1873, *ARSW* 1876, 1: 129–30.

43. D. H. Jerome, O. O. Howard, William Stickney, and A. C. Barstow, "Conference at Lapwai," November 13, 1876, *ARBIC* 1877, 211–12.

44. Flanagan, "The Invalidity of the Nez Perce Treaty," 97–98.

45. Shennon and Full, *An Evaluation Study,* 1: inset.

46. Jerome et al., "Conference at Lapwai," 212–13; O. O. Howard, "Council with Chief Joseph's Band, May 3–7, 1877," May 22, 1877, *ARSW* 1877, 1: 591–95.

47. Cohen, *Handbook of American Indian Law,* 173, 178.

48. P. H. Sheridan to W. T. Sherman, *Emporia News,* November 16, 1868; P. H. Sheridan, "Indian Matters," *Emporia News,* July 9, 1869; Cohen, *Handbook of American Indian Law,* 93; Hare, "Foreword," 45.

49. Hare, "Foreword," 45; J. M. Schofield, "Report #5," September 20, 1875, *ARSW* 1875, 1: 122.

50. G. W. McCrary, "Report," November 19, 1877, *ARSW* 1877, 1: xxi; P. H. Sheridan to Secretary of War, October 25, 1878, *ARSW* 1878, 1: 34–39.

51. "Washington Happenings," *Arkansas City Traveler,* April 26, 1876; "Appendix II: Lt.-Col. Bowen's Account of Custer's Defeat on the Little Big Horn," in Brady, *Northwestern Fights and Fighters,* 336.

52. Sewall S. Cutting, M. E. Strieby, John C. Lowrie, Benjamin Tatham, and Samuel L. Jenney, "A. B. Meacham," *Journal of the 8th Annual Conference with Representatives of Missionary Boards,* Washington, D.C., January 15, 1879, *ARBIC* 1879, 125.

53. Howard, "A Practical View of the Indian Problem."

54. Blase, "Political History of Idaho Territory," 52.

55. O. O. Howard to Division H.Q., June 14, 1876, *ARSW* 1877, 1: 114–18; Jerome et al., "Conference at Lapwai," 212–13.

56. Cohen, *Handbook of American Indian Law,* 93, 39.

57. O. O. Howard, "Supplemental Report, Non-Treaty Nez Perce Campaign," December 26, 1877, *ARSW* 1877, 1: 613.

58. Cohen, *Handbook of American Indian Law,* 274.

59. J. Q. Smith, "Report and Submission of Letters," January 16, 1877, February 2, 1877, *ARSW* 1877, 1: 114–15, 116.

60. J. Q. Smith to Secretary of Interior, March 6, 1877, *ARSW* 1877, 1: 115; C. T. Gorham, March 7, 1877, ibid., 113.

61. E. D. Townsend to McDowell, March 13, 1877, *ARSW* 1877, 1: 116; S. Breck, "H. Q., Military Division of the Pacific and Department of California," March 24, 1877, ibid., 116–17; E. D. Townsend, "Copy and Instructions," April 26, 1877, ibid., 117.

62. O. O. Howard, May 21, 1877, *ARSW* 1877, 1: 117.

Chapter 2

1. "Sioux War," *Arkansas City Traveler,* July 19, 1876; E. A. Hayt, "Annual Report," *ARCIA* 1879, v–vi; "Bill to Transfer Control of the Indian Bureau," *New York Tribune,* July 12, 1876.

2. Zimmer, *Frontier Soldier,* 69, 68; N. A. Miles, "Report," *ARSW* 1877, 1: 523–29; J. A. Brisbin to Adj. Gen., ibid., 552–53; Marquis, *Wooden Leg,* 325; Stands in Timber and Liberty, *Cheyenne Memories,* 226.

3. FitzGerald, *An Army Doctor's Wife,* 220.

4. Ibid., 221.

5. Ibid., 219, 220, 221, 223, 259.

6. Ibid., 262.

7. Ibid., 221, 259, 219, 250; John FitzGerald, quoted in ibid., 304.

8. Ray, "Ethnohistory of the Joseph Band," 216–17; McWhorter, *Yellow Wolf,* 36; H. M. Painter to L. V. McWhorter, undated letter, 1929, McW, folder 93.

9. O. O. Howard, "Report," *ARSW* 1877, 1: 590; Gibson, *The Life of General George M. Sternberg,* 92, 93; John FitzGerald, quoted in FitzGerald, *An Army Doctor's Wife,* 304.

10. Painter to McWhorter, undated letter, 1929.

11. Ibid.

12. "Details of Operations," May 22, 1877, *ARSW* 1877, 1: 589–90.

13. Howard, "Report," 593; FitzGerald, *An Army Doctor's Wife,* 246–47; Howard, *Nez Percé Joseph,* 51, 75; Grafe, "Museum Collections," 31; Alcorn and Alcorn, "Aged Nez Perce Recalls the 1877 Tragedy," 59; Wood, "Chief Joseph, the Nez Percé," 135.

14. FitzGerald, *An Army Doctor's Wife,* 248, 249, 260; Gibson, *The Life of General George M. Sternberg,* 93; Evans, *Voice of the Old Wolf*, 39–40; Cyrus Townsend Brady, "The Epic of the Nez Percés," in Brady, *Northwestern Fights and Fighters,* 39–40.

15. Meacham, "Visit among the Indians in the Indian Territory."

16. G. Crook, "Report, Howard's Scouts," September 23, 1878, *ARSW* 1878, 1: 89; McGillycuddy, "Dr. Valentine T. McGillycuddy's Recollections," 43; Lee, "To General James N. Allison."

17. "Sheridan's Report," *Emporia News,* November 16, 1868; "Custer's Official Report," *Walnut Valley Times,* September 12, 1873.

18. James, *Nez Perce Women in Transition,* 119, 139; Alcorn and Alcorn, "Aged Nez Perce Recalls the 1877 Tragedy," 59; Gidley, *With One Sky above Us,* 90.

19. A. H. Terry, "Report," *ARSW* 1877, 1: 487; P. H. Sheridan to Townsend, "Report, Captured Band of Hostiles," October 25, 1877, ibid., 57.

20. Brown, *The Flight of the Nez Perce,* 91–94; M. C. Meigs, "Quartermaster's Report," *ARSW* 1877, 1: 183; "General of the Army," ibid., 12–23; N. A. Miles to A. H. Terry, "Report," September 17, 1877, ibid., 73; Theodore W. Goldin, "The Seventh Cavalry at Cañon Creek," in Brady, *Northwestern Fights and Fighters,* 203–205; Sheridan to Townsend, October 25, 1877, *ARSW* 1878, 1: 58; M. C. Meigs, "Appropriations," ibid., 296; Benj. Alvord to McCrary, ibid., 438; M. C. Meigs, "Report," ibid., 254–55.

21. Hunn with Selam and Family, *Nch'i-Wána,* 175–79; James, *Nez Perce Women in Transition,* 20–23, 14, 17, 19; Gidley, *Kopet,* 63; McWhorter, *Hear Me, My Chiefs!* 394.

22. G. W. McCrary, "Report, Nez Perce Resistance," November 19, 1877, *ARSW* 1877, 1: xv; W. T. Sherman, "Report, Nez Perce," November 7, 1877, ibid., 15.

23. P. H. Sheridan to E. G. Townsend, "Colonel Miles Captured Hostiles," October 25, 1877, *ARSW* 1877, 1: 55; J. Pope, "Nez Perce Population," December 4, 1877, NPWF, 339.

24. J. Gibbon, "Report 3A," September 2, 1877, *ARSW* 1877, 1: 73; Haines, *Red Eagles of the Northwest,* 292; Howard, *Nez Percé Joseph,* 210; McWhorter, *Hear Me, My Chiefs!* 400; J. T. Van Orsdale to C. Rawn, "Reburials at Big Hole," *ARSW* 1877, 1: 549–50.

25. John FitzGerald quoted in FitzGerald, *An Army Doctor's Wife,* 290; McWhorter, *Yellow Wolf,* 112–25; Many Wounds and Black Eagle, "Women Wounded at the Big Hole," 1928, McW, folder 79; Owyen, interview with Lucullus McWhorter, November 1926, McW, folder 41–43; *James Reuben's Record Book,* University of Idaho Library, 9: lines 6, 14.

26. W. Otis Halfmoon, interview with author, July 20, 2005.

27. Shields, *The Battle of the Big Hole,* 166–67, 172–73, 179, 181–83.

28. McWhorter, *Yellow Wolf,* 136.

29. Gibbon, "Report 3A," 68–71; Gibbon, *Adventures on the Western Frontier,* 217; Wood, *Days with Chief Joseph,* 360–61; Owyen, interview with McWhorter; Brown, *The Flight of the Nez Perce,* 254.

30. McWhorter, *Hear Me, My Chiefs!* 381.

31. Edward S. Curtis, "Tom Hill," in Curtis, *The Nez Perces,* 171.

32. Many Wounds and Black Eagle, "Women Wounded at the Big Hole"; Owyen, interview with McWhorter; Edward S. Curtis, "Yellow Bull," in Curtis,

The Nez Perces, 167; McWhorter, *Hear Me, My Chiefs!* 405, 484–85, 486; Wood, *Days with Chief Joseph,* 362.

33. Alcorn and Alcorn, "Aged Nez Perce Recalls the 1877 Tragedy," 59, 63–64; Pahit Palikt, in McWhorter, *Yellow Wolf,* 143; David Williams, ibid., 142; Many Wounds and Black Eagle, "Women Wounded at the Big Hole"; McWhorter, *Yellow Wolf,* 162.

34. Chief Joseph, "An Indian's View," 427.

35. Pinkham, *100th Anniversary of the Nez Perce War;* Scott, *Some Memories of a Soldier,* 82; McWhorter, *Hear Me, My Chiefs!* 381; Alcorn and Alcorn, "Aged Nez Perce Recalls the 1877 Tragedy," 63–64; Curtis, "Yellow Bull," 68; *James Reuben's Record Book,* February 1883, 64: line 24.

36. Garcia, *Tough Trip through Paradise,* 237.

37. McWhorter, *Yellow Wolf,* 132; McWhorter, *Hear Me, My Chiefs!* 405; Garcia, *Tough Trip through Paradise,* 237–39.

38. Nelson A. Miles, "Report to the Assistant Adjutant General, Tongue River," *ARSW* 1877, 1: 512.

39. Noyes, *In the Land of the Chinook,* 81; In-who-lise, quoted in Garcia, *Tough Trip through Paradise,* 240; Zimmer, *Frontier Soldier,* 129; Woodruff, "We Have Joseph and All of His People," 33; Howard, *Nez Percé Joseph,* 269; W. L. Lincoln, "Fort Belknap," *ARCIA* 1880, 100; W. Otis Halfmoon, interview with author, July 25, 2005; McWhorter, *Hear Me, My Chiefs!* 514; Zimmer, *Frontier Soldier,* 129.

40. *James Reuben's Record Book,* 93: lines 9–17; 95: line 3.

41. O. O. Howard, "Battle of the Clearwater," August 12, 1877, *ARSW* 1877, 1: 606; Alcorn and Alcorn, "Aged Nez Perce Recalls the 1877 Tragedy," 61; Brown, *The Flight of the Nez Perce,* 201, 204, 214, 444; McWhorter, *Yellow Wolf,* 310–12.

42. Gibson, *The Life of General George M. Sternberg,* 106–109; FitzGerald, *An Army Doctor's Wife,* 288–89.

43. J. Reuben to O. O. Howard, December 20, 1877, NPWF, 339.

44. W. Otis Halfmoon, interview with author, February 8, 2006; E. C. Watkins to C. Schurz, September 25, 1877, NPWF, 338; O. O. Howard to J. G. Kelton, November 27, 1877, ibid.; Halfmoon, *Chief Joseph and Warriors Memorial Celebration,* 18.

45. Curtis, "Yellow Bull," 168; N. A. Miles, "Report," October 24, 1881, NPWF, 340; N. A. Miles, "Memorandum," October 28, 1877, NPWF, 338; Nez Perce Census, 1880, LDNPQA, PA 1; "Chief Joseph in the City, Together with Three of His Chiefs, Become for a Short Time Our Guests; See the Telephone and Are the First Indians to Talk to a Phonograph," *Leavenworth Times,* June 19, 1878; Sup-poon-mas, aka Charlie Moses, and John Fur Cap, He-yum-tak-mul-in, "Joseph's Brethren Taken to Fort Leavenworth," *Leavenworth Times,* December 5, 1877.

46. R. MacFeely, "Transfers and Issues to Indians," *ARSW* 1877, 1: 411.

47. McWhorter, *Yellow Wolf*, 108; McWhorter, *Hear Me, My Chiefs!* 347, 348; C. Rawn, "Post Missoula," September 19, 1877, *ARSW* 1877, 1: 549.

48. J. R. Brooke, telegram, "Case of Three Nez Perce Indians," 1878, NPWF, 339; McWhorter, *Yellow Wolf*, 108.

49. McWhorter, *Hear Me, My Chiefs!* 348; Brown, *The Flight of the Nez Perce*, 100.

50. Rawn, "Post Missoula," 549; Curtis, "Tom Hill," 169.

51. J. Gibbon, "Fort Shaw Captives," October 5, 1878, NPWF, 340; Geo. W. McCrary, "Three Nez Perce Prisoners," April 11, 1878, NPWF, 339.

52. Gibbon, "Fort Shaw Captives."

53. James Wilson, "Doings at Ponca Agency," *Arkansas City Traveler*, October 27, 1880.

54. Many Wounds and Black Eagle, "Women Wounded at the Big Hole"; Pinkham, *100th Anniversary of the Nez Perce War of 1877;* Miles, "Report," October 24, 1881. Pa-ya-wa-hiekt was also known as Hoof Necklace or Samuel Fleming; Ip-na-Not-Will-Ken was also known as Ip-na-mat-we-ken; Seelo Wahyakt was also known as Eye Necklace; and Ko-san-yum was also known as Luke Wilson.

55. C. A. Dempsey, "Going to the Reservation," *Atchison Patriot*, reprinted in *Columbus Border Star*, December 13, 1878.

56. James, *Nez Perce Women in Transition*, 132–33.

57. Evans, *Voice of the Old Wolf*, 104; Howard and McGrath, *Saga of Chief Joseph*, 355–56; Halfmoon, *Chief Joseph and Warriors Memorial Celebration*, 9, 13; James, *Nez Perce Women in Transition*, 132–33; McWhorter, *Yellow Wolf*, 63; Nez Perce Census, 1878, LDNPQA, QA 2: lines 39, 51; Nez Perce Census, 1879, LDNPQA, QA 1: lines 63, 77, 60; Nez Perce Census, 1880, LDNPQA, PA 1: lines 62, 17, 42, 99; Nez Perce Census, 1885, IINP: lines 63, 17, 111, 98.

58. C. Aubrey to C. Rawn, August 24, 1878, NPWF, 340; "Fort Shaw, Roster of Troops," *ARSW* 1878, 1: 78; Curtis, "Yellow Bull," 168–70; testimony of Tom Hill in U.S. Senate, Committee on Indian Affairs, *Memorial of the Nez Perce Indians Residing in the State of Idaho to the Congress of the United States*, 31–34.

59. E. A. Hayt to Secretary of Interior, September 30, 1878, NPWF, 340; Aubrey to Rawn, August 24, 1878, ibid.; M. L. Kendrick, "Report," September 30, 1877, ibid.; telegram, October 5, 1878, ibid.

60. P. H. Sheridan to John Gibbon, September 6, 1878, NPWF, 340; Philip T. Sheridan, untitled, September 6, 1878, ibid.

61. Telegram to Headquarters, Minneapolis, Minn., "Nez Perce Indians from Ft Shaw Arrived at St. Paul," October 5, 1878, NPWF, 340; John Gibbon, telegram, "Nez Perce Captives," October 5, 1878, ibid.; C. S. Ilsley, Special Order no. 183, October 9, 1878, ibid.; John Gibbon, "Sale of Captured Horses," October 17, 1878, ibid.

62. Camille Williams to L. V. McWhorter, March 21, 1938, McW, folder 79; W. D. Whipple, "Prisoners at Crow Camp," July 11, 1878, NPWF, 340; Edw. Smith, Special Orders no. 82, Fort Snelling, July 13, 1878, ibid. Weyat-mas Wa-hakt was also known as Swan Necklace or John Minthorn.

63. L. V. McWhorter, "Indian Relics," Parker/Fisher Collection, February 18, 1930, McW, folder 64.

64. Shields, *The Battle of the Big Hole,* 80–81; "The Surrender of Joseph"; FitzGerald, *An Army Doctor's Wife,* 102; T. A. Sutherland, "Nez Perce," *San Francisco Chronicle,* July 28, 1877; Forse, "Chief Joseph as a Commander," 11; Brown, *The Flight of the Nez Perce,* 195.

65. Gibson, *The Life of General George M. Sternberg,* 102.

66. FitzGerald, *An Army Doctor's Wife,* 290; Gibson, *The Life of General George M. Sternberg,* 102; Redfield, "Who Stole the Piano?" 292–93.

67. John Gibbon, "Report," October 18, 1877, *ARSW* 1877, 1: 522; Mueller, "The Nez Perce at Cow Island," 52; Kelly, *"Yellowstone Kelly,"* 205.

68. McWhorter, *Yellow Wolf,* 168.

69. Colonel J. W. Redington, "The Story of Bugler Brooks," in Brady, *Northwestern Fights and Fighters,* 199; H. J. Davis, "The Battle of Camas Meadows," ibid., 194–95, 197; Wood, "Chief Joseph, the Nez Percé"; McWhorter, *Yellow Wolf,* 168–69; McWhorter, *Hear Me, My Chiefs!* 420; Howard, *Nez Percé Joseph,* 269.

70. S. D. Sturgis, "Report, American Horses," September 13, 1877, *ARSW* 1877, 1: 74; N. A. Miles, "Report, on the March," ibid., 512; O. O. Howard, "Report, in Camp," September 15, 1877, ibid., 624; Goldin, "The Seventh Cavalry at Cañon Creek," 221; "The Yellowstone Park in the Early Days," pts. 1 and 2; McWhorter, *Yellow Wolf,* 62–63; Evans, *Voice of the Old Wolf,* 64, 96–97, 157; O. O. Howard, "Report," *ARSW* 1879, 1: 153.

71. Brown, *The Flight of the Nez Perce,* 167, 338; Mrs. George Cowan, "Reminiscences of Pioneer Life"; Garcia, *Tough Trip through Paradise,* 238.

72. McWhorter, *Yellow Wolf,* 43, 88; Red Feather of the Wing, "The Story of Red Feather of the Wing," 1908, McW, folder 32; James, *Nez Perce Women in Transition,* 97, 126; McWhorter, *Hear Me, My Chiefs!* 486.

73. A. I. Chapman to Hayt, letter, December 13, 1878, NPWF, 340; Lynus Walker, story shared with author by Steve and Connie Evans, September 15, 2004.

74. McWhorter, *Yellow Wolf,* 91; "Nez Perce Indians after the Battle," *Saint Paul and Minneapolis Pioneer Press,* October 17, 1877; Miles, *Personal Recollections and Observations,* 277; N. A. Miles, "Report," December 27, 1877, *ARSW* 1877, 1: 529; "Miles the Fighter," *Leavenworth Times,* November 23, 1877; G. W. McCrary to E. A. Hayt, April 22, 1879, NPWF, 340; Deward Walker, e-mail to author, June 7, 2006; Chapman to Hayt, December 13, 1878; M. C. Meigs, "Quartermaster's Report," *ARSW* 1878, 1: 260.

75. *United States Statutes at Large,* Rev. Stat., March 3, 1865, 13 Stat. L., 563, Sec. 2127.

76. Chief Joseph, in Meacham, "Visit among the Indians in the Indian Territory."

77. McCrary to Hayt, April 22, 1879; A. I. Chapman to E. A. Hayt, December 13, 1878, NPWF, 340.

78. McCrary to Hayt, April 22, 1879.

79. Phinney, *Jirah Isham Allen*, 99.

80. McWhorter, *Hear Me, My Chiefs!* 524.

Chapter 3

1. McWhorter, *Hear Me, My Chiefs!* 499.

2. Wood, "Chief Joseph, the Nez Perce," 141–42; "Nez Perce Indians after the Battle," *St. Paul and Minneapolis Pioneer Press*, October 17, 1877.

3. "The Surrender of Joseph."

4. "Nez Perces," *San Francisco Chronicle*, November 1, 1877.

5. McWhorter, *Yellow Wolf*, 211, 219–20; "Nez Perce Indians after the Battle"; McWhorter, *Hear Me, My Chiefs!* 495.

6. Thomas A. Sutherland, "The Captive Chief Joseph's Last Gallant Fight in Montana," *San Francisco Chronicle*, November 1, 1877; McWhorter, *Hear Me, My Chiefs!* 495.

7. *James Reuben's Record Book*, University of Idaho Library, 1882, 83: lines 100, 103.

8. Howard, *Nez Percé Joseph*, 273; McWhorter, *Yellow Wolf*, 211, 219–20; Chief Joseph, "An Indian's View," 264; McWhorter, *Hear Me, My Chiefs!* 501; Debo, *A History of the Indians*, 264; "Nez Perce Indians after the Battle."

9. Alcorn and Alcorn, "Aged Nez Perce Recalls the 1877 Tragedy," 67.

10. J. W. Redington to L. V. McWhorter, January 1, 1928, McW, folder 40; McWhorter, *Yellow Wolf*, 22; "The Surrender of Joseph," 906.

11. "Map," *ARSW* 1878, 1: following 660; N. A. Miles, "Report," October 6, 1877, *ARSW* 1878 1: 654.

12. Romeyn, "The Capture of Chief Joseph," 291; H. R. Tilton, "Surgeon's Report," October 1877, *ARSW* 1878, 1: 429.

13. "Miles the Fighter," *Leavenworth Times*, November 23, 1877.

14. Tilton, "Surgeon's Report."

15. "Enroute; Arrival of Miles' Indian Prisoners at Fort Buford, Dispatch from Bismarck, November 8, 1877," *St. Paul Dispatch*, November 16, 1877.

16. Scott, *Some Memories of a Soldier*, 180.

17. "Disposing of the Prisoners," *The New North-west*, October 19, 1877.

18. O. O. Howard, "Report to Division Headquarters, Red River French Half-Breeds," October 8, 1877, *ARSW* 1877, 1: 632–33; Howard, *Strange Empire*,

278, 281, 284; Stegner, *Wolf Willow,* 117–19; Brown, *The Flight of the Nez Perce,* 309; Scott, *Some Memories of a Soldier,* 76.

19. Kelly, *"Yellowstone Kelly,"* 205; "Nez Perce Indians after the Battle"; Scott, *Some Memories of a Soldier,* 76–77.

20. Scott, *Some Memories of a Soldier,* 77–79; Steve Grafe, interview with author, May 19, 2004.

21. Scott, *Some Memories of a Soldier,* 83.

22. Reed, in Carroll, *The Recollections of Colonel Hugh T. Reed,* 16.

23. Brown, *The Flight of the Nez Perce,* 423–24; "Miles the Fighter."

24. Relander, *Drummers and Dreamers,* 82; J. T., "A Nez Perce Funeral," 258, 260–61.

25. "Miles the Fighter."

26. Miles, *Personal Recollections and Observations,* 277.

27. Baldwin, *Memoirs of the Late Frank D. Baldwin,* 194.

28. Brust, "John H. Fouch," 8.

29. Lang, "Where Did the Nez Perce Go?" 22.

30. Brust, "John H. Fouch," 8.

31. Brown, *The Flight of the Nez Perce,* 423–25.

32. "Chief Joseph and His Tribe, Special Dispatch," *New York Times,* November 8, 1877.

33. A. I. Chapman to E. A. Hayt, "Nez Perce Saddles and Equipment," December 13, 1878, NPWF, 340.

34. Bond, *Flatboating on the Yellowstone,* 3–22; F. G. Bond to L. V. McWhorter, letter, September 29, 1928, McW, folder 79; Bond to McWhorter, letter, January 12, 1929, McW, folder 256.

35. Brown, *The Flight of the Nez Perce,* 456.

36. Bond, *Flatboating on the Yellowstone,* 9–11, 15, 19; Ray, "Ethnohistory of the Joseph Band," 230; F. G. Bond to L. V. McWhorter, "Notes," September 29, 1928; L. V. McWhorter, "Notes," n.d., McW, folder 79; Bond to McWhorter, January 12, 1929.

37. Bond, *Flatboating on the Yellowstone,* 5–6; G. W. McCrary, "Roster," *ARSW* 1878, 1: 58–59, 62–63, 79; R. G. Redd, "To Fort Keogh," *ARSW* 1878, 1: 79.

38. James, *Nez Perce Women in Transition,* 80–81.

39. Bond, *Flatboating on the Yellowstone,* 6–10, 15.

40. Ibid., 5, 8, 12–13, 15–16.

41. Ibid., 11, 13.

42. Ibid., 5.

43. Ibid., 6–8, 17–18; Edward M. Bruner, "Mandan," in *Perspectives in American Indian Culture Change,* ed. Edward H. Spicer (Chicago: University of Chicago Press, 1956), 239; Miles, *Personal Recollections and Observations,* 280.

44. Scott, *Some Memories of a Soldier,* 83–84.

45. Bond, *Flatboating on the Yellowstone,* 19.

46. Stands in Timber and Liberty, *Cheyenne Memories,* 228; Miles, *Personal Recollections and Observations,* 277; "Joseph's Arrival," *Bismarck Tribune,* November 21, 1877; Bond, *Flatboating on the Yellowstone,* 21.

47. Holm, *Strong Hearts, Wounded Souls,* 2–9, 17, 25, 184–87; Bond, *Flatboating on the Yellowstone,* 15, 19, 20.

48. Bond, *Flatboating on the Yellowstone,* 15, 19, 20, 22.

49. J. T., "A Nez Perce Funeral," 259.

50. Bond, *Flatboating on the Yellowstone,* 10, 17–19; *James Reuben's Record Book,* 1882: lines 64, 69, 96, 140, 141, 169, 172; Nez Perce Census, 1885, IINP: line 52; "George Washington, Herald of the Nez Perce," *Winfield Courier,* June 20, 1878; Relander, *Drummers and Dreamers,* 89, 105; O. O. Howard, "Council with Chief Joseph's Band," May 3–7, 1877, May 22, 1877, *ARSW* 1877, 1: 591; FitzGerald, *An Army Doctor's Wife,* 223; Bond, *Flatboating on the Yellowstone,* 15–16, 18; Miles, *Personal Recollections and Observations,* 280.

51. Bond, *Flatboating on the Yellowstone,* 7, 8, 22, 12; F. Bond to Lucullus V. McWhorter, letter, September 29, 1928, McW, folder 79.

52. Bond, *Flatboating on the Yellowstone,* 21; "Joseph's Arrival"; Reed quoted in Carroll, *The Recollections of Colonel Hugh T. Reed,* 17; Pinkham, *100th Anniversary of the Nez Perce War;* McWhorter, *Yellow Wolf,* 178; Haines, *Red Eagles of the Northwest,* 317–18; "Luncheon with the Nez Perces"; "The Last of Joseph; Interesting Incidents Connected with His Brief Sojourn at Bismarck," *St. Paul and Minneapolis Pioneer Press,* November 28, 1877; "The Banquet at the Sheridan for General Miles," *Bismarck Tribune,* November 21, 1877.

53. Pinkham, *100th Anniversary of the Nez Perce War;* McWhorter, *Yellow Wolf,* 178; Haines, *Red Eagles of the Northwest,* 317–18; "Joseph's Arrival"; "Luncheon with the Nez Perces."

54. "Chief Joseph in Bismarck," *St. Paul and Minneapolis Pioneer Press,* December 6, 1877.

55. "New Indian Outrage, Chief Joseph at the Banquet," *Brainerd Tribune,* December 8, 1877; "The *Brainerd Tribune* Is Cruel," *St. Cloud Journal-Press,* December 22, 1877; "Chief Joseph and 400 Nez Perces En Route to Fort Leavenworth, Kansas," ibid., November 24, 1877; "Chief Joseph with His Band of Nez Perces Have Arrived at Fort Leavenworth," ibid., December 1, 1877; "Is Chief Joseph a Sioux? A Well Founded Belief that the Nez Perces Warrior Is One of the Old Minnesota Indians," *St. Paul and Minneapolis Pioneer Press,* December 2, 1877.

56. "Joseph's Arrival"; "Joseph's Gone," *Bismarck Tribune,* November 23, 1877; James H. Mills, "Joseph's Grievances; The Defeated Chief Has a Talk with General Miles," Special Dispatch from the *New York Times,* in *The New North-west,* December 7, 1877.

57. "Miles the Fighter"; N. A. Miles, "Report," December 27, 1877, in Clinton B. Fisk and William Stickney, Commissioners, "Report of a Visit to Colorado and the Indian Territory," August 22, 1878, *ARBIC* 1878, 47–51; E. A. Hayt to Office of Indian Affairs, "Regarding Joseph's Return," November 24, 1877, AIC, box C, letter 191.

58. W. T. Sherman to P. H. Sheridan, "Pursue the Nez Perces to Their Deaths," August 24, 1877, NPWF, 338; Sherman to Sheridan, "Try and Execute Nez Perce Leaders, Etc.," August 31, 1877, NPWF, 339.

59. W. T. Sherman to P. H. Sheridan, "Nez Perce to Fort Leavenworth," November 19, 1877, NPWF, 339; Sheridan to Sherman, "Nez Perce Prisoners Arrive at Fort Abraham Lincoln," November 24, 1877, ibid.

60. O. O. Howard, "Report, Too Late to Return Prisoners to Idaho This Year," October 19, 1877, *ARSW* 1877, 1: 77.

61. O. O. Howard quoted in General McDowell, telegram, "Regarding: Return of the Nez Perces Prisoners from Fort Leavenworth to Their Homes in Idaho," May 20, 1878, NPWF, 340.

62. Ibid.

63. Howard, "General Howard's Comment on Joseph's Narrative," 89.

64. Carl Schurz, "Report of the Secretary of the Interior," *ARCIA* 1877, vi; Hayt, letter, November 24, 1877, AIC, box C; letter 191.

65. W. T. Sherman, telegram, "Colonel Miles Desires to Take Principal Cheyenne and Nez Perce Chiefs to Washington, D.C.," November 14, 1877, NPWF, 339; E. A. Hayt to Secretary of Interior, "Send Nez Perces to Fort Leavenworth; Denies Permission to Bring to Washington," November 16, 1877, ibid.

66. "The Nez Perces; Thirteen Carloads of Captured Red Skins Will Reach St. Paul This Afternoon, on Their Way to Leavenworth," *St. Paul and Minneapolis Pioneer Press*, November 23, 1877.

67. "The Nez Perces; The Arrival of Chief Joseph and His Band Last Night," *St Paul and Minneapolis Pioneer Press*, November 25, 1877; "Joseph's Arrival"; Mills, "Joseph's Grievances"; R. G. Redd, "To Fort Keogh," *ARSW* 1878, 1: 79; "Assignments," Capt. R. E. Johnston, Cdg. Post Co. G., 1st Infantry, Southern District, Brule Agency, *ARSW* 1877, 1: 77; Reed quoted in Carroll, *The Recollections of Colonel Hugh T. Reed*, 17–18.

68. Reed, in Carroll, *The Recollections of Colonel Hugh T. Reed*, 17; "Joseph's Gone."

69. W. P. Carlin, "Report, Headquarters, Standing Rock Post, Dakota," September 27, 1877, *ARSW* 1877, 1: 534.

70. N. A. Miles, "Report to Asst. Adj. General, Tongue River," *ARSW* 1877, 1: 512; Phinney, *Jirah Isham Allen*, 95, 97–99; McWhorter, *Yellow Wolf*, 193–94; Zimmer, *Frontier Soldier*, 91–92; Stands in Timber and Liberty, *Cheyenne Memories*, 121–26; Miles, *Personal Recollections and Observations*, 277.

71. "The Last of Joseph."

72. Ibid.

73. Ibid.

74. Mills, "Joseph's Grievances"; "The Nez Perces; The Arrival of Chief Joseph and His Band"; R. MacFeely, "Commissary General," *ARSW* 1878, 1: 411, 417–18; Bond, *Flatboating on the Yellowstone,* 4; "Joseph's Arrival"; "The Last of Joseph"; Debo, *A History of the Indians,* 263.

75. Ralph Armstrong in Evans, *Voice of the Old Wolf,* 141; "Joseph's Gone"; Svingen, *The Northern Cheyenne Indian Reservation,* 244; Bond, *Flatboating on the Yellowstone,* 22; "The Last of Joseph."

76. *Map of the Northern Pacific Railroad and Connections* (St. Paul, Minn.: Northern Pacific Railroad, 1879).

77. Reed quoted in Carroll, *The Recollections of Colonel Hugh T. Reed,* 18.

78. "Chief Joseph and 400 Nez Perces"; Reed quoted in Carroll, *The Recollections of Colonel Hugh T. Reed,* 19; "Chief Joseph's Arrival"; "The Nez Perce, Their Passage through St. Paul," *St. Paul Dispatch,* November 26, 1877.

79. Reed quoted in Carroll, *The Recollections of Colonel Hugh T. Reed,* 19.

80. John Pope, "Nez Perce Population Statistics," December 4, 1877, NPWF, 339; "Chief Joseph's Arrival."

81. "Joseph and His Brethren at Mason City, Etc.," *Saint Paul and Minneapolis Pioneer Press,* November 29, 1877; "Lo' the Poor Indian," *Cerro Gordo Republican,* November 19, 1877; "Nez Perces," *Mason City Express,* November 18, 1877.

82. "The Nez Perces; Thirteen Carloads"; R. E. Johnston to J. W. Crippen, letter to the editor, *St. Paul and Minneapolis Pioneer Press,* December 4, 1877; C. A. Dempsey, "Going to the Reservation," *Atchison Patriot,* reprinted in *Columbus Border Star,* December 13, 1878; "Joseph's Band, Arrival at Fort Leavenworth," *Leavenworth Times,* November 27, 1877; "Map of Indian Country and Railroads," *ARBIC* 1879, inset.

83. Johnston to Crippen.

84. "Assignments," Capt. R. E. Johnston, Records of Capt. Robert E. Johnston, Indian Agent at Standing Rock Agency, William Passmore Carlin Papers, State Historical Society of North Dakota Archives, MSS 20044, 1–10; Chief Joseph, "An Indian's View," 430.

Chapter 4

1. Hunt and Lorence, *History of Fort Leavenworth,* 128–29.

2. "Medical Officers Serving at Fort Leavenworth," *ARSW* 1878, 1: 58–59.

3. "Joseph's Band, Arrival at Fort Leavenworth," *Leavenworth Times,* November 27, 1877.

4. E. R. Platt, "Special Orders 211," November 21, 1877, NPWF, 339; P. H. Sheridan, "Nez Perce Arrived at Fort Leavenworth," November 27, 1877, ibid.

5. Sherman, telegram, November 14, 1877; Zimmer, *Frontier Soldier,* 70.

6. "Joseph's Band, Arrival at Fort Leavenworth."

7. J. P. Coffin, "Special Local Notes, Chief Joseph and His Band," *Daily Out-look,* November 27, 1877.

8. "Joseph's Band, Arrival at Fort Leavenworth."

9. J. H. Johnson III, "Nez Perce Indians Spent Eight Months at the Fort," *Times Weekend,* April 10, 1988; "The Nez Perce, Their Passage through St. Paul," *St. Paul Dispatch,* November 26, 1877.

10. J. P. Coffin, "Chief Joseph and His band as Mentioned in the *Public Press,*" *Daily Out-look,* November 27, 1877; "Joseph's Band, Arrival at Fort Leavenworth."

11. Coffin, "Chief Joseph and His Band."

12. Nowak, "Chief Joseph's Racetrack"; Hunt and Lorence, *History of Fort Leavenworth,* 128.

13. P. H. Sheridan, telegram, "Hold Nez Perce Prisoners at Fort Leavenworth," November 24, 1877, NPWF, 339.

14. E. Hayt, "Report, Chief Joseph," November 1, 1878, *ARCIA* 1878, xxxii, xxxiii.

15. Chief Joseph, "An Indian's View," 430.

16. Gibson, *The Life of General George M. Sternberg,* 194–95.

17. P. H. Sheridan, telegram, "Issue Old Clothing to Prisoners," January 18, 1878, NPWF, 336.

18. "The Nez Perces Are Visited by 5,000 People from the Country on Sunday; Their Religious Services as Witnessed by a Times Reporter," *Leavenworth Times,* December 11, 1877; N. A. Miles, "Report," December 27, 1877, in Clinton B. Fisk and William Stickney, Commissioners, "Report of a Visit to Colorado and the Indian Territory," August 22, 1878, *ARBIC* 1878, 47; P. H. Sheridan, telegram, "Re: Old Clothing," December 29, 1877, NPWF, 339; "The Indians," *Leavenworth Times,* May 6, 1878; C. Hoyt, "Supplies, Issues to Nez Perces," January and February 1878, NPWF, 339; "The Indians," *Leavenworth Times,* December 5, 1877; "A Perfect Fac Simile of the Autograph of the Noted Chieftain as Voluntarily Written and Given to a *Times* Reporter," ibid., December 18, 1877.

19. C. Hoyt, "Subsistence Issues," NPWF, 340; "Camp Joseph; A Short Visit to the Nez Perces," *Leavenworth Times,* December 4, 1877; G. W. McCrary, "Requests for Payment from the Indian Department," January 25, 1878, NPWF, 339; E. A. Hayt, "Debts Incurred for Nez Perce, Indian Bureau Will Not Pay," May 29, 1878, NPWF, 340; R. MacFeely, "Transfers and Issues to Indians," *ARSW* 1878, 1: 411; W. T. Sherman, "Nez Perce Remain at War Department's Expense," March 8, 1878, NPWF, 339; "Transfers," *ARSW* 1879, 1: 385.

20. J. K. Barnes, "Medical and Hospital Supplies," 1878, NPWF, 340; C. Hoyt, "Stores Transferred," December 1877, January 1878, NPWF, 339; A. P. Blunt, "Prisoners and Prison Labor," *ARSW* 1877, 1: 468; "A Perfect Fac Simile of the Autograph."

21. "Camp Joseph"; "The Indians," *Leavenworth Times,* May 8, 1878.

22. McWhorter, *Yellow Wolf,* 104, 123; McWhorter, *Hear Me, My Chiefs!* 154; H. M. Painter to L. V. McWhorter, letter, 1929, McW, folder 93.

23. A. I. Comfort, "Medical and Hospital Supplies," December 1877, January, February, March, May, July 1878, NPWF, 339, 340; J. Thomas, M.D. *A Comprehensive Medical Dictionary: With an Appendix, Comprising a Complete List of All the More Important Articles of the* Materia Medica; *with the Necessary Directions for Writing Latin Prescriptions, etc.* (Philadelphia: J. B. Lippincott, 1876), 341, 375–76, 563, 624–35, 653.

24. James, *Nez Perce Women in Transition,* 171; "Medical Statistics, Lapwai," *ARCIA* 1879, 263.

25. "George Washington, Herald of the Nez Perce," *Winfield Courier,* June 20, 1878.

26. "Camp Joseph"; Comfort, "Medical and Hospital Supplies"; J. P. Wright, "Report from the Military Prison," July 8, 1878, *ARSW* 1878, 1: 523.

27. "The Indians," May 8, 1878.

28. Chief Joseph and H. H. Gregg, in U.S. Senate, *Testimony Taken by the Joint Committee Appointed to Take into Consideration the Expediency of Transferring the Indian Bureau to the War Department,* 77–90.

29. S. T. T, "Letter"; Frederick L. Bruier, Jose Llopis, and Bob Dun, "Project 19: U.S. Army, Fort Leavenworth, Kansas," http://www.wes.army.mil/el/ccspt/milproj.html (accessed December 4, 1999); King, "WES Aids Research for Historic Graves"; Nowak, "Chief Joseph's Racetrack."

30. The Ponca remains were finally returned under provisions of the Native American Graves Protection and Repatriation Act, which was passed in 1990. Robbins, "Notice of Intent to Repatriate Cultural Items"; Grafe, interview with author, May 19, 2004.

31. "Inventory and Assessment of Human Remains"; Corbusier, *Verde to San Carlos,* 7, 278; United States Army Medical Museum, Anatomical Section, Records Relating to Specimens Transferred to the Smithsonian Institution, "Guide to the Collections of the National Anthropological Archives (SUV)," http://www.nmnh.si.edu/naa/guide/_uv.htm#jrg514 (accessed August 27, 2007).

32. Morton, *Catalogue of Skulls,* v, vi, 108–109, 707–708, 726–33, 738–39, 1227–31, 1447–49; Gillett, *The Army Medical Department,* 54–55; James Riding In, "Six Pawnee Crania."

33. "The Indians," May 8, 1878; McWhorter, *Yellow Wolf,* 142; L. V. McWhorter, "Nez Perces Escaping from Last Stand," 1928, McW, folder 79; Alcorn and Alcorn,

"Aged Nez Perce Recalls the 1877 Tragedy," 54–67. Chief Joseph took a second wife on February 19, and his unhappy wife Toma Alwawinmi and their infant daughter were alive at that time. "Chief Joseph's New Wife," *Leavenworth Times,* February 19, 1878.

34. "Notes Gathered with Regard to the Indian Camp," *Leavenworth Times,* December 28, 1877; Martin, "A Visit to Chief Joseph's Band," 303; Nowak, "Chief Joseph's Racetrack"; "The Indians Catch Everybody," *Leavenworth Times,* December 2, 1877; "Joseph's Camp," *Leavenworth Times,* January 8, 1878.

35. Martin, "A Visit to Chief Joseph's Band," 302.

36. "The Nez Perces Are Visited by 5,000 People"; "Chief Joseph," *Winfield Courier,* December 20, 1877; "Camp Joseph."

37. Marshall, "Nez Perce Groups," 23–24; Ray, *The Sanpoil and Nespelem,* 29; Ray, *Plateau Culture Element Distributions,* 248–50; Slickpoo and Walker, *Noon Nee-Me-Poo,* 61; James, *Nez Perce Women in Transition,* 142–43; "The Nez Perces Are Visited by 5,000 People."

38. Howard, *Nez Percé Joseph,* 62; Howard, "General Howard's Comment on Joseph's Narrative," 80–81.

39. "The Nez Perces; A Dance in Memory of the Warrior Who Was Killed at the Battle of Bear Paw Mountain," *Leavenworth Times,* December 23, 1877.

40. Chief Joseph, I-sa-nu-well-wacket, Ho Hats Mox Mox, Húsus Kute, Cool Cool Sneany, Tou-as-pat-lew, Chulum Mox Mox, and Him in Mox Mox, "Affidavit, Seeking Return to Northwest," December 10, 1877, NPWF, 339.

41. E. A. Hayt to Secretary of Interior, "James Reuben and General Howard Want to Send Nez Perces to the Indian Territory," January 30, 1878, AIC, box D, letter 125.

42. McWhorter, *Yellow Wolf,* 55; "Camp Joseph"; Josephy, *The Nez Perce Indians,* 637.

43. Martin, "A Visit to Chief Joseph's Band," 302–303.

44. "Camp Joseph"; "The Indians," May 8, 1878.

45. Walker, "The Nez Perce Sweat Bath Complex," 137; "Camp Joseph."

46. Teit, "The Salishan Tribes of the Western Plateau," 133, 135; "Nez Perces," *Winfield Courier,* December 27, 1877; "Camp Joseph."

47. "Notes Gathered with Regard to the Indian Camp"; Nez Perce Census, 1885, IINP: line 79; "Camp Joseph"; "The Indians," May 8, 1878; D. G. Vose to Col. A. B. Meacham, December 6, 1878, NARA, Washington, D.C., RG 75, entry 1377, Correspondence of Agent A. B. Meacham, folder 11E3; "Among Captive Indians; Scattered Remnants of Tribes, a Visit to the Nez Perces and Modocs," *New York Times,* November 8, 1878; testimony of Yellow Bull in U.S. Senate, Committee on Indian Affairs, *Memorial of the Nez Perce Indians Residing in the State of Idaho to the Congress of the United States,* 43–44.

48. "Chief Joseph in the City, Together with Three of His Chiefs, Become for a Short Time Our Guests; See the Telephone and Are the First Indians to

Talk to a Phonograph," *Leavenworth Times,* June 19, 1878; Baird, Mallickan, and Swagerty, *The Nez Perce Nation Divided,* 268–72, 276, 450, 447; "Five Indians in Confinement in Walla Walla," *Washington Statesman,* April 8, 1864; Lawyer, "Indian Treaty at Lapwai Agency, Idaho, May 16, 1863," *Portland Oregonian,* May 20, 1863; "Sha-poon-mash Discharged," *Washington Statesman,* October 7, 1864; N. A. Miles, telegram, "Our Usual Success," reprinted in *St. Paul and Minneapolis Pioneer Press,* October 9, 1877; "Joseph's Brethren White Feather and Bugle Taken to Fort Leavenworth," *Leavenworth Times,* December 5, 1877; Wood, "Chief Joseph, the Nez Perce."

49. DiLorenzo, "How Lincoln's Army 'Liberated' the Indians."

50. J. P. Wright, "Medical Conditions at the Prison," July 15, 1877, *ARSW* 1877, 1: 468; Blunt, "Prisoners and Prison Labor," 469–70.

51. Chief Joseph, "An Indian's View," 427.

52. Platter, Fleming, and Wilson, *A Memorial from the Synod of Kansas.*

53. Comfort, "Medical and Hospital Supplies."

54. DeSmet, *Life, Letters and Travels,* 817.

55. DiLorenzo, "How Lincoln's Army 'Liberated' the Indians"; Tom Holm, interview with author, November 5, 2005.

56. McWhorter, *Yellow Wolf,* 222; testimony of Tom Hill in U.S. Senate, Committee on Indian Affairs, *Memorial of the Nez Perce Indians Residing in the State of Idaho to the Congress of the United States,* 31–34; Ronan, "Indian Affairs."

57. Henry Covington, "Interview, May 18, 1958," in Ruby and Brown, *Half-Sun on the Columbia,* 222.

58. McWhorter, *Yellow Wolf,* 288; Wm. Falck to Asst. Adj. General, "Chief Joseph's Daughter," August 1, 1878, *ARSW* 1878, 1: 180.

59. G. Baird, "Mission to Canada to Interview White Bird," July 22, 1878, NPWF, 340; Gidley, *Kopet,* 83; H. M. Painter to L. V. McWhorter, letter, 1929, McW, folder 93.

60. Reed quoted in Carroll, *The Recollections of Colonel Hugh T. Reed,* 19.

61. Brown, *The Flight of the Nez Perce,* 287, 303.

62. Reed quoted in Carroll, *The Recollections of Colonel Hugh T. Reed,* 19.

63. Garcia, *Tough Trip through Paradise,* 212, 231.

64. "Chief Joseph in the City."

65. "Special Dispatch; The Edison Speaking Machine Exhibition before Members of Congress," *New York Times,* April 10, 1878; Lisa Gitelman, "Matters of Record: On the Status of Print at the Origin of Recorded Sound," http://mediastudies.cua.edu/faculty_sites/gitelman/matters.htm (accessed August 27, 2007); "A Night with Edison," *Baxter Springs Times,* October 24, 1878.

66. "Chief Joseph in the City."

67. Ibid.

68. Ibid.

69. Ibid.

70. Ibid.

71. Ibid.

72. Steve Schoenherr, "Recording Technology History," http://history.sandiego.edu/GEN/recording/notes.html#origins (accessed August 27, 2007).

73. G. Baird, "Visit to Nez Perces in Canada," July 11, 1878, NPWF, 340.

74. D. McDonald, "The Nez Perces War of 1877; The Inside History from Indian Sources," *New North-west,* March 28, 1879; J. Gibbon in P. H. Sheridan, "Canadian Refugees," December 27, 1877, NPWF, 339; "Nez Perce Deserting Sitting Bull's Camp," *Leavenworth Times,* December 29, 1877; E. A. Hayt, "Refuses Permission for Nez Perces Mission to Canada," January 16, 1878, NPWF, 339.

75. Greene, *Nez Perce Summer,* chap. 14.

76. "Send Joseph," *Leavenworth Times,* January 30, 1878; "A Plan for Utilizing Joseph," *Saturday Evening Post* 57, no. 14 (1877): 8.

77. "Indian Affairs, the Nez Perce."

78. McWhorter, *Yellow Wolf,* 150; McWhorter, *Hear Me, My Chiefs!* 216.

79. P. H. Sheridan, "Forwarding Letter from Commanding Officer, Ft. Benton, and Suggestions to Major Irvine, Regarding Nez Perces in Canada," April 24, 1878, NPWF, 339; McWhorter, *Yellow Wolf,* 150, 160.

80. Baird, "The Capture of Chief Joseph and the Nez Perces," 214; "The Indians, Leavenworth, Kansas, April 30, 1878," *New York Times,* May 1, 1878; G. W. Baird, July 28, 1878, in Brown, *The Flight of the Nez Perce,* 225; Greene, *Nez Perce Summer,* chap. 14; McDonald, "The Nez Perces War of 1877"; Baird, "Visit to Nez Perces in Canada"; "The Embassy Returns," *Leavenworth Times,* July 27, 1878.

81. Baird, "The Capture of Chief Joseph and the Nez Perces," 214; "The Indians, Leavenworth, Kansas"; Baird, in Brown, *The Flight of the Nez Perce,* 225; Greene, *Nez Perce Summer,* chap. 14; McDonald, "The Nez Perces War of 1877"; Baird, "Visit to Nez Perces in Canada"; "The Embassy Returns"; D. McDonald, "From Over the Line," *New North-west,* October 24, 1878.

82. Hayt to Secretary of Interior, January 30, 1878; E. A. Hayt to Secretary of Interior, "Removal of the Nez Perce Prisoners," February 27, 1878, NPWF, 339; W. T. Sherman, "Fourth Endorsement, Will the Indian Department Take the Nez Perces," March 18, 1878, ibid.; G. W. McCrary, telegram, "Relocation of the Nez Perces," March 20, 1878, ibid.; I. McDowell, "Removal or Return?" May 20, 1878, NPWF, 340.

83. Meacham, "Nez Perces Joseph."

84. Svingen, *The Northern Cheyenne Indian Reservation,* 244; Debo, *A History of the Indians,* 241; "Cheyenne," *Winfield Courier,* December 20, 1877.

85. Chapman, "The Nez Perce in the Indian Territory," 112; "Ponca Prepare," *Columbus Border Star,* July 19, 1878; Wm. W. Leeds, telegram, July 11, 1878, NPWF, 340; "Ponca," *Arkansas City Traveler,* February 14, 1878, July 14, 1878, July 19, 1878, July 4, 1877; "Ponca Will Reside on Quapaw," ibid., June 13, 1877; "Ponca," *Chetopa Herald,* February 28, 1878; "Ponca," *Arkansas City Traveler,* July

10, 1878; C. Schurz, "Ponca Removal," ibid., September 24, 1879; Debo, *A History of the Indians*, 210–11.

Chapter 5

1. A. I. Comfort, "Receipt for Medical Supplies," July 23, 1878, NPWF, 340.

2. S. T. T., "Letter to the Editor"; Jackson, *The Indian Reform Letters of Helen Hunt Jackson*, December 11, 1879, 32.

3. Pearson, "Numipu Narratives," 75; Wm. M. Leeds to Jones, July 5, 1878, and July 9, 1878, LDNPQA, QA 7; J. McNeil, "Report, Train Trip," July 24, 1878, NPS; Clark, "The Nez Perces in Exile," 215; E. A. Hayt, "Annual Report," *ARCIA* 1878, 464–65; J. Pope, "Report," May 6, 1878, NPWF, 339.

4. McNeil, "Report, Train Trip"; J. McNeil, "Train Fares," August 1, 1878, NPWF, 340; W. D. Whipple to Adjutant General, July 12, 1878, ibid.

5. John Pope, telegram, "Nez Perce Prisoners Sent to the Indian Territory," July 22, 1878, NPWF, 340; "Map, Indian Country and Railroads," *ARBIC* 1879, inset; Meacham, "Home at Last."

6. Clark, "The Nez Perces in Exile," 214; J. E. Rhoads, "Statement of Conditions at Agencies by Religious Groups," *ARBIC* 1879, 107–109; McNeil, "Report, Train Trip"; "Baxter Items," *Columbus Border Star*, August 23, 1878.

7. McNeil, "Report, Train Trip"; Tuttle and Tuttle, "Quapaw and Modoc Mission"; M. C. Meigs to Secretary of War, April 8, 1878, NPWF, 339; H. H. Gregg, in U.S. Senate, *Testimony Taken by the Joint Committee Appointed to Take into Consideration the Expediency of Transferring the Indian Bureau to the War Department*, 77–90.

8. H. W. Jones, "Quapaw Report, Nez Perce Relocation," August 30, 1878, *ARCIA* 1878, 65–68; Wm. M. Leeds, telegram, "Purchase Hay; Hire Employees," September 14, 1878, LDNPQA, QA 7; "Weather Report," *Baxter Springs Times*, December 26, 1878, January 9, 1879, January 6, 1879; P. B. Hunt, "Kiowa, Comanche, Wichita," *ARCIA* 1879, 62–66; E. M. Kingsley, "Visit to the IT," October 15, 1878, *ARBIC* 1879, 50; "Among Captive Indians; Scattered Remnants of Tribes; A Visit to the Nez Perces and Modocs," *New York Times*, November 8, 1878; H. W. Jones, "Quapaw Agency," August 30, 1878, *ARCIA* 1879, 439.

9. H. W. Jones to Hayt, March 24, 1879, LROIA, Quapaw, 1-4995, 709; Hayt, Orders to Jones, March 6, 1879, ibid.; Jones, "Ration Portions," ibid.; Jones to Hayt, March 15, 1879, ibid., 708.

10. Wm. W. Leeds to Jones, "Supplies Exhausted," August 10, 1878, LDNPQA, QA 7; Leeds, telegram, "Purchase Supplies," August 16, 1878, ibid.; E. A. Hayt to Jones, "Subsistence Supplies," September 3, 1878, ibid.; "Invoices, White Beans and Soap," September 20, 1878, ibid.; H. W. Jones to Hayt, telegram, October 27, 1878, ibid.; Receipt, October 24, 1878, ibid.; McNeil, "Report,

Train Trip"; Tuttle and Tuttle, "Quapaw and Modoc Mission"; "Among Captive Indians"; Edward Peckham, "Interview," in Foreman, *Indian Pioneer History Collection,* 98: 181; E. A. Hayt, "Nez Perces, Annual Report," *ARCIA* 1879, xlvii; Hayt to Jones, telegram, "Stop Nez Perce Trade with Whites," November 8, 1878, LDNPQA, QA 4; Wm. C. Krohler to Schurz, "Claim for Land," February 10, 1879, ibid., QA 7; H. W. Jones, "Affidavits and Certificates, Claims Due Recton, Kerding, and Milton Drake's Improvements," n.d., ibid.; Z. P. Cogswell, "Bid," 1878, ibid.

11. Peckham, "Interview," 182; Hunn with Selam and Family, *Nch'i-Wána,* 162; Conservation Commission of Missouri, "Biotic Communities," January 22, 2001, http://www.conservation.state.mo.us/fish/watershed/spring/biotic/370bctxt.htm (accessed December 20, 2001); Willis Lykins, "Interview," in Foreman, *Indian Pioneer History Collection,* 33: 46; Dave Geboe, "Interview," ibid., 4: 19–20; Emily Easeworth, "Interview," ibid., 23: 455; Sarah Hollingworth, "Interview," ibid., 62: 240.

12. Schlick, *Columbia River Basketry,* 115, 117, 120–21, 123–26, 128–30; Peckham, "Interview," 181.

13. Peckham, "Interview," 181–83.

14. Hunt, "Kiowa, Comanche, Wichita"; J. W. Griest, "Otoe Agency, NB, Annual Report," *ARCIA* 1874, 205–206; Griest, "Great Nemeha, Annual Report," *ARCIA* 1879, 104; J. Hertford, "Sac and Fox, Annual Report," ibid., 80; Wm. Whiteman, "Ponca," ibid., 72; H. Price, "Medical and Vital Statistics for American Indians," *ARCIA* 1880, 410–20.

15. E. M. Kingsley, "Report to the Executive Committee; Purchasing," January 15, 1879, *ARBIC* 1879, 19.

16. E. A. Hayt, "Physicians, Medical Conditions," *ARCIA* 1879, xliii.

17. McNeil, "Report, Train Trip"; A. I. Chapman, letter to the *Leavenworth Times,* reprinted in the *New York Times,* August 29, 1878; Clinton B. Fisk and William Stickney, Commissioners, "Report of a Visit to Colorado and the Indian Territory," August 22, 1878, *ARBIC* 1878, 47–51; "Tables of Statistics," *ARCIA* 1879, 286; Meacham, "Visit among the Indians in the Indian Territory," 162.

18. Fisk and Stickney, "Report of a Visit," 47; H. W. Jones, "Medicines Purchased," November 1878, December 1878, January 2, 1879, January 29, 1879, LDNPQA, QA 7; E. A. Hayt to Jones, March 13, 1879, LROIA, Quapaw, 1-4995, 709; Jones to Hayt, March 13, 1879, ibid.; C. Schurz to Hayt, March 17, 1879, ibid.; Jones to Hayt, March 17, 1879, ibid.; Jones to Hayt, April 14, 1879, ibid.; Nez Perce Census, 1879, LDNPQA, QA 1: lines 2, 43, 60.

19. H. W. Jones, "Quapaw Agency, Annual Report," August 30, 1878, *ARCIA* 1878, 65–68; Corbusier, *Verde to San Carlos,* 278, 287, 285; H. Price, "Medical and Vital Statistics," *ARCIA* 1880, 410–20.

20. "Lewis and Clark Diary," *Great Falls Tribune,* September 30, 2005; "What Are the Facts?" 37; Steven Ross Evans, interview with author, January 29, 2006.

21. William N. Aiman, "Interview," in Foreman, *Indian Pioneer History Collection,* 12: 152–53; Wm. Whiteman to Hayt, November 4, 1879, Ponca Agency Letterpress, Oklahoma Historical Society, Archives Division, PA 11; "Among Captive Indians."

22. Neiberding, "The Nez Perce at the Quapaw Agency, " 25; H. W. Jones, telegram, November 4, 1878, LDNPQA, QA 7; Walker, "Nez Perce Sweat Bath Complex," 134–35.

23. "Employees at Quapaw Agency, 2nd Quarter 1879," n.d., LROIA, Quapaw, 1-4995, 708; E. A. Hayt to Mrs. Dr. F. B. Culver, April 1, 1879, ibid.; H. E. Coleman to Hayt, April 29, 1879, ibid.; Coleman to Hayt, June 2, 1879, ibid.; W. W. Johnston to Hayt, May 8, 1879, ibid., 709.

24. Lykins, "Interview," 467.

25. "Among Captive Indians"; Meacham, "Visit among the Indians in the Indian Territory."

26. Senator Thomas C. McCreery, "McCreery's Speech, Senate Floor," February 10, 1879, *Congressional Record,* 45th Cong., 3rd sess., 8, pt. 2: 1115–55.

27. Peckham, "Interview," 181–83; C. L. Gilkeson, "Interview," in Foreman, *Indian Pioneer History Collection,* 105: 371–72; Sprague, *Aboriginal Burial Practices,* 72, 155, 158–59, 162–64; A. R. Satterthwaite to E. A. Hayt, January 12, 1880, LDNPOA, PA 11.

28. Pearson, *The Politics of Disease,* 428; Abel, *Chardon's Journal at Fort Clark,* 128.

29. Nez Perce Census, 1878, LDNPQA, QA 2; 1879, LDNPQA, QA 1; 1880, LDNPQA, PA 1.

30. Ibid.

31. Packard, "Mythology and Religion of the Nez Perces," 330.

32. Ibid., 327–28.

33. Nez Perce Census, 1878, LDNPQA, QA 2; 1879, LDNPQA, QA 1; 1880, LDNPQA, PA 1; Pinkham, *100th Anniversary of the Nez Perce War;* George L. Spining, "The Unhappy Nez Perces," *New York Times,* October 29, 1883; "Among Captive Indians"; Chapman, letter to the *Leavenworth Times;* Walker, "Nez Perce Sweat Bath Complex," 134–35.

34. Colville Census, 1885, CC.

35. McNeil, "Report, Train Trip"; Tuttle and Tuttle, "Visit to the Nez Perces," 126; Meacham, "Exiled Nez Perces"; Meacham, "Home at Last."

36. Ridley, *The Freemasons,* 216.

37. Schurz, "Present Aspects of the Indian Problem."

38. H. H. Jackson, "To Ward," March 23, 1881, in *The Indian Reform Letters of Helen Hunt Jackson,* 194; Ridley, *Freemasons,* 216.

39. Schurz, "Present Aspects of the Indian Problem."

40. Ibid.

41. Meyer, "Ezra A. Hayt," 155; Fisk and Stickney, "Report of a Visit," 48; E. A. Hayt, telegram, "Nez Perces Remain in Indian Territory," ca. July 1878, LDNPQA, QA 7; Hayt, "Request to Visit Washington, D.C., Denied," September 17, 1878, ibid.; Wm. Leeds, telegram, "The Nez Perces Must Remain on the Quapaw Reservation Permanently," August 12, 1878, ibid.

42. "Indictment, Charges against Agent Jones," n.d., LDNPQA, QA 4; H. H. Gregg, in *Testimony Taken by the Joint Committee.*

43. H. W. Jones, "Certificate," April 19, 1879, LDNPQA, QA 7.

44. F. King, Nelson Grant, Emosley Jones, and George W. Linsley, "Affidavits," February 6, 1879, LDNPQA, QA 7; "Certificate of True Copy," February 8, 1879, ibid.

45. A. I. Chapman to Hayt, "Beef Issues to Nez Perce Prisoners," November 1, 1878, NPS; Hayt to H. Jones, telegram, November 16, 1878, LDNPQA, QA 7; Neiberding, "The Nez Perce at the Quapaw Agency," 26.

46. H. Jones to Hayt, "Modocs Seek Payment for Timber Used by Nez Perces," April 8, 1879, LROIA, Quapaw, 1-4995, 709.

47. Wm. M. Leeds, telegram, August 12, 1878; Fisk and Stickney, "Report of a Visit," 47–49.

48. Fisk and Stickney, "Report of a Visit," 50; Neiberding, "The Nez Perce at the Quapaw Agency," 23.

49. "Beef Contracts for the Indian Bureau," *ARCIA* 1879, 272; Gregg, in *Testimony Taken by the Joint Committee,* 77, 80–81, 84, 87–89; "Camps of the Nez Percés, Near Seneca Mission," November 17, 1878, in Testimony Taken by the Subcommittee of the Committee on Territories, in U.S. Senate, Committee on Territories, *To Establish United States Court in Indian Territory,* 810–813.

50. "Petition to Ezra Hayt Regarding Hiram Jones," January 18, 1879, LROIA, Quapaw, 1-4995, 708; F. M. Cockrell to Hayt, "Regarding Agent Jones," February 13, 1879, ibid.; Cockrell to Hayt, "Citizens' Petition to Investigate Hiram Jones," March 11, 1878 [1879], ibid.

51. A. I. Chapman to Meacham, February 27, 1879, LROIA, Quapaw, 1-4995, 708; C. Schurz to Hayt, "Agent Jones Will Be Fired," July 23, 1879, ibid., 709; Z. Cogswell, "Invoice," April 1879, LDNPQA, QA 7.

52. H. H. Gregg, "Agent Jones," *Baxter Springs Times,* November 4, 1878.

53. Wm. M. Leeds to Schurz, "Impossible to Reconcile Joseph to Selected Reservation," October 23, 1878, NPWF, 340.

54. J. W. Haworth, "Quapaw Agency, Annual Report," August 27, 1879, *ARCIA* 1879, 77.

55. E. A. Hayt, "Chief Joseph, Annual Report," November 1, 1878, *ARCIA* 1878, iii–xlv; "Chief Joseph," October 15, 1878, ibid., 464–65; E. M. Kingsley, "Report, October 15, 1878," December 1878, *ARBIC* 1879, 50–52; Leeds to Schurz, October 23, 1878; Rhoads, "Statement of Conditions," 107; Neiberding, "The

Nez Perce at the Quapaw Agency," 26; testimony of former Indian agent P. P. Elder, August 12, 1865, in *Condition of the Indian Tribes: Report of the Joint Special Committee Appointed under Joint Resolution of March 3, 1865 with an Appendix*, 39th Cong., 2nd sess., 1867, Sen. Rpt. 156, ser. 1279, 476–77; Gregg, in *Testimony Taken by the Joint Committee;* H. W. Jones, telegram, November 8, 1878, LDNPQA, QA 7; E. M. Kingsley, "Ponca Agency, Report to the Board," December 1878, *ARBIC* 1879, 52.

56. Chapman to Meacham, February 27, 1879; H. W. Jones to Hayt, March 5, 1879, LROIA, Quapaw, 1-4995, 709; Jones to Hayt, February 26, 1879, ibid.

57. Statute, March 13, 1875, *United States Statutes at Large,* 18 Stat. L., 451; H. W. Jones to Hayt, January 6, 1879, LDNPQA, QA 4; Chief Joseph and Yellow Bull to Hayt, February 26, 1879, NPS; Arthur Taylor, e-mail to author, June 29, 2005; Geboe, "Interview"; E. J. Brooks to Jones, March 9, 1879, LDNPQA, QA 7; Chapman to Meacham, February 27, 1879; Jones to Hayt, February 26, 1879; Schmeckebier, *The Office of Indian Affairs,* 410; Jones to Hayt, March 5, 1879.

58. Wm. Whiting, "To Commissioner of Indian Affairs," March 12, 1881, LDNPOA, PA 11.

59. C. A. Dempsey, "Going to the Reservation," *Atchison Patriot,* reprinted in *Columbus Border Star,* December 13, 1878; J. F. McDowell, "Nez Perce Prisoners," *Baxter Springs Times,* December 19, 1878; Chief Joseph and Yellow Bull to Hayt, February 26, 1879; "Interview," *Leavenworth Times,* December 5, 1877; Many Wounds to L. V. McWhorter, 1928, McW, folder 79; Whiting, "To Commissioner of Indian Affairs," March 12, 1881; Meyer, "Ezra A. Hayt," 160; E. A. Hayt, "Instructions," August 8, 1878, LDNPQA, QA 7.

60. Neiberding, "The Nez Perce at the Quapaw Agency," 25; Frank G. Audrain, "Interview," in Foreman, *Indian Pioneer History Collection,* 12: 534; "Among Captive Indians."

61. "Invoices, Favorite Balmoral Skirts," January 23, 1879, and "Invoices, 108 Pairs of Pants," February 9, 1879, LDNPQA, QA 7; "Purchase Order, Black Coats," February 4, 1879, ibid.; "Contracts Fiscal Year 1879–1880," *ARCIA* 1879, 298–302.

62. J. C. Lowrie, D. D., to S. N. D. Martin, "Nez Perces at Fort Leavenworth," December 14, 1877, AIC, box K, letter 388; Lowrie to Martin, December 18, 1877, ibid., letter 393; S. Baker, W. M. Burr, M. Breaker, W. A. Clark, M. B. Pilcher, and J. H. Foster, "Report of Missionary Societies, Presbyterian Home Missions for the Year 1878," *ARBIC* 1879, 88; Martin, "A Visit to Chief Joseph's Band," 302–303; McBeth, *The Nez Perces since Lewis and Clark,* 82.

63. Mylie Lawyer, as relayed by Steve Evans, February 3, 2005; Wm. Whiteman to Haworth, July 2, 1879, ibid.

64. J. Reuben to Hayt, "Missing Paycheck," October 16, 1879, NPS; Packard, "Mythology and Religion of the Nez Perces," 327; H. W. Jones to Hayt, "Chapman's Adultery; Fired, Rehired," August 23, 1879, LROIA, Quapaw, 1-4995,

708; James M. Haworth to Hayt, "Employees," August 28, 1879, ibid., 709; "Roster of Employees, Quapaw, 2nd Quarter," 1879, ibid.

65. James Reuben, "Scouting Report," November 8, 1877, *ARBIC* 1878, 92–95; J. B. Monteith to J. Q. Smith, "Instructions to Come onto Reservation," February 9, 1877, *ARSW* 1877, 1: 115; Neiberding, "The Nez Perce at the Quapaw Agency," 26; J. Reuben, A. Lawyer, and M. Williams to W. Stickney, "Nez Perce Indians from Idaho," December 15, 1878, NPS; Ezra A. Hayt, copy of letter sent by J. Reuben, January 30, 1878, AIC, box D, letter 125; Jerome et al., "Conference at Lapwai," 211–17.

66. Lewis, *Creating Christian Indians*, 105, 111–12, 124–25.

67. Chief Joseph by James Reuben, "To Oliver O. Howard, June 30 1880," in Venn, *Soldier to Advocate*, 74.

68. Wortman, Wortman, and Bottorff, *The Indians*, 184–85.

69. Chief Joseph by James Reuben, "To General O. O. Howard, June 30, 1880."

70. Ibid.

71. McWhorter, *Yellow Wolf*, 67–68, 279–80, 304; Neiberding, "The Nez Perce at the Quapaw Agency," 26.

72. As reported by the *San Francisco Chronicle*, November 1, 1877.

73. Schmeckebier, *The Office of Indian Affairs*, 515; *United States Statutes at Large*, Rev. Stat. April 10, 1896, 16 Stat. L., section 264, 39, 474–75.

74. Reuben, Williams, and Lawyer to Stickney, December 15, 1878; Reuben to Hayt, October 16, 1879; J. Haworth to Hayt, May 26, 1879, LROIA, Quapaw, 1-4995, 708; H. W. Jones to Hayt, August 23, 1879, ibid.; Nez Perce Census, 1879, LDNPQA, QA 1.

75. Asa C. Tuttle, "Union Meeting, Wyandotte Church," *Baxter Springs Times*, February 20, 1879.

76. E. Kirk, "Teachers' Institute," *Baxter Springs Times*, March 6, 1879; E. Kirk, "Mission Teacher's Institute," ibid., March 20, 1879.

77. Mylie Lawyer, interview with author, February 3, 2005.

78. J. F. McDowell, "Chief Joseph and Interpreter Chapman Returned Friday," *Baxter Springs Times*, October 31, 1878; "Baxter Springs Items," *Empire City Echo*, December 5, 1878.

79. J. F. McDowell, "Tourists Visit Nez Perce Camps," *Baxter Springs Times*, October 17, 1878; J. F. McDowell, "Mr. Hayt and Mr. Kingsley, Purchasing Commission, Accompany Chief Joseph and Husus Kute to the Ponca Agency," *Baxter Springs Times*, October 17, 1878.

80. N. D. Ingraham, "To the Editor," *Baxter Springs Times*, October 24, 1878; H. H. Gregg, "Letter Regarding Hiram Jones," *Baxter Springs Times*, November 4, 1878.

81. "Baxter Springs Items," December 5, 1878; McBeth, *The Nez Perces since Lewis and Clark*, 97.

82. J. H. Sherburne to L. V. McWhorter, letter, May 9, 1927, McW, folder 255.

83. "Among Captive Indians."

84. Bob Sands's letter quoted in Neiberding, "The Nez Perce at the Quapaw Agency," 24–25.

85. Ibid.

86. Haworth, "Quapaw Agency, Annual Report," August 27, 1879; J. Haworth to Ezra Hayt, "Modoc Boy Killed," May 31, 1879, LROIA, Quapaw, 1-4995, 708.

87. J. Wilson, articles in *Columbus Border Star,* July 19, 1878, August 12, 1878, December 13, 1878; article in *Galena Miner,* August 29, 1878; W. W. Johnston to Hayt, "Modoc Killed," June 4, 1879, LROIA, Quapaw, 1-4995, 708; J. F. McDowell. "Modocs Aroused," *Baxter Springs Times,* June 5, 1879; Haworth to Hayt, May 31, 1879.

88. Johnston to Hayt, June 4, 1879; Haworth to Hayt, May 31, 1879; Haworth to Hayt, "Modoc Murdered," August 16, 1879, LROIA, Quapaw, 1-4995, 709; Haworth to Hayt, May 30, 1879.

89. J. F. McDowell, "Quapaw Strip," *Baxter Springs Times,* February 20, 1879; "Quapaw Lands Opened for Settlement," *Baxter Springs Times,* May 1, 1879.

Chapter 6

1. Prucha, *The Great Father,* 163.

2. Schmeckebier, *The Office of Indian Affairs,* 42, 48; "James A. Garfield," http://www.whitehouse.gov/history/presidents/jg20.html (accessed August 27, 2007).

3. Chester Arthur, "President Arthur's Message," *Advocate of Peace* 13, no. 1 (1882): 7.

4. Prucha, *The Great Father,* 246.

5. Schmeckebier, *The Office of Indian Affairs,* 66, 70, 76–77.

6. Hill, "John Q. Smith."

7. E. A. Hayt, "Annual Report," November 1, 1877, *ARCIA* 1877, 397–98, 406; J. F. McDowell, "President's Speech," *Baxter Springs Times,* December 5, 1878.

8. *An Act to Provide for Exchange of Lands with the Indians,* 4 Stat. 411–12; Carrico, *Strangers in a Stolen Land,* 47–48.

9. E. A. Hayt, "Chief Joseph, Annual Report," *ARCIA* 1878, iv.

10. Debo, *A History of the Indians,* 266.

11. Meyer, "Ezra A. Hayt," 162.

12. Goldman, "Rowland E. Trowbridge," 167–72.

13. O'Neil, "Hiram Price"; Prucha, *The Great Father,* 218.

14. Thompson, "John D. C. Atkins."

15. J. Esaw, "Examination, Senate Investigating Committee," March 11, 1880, in U.S. Senate, Committee on Indian Affairs, *Letter from the Secretary of the*

Interior . . . Relating to Leases of Lands in the Indian Territory to Citizens of the United States for Cattle-Grazing and Other Purposes; Carl Schurz to Henry L. Dawes, February 7, 1881, in Schurz, *Speeches, Correspondence and Political Papers,* 4: 91–92.

16. Schmeckebier, *The Office of Indian Affairs,* 258; "Indian Ruffian Shot," *New York Times,* November 2, 1879; "Standing Bear," November 26, 1879, in Wortman, Wortman, and Bottorff, *The Indians,* 156–57; "For the Ponca Indians," *New York Times,* December 13, 1879; "Ponca Agent Wm. Whiteman Retiring," January 7, 1880, in Wortman, Wortman, and Bottorff, *The Indians,* 152; "The Wrongs of the Poncas," *New York Times,* March 12, 1880; "Mason Waiting for Payne," December 8, 1880, in Wortman, Wortman, and Bottorff, *The Indians,* 168; "Ponca Indians, Justice," February 23, 1881, ibid., 172–73; Mary Ann Wortman, interview with author, March 31, 2005; J. Sherburne to L. V. McWhorter, letter, September 10, 1927, McW, folder 255; "Senate Commission Today Examines the Question of Big Snake's Killing," *New York Times,* March 11, 1881; Esaw, "Examination, Senate Investigating Committee"; Schurz to Dawes, February 7, 1881.

17. "Ponca Agent Wm. Whiteman Retiring"; Criminal Defendant Case File, William H. Whiteman, June 3, 1880, July 24, 1880, NARA, Fort Worth, ARC-24937.

18. Ezra A. Hayt, "To Associated Press," April 10, 1879, in Tibbles, *The Ponca Chiefs,* 124; Schmeckebier, *The Office of Indian Affairs,* 258.

19. Clark, "The Nez Perces in Exile," 223.

20. L. Woodin to Price, November 23, 1882, LDNPOA, PA 13.

21. E. A. Hayt, "Annual Report," *ARCIA* 1877, 401–402; J. D. Miles, "Cheyenne and Arapaho," August 31, 1878, *ARCIA* 1878, 56; Debo, *A History of the Indians,* 241–42.

22. E. M. Kingsley, "Ponca Agency," December 1878, *ARBIC* 1879, 51–53.

23. Chief Joseph, in U.S. Senate, *Testimony Taken by the Joint Committee,* 78.

24. Ibid., 78–79.

25. E. A. Hayt, "Annual Report, Chief Joseph," *ARCIA* 1878, xxxii.

26. Ibid.

27. Ibid.

28. Osborn, "The Exile of the Nez Perce in Indian Territory," 465–66; A. I. Chapman to Meacham, February 4, 1879, LROIA, Quapaw, 1-4995, 708; Chapman to Board of Indian Commissioners, April 1, 1879, ibid.; Chapman to E. A. Hayt, May 13, 1879, ibid.; C. Schurz to Hayt, June 7, 1879, ibid.

29. Meacham, "Nez Perce Joseph," 22–23; "Arrival of Chief Joseph," *The Washington Post,* January 14, 1879.

30. "Chief Joseph as Lecturer," *New York Times,* January 18, 1879.

31. "Mr. Hayes' Reception, the Number and Social Standing of the Guests—Scenes and Incidents," *The Washington Post,* January 15, 1879.

32. Geer, *First Lady,* 200; Kirk, *Music at the White House,* 108, 111, 114; Ryan and Guinness, *The White House,* 138; Holloway, *The Ladies of the White House,*

636, 640–41, 649; Jensen, *The White House and Its Thirty-Two Families*, 113; Lewis, *The White House*, 202, 206–207.

33. S. S. Cutting, M. E. Strieby, J. C. Lowrie, B. Tatham, and S. L. Jenney, " A. B. Meacham," *Journal of the 8th Annual Conference with Representatives of Missionary Boards*, Washington, D.C., January 15, 1879, *ARBIC* 1879, 123–26; S., "Correspondence to the Editors of the *Friends' Intelligencer*"; E A. Hayt, "Ute Outbreak," November 1, 1879, *ARCIA* 1879, xviii; Hayt, "Pawnee and Northern Cheyenne Removal," *ARCIA* 1877, 404–402.

34. "Chief Joseph as Lecturer"; Clark, "The Nez Perces in Exile," 218.

35. "Chief Joseph as Lecturer"; Meacham, "Nez Perce Joseph"; Chief Joseph, "An Indian's View," 430–32; "Broken Pledges," *The Washington Post*, January 18, 1879; A. I. Chapman, letter to General Howard, copy provided to author by George Venn, August 29, 2006.

36. "Broken Pledges."

37. Ibid.

38. Howard, "General Howard's Comment on Joseph's Narrative," 76, 79–81; Chief Joseph by James Reuben, "To Oliver O. Howard, June 30 1880," in Venn, *Soldier to Advocate*, 75.

39. "Reception at the White House," *New York Times*, February 13, 1903.

40. "Agreement with the Chief Joseph Band, January 31, 1879," in Deloria and DeMallie, *Documents of American Indian Diplomacy*, 2: 1418–19; H. Price, "Nez Perce Indians of Joseph's Band," *ARCIA* 1882, lxiii.

41. "Agreement with the Tabaguache, Yampa, Grand River, and Uintah Ute, January 14, 1879," in Deloria and Demallie, *Documents of American Indian Diplomacy*, 2: 1416–17; "Buying Land of the Indians," *New York Times*, February 2, 1879; B. Chapman, "The Nez Perce in the Indian Territory," 98–121.

42. W. Stanley, "Los Pinos," August 16, 1879, *ARCIA* 1879, 16.

43. Nez Perce Census, 1878, LDNPQA, QA 2: line 2.

44. "Agreement with the Chief Joseph Band."

45. Ibid.

46. Ibid.

47. A. Chapman to A. B. Meacham, February 7, 1879, LROIA, Quapaw, 1-4995, 708.

48. H. Price, "Joseph's Band," *ARCIA* 1882, lxiii.

49. Beal, *I Will Fight No More Forever*, 285–86; Neiberding, "The Nez Perce at the Quapaw Agency," 24.

50. "Yellow Bull's Speech at the Cowley County Fair," October 8, 1879, in Wortman, Wortman, and Bottorff, *The Indians*, 181.

51. Ibid.; Wm. W. Bottorff, "The President and Governor," *Winfield Courier*, August 28, 1879; Historical Resources, Cowley County, Kansas, http://www.ausbcomp.com/~bbott/wortman/index.html (accessed August 27, 2007).

52. Testimony of Yellow Bull in U.S. Senate, Committee on Indian Affairs, *Memorial of the Nez Perce Indians Residing in the State of Idaho to the Congress of the United States*, 43–44.

53. Wortman, Wortman, and Bottorff, *The Indians*, 181.

54. Meacham, "Letters," 47; "Wards of the Government."

55. Frost, "Indian Law Suit," 36–37.

56. Meacham, "Chief Joseph, Visit," 145.

57. Wm. Stickney and N. A. Miles, "The Nez Perce Tribe," *ARBIC* 1881, 7.

58. J. H. Sherburne to L. V. McWhorter, letter, December 1, 1926, McW, folder 48; Sherburne to McWhorter, letter, September 10, 1927, ibid., folder 255.

59. N. A. Miles to Rutherford B. Hayes, "Nez Perce Indians," January 19, 1881, NPWF, 340.

60. C. Schurz to the President, letters, "Nez Perce Indians," February 2, 1881, March 1, 1881, March 14, 1881, NPWF, 340; copies of N. A. Miles's letters forwarded to General Irvin McDowell, March 15, 1881, ibid.

61. Miles quoted in Jackson, *The Indian Reform Letters of Helen Hunt Jackson*, 195.

62. Ibid., 13–14, 16–17, 64, 72, 78–79, 83, 93, 104–105.

63. Jackson, *The Indian Reform Letters of Helen Hunt Jackson*, 195.

64. Brown, *The Flight of the Nez Perce*, 430.

65. Price, "Joseph's Band," lxiii.

66. Ibid.

67. Ibid.

68. N. A. Miles, "Idaho Indictments," October 24, 1881, NPWF, 340.

69. George L. Spining, "The Unhappy Nez Perces," *New York Times*, October 29, 1883.

Chapter 7

1. J. M. Haworth to Hayt, "Council with the Nez Perces," April 23, 1879, LROIA, Quapaw, 1-4995, 708.

2. J. M. Haworth to Hayt, "Nez Perce Council; Will Relocate," April 24, 1879, ibid.

3. Clark, "The Nez Perces in Exile," 218–19; Wortman, Wortman, and Bottorff, *The Indians*, 147, 208; E. A. Howard, "Journal of the March, Ponca Agency, Indian Territory," August 25, 1877, *ARCIA* 1877, 97–99.

4. Pearson, "Numipu Narratives," 77.

5. Haworth to Hayt, April 24, 1879.

6. A. I. Chapman to Hayt, May 13, 1879, LROIA, Quapaw, 1-4995, 708; J. M. Haworth to Hayt, "Nez Perce Restless," May 6, 1879, ibid., 709.

7. H. E. Coleman, "Medical Supplies," June 26, 1879, LDNPQA, QA 4; E. J. Brooks to Haworth, "Ex-Agent Jones," July 3, 1879, ibid.; "Receipt," June 3, 1879, ibid.

8. J. M. Haworth, "Horses Wanted," *Baxter Springs Times,* May 22, 1879; Haworth to E. Hayt, May 24, 1879, LROIA, Quapaw, 1-4995, 708; E. J. Brooks to Haworth, May 6, 1879, LDNPQA, QA 4.

9. Haworth to Hayt, April 24, 1879; Haworth to Hayt, "When Will Wagons Arrive," May 19, 1879, LROIA, Quapaw, 1-4995, 708; Haworth to Hayt, "Nez Perce Removal," May 24, 1879, May 31, 1879, ibid.

10. "Baxter Items," *Columbus Border Star,* June 20, 1878.

11. J. M. Haworth to Ezra Hayt, "Nez Perce Removal," June 6, 1879, LROIA, Quapaw, 1-4995, 709; Haworth to Hayt, May 24, 1879.

12. Haworth to Hayt, "Nez Perce Removal," June 6, 1879, ibid.

13. J. M. Haworth to Hayt, "Journal," June 25, 1879, NPS; C. Schurz to Hayt, "Agent Jones," July 23, 1879, LROIA, Quapaw, 1-4995, 709; Haworth to Hayt, May 31, 1879.

14. "Nez Perces," *Baxter Springs Times,* June 5, 1879; Haworth to Hayt, June 25, 1879, 1, 2, 3; Wm. Whiteman to Haworth, "Nez Perce Employees," July 2, 1879, LDNPQA, QA 4; J. Reuben to Hayt, "Paycheck," October 16, 1879, NPS; J. M. Haworth to Hayt, April 24, 1879, LROIA, Quapaw, 1-4995, 708.

15. J. M. Haworth to Hayt, May 31, 1879, LROIA, Quapaw, 1-4995, 708.

16. Haworth to Hayt, June 25, 1879, 1, 2.

17. Brooks to Haworth, July 3, 1879; E. A. Hayt to Haworth, June 30, 1879, LDNPQA, QA 4.

18. C. Schurz to Hayt, July 21, 1879, LROIA, Quapaw, 1-4995, 709; Schmeckebier, *The Office of Indian Affairs,* 475.

19. Haworth to Hayt, June 25, 1879, 1–3; Josephine Spence, "Interview," in Foreman, *Indian Pioneer History Collection,* 58: 341; C. Schurz to Hayt, "Nez Perce Removal," July 17, 1879, LROIA, Quapaw, 1-4995, 709; J. M. Haworth to Hayt, "Nez Perce Removal," May 10, 1879, ibid.

20. "Ponca War Dance," *Arkansas City Traveler,* May 15, 1878.

21. Haworth to Hayt, June 25, 1879, 4–5; Florence D. Richmond, "Interview," in Foreman, *Indian Pioneer History Collection,* 107: 446.

22. Haworth to Hayt, June 25, 1879, 5, 6, 8.

23. Ibid., 7; Clark, "The Nez Perces in Exile," 221; Coleman, "Medical Supplies," June 26, 1879.

24. J. M. Haworth to Ezra Hayt, May 24, 1879, LROIA, Quapaw, 1-4995, 708.

25. Debo, *A History of the Indians,* 210; Wortman, Wortman, and Bottorff, *The Indians,* 130–31, 147, 208–209, 218; John Pope, "Report," *ARSW* 1878, 1: 40; J. D. Miles, "Cheyenne and Arapaho," September 21, 1878, ibid., 49.

26. Wortman, Wortman, and Bottorff, *The Indians,* 209, 213.

27. Ibid., 19, 72, 77, 91, 208, 212, 273, 317, 271, 274–304.

28. "Beef Contracts," *ARCIA* 1879, 272.

29. Wortman, Wortman, and Bottorff, *The Indians,* 131–32, 150, 199–201, 202–203, 205–206, 213, 272, 303.

30. Ibid., 202, 218.

31. Ibid., 131, 220, 223; Margaret Gardiner Mack Vanderlip quoted in ibid., 430.

32. Ibid., 141.

33. Ibid., 15, 19–20, 52, 155, 183, 221–22, 277, 366, 393, 397, 415.

34. P. J. Noble in ibid., 43–47; Haworth to Hayt, June 25, 1879, 6; Wortman, Wortman, and Bottorff, *The Indians,* 179–80.

35. "Statistics, Kansas and Indian Territory," *Arkansas City Traveler,* December 10, 1879; "Cherokee Nation," *Arkansas City Traveler,* December 24, 1879.

36. Root, "Ferries in Kansas," 39–42; Wortman, Wortman, and Bottorff, *The Indians,* 149; "Arkansas River Bridge," *Arkansas City Traveler,* October 1, 1884, October 4, 1884; "Joseph H. Sherburne Family," http://www.ausbcomp.com/~bbott/wortman/SherburneJH.htm (accessed August 27, 2007).

37. Haworth to Hayt, June 25, 1879, 6, 7.

38. J. H. Sherburne to L. V. McWhorter, letter, March 5, 1926, McW, folder 243; Sherburne to McWhorter, letter, May 19, 1927, ibid.; Wortman, Wortman, and Bottorff, *The Indians,* 154.

39. Sherburne to McWhorter, May 19, 1927.

40. Sherburne to McWhorter, March 5, 1926.

41. N. Hughes, "Nez Perce Wagon Train," *Arkansas City Traveler,* June 18, 1879; Nez Perce Census, 1880, LDNPQA, PA 1: lines 2, 3, 4, 17, 10, 55, 7.

42. Nez Perce Census, 1879, LDNPQA, QA 1: lines 4, 22, 25.

43. Ibid., line 60.

44. Ibid., lines 10, 11, 15, 52, 67, 80.

45. Nez Perce Census, 1880, LDNPQA, PA 1: lines 20, 52.

46. Ibid., lines 1, 3, 71, 55, 17, 34, 27, 2, 88, 4, 11; L. E. Woodin, "Teamster Payroll Report," February 24, 1884, LDNPOA, PA 13.

47. Wm. Whiteman, "Receipt of Nez Perce," June 16, 1879, LDNPQA, QA 4; Haworth to Hayt, June 25, 1879, 6, 7.

48. Haworth to Hayt, June 25, 1879, 8; Ezra Hayt to Haworth, July 16, 1879, LDNPQA, QA 4.

49. Haworth to Hayt, June 25, 1879, 8; Nez Perce Census, 1879, LDNPQA, QA 1; "Table of Statistics, Population, Dress, Agriculture and Schools," *ARCIA* 1879, 232.

50. C. Schurz to Hayt, "Nez Perce Removal," July 17, 1879, LROIA, Quapaw, 1-4995, 709; Clark, "The Nez Perces in Exile," 222; "Table: Prevailing Diseases," August 1879, *ARCIA* 1879, 263–64; "Table: Prevailing Diseases," August 1880, *ARCIA* 1880, 275.

51. Wm. Whiteman to Hayt, "Several Older Nez Perces Have Consumption," November 4, 1879, LDNPOA, PA 11; Wortman, Wortman, and Bottorff, *The Indians,* 164.

52. "Table: Prevailing Diseases," August 1879; "Table: Prevailing Diseases," August 1880; J. D. Miles, "Cheyenne and Arapaho Agency," *ARCIA* 1880, 70.

53. "Oakland Agency, Annual Report," *ARCIA* 1884, 338–39.

54. Bland, "Visit to the Indian Territory."

55. T. J. Jordan, "Condition of Nez Perce," *ARCIA* 1881, 94; Jordan, "Death of John Bull"; Hampton, *Children of Grace,* 328; "Population, Sources of Subsistence, Religious, Vital and Crime Statistics," *ARCIA* 1882, 334.

56. J. H. Sherburne to L. V. McWhorter, letter, May 6, 1927, McW, folder 255.

57. L. J. Miles, "Osage and Kaw Agency," *ARCIA* 1879, 69–70; E. H. Bowman, "Pawnee Agency," *ARCIA* 1880, 77; Wm. Whiteman, "Ponca, Agency Report," ibid., 244; J. D. Miles, "Cheyenne and Arapaho Agency, Population Statistics," ibid., 67; P. B. Hunt, "Kiowa, Comanche and Wichita," ibid., 77; John Pope, "Report; Northern Cheyennes, Nez Perces," October 4, 1878, *ARSW* 1878, 1: 40, 43.

58. J. D. Miles, "Cheyenne and Arapaho," September 21, 1878, *ARSW* 1878, 1: 49; Debo, *A History of the Indians,* 241–42; James E. Rhoads, "Statement of Conditions at Agencies by Religious Groups," *ARBIC* 1879, 108–109.

59. "Table Showing Agriculture Improvements, Stock, Production, and Sources of Subsistence," *ARCIA* 1880, 384–85.

60. Wortman, Wortman, and Bottorff, *The Indians,* 44–45, 49, 145; Miles, "Cheyenne and Arapaho," 49; John Pope, "Report," 40, 43.

61. Wm. Whiting, "Permit to Visit Cheyenne and Arapaho," June 18, 1880, LDNPOA, PA 11; Whiting, "Permission to Visit Arapaho and Cheyenne," September 27, 1880, ibid.; Wortman, Wortman, and Bottorff, *The Indians,* 46–47, 49.

62. Chapman, "How the Cherokee Acquired and Disposed of the Outlet," 216; Wortman, Wortman, and Bottorff, *The Indians,* 153; G. F. Towle, June 22, 1879, LDNPQA, QA 7; Clark, "The Nez Perces in Exile," 219.

63. Wortman, Wortman, and Bottorff, *The Indians,* 155, 181; "Lumber," *Winfield Courier,* September 25, 1879; "Civilized Indians," *Arkansas Valley Democrat,* August 28, 1879; J. H. Sherburne to L. V. McWhorter, letter, May 19, 1927, McW, folder 40.

Chapter 8

1. Wm. H. Whiteman, "Ponca Agency Report," August 31, 1879, *ARCIA* 1879, 73–74.

2. J. H. Sherburne to L. V. McWhorter, letter, January 4, 1927, McW, folder 243; Sherburne to McWhorter May 19, 1927, ibid., folder 240; Sherburne to

McWhorter, September 10, 1927, ibid., folder 255; "Joe Sherburne, Trader," *Arkansas City Traveler,* October 16, 1878; "Joseph H. Sherburne Family," http://www.ausbcomp.com/~bbott/wortman/SherburneJH.htm (accessed August 27, 2007); Wortman, Wortman, and Bottorff, *The Indians,* 156.

3. Clark, "The Nez Perces in Exile," 223; Wortman, Wortman, and Bottorff, *The Indians,* 158; "Statistics," *ARCIA* 1881, 354–55; "Statistics," *ARCIA* 1882, 352–53; "Statistics," *ARCIA* 1883, 2901–11; "Statistics," *ARCIA* 1884, 308–309.

4. A. R. Satterthwaite to Commissioner of Indian Affairs, February 24, 1880, LDNPOA, PA 11; Wm. Whiting, "Nez Perce," *ARCIA* 1880, 85, 244; "Nez Perces Houses," February 20, 1880, LDNPOA, PA 11; H. E. Horne, "Interview," in Foreman, *Indian Pioneer History Collection,* 106: 155; Wortman, Wortman, and Bottorff, *The Indians,* 182; T. J. Jordan, "Nez Perce," *ARCIA* 1881, 94; Wm. J. Pollock to S. J. Kirkwood, "Nez Perces Have Been Horribly Wronged," May 30, 1881, LROIA, Ponca, 1881-9711; R. L. Bonewell, "Interview," in Foreman, *Indian Pioneer History Collection,* 66: 273–74; "Sac and Fox, Indian Territory," *ARCIA* 1881, 100–103.

5. T. J. Jordan, "Nez Perce, Annual Report," *ARCIA* 1882, 76–77; L. E. Woodin, "Nez Perces Must Have Homes," September 1882, LDNPOA, PA 14; "Population, Sources of Subsistence, Religious, Vital and Criminal Statistics," *ARCIA* 1883, 272; "Statistical Report, Nez Perces, Indian Territory," *ARCIA* 1884, 290–91; J. W. Scott to Price, "Terribly Cold; Three Nez Perce Families No Stoves or Heat," February 24, 1884, LDNPOA, PA 13.

6. Wortman, Wortman, and Bottorff, *The Indians,* 30–31; J. D. Miles, "Cheyenne and Arapaho," *ARCIA* 1879, 59; P. B. Hunt, "Kiowa, Wichita and Comanche," ibid., 67; L. J. Miles, "Osage and Kaw Agency Report," ibid., 69; Wm. Whiteman, "Ponca Agency Report," ibid., 72–73; "Civilized Indians," *Arkansas Valley Democrat,* August 28, 1879.

7. Wortman, Wortman, and Bottorff, *The Indians,* 412.

8. J. D. Miles, "Cheyenne and Arapaho Report," *ARCIA* 1880, 70–71; L. J. Miles, United States Indian Agent (USIA), Osage Agency, Indian Territory, "Osage Report," ibid., 76–77; "Pawnee Report," ibid., 81; Wm. Whiting, "Ponca Agency Report," ibid., 83–86.

9. P. B. Hunt, "Kiowa, Comanche and Wichita," *ARCIA* 1881, 77–83; J. D. Miles, "Osage," ibid., 85–86; James Rhoads, "Cheyenne and Arapaho," *ARBIC* 1881, 78–79.

10. Wm. Whiting, "Nez Perce Annual Report," *ARCIA* 1880, 85.

11. Wortman, Wortman, and Bottorff, *The Indians,* 282; Thomas J. Jordan, "Nez Perce Annual Report," *ARCIA* 1881, 93–94.

12. E. Whittlesey, "Nez Perce Report," *ARBIC* 1883, 34; D. B. Dyer, "Cheyenne and Arapaho," *ARCIA* 1884, 74–75; J. W. Scott, "Nez Perce," January 1884, February 1, 1884, LDNPOA, PA 13; Wortman, Wortman, and Bottorff, *The Indians,* 428–29; J. W. Scott, "Report," January 1, 1885, LDNPOA, PA 13.

13. Pearson, "Developing Reservation Economies."

14. "Indian Bureau Awards and Contracts," *ARBIC* 1880, 21–22; E. A. Hayt, "Report," *ARCIA* 1879, 197, 278–79, 297; Wm. Whiting, "Nez Perce, Annual Report," *ARCIA* 1880, 85; Wortman, Wortman, and Bottorff, *The Indians,* 163, 203, 278–70, 297; "Cheyenne and Arapaho," *Arkansas City Traveler,* May 10, 1881; "Major Woodin and Wagon Trains," ibid., August 29, 1883; John W. Scott, "Ponca, Pawnee and Otoe, Annual Report," *ARCIA* 1884, 90.

15. "Statistics," *ARCIA* 1879, 342; "Pine Ridge, Dakota," *ARCIA* 1883, 34–36; J. D. Miles, "Cheyenne and Arapaho, Annual Report," *ARCIA* 1880, 61; "Statistics," ibid., 342; L. E. Woodin, "Agricultural Operations," October 16, 1883, LDNPOA, PA 13; Mary Ann Wortman, interview with author, August 26, 2004; Pearson, "Developing Economies," 158.

16. William N. Aiman, "Interview," in Foreman, *Indian Pioneer History Collection,* 12: 152–53.

17. Wortman, Wortman, and Bottorff, *The Indians,* 84, 93, 95, 100, 108, 111, 137, 164, 276, 410, 418; D. W. Miller, "Interview," in Foreman, *Indian Pioneer History Collection,* 106: 54–55.

18. Aiman, "Interview"; Wortman, Wortman, and Bottorff, *The Indians,* 168, 204.

19. Wm. Whiteman, "Nez Perces," *ARCIA* 1879, 75; L. E. Woodin, "Nez Perces," *ARCIA* 1883, 79; H. Price, "Indian Bureau Statistics," ibid., 291.

20. Wortman, Wortman, and Bottorff, *The Indians,* 191; "Proposals Received and Contracts," *ARCIA* 1879, 310–11; J. Reuben to J. M. Haworth, "Nez Perce Widows and Orphans," August 30, 1882, LROIA, Ponca, 1882-17594.

21. Wm. Whiteman, "Nez Perce," *ARCIA* 1879, 75; T. J. Jordan, "Condition of the Nez Perce," *ARCIA* 1881, 94; Florence D. Richmond, "Interview," in Foreman, *Indian Pioneer History Collection,* 107: 446; J. H. Sherburne to McWhorter, letter, September 10, 1927, McW, folder 79.

22. "Mammoth Clothing House," *Cowley County Courant,* April 6, 1882; Historical Resources, Cowley County, Kansas, http://www.ausbcomp.com/~bbott/wortman/index.html (accessed August 27, 2007).

23. Edward Peckham, "Interview," in Foreman, *Indian Pioneer History Collection,* 98: 181; Wortman, Wortman, and Bottorff, *The Indians,* 186, photograph 443; Steve Grafe, interview with author, December 14, 2004; "Nez Perce Ladies," *Arkansas City Traveler,* May 11, 1881; Henderson, "Reminiscences of a Range Rider."

24. Wortman, Wortman, and Bottorff, *The Indians,* 182, 192, 443; J. H. Sherburne to McWhorter, letter, May 9, 1927, McW, folder 255; A. H. Kenney, "Interview," in Foreman, *Indian Pioneer History Collection,* 62: 495–96; "Nez Perce," *Winfield Courant,* August 25, 1881.

25. "Indian Bureau Contracts," *ARCIA* 1880, 286–87; Wm. Whiting, "Butcher to Oakland," October 1, 1880, LDNPOA, PA 11; "Cartridges for Slaughter," January 21, 1881, ibid.

26. Whiting, "Butcher to Oakland"; Wm. Whiting to Price, "School Children," October 15, 1881, LDNPOA, PA 11; Whiting to Price, "Cayuse Held with Nez Perce Prisoners," March 12, 1881, ibid.; "Note," June 6, 1881, ibid.; Wortman, Wortman, and Bottorff, *The Indians,* 182.

27. N. K. Barnum, "Spotted Tail Agency, Purchasing Commission Report," *ARBIC* 1876, 161–62; Wm. Whiteman, "Nez Perce," *ARCIA* 1879, 75; L. E. Woodin to H. Price, "Cartridges," November 12, 1882, LDNPOA, PA 14; Woodin to Hayt, letter, October 1882, ibid.

28. "Statistics, Agricultural Improvements, Etc.," *ARCIA* 1880, 384–85, *ARCIA* 1881, 354–55, *ARCIA* 1884, 290–91; Wm. S. Whiting, "Rations Not Sufficient for Laboring Men," March 26, 1881, LDNPOA, PA 11.

29. E. A. Hayt to Whiteman, "Hire Plowing Done," December 1, 1879, LDNPOA, PA 11; Wm. Whiting, "Nez Perce, Annual Report," *ARCIA* 1880, 85.

30. Wm. Whiteman, "Ponca Agency Report," *ARCIA* 1879, 75; James, *Nez Perce Women in Transition,* 65–67; Report to CIA, "Women Thresh Grain," August 1, 1883, LDNPOA, PA 13.

31. Meacham, "Chief Joseph, Visit," 145; "Nez Perce, Oakland, Annual Report," *ARCIA* 1884, 308–309; Whiting, "Receipt," April 7, 1881, LDNPOA, PA 11.

32. "Statistics, Agricultural Improvements, Etc.," *ARCIA* 1880, 385, *ARCIA* 1881, 354–55, *ARCIA* 1883, 272, *ARCIA* 1884, 290–91; L. E. Woodin to Price, "Crops and Farming," October 1, 1882, LDNPOA, PA 13; Wm. J. Pollock to Price, "Agriculture," May 30, 1881, LROIA, Ponca, 1881-9711.

33. George L. Spining, "The Unhappy Nez Perces," *New York Times,* October 29, 1883; Wm. Whiting, "Nez Perce Farmers," October 1, 1880, LDNPOA, PA 11; James, *Nez Perce Women in Transition,* 69; L. E. Woodin, "Nez Perce," *ARCIA* 1883, 290–91; Slickpoo and Walker, *Noon Nee-Me-Poo,* 199.

34. Wm. Whiting, "Report," October 14, 1880, LDNPOA, PA 11.

35. Spining, "The Unhappy Nez Perces."

36. Ibid.; "Statistics, Livestock Owned, Acres Cultivated, Crops, Etc.," *ARCIA* 1882, 352–53, *ARCIA* 1883, 290–91, *ARCIA* 1881, 354–55, *ARCIA* 1884, 308; J. W. Scott, "Permission to Buy Stove Wood," August 30, 1884, LDNPOA, PA 13.

37. Wortman, Wortman, and Bottorff, *The Indians,* 174, 220; "Medical Statistics," *ARCIA* 1882, following 366; McWhorter, *Yellow Wolf,* 118, 143–44.

38. "Requests to Hiram Price," March 18, 1880, October 1, 1880, LDNPOA, PA 11; Wm. Whiteman, "Nez Perce," *ARCIA* 1879, 75; Wm. Whiting, "Authority to Purchase," December 16, 1880, January 21, 1881, LDNPOA, PA 11; Wm. J. Pollock to Price, May 30, 1881, LROIA, Ponca, 1881-9711; "Statistics, Agricultural Improvements, Etc.," *ARCIA* 1881, 354–55, *ARCIA* 1882, 352–53, *ARCIA* 1883, 290–91, *ARCIA* 1884, 308–309; Wortman, Wortman, and Bottorff, *The Indians,* 182, 284.

39. Lynus Walker, story shared with author by Steve and Connie Evans, September 15, 2004.

40. Steve Grafe, interview with author, December 2, 2004; C. D. Warner, "Nez Perce Agency, Lapwai," August 14, 1880, *ARCIA* 1880, 64–67.

41. Wm. Whiting, "Nez Perce, Annual Report," *ARCIA* 1880, 85.

42. "Statistics, Agricultural," *ARCIA* 1881, 354–55; L. E. Woodin, "Memo," August 7, 1883, LDNPOA, PA 13; "Statistics of Livestock Owned," *ARCIA* 1882, 352–53, *ARCIA* 1883, 290–91; "Statistics of Livestock Owned, Acreage Cultivated, Crops, Etc.," *ARCIA* 1884, 308–309; Wortman, Wortman, and Bottorff, *The Indians*, 188, 287.

43. E. A. Hayt, "Report to Secretary of the Interior," *ARCIA* 1879, xlvii; Nez Perce Census, 1885, IINP: line 96; J. Lee Hall, "Kiowa, Comanche, Wichita," *ARCIA* 1886, 131; "Stolen Nez Perce Cattle," *Arkansas City Traveler*, August 2, 1881; Wortman, Wortman, and Bottorff, *The Indians*, 190; Criminal Defendant Case File, John T. Bennett, U.S. District Court for the Fort Smith Division of the Western District of Arkansas, September 13, 1881, NARA, Fort Worth, ARC-204756, ARC-204754, ARC-204755.

44. Tom Hill to Commissioner of Indian Affairs, June 4, 1881, LROIA, Ponca, 1881-9711.

45. Ibid.

46. U.S. Senate, Committee on Indian Affairs, *Letter from the Secretary of the Interior . . . Relating to Leases of Lands in the Indian Territory to Citizens of the United States for Cattle-Grazing and Other Purposes;* "Item, Rube Houghton's Cattle in the Indian Territory," *Arkansas City Traveler*, May 26, 1880.

47. Edward Everett Dale, "Ranching on the Cheyenne and Arapaho Reservation, 1880–1885," *Chronicles of Oklahoma* 6, no. 1 (March 1928): 35–59; "Interior Does Not Approve Standard Oil Cattle Leases," *Arkansas City Traveler*, January 10, 1883; J. D. C. Atkins, "Leases of Indian Lands for Grazing," *ARCIA* 1885, xvi–xix.

48. Wortman, Wortman, and Bottorff, *The Indians*, 149, 195, 299, 429; "Cattle Leases," *Arkansas City Traveler*, January 23, 1884; E. S. Torrance, "Leases of Lands in the Indian Territory, State of Kansas, County of Cowley, City of Winfield, Court of Record," February 22, 1884, in U.S. Senate, *Leases of Land in the Indian Territory.*

49. Wortman, Wortman, and Bottorff, *The Indians*, 183.

50. Young Joseph (Chief Joseph), Yellow Bull, and A. I. Chapman to Commissioner of Indian Affairs, February 26, 1878, NPS; Schmeckebier, *The Office of Indian Affairs*, 262; E. W. Marble, "Report," *ARCIA* 1880, iv, x; Leupp, *The Indian and His Problem*, 242; "Index," *ARCIA* 1879, 386; "Proposals and Contracts," *ARCIA* 1884, 406; E. A. Hayt, "Report," *ARCIA* 1879, xii.

51. McWhorter, *Yellow Wolf*, Appendix C, 305–306.

52. Wortman, Wortman, and Bottorff, *The Indians*, 183; "Indian Police Required, Fiscal Year 1885," *ARCIA* 1886, 71; Thomas J. Jordan, "Earth Blanket

Deposed," July 10, 1881, LDNPOA, PA 11; Jordan, "Crow Blanket Deposed," July 14, 1881, ibid., PA 13; J. W. Scott, "Thomas Peters," February 25, 1884, ibid.; T. J. Jordan, "Changes in Police Force," July 11, 1881, ibid., PA 11; J. W. Scott, letter, April 8, 1884, ibid., PA 13; Thomas H. P. Lindsley to Price, February 6, 1884, LROIA, Ponca, 1884-3168; Lindsley to Price, February 24, 1884, ibid., 1884-4180; Lindsley to Price, March 3, 1884, ibid., 1884-7319; T. H. P. Lindsley, Yellow Bear, and Húsus Kute to Commissioner of Indian Affairs, April 25, 1884, ibid., 1884-8059; J. W. Scott to Price, February 22, 1884, ibid., 1884-4118; Scott to Price, April 8, 1884, ibid., 1884-7319.

53. J. W. Scott to Price, August 21, 1884, LDNPOA, PA 13; "Oakland Agency, August, 1884," September 1, 1884, ibid.; James, *Nez Perce Women in Transition*, 76.

54. J. W. Scott to Price, "Nez Perce Judges Appointed to Court," February 28, 1885, LDNPOA, PA 13; J. D. C. Atkins, "Court of Indian Offenses," *ARCIA* 1885, xxiii.

55. Prucha, *The Great Father*, 219; Leupp, *The Indian and His Problem*, 241–42; Deloria and Lytle, *American Indians, American Justice*, 115; Nez Perce Census, 1885, IINP: line 72.

56. Wortman, Wortman, and Bottorff, *The Indians*, 162–63, 187, 190; Lewis, *Creating Christian Indians*, 100.

57. Lewis, *Creating Christian Indians*, 100; Wortman, Wortman, and Bottorff, *The Indians*, 162–63, 187, 190.

58. Bland, "Visit to the Indian Territory."

59. Wortman, Wortman, and Bottorff, *The Indians*, 182.

60. J. Ashley Thompson, M.D., "Pine Ridge Agency, Report," August 20, 1884, *ARCIA* 1884, 211, 338–48.

61. "Medical Statistics," *ARCIA* 1885, 314, 318, 250, 396–405, *ARCIA* 1884, 344–45, 347, *ARCIA* 1883, 310, 313.

62. Wortman, Wortman, and Bottorff, *The Indians*, 193.

63. "Medical Statistics," *ARCIA* 1885, 396–405; Wortman, Wortman, and Bottorff, *The Indians*, 196; "Statistics Showing Population, Schools, Churches, and General Conditions," *ARCIA* 1879, 232–33; "Indian Items," *Arkansas City Traveler*, November 26, 1879; "Medical Statistics," *ARCIA* 1880, 275; Wm. Whiting, "Table of Statistics Regarding Population, Etc.," ibid., 244; "Statistics, Agricultural Improvements, Etc.," *ARCIA* 1881, 354–55, 366; "Medical Statistics," *ARCIA* 1882, following 366; "Population, Sources of Subsistence, Religious, Etc.," ibid., 334; T. J. Jordan, "Nez Perces, Annual Report," ibid., 76–77; "Medical Statistics," *ARCIA* 1883, 304–11; "Population, Sources of Subsistence, Religious, Vital and Criminal Statistics," ibid., 272; L. E. Woodin, "Nez Perce, Annual Report," ibid., 75; Wortman, Wortman, and Bottorff, *The Indians*, 193; "Nez Perces, Report," *ARCIA* 1884, 290, 308; "Medical Statistics," ibid., 338–42, 346–47; "Population, Sources of Subsistence, Religious and Vital

Statistics," ibid., 287; J. W. Scott, "Nez Perce, Annual Report," *ARCIA* 1885, 96; "Medical Statistics," ibid., 396–405; Nez Perce Census, 1885, IINP.

64. L. E. Woodin, "Nez Perces, Annual Report," August 1883, *ARCIA* 1883, 75, 79.

65. McWhorter, *Hear Me, My Chiefs!* 270; Nez Perce Census, 1885, IINP: lines 5, 6, 81, 96, 108.

66. "Medical Statistics," *ARCIA* 1879, 263.

67. Wm. Whiteman, "Ponca Agency Report," *ARCIA* 1879, 74–75; "Medical Statistics," *ARCIA* 1882, 366 inset, *ARCIA* 1883, 304, *ARCIA* 1884, 338, *ARCIA* 1885, 396; W. H. Robb, "Quapaw, Annual Report," *ARCIA* 1884, 91; Thornton, *American Indian Holocaust and Survival,* 54, 62; Curtin, "Epidemiology and the Slave Trade," 141; Ray, "Ethnohistory of the Joseph Band," 231.

68. Nez Perce Census, 1878, LDNPQA, QA 2; 1879, LDNPQA, QA 1; 1880, LDNPQA, PA 1; 1885, IINP.

69. "Medical Statistics," *ARCIA* 1879, 263, 264.

70. Wortman, Wortman, and Bottorff, *The Indians,* 188.

71. B. P. Moore, "Chief Joseph's Band, Colville," *ARCIA* 1886, 232–33; Wm. Whiteman to Hayt, "Older Nez Perces Have Consumption," November 4, 1879, LDNPOA, PA 11; "Medical Statistics," *ARCIA* 1885, 396.

72. Records of the Bureau of Indian Affairs, Chemawa (Forest Grove) Indian School, NARA, Seattle; Pearson, "Numipu Narratives," 82.

73. T. J. Jordan, "Requests Vaccines," June 20, 1881, LDNPOA, PA 11.

74. T. J. Jordan, letter, June 20, 1881, LDNPOA, PA 11; Ruby and Brown, *Half-Sun on the Columbia,* 313.

75. Wortman, Wortman, and Bottorff, *The Indians,* 137; L. E. Woodin to Commissioner of Indian Affairs, letter, "Smallpox at Kaw Agency," LDNPOA, PA 12; T. J. Jordan, "Vaccine," February 15, 1882, LROIA, P2186, 5.

76. Colville Census, 1885, CC.

Chapter 9

1. S. C. Armstrong, Lecture at Hampton Institute, January 18, 1879, http://home.epix.net/~landis/prattletters.html (accessed August 27, 2007).

2. Lindsey, *Indians at Hampton Institute,* 21, 34; R. H. Pratt to Townsend, "Speedy Civilization of Nez Perce Prisoners," June 24, 1878, NPWF, 340; Wortman, Wortman, and Bottorff, *The Indians,* 318.

3. E. A. Hayt, "Annual Report," November 1, 1877, *ARCIA* 1877, 397–98; Lindsey, *Indians at Hampton Institute,* 21, 34; Pratt to Townsend, June 24, 1878; Wortman, Wortman, and Bottorff, *The Indians,* 318.

4. Pratt to Townsend, June 24, 1878.

5. G. McCrary, "Orders," June 3, 1878, NPWF, 340; R. H. Pratt to Townsend, June 15, 1878, ibid.

6. Pratt to Townsend, June 24, 1878.

7. Ibid.

8. J. Reuben to Barstow, November 8, 1877, *ARBIC* 1877, 95.

9. Wm. Whiting, "Nez Perce," *ARCIA* 1880, 85, 244.

10. E. Whittlesey, "Visit to Oakland," December 1, 1882, *ARBIC* 1882, 34; J. W. Scott, "Nez Perce, Annual Report," *ARCIA* 1884, 90; T. J. Jordan, "Nez Perce," *ARCIA* 1882, 76–77; L. E. Woodin, "Nez Perce, Annual Report," *ARCIA* 1883, 79; J. W. Scott to Price, "School Building," January 7, 1884, LDNPOA, PA 13.

11. Tom Hill to H. Price, letter, June 4, 1881, LROIA, Ponca, 1881-9711.

12. W. J. Pollock to Secretary of Interior S. J. Kirkwood, May 30, 1881, LROIA, Ponca, 1881-9711.

13. J. W. Scott to Price, May 1, 1884, LDNPOA, PA 13; Scott, "Nez Perce," August 15, 1884, ibid.

14. W. Whiting, "Nez Perce, Annual Report," August 1880, *ARCIA* 1880, 244; "Cost of the School This Year," *ARCIA* 1881, 336.

15. J. W. Scott to Price, "Lumber at Oakland," November 28, 1884, LDNPOA, PA 13; Scott to Price, letter, "Materials Transferred," March 1, 1884, ibid.

16. T. J. Jordan, "Nez Perce, Table of Statistics, Etc.," *ARCIA* 1881, 336; E. Whittlesey, "Visit to Nez Perce November 30," December 1, 1882, *ARBIC* 1883, 34; L. E. Woodin, "Nez Perce," *ARCIA* 1883, 79; J. W. Scott, "March 1884," LDNPOA, PA 13.

17. Wm. Whiting, "Report," December 16, 1880, LDNPOA, PA 13.

18. *James Reuben's Record Book,* University of Idaho Library, 42: line 13; 50: line 20; 56: line 23; 60: line 23; 64: line 24; 42: line 16; 46: line 14; 66: line 8; 70: line 7; 74: line 8; 78: line 8; 64: line 1; 68: line 1; 72: line 1; 76: line 1.

19. J. W. Scott, "Nez Perce, Annual Report," August 15, 1884, *ARCIA* 1884, 90; Scott to Price, May 1, 1884, LDNPOA, PA 13; Scott, letter, February 1, 1884, ibid.; Scott, letter, January 5, 1885, ibid.; Scott, "Reply to Price," February 1, 1885, ibid.; Scott to Price, February 6, 1885, ibid.

20. J. W. Scott to Price, March 2, 1885, LDNPOA, PA 13; J. M. Haworth, letter, June 25, 1883, LROIA, Ponca, 1883-11859; July 13, 1892, *United States Statutes at Large,* 27 Stat. L., 143.

21. *James Reuben's Record Book,* 8: line 4; Wm. Whiting, letter, March 12, 1881, LDNPOA, PA 11; T. J. Jordan, letter, July 14, 1881, ibid., PA 13; *James Reuben's Record Book,* front label; T. J. Jordan, "Nez Perce," *ARCIA* 1882, 76–77; J. W. Scott to Price, letter, March 11, 1884, LDNPOA, PA 13; "W. H. and Mrs. Nelson," *Winfield Courier,* January 12, 1882.

22. Wortman, Wortman, and Bottorff, *The Indians,* 188; *James Reuben's Record Book,* 42: line 13; 50: line 20; 56: line 23; 60: line 23; 64: line 24; 42: line 16; 46:

line 14; 66: line 8; 70: line 7; 74: line 8; 78: line 8; 64: line 1; Nez Perce Census, 1885, IINP: lines 31, 81, 74, 90, 100, 113.

23. R. H. Pratt, "Carlisle Indian Training School, 1st AR," October 5, 1880, *ARCIA* 1880, 178–79; *James Reuben's Record Book,* 34: line 3; Clark, "The Nez Perces in Exile," 228; Wortman, Wortman, and Bottorff, *The Indians,* 322.

24. A. R. Satterthwaite to Commissioner of Indian Affairs, May 1880, LDNPOA, PA 11; *James Reuben's Record Book,* 82–100, 103.

25. *James Reuben's Record Book,* 99–100, 103.

26. A. R. Satterthwaite to Commissioner of Indian Affairs, June 1880, LDNPOA, PA 11; J. Reuben to J. M. Haworth, "Is There News of Return to Idaho," February 4, 1884, LROIA, Ponca, 1884-5212.

27. L. E. Woodin, "Reuben's Return," June 4, 1883, LDNPOA, PA 13; Woodin, "Report, Oakland Reservation," August 10, 1883, ibid.; "Great Drawback to J. Reuben," August 1, 1883, ibid.; "Table A: Indian School Employees," *ARCIA* 1885, xlvii–clix.

28. T. Hill to Price, "Hill Wishes to Attend School," June 14, 1884, LROIA, Ponca, 1884-11132.

29. Ibid.

30. Nez Perce Census, 1885, IINP: line 113.

31. J. W. Scott, "Carrie Shutts [Shults], Hired," July 6, 1884, LDNPOA, PA 13; Scott, letter, March 11, 1884, ibid.; Scott, "Recommendation and Request," June 30, 1884, ibid.; Tom Hill, "Letter to Miss Fannie Skinner," *Arkansas City Traveler,* February 13, 1884; Hill to Price, June 14, 1884; Scott to Price, June 30, 1884, LROIA, Ponca, 1884-12567.

32. "Table A: Indian School Employees," *ARCIA* 1885, clix, clviii,; "Table B: Government and Contract Schools," ibid., cxcvi, cxcvii; "Table D: Government Day-Schools, Etc.," ibid., ccx, ccxi.

33. L. E. Woodin to Price, November 1, 1883, LDNPOA, PA 13.

34. J. W. Scott, "February," February 16, 1884, LDNPOA, PA 13; Scott to Price, February 6, 1885, ibid.

35. Scott to Price, February 6, 1885.

36. Lomawaima, *They Called It Prairie Light,* 9–10.

37. Scott to Price, February 6, 1885.

38. Ibid.; Descriptive Record of Students Admitted, Enrollment Records of Chilocco School, NARA, Fort Worth, 7RA61, vols. 1–8; Nez Perce Census, 1885, IINP: line 108.

39. Descriptive Record of Students Admitted; Nez Perce Census, 1885, IINP: lines 108, 40; K. McBeth to J. S. Lowrie, November 9, 1880, AIC, box D, letter 329; Kate McBeth, *Called to Evangelize: James Hayes* (New York: Board of National Missions of the Presbyterian Church in the U.S.A., 1928), 6; Evans, *Voice of the Old Wolf,* 104–105; Olsen, *Qillíowawya,* 24; McWhorter, *Yellow Wolf,*

311; Pierson, "Indian Progression"; McBeth, *The Nez Perces since Lewis and Clark,* 209–10, 212, 215; J. Hayes quoted in ibid., 209; "Undated Letter Signed 'Mark' to Dr. Clifford Drury: Doctorate of Divinity Awarded to James Hayes," Whitworth College, Spokane, Wash.; Julia Frazer, *Y. P. Secretary of Synod of California, to Sunday School Superintendents of the Synod of California* (pamphlet, Oakland, Calif., 1905); Lewis, *Creating Christian Indians,* 132–33.

40. "Table A: Indian School Employees," *ARCIA* 1885, clxxxii, clxxxiii, clxxxiv, clxxxv.

41. "Chilocco Indian School," *Arkansas City Traveler,* 1885; Historical Resources, Cowley County, Kansas, http://www.ausbcomp.com/~bbott/wortman/index.html (accessed August 27, 2007).

42. Lomawaima, *They Called It Prairie Light,* 9, 25; "Table A: Indian School Employees," clxxx, clxxxi.

43. Wortman, Wortman, and Bottorff, *The Indians,* 322; Pearson, "Reservation Economies," 160; W. J. Hadley, "Chilocco School," July 15, 1884, *ARCIA* 1884, 209–10; H. J. Minthorn, "Chilocco School," July 15, 1884, ibid., 222; J. B. Riley, "Chilocco School," *ARCIA* 1886, lxii; Wortman, Wortman, and Bottorff, *The Indians,* 156, 322; Emma D. K. Sleeth quoted in Lomawaima, *They Called It Prairie Light,* 23.

44. Lomawaima, *They Called It Prairie Light,* 23; Nez Perce Students Enrolled at Chilocco, 1910, NARA, Fort Worth, CHL-11; Jesse Paul, interview with author, October 12, 2004.

45. R. H. Pratt, "Speech at Association Hall, Philadelphia, Items: The Carlisle Indian School," *Friend's Intelligencer* 38, no. 12 (May 1881): 186–88.

46. Ibid.; Vine Deloria, Jr., "Foreword," in Cajete, *Look to the Mountain,* 11; Evans, *Voice of the Old Wolf,* 109; Harriet Mary, "Letter from the Country, Bellefonte, Centre Co., PA," *School News,* November 1882, http://home.epix.net/~landis/mary.html (accessed August 27, 2007); Cumberland County Historical Society, http://www.historicalsociety.com/ (accessed August 27, 2007).

47. W. Whiting, Carlisle Indian School, October 15, 1880, LDNPOA, PA 11.

48. L. E. Woodin, letter, April 16, 1883, LDNPOA, PA 13; Woodin to R. H. Pratt, June 20, 1883, ibid.; Woodin to Pratt, July 2, 1883, ibid.; Records of the Bureau of Indian Affairs, Chemawa (Forest Grove) Indian School, NARA, Seattle; "Carlisle Indian School Enrollments," http://members.aol.com/tawodi/carlisle/page5.htm (accessed August 27, 2007); Cumberland County Historical Society, http://www.historicalsociety.com/.

49. Harriet Mary, "Letter from the Country."

50. Ibid.; Harriet Mary, letter in the *Red Man,* November 8, 1889, http://home.epix.net/~landis/mary.html (accessed August 27, 2007); Harriet Mary, letter in the *Indian Helper,* January 10, 1890, ibid.; Cumberland County Historical Society, http://www.historicalsociety.com/; Gay, *With the Nez Perces,* 28; Evans, *Voice of the Old Wolf,* 109.

51. "Camp Items," *Indian Helper,* August 12, 1887, http://home.epix.net/~landis/phillips.html (accessed August 27, 2007); Cumberland County Historical Society, http://www.historicalsociety.com/.

52. Luke Phillips, letter, *School News,* November 1882; Phillips, letter, *Morning Star,* February 1885; Luke Phillips, obituary, *Indian Helper,* January 13, 1888; all at http://home.epix.net/~landis/phillips.html (accessed August 27, 2007); Cumberland County Historical Society, http://www.historicalsociety.com/.

53. Samuel Johns, Carlisle Indian School, http://home.epix.net/~landis/john.html (accessed August 27, 2007); *Indian Helper,* March 25, 1888, http://home.epix.net/~landis/paul.html (accessed August 27, 2007); Cumberland County Historical Society, http://www.historicalsociety.com/; "Health Statistics, Carlisle," *ARCIA* 1880, 275–76; George L. Spining, "The Unhappy Nez Perces," *New York Times,* October 29, 1883; R. H. Pratt, "Carlisle Training School for Youth," *ARCIA* 1880, 178–79; Pratt, "Carlisle Indian School," *ARCIA* 1888, 277–78; Pratt, "Carlisle Indian School," *ARCIA* 1884, 187.

54. Information on Charles Wolf, Jesse Paul, and the Carlisle Indian School obtained from the Cumberland County Historical Society, http://www.historicalsociety.com/.

55. Jesse Paul, interviews with author, October 31, 2003, October 12, 2004.

56. Scott, *Some Memories of a Soldier,* 82–83.

57. R. H. Pratt, "Carlisle Indian School, Statistics," September 12, 1884, *ARCIA* 1884, 187; "Carlisle Indian School, Statistics," *ARCIA* 1889, 365; "Carlisle Indian School, AR," *ARCIA* 1892, 691.

Chapter 10

1. George L. Spining, "The Unhappy Nez Perces," *New York Times,* October 29, 1883.

2. Elder Billy Williams quoted in "Nez Perce History," McBeth Journals; Walker, *Conflict and Schism in Nez Percé Acculturation,* 34; William Willard, interview with author, October 11, 2005.

3. McBeth, *The Nez Perces since Lewis and Clark,* 28; W. Otis Halfmoon, interview with author, August 9, 2005.

4. Dorsey, "The Ponca Sun Dance," 86–87.

5. Wortman, Wortman, and Bottorff, *The Indians,* 160–61.

6. J. W. Scott to Commissioner of Indian Affairs, June 6, 1884, LDNPOA, PA 13; Daily, *Battle for the BIA,* 38; Scott, "Ponca," *ARCIA* 1884, 86.

7. Berthrong, *The Cheyenne and Arapaho Ordeal,* 134; D. B. Dyer, "Cheyenne and Arapaho," *ARCIA* 1884, 72.

8. Wm. Whiting, "Permit to Visit Cheyenne and Arapaho," June 18, 1880, LDNPOA, PA 11; "Permit to Visit," September 27, 1880, ibid.

9. "Permit to Visit the Cheyenne and Arapaho," January 22, 1881, LDNPOA, PA 11.

10. "Editorial," *Arkansas City Traveler*, June 29, 1881.

11. Wortman, Wortman, and Bottorff, *The Indians*, 49.

12. Ibid., 185–86; Nez Perce Census, 1885, IINP: line 32, Ow-hi.

13. La Barre, *The Ghost Dance*, 128–29, 136.

14. Mooney, "Ghost Dance," 256, 295, 344–47, 249, 352.

15. Ibid., 154, 351; Harrington, *Vocabulary of the Kiowa Language*, 1.

16. Harrington, *Vocabulary of the Kiowa Language*, 1; William Willard, interview with author, May 2004.

17. Steve Grafe, interview with author, September 2, 2004.

18. Mooney, "Ghost Dance," 351.

19. Wortman, Wortman, and Bottorff, *The Indians*, 194.

20. Steve Grafe, interview with author, December 14, 2004.

21. Mooney, "Ghost Dance," 351; Hunt and Nye, "The Annual Sun Dance of the Kiowa Indians," 357.

22. *James Reuben's Record Book*, University of Idaho Library, 56: lines 25, 26, 27, 60: line 29.

23. Clark, "The Nez Perces in Exile," 227; T. Jordan, "Nez Perce," *ARCIA* 1881, 94.

24. Ewers, "The Substitution of the Bone Hair Pipe"; Spinden, *The Nez Percé Indians*, 217–18; Olsen, *A Legacy from Sam Morris*, 23, 26, CD1, 27.

25. "The Nez Perces Are Visited by 5,000 People from the Country on Sunday; Their Religious Services as Witnessed by a Times Reporter," *Leavenworth Times*, December 11, 1877; John B. Monteith, "Lapwai," August 15, 1877, *ARCIA* 1877, 81; McBeth, *The Nez Perces since Lewis and Clark*, 89, 90; John C. Lowrie to Samuel N. D. Martin, December 14, 1877, AIC, box K-1, letter 388; W. O. Halfmoon, interview with author, August 26, 2005.

26. Samuel Baker, W. M. Burr, Manly Breaker, W. A. Clark, M. B. Pilcher, and J. H. Foster, "Report of Missionary Societies, Presbyterian Homes Missions for the Year 1878," *ARBIC* 1879, 88.

27. Wortman, Wortman, and Bottorff, *The Indians*, 189.

28. Ibid., 185.

29. Mark Williams had come to the Indian Territory in 1878 in place of his brother Robert. Missionary Sue McBeth regarded Robert as her special pupil and thus resisted his being sent to the Indian Territory, so Mark Williams was hired as the assistant farmer and assisted the agency clerk. Archie Lawyer, who was supposed to have served as Williams's spiritual advisor, became the pastor of the Oakland Presbyterian Church and an Indian rights activist. James Reuben, who was intended to serve as Williams's other advisor and mentor, became the deacon of the Oakland Presbyterian Church. Morrill and Morrill, *Out of the Blanket*, 184.

30. Spining, "The Unhappy Nez Perces"; James, *Nez Perce Women in Transition,* following 81, 82, 84.

31. M. Hopkins, "Meeting Notes, Kendall Reporting," *ARBIC* 1880, 99–100.

32. Wortman, Wortman, and Bottorff, *The Indians,* 182, 184–85, 185–87.

33. Ibid., 184–85.

34. Ibid.

35. Ibid.

36. Ibid.

37. Ibid.

38. Lewis, *Creating Christian Indians,* 47, 51, 115; Walker, *Conflict and Schism in Nez Percé Acculturation,* 64.

39. Lewis, *Creating Christian Indians,* 111–13, 115–19.

40. Wortman, Wortman, and Bottorff, *The Indians,* 185–87.

41. Lawyer, *Letter, and Memorial, from the Synod of Kansas of the Presbyterian Church,* 1; Slickpoo and Walker, *Noon Nee-Me-Poo,* 209.

42. Arthur Taylor, interview with author, November 5, 2005.

43. Wortman, Wortman, and Bottorff, *The Indians,* 189, 190; T. J. Jordan, "Nez Perce," *ARCIA* 1881, 94; J. W. Scott to Price, April 8, 1884, LDNPOA, PA 13; Lawyer, *Letter, and Memorial, from the Synod of Kansas of the Presbyterian Church,* 1; Wortman, Wortman, and Bottorff, *The Indians,* 193; E. Whittlesey, "Visit to Oakland," November 30, 1882, *ARBIC* 1882, 35.

44. Wortman, Wortman, and Bottorff, *The Indians,* 194, 195.

45. Packard, "Mythology and Religion of the Nez Perces," 327.

46. Wortman, Wortman, and Bottorff, *The Indians,* 185–87.

47. T. J. Jordan, "Nez Perces, Annual Report," *ARCIA* 1881, 94.

48. Nez Perce Census, 1885, IINP.

49. Dean A. Ferguson, "Lawyer Lore Was Told in Fireside Chats: Interview with Mylie Lawyer," http://robschmidt3.freewebpage.org/mylie.htm (accessed December 20, 2004); Mylie Lawyer, interview with author, February 3, 2005.

50. Wortman, Wortman, and Bottorff, *The Indians,* 192; Lawyer, *Letter, and Memorial, from the Synod of Kansas of the Presbyterian Church,* 1; Henderson, "Reminiscences of a Range Rider."

51. "Wedding Bells at Ponca Agency," *Arkansas City Traveler,* October 5, 1881.

52. Mylie Lawyer, as relayed by Steve Evans, February 3, 2005, October 1, 2005.

53. Wortman, Wortman, and Bottorff, *The Indians,* 194.

54. Mylie Lawyer, as relayed by Steve Evans, February 3, 2005.

55. Spining, "The Unhappy Nez Perces."

56. A. Lawyer to [F. F.] Ellinwood, September 9, 1884, AIC, box 1-1, letter 289.

57. Lewis, *Creating Christian Indians,* 106, 123, 125–27; Evans, *Voice of the Old Wolf,* 84; K. McBeth to F. F. Ellinwood, July 12, 1887, AIC, box 1-1, letters 254 and 260; A. Lawyer to [F. F.] Ellinwood September 9, 1884, ibid., letter 289;

Lawyer to Ellinwood, August 13, 1886, AIC, box 1-2, letter 198; Lawyer, "A Christian Indian's Plea."

Chapter 11

1. Wortman, Wortman, and Bottorff, *The Indians,* 173, 223.

2. Records of the Bureau of Indian Affairs: Indexes to Letters Received, 1881–1886, Ponca Agency, Indian Territory, NARA, Washington, D.C., reel 2.

3. Wortman, Wortman, and Bottorff, *The Indians,* 159–60, 165; Wm. Whiting, "Ponca Agency Report," *ARCIA* 1889, 85; Wm. Whiting to Carlisle Industrial School, "Huses Kute Wants to Know Why His Son Does Not Spend More Time in Class," October 15, 1880, LDNPOA, PA 11; T. J. Jordan, "Permit for Reuben to Attend Teacher's Institute," July 13, 1881, ibid.

4. J. M. Haworth to Commissioner of Indian Affairs, letter, "H. J. Minthorn at Oakland," March 29, 1882, LROIA, Ponca, 1882-6008; L. E. Woodin, letter, "Nez Perce School Children," April 16, 1883, LDNPOA, PA 13; Woodin to R. H. Pratt, letter, "Nez Perce Students," July 2, 1883, ibid.

5. J. W. Scott to Hadley, "Charley Moses to Deliver School Children to Chilocco School," February 16, 1884, LDNPOA, PA 13; J. W. Scott to Price, "Oakland Report for February 1884," March 14, 1884, ibid.; Scott to Price, "Archie Lawyer to Return to Idaho," *Arkansas City Traveler,* July 16, 1884; J. W. Scott, "Oakland Report for January," February 1, 1885, LDNPOA, PA 13; L. W. Woodin, "Oakland Report," August 1883, *ARCIA* 1883, 79.

6. Wm. Whiting, "Permit to Visit," June 18, 1880, LDNPOA, PA 11; Wm. Whiting, "Ponca Visit Cheyennes and Arapahos," September 27, 1880, ibid.; Wm. Whiting, "Ponca, Annual Report," *ARCIA* 1880, 85; Wortman, Wortman, and Bottorff, *The Indians,* 183–87; Whiting, "Ponca, Annual Report," *ARCIA* 1882, 76–77.

7. T. Jordan, "Nez Perce, Indian Territory, Report," August, 1881, *ARCIA* 1881, 94.

8. L. E. Woodin, "Permit," October 2, 1882, LDNPOA, PA 13.

9. J. W. Scott to Price, letter, April 4, 1884, LDNPOA, PA 13; Scott, letter, June 16, 1884, ibid.

10. Wortman, Wortman, and Bottorff, *The Indians,* 159–60; Wm. Whiting, "Ponca, Annual Report," *ARCIA* 1880, 85–86.

11. T. J. Jordan, "Ponca, Annual Report," *ARCIA* 1882, 76–77; Wortman, Wortman, and Bottorff, *The Indians,* 174; Jordan, "Nez Perces Must Have More Horses," *ARCIA* 1881, 94; J. M. Haworth to CIA, Dr. Minthorn, letter, March 29, 1882, LROIA, Ponca, 1882-6008.

12. L. E. Woodin, "Ponca, Annual Report," 79, *ARCIA* 1883, 75–79, 290, 291.

13. Ibid.

14. J. W. Scott to Commissioner of Indian Affairs, "Needs Farm Implements," March 5, 1884, LDNPOA, PA 13; Scott to H. Price, "Indian Freighters," December 9, 1884, ibid.; Scott to Price, "Teacher and Matron at Oakland," March 11, 1884, ibid.; "Land Leases," *Arkansas City Traveler,* January 10, 1885.

15. T. J. Jordan to Commissioner of Indian Affairs, July 4, 1881, LDNPOA, PA 11; L. E. Woodin, "Memo," October 1882, ibid., PA 14.

16. Wm. Whiting, "Nez Perce, Ponca Agency, Indian Territory," August 1880, *ARCIA* 1880, 85.

17. J. W. Scott to Price, "Police Discharged," February 25, 1884, LDNPOA, PA 13; Scott to Price, "Change in Oakland Police," April 8, 1884, ibid.

18. J. W. Scott to Price, "Agency Administration," February 28, 1884, LDNPOA, PA 13.

19. T. J. Jordan to Commissioner of Indian Affairs, letter, "Tribal Police," September 17, 1881, LDNPOA, PA 11.

20. Wm. Whiting, letter, "Re: Lost Children," January 7, 1881, LDNPOA, PA 11; Whiting, letter, "Cayuse in Indian Territory," March 12, 1881, ibid.

21. Wm. Whiting, letter, "Insufficient Rations," March 26, 1881, LDNPOA, PA 11; Whiting, "Receipt, Payment for Destroyed Hay Crop," April 7, 1881, ibid.

22. T. J. Jordan, "Ponca, Annual Report," *ARCIA* 1881, 94, *ARCIA* 1882, 76–77; L. E. Woodin to Price, letter, "Widows Return to Idaho," October 19, 1882, LDNPOA, PA 13.

23. Criminal Defendant Case File, John T. Bennett, U.S. District Court for the Fort Smith Division of the Western District of Arkansas, September 13, 1881, NARA, Fort Worth, ARC-204756, ARC-204754, ARC-204755; George L. Spining, "The Unhappy Nez Perces," *New York Times,* October 29, 1883.

24. Spining, "The Unhappy Nez Perces."

25. T. J. Jordan, "Ponca, Annual Report," *ARCIA* 1881, 94.

26. Spining, "The Unhappy Nez Perces."

27. Wortman, Wortman, and Bottorff, *The Indians,* 156; "Minthorn's Family," *Arkansas City Traveler,* October 29, 1879; "Dr. Minthorn," *Arkansas City Traveler,* March 11, 1885.

28. Wortman, Wortman, and Bottorff, *The Indians,* 181, 164, 173, 204; "Dr. Minthorn"; "Minthorn, H. J."

29. L. E. Woodin to Price, "Physician's Duties," November 23, 1882, LDNPOA, PA 13; Wortman, Wortman, and Bottorff, *The Indians,* 205; Woodin to J. S. Woodward, letter, "Transfer," December 11, 1882, LDNPOA, PA 13; Woodward quoted in Spining, "The Unhappy Nez Perces"; Thomas H. P. Lindsley to Price, letter, "Complaints about Tom Hill," February 6, 1884, LROIA, Ponca, 1884-316; Lindsley to Price, letter, "Oakland Police," February 24, 1884, ibid., 1884-4180; Lindsley to Price, "Oakland Complaints," March 3, 1884, ibid., 1884-7319; T. H. P. Lindsley, Yellow Bear, and Húsus Kute to Commissioner of Indian Affairs, letter, "Problems at Oakland," April 25, 1884, LROIA, Ponca, 1884-8059.

30. L. E. Woodin, "Nez Perces, Annual Report," *ARCIA* 1883, 79.

31. J. W. Scott, letter, "Dr. Woodward Serves Three Reservations," January 14, 1884, LDNPOA, PA 13.

32. Wortman, Wortman, and Bottorff, *The Indians,* 151, 156, 406; J. M. Haworth to Office of Indian Affairs, "Nez Perce Request Keep Mrs. Nelson at Oakland," April 4, 1881, LROIA, Ponca, 1881-5798.

33. Haworth to Office of Indian Affairs, April 4, 1881; Emily S. Cook, "Field Matrons," *ARBIC* 1893, 50.

34. J. M. Haworth to Indian Bureau, letter, "Nez Perce Request," April 4, 1881, LROIA, Ponca, 1884-5798; "W. H. and Mrs. Nelson," *Winfield Courier,* January 12, 1882; Emily S. Cook, "How the ID Undertakes to Teach the Indian Woman to Shoulder the White Woman's Burden," *ARBIC* 1901, 84–85; Birney, "Address of Welcome"; Emily S. Cook, "Matron's Report," *ARBIC* 1892, 50–62; Louise H. Douglas, "Matron's Report, Ponca," *ARCIA* 1892, 316.

35. J. W. Scott, "Report, Oakland Agency," April 15, 1884, LDNPOA, PA 13; W. Rouse to Price, "Requests Transfer," June 20, 1884, ibid.; Rouse to Price, "Rouse Resigned," April 9, 1885, ibid.; Tom Hill to Price, "Asks to Attend School," June 14, 1884, LROIA, Ponca, 1884-11132.

36. "Wedding," *Arkansas City Traveler,* December 6, 1882; "Houghton Family," http://www.ausbcomp.com/~bbott/wortman/AcLeadersHoughtonFamily.htm (accessed August 27, 2007).

37. J. H. Sherburne to Lucullus McWhorter, letter, May 19, 1927, McW, folder 40; Sherburne to McWhorter, letter, May 9, 1927, ibid., folder 255; Sherburne to McWhorter, letter, September 10, 1927, ibid.; Sherburne to McWhorter, letter, April 10, 1936, ibid.; Sherburne to McWhorter, letter, April 10, 1936, ibid., folder 258.

38. Sherburne, "Chief Joseph Presented Gifts to Browning Man."

39. Wortman, Wortman, and Bottorff, *The Indians,* 165–67, 173.

40. Ibid., 399–412.

41. Ibid., 402.

42. Ibid., 95–96, 169, 318, 319, 333, 402; Cutler, "James A. Haworth"; J. Oberly, "Report of Indian School Superintendent," *ARCIA* 1885, lxx–cxxvii.

43. "R. A. Houghton, Joe Sherburne, Brand Cards, Pollock, Etc.," obtained from Mary A. Wortman, http://www.ausbcomp.com/~bbott/wortman/index.html (accessed August 27, 2007).

44. Ibid.

45. Webb, "Henry County History," 1.

46. "Joseph H. Sherburne Family," http://www.ausbcomp.com/~bbott/wortman/SherburneJH.htm (accessed August 27, 2007).

47. "Indian Traderships, Leases, Scandals, Etc., from Local Newspapers," obtained from Mary A. Wortman, http://www.ausbcomp.com/~bbott/wortman/index.html; Allison-Bunnell and Rowan, "Guide to the Sherburne Family Papers," 1.

48. Wortman, "Indian Traderships"; Allison-Bunnell and Rowan, "Guide to the Sherburne Family Papers," 1.

49. Allison-Bunnell and Rowan, "Guide to the Sherburne Family Papers," 1.

50. J. H. Sherburne to L. V. McWhorter, letter, May 6, 1927, McW, folder 255; E. A. Brininstool to McWhorter, letter, September 16, 1938, ibid., folder 358.

51. David B. Custeahoot, "Statement," n.d., McW, folder 66, ms. 189, 24; Brown, *The Flight of the Nez Perce,* 63; contributions from J. W. Redington to L. V. McWhorter, 1927–1932, McW, folder 66, ms. 189, 3; Corbet Lawyer, "Statement," n.d., ibid., folder 66; Henderson, "Reminiscences of a Range Rider"; McWhorter, *Yellow Wolf,* 55; Many Wounds, letter, November 26 [no year], McW, folder 66; Raven Spy, "Statement," n.d., ibid.; Aoki, "Nez Perce Texts," 98.

52. L. V. McWhorter to D. McDonald, letter, March 16, 1928, McW, folder 40; Brown, *The Flight of the Nez Perce,* 63; Aoki, "Nez Perce Texts," 114–15; Thomas Beal, "Statement," n.d., McW, folder 66, ms. 189, 6; Yellow Wolf, "Statement," September 28, 1930, ibid., folder 66; Arthur Simon, "Statement," n.d., ibid.

53. Many Wounds, "Statement," n.d., McW, folder 66, ms. 189, 5; Brown, *The Flight of the Nez Perce,* 63; Many Wounds, "Statement," 1926, McW, folder 66, ms. 189, 15.

54. McWhorter, *Yellow Wolf,* 55.

55. Arthur Simon, "Statement," September 22, 1941, McW, folder 66; Red Elk, "Statement," n.d., ibid.; Philip Williams, "Statement," n.d., ibid., ms. 189, 8.

56. Redfield, "Reminiscences," 73–76.

57. McWhorter, *Yellow Wolf,* 289; H. W. Jones to Ezra Hayt, August 23, 1879, LROIA, Quapaw, 1-4995, 709; Redfield, "Reminiscences," 76; Arthur I. Chapman, letter to Editor Alfred B. Meacham, *Council Fire* 4, no. 8 (August 1881): 122; J. M. Redington, "Statement," n.d., McW, folder 66, ms. 189, 3, article 1; David B. Custeahoot, "Statement," ibid., folder 66, ms. 189, 4.

58. Meacham, "Exiled Nez Perces," 125.

59. Henderson, "Reminiscences of a Range Rider."

60. Young Joseph, Yellow Bull, Espowis, et al., "Notarized Statement Submitted to the Honorable Commissioner of Indian Affairs," February 24, 1878, NPS; A. I. Chapman to Meacham, February 5, 1879, LROIA, Quapaw, 1-4995, 708.

61. A. I. Chapman, "The Nez Perces and the Modocs, Nez Perces Camp, Quapaw Agency," *Leavenworth Times,* August 28, 1879, reprinted in the *New York Times,* September 28, 1879.

62. Wortman, Wortman, and Bottorff, *The Indians,* 180, 181; Henderson, "Reminiscences of a Range Rider"; E. C. Osborn to A. I. Chapman, letter, March 28, 1888, LDNPOA, PA 15.

Chapter 12

1. Wortman, Wortman, and Bottorff, *The Indians,* 165–67, 183–85.

2. Ibid.; Reuben, "Documents from the Cornerstone," 363.

3. Wortman, Wortman, and Bottorff, *The Indians,* 165–67, 183–85.

4. Ibid., 165–67, 410; "Brick Work and Foundation," *Cowley County Courant,* December 29, 1881; *James Reuben's Record Book,* University of Idaho Library, 82.

5. E. A. Hayt to Jones, letter, "Skou-cum-Joe," August 8, 1878, LDNPQA, QA 7; J. McNeil to Hayt, letter, "Skou-cum-Joe," August 2, 1878, NPWF, 340; Hayt to Secretary of Interior, letter, "Skou-cum-Joe," August 8, 1878, ibid.; C. Schurz to Secretary of War, letter, "Skou-cum-Joe," August 10, 1878, ibid.; Lt. Crowley to N. A. Miles, memo, November 30, 1878, ibid.; G. C. Doane to Asst. Adj. General, "Skou-cum-Joe," September 26, 1878, ibid.; G. McCrary to Secretary of Interior, letter, "Skou-cum-Joe," February 5, 1879, ibid.; N. A. Miles, "Skou-cum-Joe," January 16, 1879, ibid.

6. Nez Perce Census, 1880, LDNPQA, PA 1: lines 70, 94; Nez Perce Census, 1885, IINP: lines 71, 93, 4, 10; Wm. Whiting, letter, "Inquiries, Cayuse Held in Indian Territory," March 12, 1881, LDNPOA, PA 11; O. O. Howard, transmitting letter, "Little Man Chief," January 30, 1879, NPWF, 340; C. Schurz to Secretary of War, "Little Man Chief," January 30, 1879, ibid.; Trafzer, "Chief Joseph's Allies," 7.

7. Arthur I. Chapman, letter to Editor Alfred B. Meacham, *Council Fire* 4, no. 8 (August 1881): 122; Nez Perce Census, 1885, IINP: line 4.

8. L. E. Woodin to Price, letter, "Jim Horn," January 23, 1882, LDNPOA, PA 13.

9. McWhorter, *Yellow Wolf,* 134, 139.

10. Wm. Whiting, "Permit," September 27, 1880, LDNPOA, PA 11; McWhorter, *Yellow Wolf,* 187; testimony of Joe Albert in U.S. Senate, Committee on Indian Affairs, *Memorial of the Nez Perce Indians Residing in the State of Idaho to the Congress of the United States,* 103–104; "Visitor's Pass," September 12, 1882, LDNPOA, PA 13; "Memo to Hiram Price," October 1882, ibid., PA 14.

11. Yellow Bear to CIA, letter, June 4, 1881, LROIA, Ponca, 1881-9711.

12. Tom Hill to CIA, letter, June 4, 1881, ibid.

13. Chief Joseph, "Letter and Request," June 4, 1881, ibid.

14. T. J. Jordan, "Oakland, Annual Report," *ARCIA* 1881, 94.

15. "Reverend Lawyer and Others Visit," *Winfield Courier,* August 25, 1881; "James Ruben," *Winfield Courier,* August 24, 1882; Wortman, Wortman, and Bottorff, *The Indians,* 188.

16. Chief Joseph by James Reuben, "To Oliver O. Howard, June 30 1880," in Venn, *Soldier to Advocate,* 74.

17. L. E. Woodin to Price, letter, "Widows and Orphans," October 19, 1882, LDNPOA, PA 13.

18. Ibid.; Haines, *Red Eagles of the Northwest,* 323.

19. Woodin, letter, October 19, 1882; testimony of Three Eagles in U.S. Senate, Committee on Indian Affairs, *Memorial of the Nez Perce Indians Residing in the State of Idaho to the Congress of the United States,* 114–15; Evans, *Voice of the Old Wolf,* 39; McWhorter, *Hear Me, My Chiefs!* 270; Colville Census, 1885, CC; J. Reuben to Haworth, letter, "Widows and Orphans," August 30, 1882, LROIA, Ponca, 1882-17594; Nez Perce Census, 1885, IINP: lines 6, 5, 81, 86, 21, 29, 47, 55, 70, 80, 81, 85, 86, 88, 96, 108, 113, 115.

20. "James Reuben," *Arkansas City Traveler,* May 23, 1883.

21. *James Reuben's Record Book,* 70–71, 74–81; McBeth, *The Nez Perces since Lewis and Clark,* 99–100.

22. Telegrams, C. Monteith to Commissioner of Indian Affairs, June 18, 1883, NPWF, 340; H. Teller to R. Lincoln, June 20, 1883, ibid.; Lincoln to Teller, June 21, 1883, ibid.; H. A. Price to Teller, June 22, 1883, ibid.; and O. O. Howard to Adj. General, July 3, 1883, ibid.

23. George L. Spining, "The Unhappy Nez Perces," *New York Times,* October 29, 1883; *James Reuben's Record Book,* 70–71, 74–75, 78–81; McBeth, *The Nez Perces since Lewis and Clark,* 100.

24. McBeth, *The Nez Perces since Lewis and Clark,* 100; *James Reuben's Record Book,* 81; Wortman, Wortman, and Bottorff, *The Indians,* 195–96.

25. C. E. Monteith, "Nez Perce Agency," August 20, 1883, *ARCIA* 1883, 57.

26. Records of the Bureau of Indian Affairs, Chemawa (Forest Grove) Indian School, Register of Students, 1880–1928, NARA, Seattle, 92: 187–94; H. J. Minthorn, "Forest Grove, Annual Report," *ARCIA* 1883, 180–83.

27. Loran Olsen, "Levi Jonas," in Olsen, *Qillóowawya,* 24; Olsen, *Guide to the Nez Perce Music Archive,* 8.

28. *James Reuben's Record Book,* title page.

29. Wortman, Wortman, and Bottorff, *The Indians,* 192.

30. Platter, Fleming, and Wilson, *A Memorial from the Synod of Kansas.*

31. Ibid.

32. Wortman, Wortman, and Bottorff, *The Indians,* 191, 192.

33. Ibid., 193; testimony of Three Eagles in U.S. Senate, Committee on Indian Affairs, *Memorial of the Nez Perce Indians Residing in the State of Idaho to the Congress of the United States,* 114–15.

34. Wortman, Wortman, and Bottorff, *The Indians,* 193–94; U.S. Senate, Committee on Indian Affairs, *Message from the President of the United States, Transmitting . . . Draft of a Bill "For the Relief of the Nez Perce Indians in the Territory of Idaho."*

35. Luke Phillips, letter, *Morning Star,* February 1885, http://home.epix.net/~landis/phillips.html (accessed August 27, 2007); Cumberland County Historical Society, http://www.historicalsociety.com/ (accessed August 27, 2007).

36. Wm. J. Pollock to Price, "Asks Permission to Take Nez Perces Home," April 13, 1883, LROIA, Ponca, 1883-6796.

37. Spining, "The Unhappy Nez Perces."

38. E. Whittlesey, "Report, Nez Perce Agency, Oakland," *ARBIC* 1883, 34.

39. Wortman, Wortman, and Bottorff, *The Indians,* 194.

40. Ibid.; Nez Perce Census, 1885, IINP: line 11.

41. J. W. Scott to Commissioner of Indian Affairs, "Report for March," March 31, 1884, LDNPOA, PA 13; Scott, "Monthly Report, May," May 31, 1884, ibid.

42. Wortman, Wortman, and Bottorff, *The Indians,* 195–96.

43. Ibid., 194; J. W. Scott to Price, letter, June 30, 1884, LDNPOA, PA 13.

44. Scott to Price, "Nez Perce Excited," June 30, 1884; Scott to Price, letter, August 6, 1884, LDNPOA, PA 13.

45. J. Reuben to Haworth, letter, February 4, 1884, LROIA, Ponca, 1884-5212; Clark, "The Nez Perces in Exile," 229; U.S. Senate, *Message from the President of the United States, Transmitting . . . Draft of a Bill "For the Relief of the Nez Perce Indians in the Territory of Idaho"*; B. Chapman, "The Nez Perce in the Indian Territory," 119.

46. "Mr. and Mrs. Lawyer and Mrs. Husis Kute," *Arkansas City Traveler,* July 16, 1884; J. Reuben to Price, letter, June 30, 1884, LROIA, Ponca, 1884-12663.

47. J. W. Scott to Price, telegram, August 6, 1884, LDNPOA, PA 13; Scott to Price, telegram, September 1, 1884, ibid.; Scott, "Nez Perce, Annual Report," *ARCIA* 1885, 96.

48. H. Price, telegram, "Nez Perces to Colville," September 18, 1884, LRNPOA, PA 13; J. W. Scott, "In Response to Hiram Price's Telegram of Same Date Demanding Prisoners Be Separated," September 18, 1884, ibid.

49. Chief Joseph quoted in Scott, "Instructions, Colville."

50. Scott, "Instructions, Colville"; J. W. Scott to Price, September 18, 1884, LDNPOA, PA 13; J. Haworth, "Re: J. Reuben's Letter Recommending Chief Joseph et al. Visit Washington," February 9, 1883, Records of the Bureau of Indian Affairs: Indexes to Letters Received, 1881–1907, NARA, Washington, D.C., reel 8; T. S. Stover, telegram to Price, September 18, ibid.

51. Alcorn and Alcorn, "Aged Nez Perce Recalls the 1877 Tragedy," 65.

52. McWhorter, *Yellow Wolf,* 290.

53. T. S. Stover to the Reverend S. D. Fleming, letter, October 10, 1884, LDNPOA, PA 13; L Q. C. Lamar to Rev. G. L. Spining, May 12, 1885, LROIA, Ponca, 10823-1885.

54. G. L. Spining to L. Q. C. Lamar, May 13, 1885, LROIA, Ponca, 10823-1885.

55. J. W. Scott, "Report, Nez Perces Disappointed," November 10, 1884, LDNPOA, PA 13.

56. J. W. Scott to Price, "Letter, Nez Perces Calm," November 1, 1884, LDNPOA, PA 13; Scott to Price, "Acknowledgement," November 7, 1884, ibid.; Scott, "Nez Perce, Annual Report," *ARCIA* 1885, 96.

57. J. W. Scott, "Report to CIA, Nez Perce Waiting," January 1, 1885, LDNPOA, PA 13.

58. *Letter from the Secretary of the Treasury, Transmitting an Estimate from the Secretary of the Interior of an Appropriation for the Removal of the Nez Perce Indians from the Indian Territory,* 48th Cong., 2nd sess., 1885, H. Ex. Doc. 88, ser. 2302; Price, "Estimates, Nez Perces Removal," January 14, 1885, ibid.

59. R. D. Drum, "Copies of Indictments, Etc.," March 15, 1881, NPWF, 340; N. A. Miles, "Investigation," October 24, 1881, ibid.; R. Lincoln, "Miles's Report," November 23, 1881, ibid.; W. R. White, "Letter and Investigation," February 11, 1882, ibid.; W. H. Faulkner, "Report," June 24, 1885, LROIA, Ponca, 14242-1885; F. Lockley, "Visit to Ponca," *Arkansas City Traveler,* April 8, 1885; Historical Resources, Cowley County, Kansas, http://www.ausbcomp.com/~bbott/wortman/index.html (accessed August 27, 2007).

60. L. Q. C. Lamar to Spining, May 13, 1885, LROIA, Ponca, 10823-1885; Albert Andrews, interview with author, March 21, 2006.

61. B. F. Morris and L. P. Brown to C. E. Monteith, May 7, 1885, LROIA, Ponca, 11472-1885.

62. J. D. C. Atkins, "Nez Perces, Annual Report," *ARCIA* 1886, lviii.

63. W. R. White to B. H. Brewster, February 11, 1882, NPWF, 340; Miles, "Investigation," October 24, 1881, ibid.

64. C. Schurz to the President, letter, "Nez Perces in the Indian Territory," February 21, 1881, NPWF, 340; L. Q. C. Lamar to R. Lincoln, letter, "Concurs," April 15, 1882, ibid.; Lincoln to Lamar, letter, November 23, 1881, ibid.; Miles, *Serving the Republic,* 181.

65. S. Querry, "Interview," in Foreman, *Indian Pioneer History Collection,* 113: 44; Wood, *Days with Chief Joseph,* 559; Patricia Penn-Hilden, conversations with author, 2003 and 2004; Susan E. Harless, "Doris Swayze Bounds," in Harless, *Native Arts of the Columbia Plateau,* 7–9; Penn-Hilden, interviews with author, April 12, 2004, March 12, 2005, August 10, 2006; Tom Holm, interview with author, October 2004.

66. Lynus Walker, story shared with author by Steve and Connie Evans, September 15, 2004, October 1, 2004; Evans, *Voice of the Old Wolf,* 81.

67. J. W. Scott, "Report to Indian Bureau," April 1, 1885, LDNPOA, PA 13; Nez Perce Census, 1885, IINP: following line 120; "Leaving the Indian Territory," *Arkansas City Traveler,* April 15, 1885; Sidney D. Waters, "Received," May 28, 1885, LROIA, Ponca, 14242-1885.

68. Colville Census, 1885, CC; Lockley, "Visit to Ponca"; Wortman, Wortman, and Bottorff, *The Indians,* 197; Wm. H. Faulkner, telegram, May 21, 1885, LROIA, Ponca, 1885-11439; Faulkner to CIA, telegram, "Nez Perces," May 22, 1885, ibid., 1885-11551; Faulkner, "Report," June 24, 1885, 2, 3, 6; R. K. Small, "Burials," in Foreman, *Indian Pioneer History Collection,* 57: 343–45, 350–51.

69. J. W. Scott to Atkins, letter, May 25, 1885, LDNPOA, PA 13; Wortman, Wortman, and Bottorff, *The Indians,* 197–98; Faulkner, "Report," June 24, 1885, 4, 5.

70. Scott to Atkins, May 25, 1885; Wortman, Wortman, and Bottorff, *The Indians,* 197–98; Faulkner, "Report," June 24, 1885, 4, 5; "Property Left at Oakland," July 7, 1885, LDNPOA, PA 14; E. E. Osborn to A. I. Chapman, March 28, 1888, ibid., PA 15.

71. J. D. C. Atkins, "Nez Perces, Annual Report," *ARCIA* 1886, lviii.

72. J. W. Scott, "Deed of Relinquishment," May 25, 1885, LDNPOA, PA 14.

73. Testimony of Three Eagles and Yellow Bull in U.S. Senate, Committee on Indian Affairs, *Memorial of the Nez Perce Indians Residing in the State of Idaho to the Congress of the United States,* 114–15, 43–44.

74. McWhorter, *Yellow Wolf,* 290.

75. Wortman, Wortman, and Bottorff, *The Indians,* 197–98; Sherburne, "Chief Joseph Presented Gifts to Browning Man"; J. H. Sherburne to L. V. McWhorter, April 10, 1936, McW, folder 258.

76. J. H. Sherburne to McWhorter, letter, December 1, 1926, McW, folder 48.

77. J. W. Scott, "Report, Nez Perces Are Gone," June 1, 1885, LDNPOA, PA 14; Wortman, Wortman, and Bottorff, *The Indians,* 197–98.

78. Nez Perce Census, 1885, IINP: lines 22, 41, 14, 30, 40, 56.

79. Ibid., lines 2, 8, 9, 14, 21, 22, 33, 40, 41, 73, 93, 108, following 120; Wortman, Wortman, and Bottorff, *The Indians,* 197–98; Descriptive Record of Students Admitted, Enrollment Records of Chilocco School, NARA, Fort Worth, 7RA61, vols. 1–8; McWhorter, *Yellow Wolf,* 153; Nez Perce Census, 1878, LDNPQA, QA 2: line 2; 1879, LDNPQA, QA 1: line 2; 1880, LDNPQA, PA 1: line 2; Colville Census, 1885, CC.

80. Wortman, Wortman, and Bottorff, *The Indians,* 197–98; Faulkner, "Report," June 24, 1885, 7, 8, 10, 11, 13.

81. "Aborigines," *Laramie Weekly Sentinel,* May 30, 1885.

82. Faulkner, "Report," June 24, 1885, 9, 10.

83. Baldwin, *Memoirs of the Late Frank D. Baldwin,* 194; C. A. Dempsey, "Going to the Reservation," *Atchison Patriot,* reprinted in *Columbus Border Star,* December 13, 1878.

84. C. E. Monteith, "Travel Receipt," May 27, 1885, LROIA, Ponca, 1885-14242; "Aborigines"; Dozier, "Idaho Homecoming," 23–24; "Joseph and Retinue," *Walla Walla Journal and Weekly Magazine,* June 5, 1885; "Are Troops Needed at Lapwai," *Walla Walla Weekly Journal and Watchman,* May 29, 1885; Slickpoo and Walker, *Noon Nee-Me-Poo,* 201; "Chief Joseph Returns," *Walla Walla Weekly Journal and Watchman,* May 22, 1885; "Arrival of Chief Joseph and His Once Famous Band," *Morning Oregonian,* May 28, 1885; Deffenbaugh, "The Return of the Nez Perces," 71.

85. C. E. Monteith to Atkins, letter, December 4, 1885, LROIA, Nez Perce, 1885-29590; Monteith to Atkins, telegram, March 9, 1886, ibid., 1886-8224; Monteith to Atkins, telegram, April 2, 1886, ibid., 1886-9063; Monteith to Atkins, telegram, April 12, 1886, ibid., 1886-10768, 1886-10769.

86. Faulkner, "Report," June 24, 1885, 13; "Return of Joseph's People," *Morning Oregonian,* May 29, 1885; Nez Perce Census, 1885, IINP: lines 1–116, following line 120; Colville Census, 1885, CC.

87. Deffenbaugh, "The Return of the Nez Perces," 71–72; Morrill and Morrill, *Out of the Blanket,* 227–30.

88. Deffenbaugh, "The Return of the Nez Perces," 71–72.

89. Evans, *Voice of the Old Wolf,* 105.

90. Deffenbaugh, "The Return of the Nez Perces," 71–73; Morrill and Morrill, *Out of the Blanket,* 227–30; George L. Deffenbaugh, "Nez Perce Agency," August 14, 1885, *ARCIA* 1885, 73; Ellinwood, "Descriptive Sketches of Missions," 422; Coleman, *Presbyterian Missionary Attitudes toward American Indians,* 122–23.

91. C. E. Monteith, "Nez Perces Agency, Annual Report," August 14, 1885, *ARCIA* 1885, 72.

92. Deffenbaugh, "The Return of the Nez Perces," 71–73; Robertson, *Washington and Oregon,* 181; Colville Census, 1885, CC.

93. Colville Census, 1885, CC; Faulkner, "Report," June 24, 1885, 13; S. D. Waters, "Receipt, Spokane Falls," May 28, 1885, LROIA, Ponca, 1885-14242; Colville Census, 1886, 1887, 1888, 1890, 1891, CC.

94. S. D. Waters, "Nez Perces, Annual Report," *ARCIA* 1885, 185–87; "Colville Agency, WT, 1881–1886," in Records of the Bureau of Indian Affairs: Indexes to Letters Received, 1881–1907, NARA, Washington, D.C., roll 1, A–K.

95. B. Moore, "Nez Perces, Colville," *ARCIA* 1886, 232.

96. H. J. Cole, "Colville Agency," *ARCIA* 1891, 443.

97. Faulkner, "Report," June 24, 1885, 11–13; R. D. Gwydir, "Nez Perces, Colville," *ARCIA* 1887, 206; Gidley, *With One Sky above Us,* 31; Gibbon, *Adventures on the Western Frontier,* 220–23.

Epilogue

1. Nez Perce Census, 1885, IINP, 23; Colville Census, 1885, CC.
2. Colville Census, 1885, 1887, 1890, 1891, 1892, CC.
3. Nez Perce Census, 1885, IINP, 3; Greene, "Nez Perce Summer," 3.
4. Colville Census, 1885, 1888, 1890, 1891, 1892, CC; Nez Perce Census, 1885, IINP, line 103.
5. Colville Census, 1885, 1887, 1890, 1891, CC.
6. Colville Census, 1885, CC.
7. Gidley, *With One Sky above Us,* 94.

8. Evans, *Voice of the Old Wolf,* 73.

9. Hal. J. Cole, "Colville Agency, W. T., Annual Report," *ARCIA* 1890, 218.

10. Ibid.

11. Cole, "Colville Agency, W. T., Annual Report," August 15, 1891, *ARCIA* 1891, 445.

12. Cole, "Colville Agency," *ARCIA* 1890, 218.

13. Evans, *Voice of the Old Wolf,* 142.

14. Cole, "Colville Agency," *ARCIA* 1891, 442.

15. Evans, *Voice of the Old Wolf,* 15.

16. "Anecdotes of Chief Joseph," in Brady, *Northwestern Fights and Fighters,* 225; "Chief Joseph," *New York Times,* April 24, 1897; "Chief Joseph Sightseeing," *New York Times,* April 24, 1897; "All Honor to Grant," *New York Times,* April 27, 1897.

17. McLaughlin, *My Friend the Indian,* 344; McWhorter, *Hear Me, My Chiefs!* 547, 548 n. 8; Josephy, *The Nez Perce Indians,* 643; Gidley, *Kopet,* 35.

18. "Reception at the White House," *New York Times,* February 13, 1903; "Anecdotes of Chief Joseph," 224.

19. Elizabeth P. Wilson, in Aoki, "Nez Perce Texts," 125–26.

20. Josephy, *The Nez Perce Indians,* 642.

21. Grafe, *Peoples of the Plateau,* 184–85.

Bibliography

Archival Sources

National Anthropological Archives, Smithsonian Institution, Washington, D.C.
SIRIS, NAA Inventory, "Nez Perces."
National Archives and Records Administration, Fort Worth, Tex.
Criminal Defendant Case File, John T. Bennett, U.S. District Court for the Fort Smith Division of the Western District of Arkansas. RG 21, Records of District Courts of the United States, 1865–1991, ARC Identifiers 204756, 204754, 204755.
Criminal Defendant Case File, William H. Whiteman. RG 21, Records of District Courts of the United States, 1865–1992, ARC Identifier 24937.
Descriptive Record of Students as Admitted, Enrollment Records, Chilocco Indian School. 7RA61, vols. 1-8.
Nez Perce Students Enrolled at Chilocco, 1910. Chilocco Indian School, Enrollment, Student Activities, Graduations and Letters from Ex-Students, undated and September 30, 1893–May 21, 1893. CHL-11.
National Archives and Records Administration, Seattle, Wash.
Records of the Bureau of Indian Affairs, Chemawa (Forest Grove) Indian School, Register of Students 1880–1928. RG 75, Pacific N.W. Region.
National Archives and Records Administration, Washington, D.C.
Census, Nez Perces of Joseph's Band, Colville Indian Agency, Washington Territory, 1885–1888, 1890–1893. RG 75, Indian Census Rolls, 1885–1940, M-595, reel 49.
Indian Census Rolls, 1885–1940. RG 75, M-595.
Issues to Indians, Nez Perces, Oakland, Indian Territory, 1885, Ponca, Pawnee, and Otoe Agency, Indian Territory. RG 75, 1392-1885.
Letters Received, Office of Indian Affairs, 1881–1907, Nez Perce Agency, Idaho. RG 75.

Letters Received, Office of Indian Affairs, 1881–1907, Ponca, Pawnee, and Otoe Agency, Indian Territory. RG 75.

Letters Received, Office of Indian Affairs, 1881–1907, Quapaw Agency, Indian Territory, 1870–1880. MF 1-4995, rolls 708, 709.

Minutes of Proceedings of the Commission for Holding Treaties in Washington Territory and the Blackfoot Country, Documents Relative to the Negotiations of Ratified and Unratified Treaties with the Various Tribes of Indians, 1801–1869. RG 75, MF 494, 1854.

Nez Perce War File, Records of the Adjutant General's Office. MF 666, reels 337–40, 1876, 1877, 1878, 1879, 1881, 1882, 1883.

Records of the Bureau of Indian Affairs: Indexes to Letters Received, 1881–1907. Microfilm Publication P2187.

National Park Service, Lewiston, Idaho

Letters Received, Office of Indian Affairs, Quapaw Agency.

Oklahoma Historical Society, Archives Division, Oklahoma City, Okla.

Letters and Documents concerning Nez Perce Tribal and Individual Indian Affairs, Pawnee, Ponca, Otoe, and Oakland Agency, Indian Territory. Vols. PA 2 (1882), PA 11 (1879–1880), PA 13 (1882–1885), PA 14 (1885), PA 15 (1888).

Letters and Documents concerning Nez Perce Tribal and Individual Indian Affairs, Quapaw Agency, Indian Territory. Vols. QA 1 (1879), QA 4 (1878–1879), QA 7 (1878–1879).

Office of Indian Affairs, Nez Perces Census, Letters and Documents concerning Nez Perce Tribal and Individual Indian Affairs, Pawnee, Ponca, Otoe, and Oakland Agency. Vols. QA 1 (1879), PA 1 (1880).

Office of Indian Affairs, Nez Perces Census, Letters and Documents concerning Nez Perce Tribal and Individual Indian Affairs, Quapaw Agency, Indian Territory. Vol. QA 2 (1878).

Ponca Agency Letterpress, Letters and Documents concerning Nez Perce Tribal and Individual Indian Affairs, Pawnee, Ponca, Otoe, and Oakland Agency, Indian Territory. Vol. PA 11 (1879–1881).

Presbyterian Historical Society, Philadelphia, Pa.

American Indian Correspondence, 1872–1887.

University of Idaho Library, Special Collections, Moscow, Idaho

James Reuben's Record Book, 1881–1883. MG 5369.

Washington State Archives, Olympia, Wash.

U.S. vs. Sha-poon-mas. Case no. 46, 1863.

Washington State Archives, Eastern Regional Branch, Cheney, Wash.

U.S. vs. Sha-poon-mas. Office Nez Perce Indian Agency, 1863–1864.

Washington State University Libraries, Manuscripts, Archives, and Special Collections, Pullman, Wash.

Cage 55, Lucullus Virgil McWhorter Papers, 1848–1945.

Published Government Documents

An Act to Provide for Exchange of Lands with the Indians Residing in Any of the States or Territories, and for Their Removal West of the River Mississippi. In *United States Statutes at Large,* 4 Stat. 411–12. Washington, D.C.: United States Government Printing Office, 1830.

Annual Report, Board of Indian Commissioners to the Secretary of Interior (ARBIC). Washington, D.C.: United States Government Printing Office, 1875, 1876, 1877, 1878, 1879, 1880, 1881, 1882, 1883, 1893.

Annual Report, Commissioner of Indian Affairs to the Secretary of Interior (ARCIA). Washington, D.C.: United States Government Printing Office, 1875, 1876, 1877, 1878, 1879, 1880, 1881, 1882, 1883, 1884, 1885, 1886, 1887, 1888, 1889, 1890.

Annual Report, Secretary of War (ARSW). Washington, D.C.: United States Government Printing Office, 1873, 1875, 1877, 1878, 1879, 1885.

United States Statutes at Large. Various volumes. Washington, D.C.: United States Government Printing Office.

U.S. Congress. House. *Message from the President of the United States to the Two Houses of Congress, 1843.* 28th Cong., 1st Sess., 1843. H. Ex. Doc. 2, ser. 439.

U.S. Congress. House. *Reports of Explorations and Surveys, to Ascertain the Most Practicable and Economical Route for a Railroad from the Mississippi River to the Pacific Ocean.* Vol. 1. 33rd Cong., 2nd sess., 1855. H. Ex. Doc. 91, ser. 791.

U.S. Congress. Senate. *Testimony Taken by the Joint Committee Appointed to Take into Consideration the Expediency of Transferring the Indian Bureau to the War Department.* 45th Cong., 3rd sess., 1879. S. Misc. Doc. 53, ser. 1835.

U.S. Congress. Senate. Committee on Indian Affairs. *Memorial of the Nez Perce Indians Residing in the State of Idaho to the Congress of the United States.* 62nd Cong., 1st sess., 1911. S. Doc. 97, ser. 6108.

U.S. Congress. Senate. Committee on Indian Affairs. *Letter from the Secretary of the Interior, Transmitting, in Compliance with Senate Resolution of December 4, 1883, Copies of Documents and Correspondence Relating to Leases of Lands in the Indian Territory to Citizens of the United States for Cattle-Grazing and Other Purposes.* 48th Cong., 1st sess., 1884. S. Ex. Doc. 54, ser. 2165.

U.S. Congress. Senate. Committee on Indian Affairs. *Message from the President of the United States, Transmitting a Communication from the Secretary of the Interior of 3d Instant Submitting Draft of a Bill "For the Relief of the Nez Perce Indians in the Territory of Idaho, and of the Allied Tribes Residing on the Grande Ronde Indian Reservation in the State of Oregon."* 48th Cong., 1st sess., 1884. S. Ex. Doc. 21, ser. 2162.

U.S. Congress. Senate. Committee on Territories. *To Establish United States Court in Indian Territory.* Report to Accompany Bill S. 1802. 45th Cong., third sess., 1879. S. Rpt. 744, ser. 1839.

Wood, H. Clay. *Report Submitted to General O. O. Howard on the Status of Young Joseph and his Band of Nez Perce Indians under the Treaties between the U. S. and the Nez Perce Tribe of Indians and the Indian Title to Land.* Portland, Ore.: Assistant Adjutant General's Office, Department of the Columbia, 1876.

Books and Articles

Abel, Annie H. *Chardon's Journal at Fort Clark, 1834–1839.* Pierre: Department of History, State of South Dakota, 1932.

Alcorn, Rowena, and Gordon D. Alcorn. "Aged Nez Perce Recalls the 1877 Tragedy." *Montana: The Magazine of Western History* 15, no. 5 (October 1965): 54–67.

Allison-Bunnell, Jodi, and Jack Rowan. "Guide to the Sherburne Family Papers, 1823–1962." Maureen and Mike Mansfield Library, K. Ross Toole Archives, University of Montana–Missoula. http://nwda-db.wsulibs.wsu.edu/findaid/ark:/80444/xv24627 (accessed August 27, 2007).

Aoki, Haruo. "Nez Perce Texts, Historical Texts, Told by Mrs. Agnes Moses." Recorded by Professor Sven Liljeblad, 1961. *Linguistics* 90 (1979): 1–133.

Baird, Dennis W., Diane Mallickan, and William R. Swagerty, eds. *The Nez Perce Nation Divided: Firsthand Accounts of Events Leading to the 1863 Treaty.* Moscow: University of Idaho Press, 2002.

Baird, George W. "The Capture of Chief Joseph and the Nez Perces." *International Review* 7 (1879): 209–15.

Baldwin, Alice Blackwood. *Memoirs of the Late Frank D. Baldwin, Major General, U.S.A.* Los Angeles: Wetzel Publishing Co., 1929.

Beal, Merrill D. *I Will Fight No More Forever.* Seattle: University of Washington Press, 1963.

Berthrong, Donald J. *The Cheyenne and Arapaho Ordeal: Reservation and Agency Life in the Indian Territory, 1875–1907.* Norman: University of Oklahoma Press, 1976.

Bird, Annie L. "Portrait of a Frontier Politician." *Idaho Yesterdays* 3, no. 1 (1959): 8–30.

Birney, Mrs. Theodore W. "Address of Welcome." In *The Work and Words of the National Congress of Mothers, First Annual Session.* New York: D. Appleton and Co., 1897.

Bland, Cora M. "Visit to the Indian Territory." *Council Fire* 2, no. 9 (September 29, 1879): 133.

Bond, Fred G. *Flatboating on the Yellowstone.* New York: Printed at the New York Public Library, 1925.

Brady, Cyrus Townsend. *Northwestern Fights and Fighters.* New York: Doubleday, Page and Co., 1907.

Brown, Mark H. *The Flight of the Nez Perce.* New York: Putnam, 1967.

Brust, James S. "John H. Fouch: First Post Photographer at Fort Keogh." *Montana: The Magazine of Western History* 44, no. 2 (Spring 1994): 2–17.

Cajete, Gregory A. *Look to the Mountain.* Durango, Colo.: Kivaki Press, 1994.

Carrico, Richard L. *Strangers in a Stolen Land: American Indians in San Diego, 1850–1880.* Newcastle, Calif.: Sierra Oaks Publishing Co., 1987.

Carroll, John M., ed. *The Recollections of Colonel Hugh T. Reed.* El Paso, Tex.: Little Big Horn Associates, 1989.

Chalfant, Stuart A., and Verne Frederick Ray. *The Nez Perce Indians: Aboriginal Territory of the Nez Perce Indians and Ethnohistory of the Joseph Band of Nez Perce Indians, 1805–1905.* Interstate Commerce Commission Findings. New York: Garland, 1974.

Chapman, Berlin B. "How the Cherokee Acquired and Disposed of the Outlet." *Chronicles of Oklahoma* 15, no. 2, pt. 2 (1937): 205–25.

———. "The Nez Perce in the Indian Territory: An Archival Study." *Oregon Historical Quarterly* 1, no. 2 (1949): 98–121.

Chief Joseph. "An Indian's View of Indian Affairs." *North American Review* 128 (1879): 412–34. Reprinted as "Chief Joseph's Own Story," with an introduction by the Rt. Rev. W. H. Hare, D.D., Bishop of South Dakota, in *Northwestern Fights and Fighters,* ed. Cyrus T. Brady, 44–75. New York: Doubleday, Page and Co., 1907.

Clark, J. Stanley. "The Nez Perces in Exile." *Pacific Northwest Quarterly* 36, no. 3 (July 1945): 213–32.

Cohen, Felix S. *Handbook of American Indian Law.* Albuquerque: University of New Mexico Press, 1971.

———. *Indians Are Citizens.* Washington, D.C.: Department of the Interior, 1948.

Coleman, Michael C. *Presbyterian Missionary Attitudes toward American Indians, 1837–1893.* Jackson: University Press of Mississippi, 1985.

Corbusier, William T. *Verde to San Carlos: Recollections of a Famous Army Surgeon and His Observant Family on the Western Frontier, 1869–1886.* Tucson, Ariz.: Dale Stuart King, 1968.

Cowan, Mrs. George. "Reminiscences of Pioneer Life." *Contributions to the Montana Historical Society* 4 (1903): 172.

Curtin, Phillip D. "Epidemiology and the Slave Trade." In *Biological Consequences of European Expansion, 1450–1800,* ed. Kenneth F. Kiple and Stephen V. Beck, 133–60. Ashgate: Variorum, 1997.

Curtis, Edward S. *The Nez Perces; Walla Walla; Umatilla; Cayuse; The Chinookan Tribes.* Vol. 8 of *The North American Indian.* New York: Johnson Reprint Co., 1911.

Cutler, William G. "James A. Haworth." Johnson County, Part 6: Biographical Sketches. http://www.kancoll.org/books/cutler/johnson/johnson-co-p6.html (accessed August 27, 2007).

Daily, David W. *Battle for the BIA: G. E. E. Lindquist and the Missionary Crusade against John Collier.* Tucson: University of Arizona Press, 2004.

Debo, Angie. *A History of the Indians of the United States.* Norman: University of Oklahoma Press, 1970.

Deffenbaugh, George L. "The Return of the Nez Perces." *Foreign Missionary* 39–40 (July 1885): 71–73.

Deloria, Vine, Jr., and Raymond J. Demallie. *Documents of American Indian Diplomacy: Treaties, Agreements, and Conventions, 1775–1979.* Norman: University of Oklahoma Press, 1999.

Deloria, Vine, Jr., and Clifford M. Lytle. *American Indians, American Justice.* Austin: University of Texas Press, 1983.

DeSmet, Pierre-Jean, S.J. *Life, Letters and Travels of Pierre-Jean DeSmet, S.J., 1801–1873.* New York: Francis P. Harper, 1905.

DiLorenzo, Thomas J. "How Lincoln's Army 'Liberated' the Indians." *Native History Magazine,* February 12, 2003. http://nativehistory.tripod.com/id19.html (accessed August 27, 2007).

Dorsey, George A. "The Ponca Sun Dance." *Publications of the Field Museum of Natural History* 7 (1905): 67–91.

Dozier, Jack. "Idaho Homecoming." *Idaho Yesterdays* 7, no. 3 (1963): 22–35.

Drury, Clifford M. *Chief Lawyer of the Nez Perce Indians, 1796–1876.* Glendale, Calif.: Arthur H. Clark Co., 1979.

Ellinwood, F. F. "Descriptive Sketches of Missions, the Nez Perces." *Foreign Missionary* 39–40 (February 1886): 416–23.

Evans, Steven Ross. *Voice of the Old Wolf.* Pullman: Washington State University Press, 1996.

Ewers, John C. "The Substitution of the Bone Hair Pipe." *Bureau of American Ethnology Bulletin* 164. http://www.sil.si.edu/DigitalCollections/BAE/Bulletin164/section4.htm (accessed August 27, 2007).

FitzGerald, Emily McCorkle. *An Army Doctor's Wife on the Frontier: Letters from Alaska and the Far West, 1874–1878.* Edited by Abe Laufe. Pittsburgh: University of Pittsburgh Press, 1962.

Flanagan, John K. "The Invalidity of the Nez Perce Treaty of 1863 and the Taking of the Wallowa Valley." *American Indian Law Review* 24, no. 1 (1999–2000): 75–98.

Foreman, Grant, ed. *Indian Pioneer History Collection.* 112 vols. Oklahoma City: Oklahoma Historical Society, 1937.

Forse, Albert G. "Chief Joseph as a Commander." In *Unpublished Papers of the Order of the Indian Wars,* ed. John M. Carroll, vol. 3, 1–13. New Brunswick, N.J.: Privately published, 1977.

Frost, Gideon. "Indian Law Suit." *Friend's Intelligencer* 36/37 (November 1, 1879): 586.

Garcia, Andrew. *Tough Trip through Paradise, 1878–1879.* New York: Ballantine Books, 1974.

Gay, Jane. *With the Nez Perces: Alice Fletcher in the Field, 1889–1892.* Edited by Frederick F. Hoxie and Joan T. Mark. Lincoln: University of Nebraska Press, 1981.

Geer, Emily A. *First Lady: The Life of Lucy Webb Hayes.* Fremont, Ohio: Kent State University Press, 1984.

Gibbon, John. *Adventures on the Western Frontier.* Edited by Alan Gaff and Maureen Gaff. Bloomington: Indiana University Press, 1994.

———. "The Battle of the Big Hole." *Harper's Weekly,* December 21, 1895, 1215–16.

———. "The Pursuit of Joseph." *American Catholic Quarterly Review* 4 (April 1879): 317–44.

Gibson, John M. *The Life of General George M. Sternberg.* Durham, N.C.: Duke University Press, 1958.

Gidley, Mick. *Kopet: A Documentary Narrative of Chief Joseph's Last Years.* Seattle: University of Washington Press, 1981.

———. *With One Sky above Us: Life on an American Indian Reservation at the Turn of the Century.* Seattle: University of Washington Press, 1979.

Gillett, Mary C. *The Army Medical Department, 1818–1865.* Washington, D.C.: United States Government Printing Office, 1987.

Goldman, Michael A. "Rowland E. Trowbridge, 1880–1881." In *The Commissioners of Indian Affairs, 1824–1977,* ed. Robert M. Kvasnicka and Herman J. Viola, 167–78. Lincoln: University of Nebraska Press, 1979.

Gould, Stephen J. *The Mismeasurement of Man.* New York: W. W. Norton and Co., 1981.

Grafe, Steve. "Museum Collections." *Persimmon Hill* 32, no. 4 (2004): 29–31.

———. *Peoples of the Plateau: The Indian Photographs of Lee Moorhouse, 1898–1915.* Norman: University of Oklahoma Press, 2005.

Greene, Jerome A. *Nez Perce Summer, 1877: The U.S. Army and the Nee-Me-Poo Crisis.* http://www.nps.gov/nepe/greene/ (accessed August 27, 2007).

Haines, Francis. *The Nez Percés: Tribesmen of the Columbia Plateau.* Norman: University of Oklahoma Press, 1955.

———. *Red Eagles of the Northwest: The Story of Chief Joseph and His People.* Portland, Ore.: Scholastic Press, 1939.

Halfmoon, W. Otis. *Chief Joseph and Warriors Memorial Celebration.* Lapwai, Idaho: Nez Perce Tribal Executive Committee, 1996.

Hampton, Bruce. *Children of Grace: The Nez Perce War of 1877.* New York: Henry Holt and Co., 1994.

Hare, William H. "Foreword" to Chief Joseph, "An Indian's View of Indian Affairs." In *Northwestern Fights and Fighters,* ed. Cyrus Townsend Brady, 45–46. New York: Doubleday, Page and Co., 1907.

Harless, Susan E., ed. *Native Arts of the Columbia Plateau: The Doris Swayze Bounds Collection.* Seattle: University of Washington Press, 1998.

Harrington, John P. *Vocabulary of the Kiowa Language.* Smithsonian Institution Bureau of American Ethnography Bulletin no. 84. Washington, D.C.: Smithsonian Institution, 1928.

Hawley, James H. *History of Idaho: The Gem of the Mountains.* Chicago: S. J. Clarke Publishing Co., 1920.

Heard, J. Norman. *The Far West.* Vol. 4 of *Handbook of the American Frontier.* Lanham, Md.: Scarecrow Press, 1997.

Henderson, James C. "Reminiscences of a Range Rider." *Chronicles of Oklahoma* 3, no. 4 (1925): 277–79.

Hill, Edward. "John Q. Smith, 1875–1877." In *The Commissioners of Indian Affairs, 1824–1977,* ed. Robert M. Kvasnicka and Herman J. Viola, 149–54. Lincoln: University of Nebraska Press, 1979.

Holloway, Laura C. *The Ladies of the White House.* Philadelphia: Bradley and Co., 1882.

Holm, Tom. *Strong Hearts, Wounded Souls: Native American Veterans of the Vietnam War.* Austin: University of Texas Press, 1996.

Holm, Tom, J. Diane Pearson, and Ben Chavis. "Peoplehood: A Model for American Indian Sovereignty." *Wicazo Sa Review* 18, no. 1 (Spring 2003): 43–68.

Horr, David Agee, ed. *Nez Perce Indians.* New York: Garland Publishing, 1974

Howard, Guy. "A Practical View of the Indian Problem." *California* 1, no. 6 (June 1880): 494–98.

Howard, Helen Addison, and George D. McGrath. *Saga of Chief Joseph.* Caldwell, Idaho: Caxton Printers, 1941.

Howard, Joseph K. *Strange Empire: A Narrative of the Northwest.* St. Paul: Minnesota State Historical Society, 1952.

Howard, Oliver O. "General Howard's Comment on Joseph's Narrative." In *Northwestern Fights and Fighters,* ed. Cyrus T. Brady, 76–89. New York: Doubleday, Page and Co., 1907.

———. *Nez Percé Joseph: An Account of His Ancestors, His Lands, His Confederates, His Enemies, His Murders, His War, His Pursuit and Capture.* 1881. Reprint, New York: De Capo Press, 1972.

Hunn, Eugene S., with James Selam and Family. *Nch'i-Wána, "The Big River": Mid-Columbia Indians and Their Lands.* Seattle: University of Washington Press, 1990.

Hunt, Elvid, and Walter E. Lorence. *History of Fort Leavenworth, 1827–1937.* Fort Leavenworth, Kans.: Command and General Staff School Press, 1937.

Hunt, George, and Wilbur Nye. "The Annual Sun Dance of the Kiowa Indians, as Related by George Hunt to Lt. Wilbur S. Nye, U.S. Army Historian." *Chronicles of Oklahoma* 12, no. 3 (September 1934): 340–58.

"Indian Affairs, the Nez Perce." *Army and Navy Journal and Gazette*, April 30, 1878, 641.

"Inventory and Assessment of Human Remains Identified as Nez Perce in the National Museum of Natural History." Repatriation Office, National Museum of Natural History, Smithsonian Institution. http://www.nmnh.si.edu/anthro/repatriation/reports/regional/plateau/nez_perce.htm (accessed August 27, 2007).

Jackson, Helen Hunt. *The Indian Reform Letters of Helen Hunt Jackson, 1879–1885.* Edited by Valerie Sherer Mathes. Norman: University of Oklahoma Press, 1998.

James, Caroline. *Nez Perce Women in Transition, 1877–1900.* Moscow: University of Idaho Press, 1996.

Jensen, Amy La Follette. *The White House and Its Thirty-two Families.* New York: McGraw Hill, 1958.

Jordan, David Wilson. "Death of John Bull." August 31, 1881. In "Among the Indians: Letters Written by David Wilson Jordan." Handwritten notes. From the collection of Phil Cash Cash.

Josephy, Alvin M., Jr. *The Great Patriot Chiefs.* New York: Viking Press, 1961.

———. *The Nez Perce Indians and the Opening of the Northwest.* Boston: Houghton Mifflin Co., 1965.

J. T. "A Nez Perce Funeral." *Lippincott's Magazine of Popular Literature and Science* 22 (August 1878): 258–61.

Kappler, Charles J. *Indian Affairs: Laws and Treaties.* Washington, D.C.: United States Government Printing Office, 1904.

Kelly, Luther S. *"Yellowstone Kelly": The Memoirs of Luther S. Kelly.* Edited by M. M. Quaife, with a foreword by Lieutenant-General Nelson A. Miles, U.S.A. New Haven, Conn.: Yale University Press, 1926.

King, Jennifer. "WES Aids Research for Historic Graves." http://www.hq.usace.army.mil/cepa/pubs/apr99/story15.htm (accessed August 27, 2007).

Kirk, Elise K. *Music at the White House.* Urbana: University of Illinois Press, 1986.

La Barre, Weston. *The Ghost Dance: Origins of Religion.* New York: Dell, 1972.

Lang, William L. "Where Did the Nez Perce Go in Yellowstone in 1877?" *Montana: The Magazine of Western History* 40, no. 1 (1990): 14–28.

Lawyer, Archie. "A Christian Indian's Plea." *The Church at Home and Abroad* 5 (1889): 155.

———. *Letter, and Memorial, from the Synod of Kansas of the Presbyterian Church Asking for the Restoration of the Nez Perce Indians to Their Home in Idaho Territory.* Winfield, Kans.: Winfield Courier Job Printing House, 1881.

Lee, Jesse M. "To General James N. Allison, Editor of the *Journal of the Military Service Institution.*" In *Crazy Horse: Greatest Fighting Chief of the Ogalalla*

Sioux—His Tragic End, ed. Earl A. Brininstool, 36–37. Los Angeles: Wetzel Publishing Co., 1914.

Leupp, Francis E. *The Indian and His Problem.* New York: Charles Scribner's Sons, 1910.

Lewis, Bonnie Sue. *Creating Christian Indians: Native Clergy in the Presbyterian Church.* Norman: University of Oklahoma Press, 2003.

Lewis, Ethel. *The White House: An Informal History of Its Architecture, Interiors and Gardens.* New York: Dodd, Mead and Co., 1937.

Lindsey, Donald F. *Indians at Hampton Institute, 1877–1923.* Urbana: University of Illinois Press, 1995.

Lomawaima, K. Tsianina. *They Called It Prairie Light: The Story of Chilocco Indian School.* Lincoln: University of Nebraska Press, 1994.

"Luncheon with the Nez Perces." *U.S. Army and Navy Journal and Gazette of the Regular and Volunteer Forces* 14/15 (December 1, 1877): 267.

Marquis, Thomas B. *Wooden Leg: A Warrior Who Fought Custer.* Lincoln: University of Nebraska Press, 1931.

Marr, Carolyn. "Assimilation through Education: Indian Boarding Schools in the Pacific Northwest." http://content.lib.washington.edu/aipnw/marr.html (accessed August 27, 2007).

Martin, Samuel N. D. "A Visit to Chief Joseph's Band." *Foreign Missionary* 36 (March 1878): 302–303.

McBeth, Kate. *The Nez Perces since Lewis and Clark.* With an introduction by Peter Iverson and Elizabeth James. 1908. Reprint, Moscow: University of Idaho Press, 1993.

McGillycuddy, Valentine T. "Dr. Valentine T. McGillycuddy's Recollections of the Death of Crazy Horse." In *Crazy Horse: Greatest Fighting Chief of the Ogalalla Sioux—His Tragic End*, ed. E. A. Brininstool. Los Angeles: Wetzel Publishing Co., 1949.

McLaughlin, James. *My Friend the Indian.* New York: Houghton-Mifflin, 1910.

McWhorter, Lucullus V. *Hear Me, My Chiefs! Nez Perce History and Legend.* Caldwell, Idaho: Caxton Printers, 1983.

———. *Yellow Wolf: His Own Story.* Caldwell, Idaho: Caxton Printers, 1940.

Meacham, Alfred B. "Chief Joseph, Visit." *Council Fire* 2, no. 10 (October 1879): 145–46.

———. "Exiled Nez Perces: Where to Send Chief Joseph." *Council Fire* 1, no. 8 (August 1878): 125.

———. "Home at Last." *Council Fire* 1, no. 8 (July 1878):126.

———. "Letters." *Council Fire* 2, no. 3 (March 1879): 47.

———. "Nez Perce Joseph: Visit to Washington, DC." *Council Fire* 2, no. 2 (February 1879): 22–23.

———. "Nez Perces Joseph." *Council Fire* 1, no. 7 (July 1878): 104–105.

———. "Visit among the Indians in the Indian Territory." *Council Fire* 1, no. 11 (November 1878): 162.

Meyer, Roy W. "Ezra A. Hayt, 1877–1880." In *The Commissioners of Indian Affairs, 1824–1977*, ed. Robert M. Kvasnicka and Herman J. Viola, 155–66. Lincoln: University of Nebraska Press, 1979.

Miles, Nelson A. *Personal Recollections and Observations of General Nelson A. Miles.* Chicago: Werner Co., 1896.

———. *Serving the Republic: Memoirs of the Civil and Military Life of Nelson A. Miles, Lieutenant General, U.S. Army.* New York: Harper and Bros., 1911.

"Minthorn, H. J." Gallery of the Open Frontier. http://gallery.unl.edu/picinfo/21871.html (accessed August 27, 2007).

Monteith, John B. "Civilization in Idaho, versus Chief Joseph's Band in Exile." *Council Fire* 1, no. 5 (May 1878): 76.

Mooney, James. "Ghost Dance." In *Seventeenth Annual Report of the Bureau of American Ethnology, 1895–1896*, pt. 2, 15–498. Washington, D.C.: United States Government Printing Office, 1898.

Morrill, Allen Conrad, and Eleanor Dunlap Morrill. *Out of the Blanket: The Story of Sue and Kate McBeth, Missionaries to the Nez Perces.* Moscow: University of Idaho Press, Division of the Idaho Research Foundation, 1978.

Morton, Samuel G. *Catalogue of Skulls of Man and the Inferior Animals, in the Collection of Samuel George Morton.* Philadelphia: Merrihew and Thompson, Printers, 1894.

Mueller, Oscar O. "The Nez Perce at Cow Island." *Montana: The Journal of Western History* 14, no. 2 (April 1964): 50–53.

Nabakov, Peter. *Native American Testimony.* New York: Penguin Books, 1991.

Neiberding, Velma. "The Nez Perce at the Quapaw Agency, 1878–1879." *Chronicles of Oklahoma* 44, no. 1 (Spring 1966): 22–30.

"Nelson Appleton Miles (1839–1945)." New Perspectives on the West. http://www.pbs.org/weta/thewest/people/i_r/miles.htm (accessed August 27, 2007).

"New Names Approved for 16 Central Oregon 'Squaw' Places." *Seattle Times*, January 27, 2006. http://seattletimes.nwsource.com/html/localnews/2002766461_webnames27.html (accessed August 27, 2007).

"Nez Perce History." McBeth Journals, ca. 1905. http://www.lib.uidaho.edu/mcbeth/journal/traditionback.htm (accessed August 27, 2007).

Nowak, Matt. "Chief Joseph's Racetrack: Matt Nowak Interview." March 10, 2004. http://www.hearingvoices.com/trail/plains/nowak.html (accessed August 27, 2007).

Noyes, Alva J. *In the Land of the Chinook.* Helena, Mont.: State Publishing Co., 1917.

Olsen, Loran. *Guide to the Nez Perce Music Archive: An Annotated Listing of Songs and Musical Selections Spanning the Period 1897–1974.* Pullman: Washington State University, 1989.

———. *A Legacy from Sam Morris.* To accompany compact discs I and II. Nez Perce Music Archive, Sam Morris Collection. Seattle: Northwest Interpretive Association, 1999.

———. *Qillóowawya, Hitting the Rawhide: Serenade Songs from the Nez Perce Music Archive.* Seattle: Northwest Interpretive Association, 2001.

O'Marr, Louis J., William M. Holt, Edgar E. Witt, Charles E. Williams, Joseph Red Thunder, and Harry Owhi. "Before the Indian Claims Commission." Charles E. Williams, Joseph Redthunder, and Harry Owhi as Representatives of the Nez Perce Tribe, Petitioners, Docket no. 180-A, Final Judgment, July 5, 1960, p. 48c. http://digital.library.okstate.edu/icc/v09/iccv09p048c.pdf (accessed August 27, 2007).

O'Neil, Floyd A. "Hiram Price, 1881–1885." In *The Commissioners of Indian Affairs, 1824–1977,* ed. Robert M. Kvasnicka and Herman J. Viola, 173–80. Lincoln: University of Nebraska Press, 1979.

Osborne, Alan. "The Exile of the Nez Perce in Indian Territory, 1878–1885." *Chronicles of Oklahoma* 16, no. 4 (Winter 1878–79): 450–71.

Packard, R. L. "Mythology and Religion of the Nez Perces." *Journal of American Folklore* 4, no. 15 (1891): 327–30.

Pearson, J. Diane. "Developing Reservation Economies: American Indian Teamsters, 1858–1900." *Journal of Small Business and Entrepreneurship* 18, no. 2 (Spring 2005): 153–70.

———. "Numipu Land Loss: Following Archie Phinney's Research." *Journal of Northwest Anthropology* 38, no. 1 (2004): 33–62.

———. "Numipu Narratives: The Essence of Survival in the Indian Territory." *Journal of Northwest Anthropology* 38, no. 1 (2004): 67–96.

Pearson, J. Diane, and Peter Harrington. "Numipu Winter Villages." *Journal of Northwest Anthropology* 38, no. 1 (2004): 63–66.

Phinney, Mary Allen. *Jirah Isham Allen, Montana Pioneer, 1839–1929.* Rutland, Vt.: Tuttle Publishing Co., 1946.

Picket, William D. "The Yellowstone Park in the Early Days." Pt. 1. *Forest and Stream: A Journal of Outdoor Life, Travel, Nature Study, Shooting, Fishing, Yachting* 70, no. 1 (February 1, 1908): 168–70.

———. "The Yellowstone Park in the Early Days." Pt. 2. *Forest and Stream: A Journal of Outdoor Life, Travel, Nature Study, Shooting, Fishing, Yachting* 70, no. 1 (February 8, 1908): 208–10.

Pierce, Elias D. "Orofino Gold: E. D. Pierce's Own Story." *Idaho Yesterdays* 4, no. 3 (1960): 2–5.

Pierson, Emeline S. "Indian Progression." *New York Evangelist* 71, no. 52 (December 27, 1900): 14.

Pinkham, Ron. *100th Anniversary of the Nez Perce War of 1877.* Lapwai, Idaho: Nez Perce Printing, 1977.

Platter, James E., Samuel B. Fleming, and James Wilson, eds. *A Memorial from the Synod of Kansas, of the Presbyterian Church, Asking for the Restoration of the Nez Perce Indians to Their Home in Idaho Territory.* Winfield, Kans.: Courier Job Printing House, 1881.

Pratt, Richard Henry. "Speech at Association Hall, Philadelphia—Items: The Carlisle Indian School." *Friend's Intelligencer* 38, no. 12 (May 1881): 186–88.

Prucha, Paul Frances. *The Great Father: The United States Government and the American Indians.* Lincoln: University of Nebraska Press, 1986.

Ray, Verne F. "Ethnohistory of the Joseph Band of Nez Perce Indians, 1805–1905." In *Nez Perce Indians,* ed. David Agee Horr, 165–268. New York: Garland Publishing, 1974.

———. *Plateau Culture Element Distributions.* Bureau of American Ethnology Report no. 8. Washington, D.C.: Smithsonian Institution.

———. *The Sanpoil and Nespelem: Salishan Peoples of Northwestern Washington.* University of Washington Publications in Anthropology no. 5. Seattle: University of Washington Press, 1933.

Redfield, Francis M. "Reminiscences of F. M. Redfield, Chief Joseph's War." *Pacific Northwest Quarterly* 27 (January 1936): 66–77.

———. "Who Stole the Piano?" *Sunset Magazine* 14 (November 1904–April 1905): 292–93.

Relander, Click. *Drummers and Dreamers.* Caldwell, Idaho: Caxton Printers, 1956.

Reuben, James. "Documents from the Cornerstone of the Nez Perce and Ponca Indian School." *Chronicles of Oklahoma* 12, no. 3 (1934): 359–63.

Riding In, James. "Six Pawnee Crania: Historical and Contemporary Issues Associated with the Massacre and Decapitation of Pawnee Indians in 1869." *American Indian Culture and Research Journal* 16, no. 2 (1992): 101–19.

Ridley, Jasper. *The Freemasons.* London: Constable and Robinson, 2000.

Robbins, John. "Notice of Intent to Repatriate Cultural Items in the Possession of the Peabody Museum of Archaeology and Ethnology, Harvard University, Cambridge, MA." November 17, 2000. *Federal Register* 65, no. 235 (December 6, 2000): 76282–83.

Robertson, Donald B. *Washington and Oregon.* Vol. 3 of *Encyclopedia of Western Railroad History.* Caldwell, Idaho: Caxton Printers, 1995.

Romeyn, Henry. "The Capture of Chief Joseph and His Nez Perce Indians." *Contributions to the Historical Society of Montana* 2 (1896): 283–91.

Ronan, Peter. "Indian Affairs." *Army and Navy Journal and Gazette of the Regular Forces* 16, no. 1 (1878): 5.

Root, George A. "Ferries in Kansas." *Kansas Historical Quarterly* 5, no. 1 (1936): 22–42.

Ruby, Robert H., and John A. Brown. *Half-Sun on the Columbia: A Biography of Chief Moses.* Norman: University of Oklahoma Press, 1964.

Ryan, William, and Desmond Guinness. *The White House: An Architectural History.* New York: McGraw-Hill, 1980.

S. "Correspondence to the Editors of the *Friends' Intelligencer.*" *Friends' Intelligencer* 35, no. 49 (January 25, 1879): 775–76.

Schlick, Mary Dodds. *Columbia River Basketry: Gift of the Ancestors, Gift of the Earth.* Seattle: University of Washington Press, 1994.

Schmeckebier, Laurence F. *The Office of Indian Affairs: Its History, Activities, and Organization.* Institute for Government Research, Service Monographs of the United States Government no. 48. Baltimore, Md.: Johns Hopkins Press, 1927.

Schurz, Carl. "Present Aspects of the Indian Problem." *North American Review* 132, no. 296 (July 1881): 1–24.

———. *Speeches, Correspondence and Political Papers of Carl Schurz.* Selected and edited by Frederic Bancroft on behalf of the Carl Schurz Memorial Committee. Vol. 4: *July 20, 1880–September 15, 1888.* New York: G. P. Putnam's Sons, 1913.

Scott, Hugh L. *Some Memories of a Soldier.* New York: Century Co., 1928.

Shennon, Philip J., and Roy P. Full. *An Evaluation Study of the Mineral Resources in the Lands Ceded to the United States by the Nez Perce Tribe of Indians on April 17, 1867. Nez Perce Tribe v. United States of America,* Indian Claims Commission Docket no. 175-180. Salt Lake City, Utah, 1957.

Sherburne, Joe L. "Chief Joseph Presented Gifts to Browning Man." *Glacier Reporter* (Browning, Mont.), 1932. Maureen and Mike Mansfield Library, University of Montana–Missoula, NUCMC no. MS78-1655, 1881–1995, 65 feet.

Shields, G. O. (Coquina). *The Battle of the Big Hole: A History of General Gibbon's Engagement with Nez Percés Indians in the Big Hole Valley, Montana, August 9th, 1877.* Library of American Civilization, LAC 16559. Chicago: Rand, McNally and Co., 1889.

Slickpoo, Allen P., Sr., and Deward E. Walker, Jr. *Noon Nee-Me-Poo (We, the Nez Perces): Culture and History of the Nez Perces.* Lapwai, Idaho: Nez Perce Tribe, 1973.

Spinden, Herbert J. *The Nez Percé Indians.* Lancaster, Pa.: New Era Printing Co., 1908.

S. T. T. "Letter to the Editor, from Leavenworth, Kansas." *Council Fire* 1, no. 8 (July 19, 1878): 125.

Stands in Timber and Margot Liberty. *Cheyenne Memories.* New Haven, Conn.: Yale University Press, 1967.

Stegner, Wallace. *Wolf Willow.* Lincoln: University of Nebraska Press, 1962.

"The Surrender of Joseph." *Harper's Weekly* 21, no. 1090 (November 17, 1877): 906–909.

Svingen, Orlan V. *The Northern Cheyenne Indian Reservation, 1877–1890.* Niwot: University Press of Colorado, 1993.

Teit, James A. "The Salishan Tribes of the Western Plateau." In *Forty-fifth Annual Report of the Bureau of American Ethnology to the Secretary of the Smithsonian Institution, 1927–1928,* 37–197. Washington, D.C.: United States Government Printing Office, 1930.

Thompson, Gregory. "John D. C. Atkins, 1885–1888." In *The Commissioners of Indian Affairs, 1825–1977,* ed. Robert M. Kvasnicka and Herman J. Viola, 181–88. Lincoln, Nebraska: University of Nebraska Press, 1979.

Thompson, Scott M. *I Will Tell My War Story: A Pictorial Account of the Nez Perce War.* Seattle: University of Washington Press, 2000.

Thornton, Russell. *American Indian Holocaust and Survival: A Population History since 1492.* Norman: University of Oklahoma Press, 1987.

Tibbles, Thomas Henry. *The Ponca Chiefs: An Account of the Trial of Standing Bear.* Edited by Kay Garber. Lincoln: University of Nebraska Press, 1972.

Trafzer, Cliff. "Chief Joseph's Allies: The Palouse Indians and the Nez Perce War of 1877." In *The Palouse in the Eekish Pah,* ed. Cliff Trafzer, 7–40. Sacramento, Calif.: Sierra Oaks Publishing Co., 1987.

———. *Northwestern Tribes in Exile: Modoc, Nez Perce, and Palouse Removal to the Indian Territory.* Sacramento, Calif.: Sierra Oaks Publishing Co., 1987.

Tuttle, Asa C., and Emeline H. Tuttle. "Quapaw and Modoc Mission." *Council Fire* 1, no. 8 (September 20, 1878): 126.

Venn, George. *Soldier to Advocate: C. E. S. Wood's 1877 Legacy.* La Grande, Ore.: Woodcraft of Oregon, 2006.

Walker, Deward E., Jr. *Conflict and Schism in Nez Percé Acculturation: A Study of Religion and Politics.* Pullman: Washington State University Press, 1968.

———. "The Nez Perce Sweat Bath Complex: An Acculturational Analysis." *Southwest Journal of Anthropology* 22, no. 2 (1966): 133–71.

"Wards of the Government." *Scribner's Monthly* 19, no. 5 (1880): 775.

Webb, David W. "Henry County History." Paris-Henry County Heritage Center, Paris, Tenn. http://www.phchc.com/henryco_history.htm (accessed August 27, 2007).

Wells, Donald D. "Farmers Forgotten: Nez Perce Suppliers of the North Idaho Gold Rush Days." *Idaho Yesterdays* 2, no. 2 (1958): 28–32.

"What Are the Facts? Did Capt. Wm. Clark Leave Indian Descendents?" *Montana: The Magazine of Western History* 5, no. 3 (July 1955): 36–37.

Wood, Erskine. *Days with Chief Joseph: Diary, Recollections, and Photos.* Portland: Published for the Oregon Historical Society by Binfords and Mort, 1970.

———. "Chief Joseph, the Nez Perce." *Century Illustrated Monthly Magazine* 28, no. 1 (1884): 135–42.

Woodruff, Thomas M. "We Have Joseph and All of His People: A Soldier Writes Home about the Final Battle." *Montana: The Magazine of Western History* 27, no. 4 (1977): 30–33.

Wortman, Richard Kay, Mary Ann Wortman, and William Bottorff, comps. and eds. *The Indians.* Vol. 2 of *History of Cowley County, Kansas.* Arkansas City, Kans.: Arkansas City Historical Society, 1999.

Zimmer, William F. *Frontier Soldier: An Enlisted Man's Journal of the Sioux and Nez Perce Campaigns, 1877.* Edited by Jerome Greene. Helena: Montana State Historical Society, 1998.

Newspapers

Arkansas City Republican, Arkansas City, Kans.
Arkansas City Traveler, Arkansas City, Kans.
Arkansas Valley Democrat, Arkansas City, Kans.
Atchison Patriot, Columbus, Kans.
Baxter Springs Times, Baxter Springs, Kans.
Bismarck Tribune, Bismarck, Dakota Territory
Brainerd Tribune, Brainerd, Minn.
Caldwell Journal, Caldwell, Kans.
Cerro Gordo Republican, Mason City, Iowa
Chetopa Herald, Chetopa, Kans.
Columbus Border Star, Columbus, Kans.
Cowley County Courant, Winfield, Kans.
Daily Out-look, Parsons, Kans.
Empire City Echo, Empire City, Kans.
Emporia News, Emporia, Kans.
Galena Miner, Galena, Kans.
Globe-Democrat, Arkansas City, Kans.
Great Falls Tribune, Great Falls, Mont.
Indian Helper, Carlisle, Pa.
Laramie Weekly Sentinel, Laramie, Wyo.
Mason City Express, Mason City, Iowa
Morning Oregonian, Portland, Ore.
The New North-west, Deerlodge, Mont.
New York Times, New York, N.Y.
New York Tribune, New York, N.Y.
Portland Oregonian, Portland, Ore.
The Red Man and Helper, Carlisle, Pa.
San Francisco Chronicle, San Francisco, Calif.

Saturday Evening Post, New York, N.Y.
School News, Carlisle, Pa.
St. Paul and Minneapolis Pioneer Press, St. Paul, Minn.
St. Paul Dispatch, St. Paul, Minn.
Times Weekend, Leavenworth, Kans.
Walla Walla Weekly Journal and Watchman, Walla Walla, Washington Territory
Walnut Valley Times, El Dorado, Kans.
Washington Post, Washington, D.C.
Washington Statesman, Walla Walla, Wash.
Winfield Courier, Winfield, Kans.

Dissertations and Theses

Blase, Fred W. "Political History of Idaho Territory, 1863 to 1890." Master's thesis, University of California, Berkeley, 1925.

Marshall, Alan G. "Nez Perce Groups: An Ecological Interpretation." Ph.D. diss., Washington State University, Pullman, 1977.

Pearson, J. Diane. "The Politics of Disease: Imperial Medicine and the American Indian, 1797–1871." Ph.D. diss., University of Arizona, 2001.

Sprague, Roderick. "Aboriginal Burial Practices in the Plateau Region of North America." Ph.D. diss., University of Arizona, 1967.

Interviews

Andrews, Albert. March 21, 2006, and April 2006.

Bottorff, William W. March 25, 2005, and May 12, 2005.

Evans, Steven Ross. October 1, 2005, and January 29, 2006.

Grafe, Steve. May 19, 2004, September 2, 2004, December 2, 2004, and December 14, 2004.

Halfmoon, W. Otis. July 20, 2005, July 25, 2005, August 9, 2005, August 26, 2005, and February 8, 2006.

Holm, Tom. October 17, 2004, June 10, 2005, and November 5, 2005.

Lawyer, Mylie. October 1, 2005.

Mallickan, Diana. April 24, 2004, and October 1, 2005.

Paul, Jesse. October 31, 2003, and October 12, 2004.

Penn-Hilden, Patricia. March 10, 2002, March 2, 2003, April 12, 2004, April 23, 2004, August 30, 2004, March 12, 2005, August 10, 2006, and September 2006.

Taylor, Arthur. June 29, 2005, November 4, 2005, and November 5, 2005.

Venn, George. August 25, 2006, September 9, 2006, September 10, 2006, and September 11, 2006.

Walker, Lynus. Story shared with author by Steve and Connie Evans. September 15, 2004, and October 1, 2004.

Willard, William. May 5, 2004, October 11, 2005, and March 24, 2006.

Wortman, Mary Ann. August 26, 2004, and March 31, 2005.

INDEX

All references to illustrations are set in italic type.